SACRAMENTAL THEOLOGY

SACRAMENTAL THEOLOGY

A Textbook for Advanced Students

*

CLARENCE McAULIFFE, S.J.

B. HERDER BOOK CO.

15 & 17 South Broadway, St. Louis 2, Mo.

AND *33 Queen Square, London, W.C.*

Library of Congress Catalog Card Number: 58-11740

IMPRIMI POTEST: Leo J. Burns, S.J.
*Provincial, Wisconsin Province
of the Society of Jesus*

IMPRIMATUR: ✠ Joseph E. Ritter, S.T.D.
Archbishop of St. Louis

April 25, 1958

THIS BOOK IS DEDICATED
to the many young Jesuit priests
who, for the past seventeen years
have listened so sympathetically
to the lectures of the author.

FOREWORD TO THE STUDENT

IN the following pages you will undertake, perhaps for the first time, the study of genuine theology as distinguished from religion. For this textbook differs only in minor details from the manuals used in our theological seminaries.

This book was prepared for you particularly, not for your professor. It is an act of confidence in you, because it assumes that you would like to know more about your Catholic faith and that you are willing to study diligently for this purpose.

You may, perhaps, have subconsciously come to regard your courses in religion as the easiest of all. After you read a few of the following pages, you will cancel that impression. On almost every page you will find put to the test your memory, your ingenuity, your ability to make distinctions, to think clearly and profoundly and reflectively.

During your regular class periods you will be able to cover only a portion, and perhaps only a small portion, of this book. We hope that your interest in the seven sacraments will be so stimulated that you will study the rest of it privately.

From the practical point of view, the sacraments are the most important part of your Catholic faith. You have already received at least four of them—baptism, confirmation, penance, and Communion—and you may confidently expect in God's providence to receive before you die two of the remaining three. This is a reason, not only for applying yourself to the contents of the book, but also for keeping possession of it for the rest of your life.

The only companion book which you will need for this course is the Bible, both the Old and the New Testaments. You will, however, find it helpful to purchase and retain *The Church Teaches* or *The Sources of Catholic Dogma* which will provide you with an English translation of the more noteworthy pronouncements of the Church's teaching authorities, not only with regard to the sacraments, but to the whole of theology.

Earnest application to this book will reward you in many ways. It will train you never to discuss any proposition without first understanding accurately its meaning. It will fashion your mind to orderly processes of thought. It will enable you in all branches of learning to distinguish substantials from accidentals. These advantages are an inevitable consequence of the thesis form, according to which the book is constructed.

Your outlook, too, not only upon your faith, but also upon your other courses, will be broadened, so that you will realize that any subject of consequence has innumerable ramifications which even a lifetime of study cannot fathom completely.

However, these will be mere byproducts of your study. Your other courses add to your knowledge and develop your mind. This book will amplify your knowledge of your faith, but it should also increase your appreciation for it. Other courses aim, either solely or primarily, at your mind. This course aims at both your mind and your *heart*. To achieve these co-equal objectives, you must study, reflect, and *pray*.

INTRODUCTION

THIS book, although it contains almost as much material as the average seminary manual, is written expressly for university students and for juniors and seniors in college. Hence it offers only a meagre bibliography. The mastery of this volume will keep the student so fully occupied that he will have little or no time for supplementary reading.

Technical expressions, too, are avoided as far as possible, but when necessity compels their use, they are explained, sometimes more than once.

Destined for such students, the book is necessarily written in English. Hence it should be noted that the recurring reference, DB., is not only to Denzinger's Latin work, *Enchiridion Symbolorum*, but also to its English translation, *The Sources of Catholic Dogma*. We had the professor in mind when, after patristic quotations, we refer to Rouët de Journel's *Enchiridion Patristicum* or to Migne's Latin and Greek Patrologies.

However, students sufficiently advanced in Latin may wish to consult the original texts as found in the Enchiridions and the Latin Patrology.

The book, then, is in some ways more, in others less complete than the average seminary manual. It is less complete in treating of the adversaries. For the most part we have not named adversaries occurring before the rise of Protestantism. We have, however, done so in several theses in which we felt that it was necessary.

Neither do we offer as many references to official pronouncements of the Church or to Holy Writ. To avoid overburdening the student, we present only one, or sometimes two, of the clearest and most telling declarations of the *magisterium*, but they always suffice to establish the thesis. Similarly, we limit our citations of Scripture texts to one or two, though occasionally more. We have selected the most convincing texts, most of which are sanctioned either by the *magisterium* or by the unanimous consent of exegetes and theologians.

Very few of even the seminary textbooks offer anything like an adequate proof from the Fathers. Ordinarily we quote a few, occasionally only one, of them. It is solely for uniformity of presentation that we introduce these quotations by the word "proof." We use the word loosely to mean a confirmatory or probable proof.

Nevertheless, we did not want to omit it. Our beliefs are fortified when we hear our Catholic ancestors, some of them now dead for fifteen centuries or more, professing the same faith to which we adhere today. We have tried to choose only those citations whose meaning is quite obvious.

Comments follow after many of the theses, but perhaps not as many as are found in the ordinary seminary manual. Although most of ours are practical, we have included some of a purely speculative nature.

Hence the volume contains as many theses as most of the seminary texts, but, generally speaking, it presents less, though always sufficient evidence to sustain them.

How does it happen, then, that this book is as long as the average seminary manual? Because in some respects its contents are more comprehensive.

The explanation of terms and of the meaning of the thesis is, as a rule, more complete. We thought this necessary for the students we had in mind.

Then, too, quotations from the *magisterium* which are cited under the dogmatic note are explained unless their meaning is patent. This is done only infrequently in seminary texts.

Moreover, the exegesis of the more important Scripture passages is more fully developed. We felt that this, too, was necessary for lay students, who could hardly be expected to consult the exegetes. Yet, we did not want them to take a course in theology without becoming acquainted with the science of hermeneutics.

Since the student may not be as well versed in philosophy as the seminarian, we have introduced a feature, not found to our knowledge, in any theological textbook. All of the syllogisms fall into the scholastic classification called "sub-prae." This is the simplest form of syllogism and should help the student to grasp more easily some of the rather difficult arguments from Scripture and from theological reasoning. When, in a few instances, we found it impossible to construct the syllogism according to this form, we resorted to the next simplest form, that whose major begins with an "if" clause. In cases where the matter is not complicated, we have used no syllogism at all.

A few other observations may be helpful for both professor and student.

We remind both that the most solid proof for any theological verity is the dogmatic note when this is at least certain. This truth ought to be constantly inculcated so that the student will finish the course with a genuinely Catholic mentality, which, whenever confronted by a problem pertaining to faith or morals, should spontaneously seek, first of all, to find out if the *magisterium* has pronounced upon it. It is for this reason that, whatever proof follows immediately after the dogmatic note, is designated as "proof 2," not "proof 1."

The translations of the *magisterium's* pronouncements are the author's. He had completed them before the appearance of the excellent translations presented in *The Church Teaches* and in *The Sources of Catholic Dogma*. He thought it might be better to keep his own, rather than to adopt either of these, so that the student could have access to three translations.

Concerning the Scripture proofs, we have introduced an innovation which needs some explanation. We regularly distinguish between the dogmatic and the apologetic value of texts. We consider this a vital distinction.

The Church is the sole legitimate interpreter of Holy Writ. Her word is final, a truth which should never be forgotten. But she has defined very few texts. However, we know the sure meaning of many other texts either because they are cited in documents of the *magisterium* or because their meaning is certified by the unanimous consent of exegetes and theologians. Hence the meaning of many texts is guaranteed by *authority*. This is what we signify when we say that a text is *dogmatically* certain.

Yet we know that God, and the Church also, wish all Catholics to read and profit from the Scriptures. Accordingly, God's word should convey a meaning to the *human mind* itself.

If, then, we have an authoritative interpretation of a text, every Catholic must hold that this is its meaning. But despite this fact, he may also ask whether that meaning is the one which his *reason* alone would draw from the words. He will find in some instances that a text's signification, though certain dogmatically, is perhaps only probable or more probable *apologetically,* i.e., from the viewpoint of reason. In doing this he does not in any way *doubt* the meaning of the text, since it is dogmatically determined. He merely wishes to inspect the text from another angle.

When the meaning of texts is not dogmatically established, the reader is free to understand them according to his own intelligence, provided that he reserves his final verdict to the authority of the Church. This is the procedure of our professional exegetes. They dispute briskly about the signification of some Scripture passages and even about the meaning of individual words, but all of them are ready to submit if the Church should render a decision.

Yet the rational argument from a text remains theological. An argument from the Fathers is theological and yet it is by the use of our reason that we apprehend the purport of a Father's statements. Scripture, too, like the Fathers, is a fount of the faith. Our only avenue to its meaning is our reason when its texts have not been authoritatively interpreted for us.

Some may wonder why we always put the Scripture proof in the first place after the dogmatic note. This is done in most of our theological manuals. It should not be forgotten, however, that a proof from tradition can be of equal, or even greater, value.

However, the development of such a proof requires so many complex operations involving the amassing of various sorts of historical evidence, its sifting and evaluation, that it would overtax both the author of a manual and its student. Besides, the student could hardly be expected to remember it.

Scripture proofs, on the other hand, are relatively short and their meaning for most of the important verities is authoritatively guaranteed. Moreover, in the United States our students come in almost daily contact with Protestants, who allege that Scripture alone is the rule of faith. Accordingly, the student should, especially in this country, become well acquainted with proofs from Holy Writ.

Some may wonder, too, why the theses are named "Conclusions." After some cogitation, though the matter does not strike us as consequential, we hit upon this word for two reasons. First, we thought that the science of theology should have a distinctive word for the enunciation of its verities. Since "thesis" is the name commonly used to designate the propositions of philosophy, we rejected this word, though it is appropriate in other ways.

Second, we desired a word which would connote that the verity is already known and, in most cases, believed. The word "proposition" would not be satisfactory because it suggests that the affirmed declaration is open to debate. Other words like "declaration," "affirmation," "position" could have been adopted, but we finally decided that "conclusion" was the most suited.

The author has been immensely helped by the exhaustive course, now almost completed, written by the Reverend Emmanuel Doronzo, O.M.I., of the Catholic University. He wishes to thank the Reverends Cyril O. Vollert, S.J., dean of the theologate at St. Mary's, and Malachi J. Donnelly, S.J., and Edward J. Weisenberg, S.J., for having patiently perused an original manuscript which was barely presentable, hardly readable.

Clarence McAuliffe, S.J.,
St. Mary's College,
St. Marys, Kansas

ABBREVIATIONS

CT   The Church Teaches.

DB   Denzinger, Enchiridion Symbolorum and The Sources of Catholic Dogma.

PG   Migne, Patrologia Graeca.

PL   Migne, Patrologia Latina.

RJ   Rouët de Journel, Enchiridion Patristicum.

All other abbreviations should be familiar to the student.

BIBLIOGRAPHY

1. Texts for consultation

Pohle-Preuss, The Sacraments, Four volumes (St. Louis: Herder, 1938).

Smith, D.D., Ph.D., Canon George D. (editor), The Teaching of the Catholic Church (New York: Macmillan, 1949).

2. Books in continuous discourse

Crock, Rev. Clement, Grace and the Sacraments (New York: Wagner, 1936; London: Herder).

Doyle, S.J., Rev. Francis X., The Wonderful Sacraments (New York: Benziger, 1924).

Herzog, S.J., Rev. Charles G., Channels of Redemption (New York: Benziger, 1931).

3. Books for additional objections and their answers

Conway, C.P., Rev. Bertrand L., The Question Box (New York: Paulist Press, 1929).

Goldstein, David, What Say You? (St. Paul: Radio Replies Press, 1945).

Rumble, M.S.C., Rev. Leslie, Radio Replies, Three volumes (St. Paul: Radio Replies Press, 1938, 1940, 1942).

4. Translations of Denzinger

Clarkson, S.J., Rev. John F.; Edwards, S.J., Rev. John H.; Kelly, S.J., Rev. William J.; Welch, S.J., Rev. John J.; The Church Teaches (St. Louis: Herder, 1955).

Deferrari, Roy J., The Sources of Catholic Dogma (St. Louis: Herder, 1957).

CONTENTS

Section Four: The Eucharist

Section Five: The Sacrament of Penance

Section Six: Extreme Unction

Section Seven: The Sacrament of Order

Section Eight: Matrimony

The Sacraments in General

*

Section One

THE SACRAMENTS IN GENERAL

Conclusion 1. A sacrament is a perceptible sign, instituted in perpetuity by Christ Himself, to signify and produce sanctifying grace.

Introduction. Before speaking about any object, we must have some notion of its nature. The present Conclusion explains the essential nature of a Christian sacrament. The remaining Conclusions in this section will clarify the present definition in greater detail.

In the New Testament the word "sacrament" has a rather general meaning. It is applied to any sacred and mysterious object or event (Eph. 1:9). It is used also of signs which indicate sacred and mysterious objects and events (Eph. 5:32). The early Fathers of the Church adopted these Scriptural meanings of the word.

It was not until the twelfth century that "sacrament" began to take the precise meaning expressed in the wording of this Conclusion. Peter Lombard (d. 1164) seems to have been the first to formulate the definition accurately. Christians, of course, had always known that the sacraments were perceptible signs instituted permanently by Christ Himself and of exceptional value to the soul. But Peter Lombard first expressed in his definition what this exceptional value was, namely, the causation of sanctifying grace. This power to produce grace is the distinctive note of a Christian sacrament.

Explanation of Terms

1. Sign. Every sign leads us to the knowledge of something else. A sign may be a *natural* one, such as a human footprint which tells us that a man has been present, or smoke which informs us of a fire.

Other signs are *arbitrary* or *conventional,* i.e., they depend upon some one's free will for their existence. Examples are the red light which tells the motorist to stop, or a word like "bomb" which leads us to think of an explosive.

Some signs are *mixed,* i.e., they are partly arbitrary, partly natural signs. The word "murmur," for instance, is partly an arbitrary sign. Some one freely chose it to designate a certain idea, a certain kind of sound. But it is also a natural sign, since the very sound of the word "murmur" resembles the idea it expresses.

The sacraments should be classified as mixed signs. They are mainly arbitrary, but, to some extent, natural signs. They are arbitrary in so far as they depend for their existence upon the free determination of Christ. They are natural in so far as their external rites by their very makeup symbolize in some measure their spiritual effects. Thus the washing of the head in baptism readily signifies the washing of the soul accomplished by this sacrament. The same is true of the other sacraments.

Signs may also be either *theoretical* or *practical.* The red traffic light is a theoretical sign. It informs the driver that he should stop his car, but it does not by its own action stop the car. He must himself apply the brakes.

On the other hand, a dark cloud is a sign that rain may come. It informs our minds of this possibility and so to this extent is a theoretical sign. But if it rains, the cloud itself produces the rain. It does what it signifies and so is also a practical sign. Every practical sign is likewise a theoretical sign, but not every theoretical sign is a practical sign.

The sacraments are theoretical signs because they inform the mind that grace is being transmitted. But the sacraments, like the cloud, truly produce the grace which they signify and so are also practical signs. This is an important point to remember.

2. Perceptible. This means that the sacramental rites must be

apprehensible to one or more of the five bodily senses. Generally speaking, both the matter (e.g., water in baptism), the application of this matter (e.g., the washing in baptism), and the form (the words spoken orally by the minister), are of a perceptible nature. Although the entire essential rites of the Eucharist and penance are not perceptible to the senses, a part of them is. Without some outward sign no sacrament can exist.

3. Instituted by Christ Himself. A later Conclusion will explain this point more precisely. Christ as God is the principal institutor of the sacraments. Christ as man is the ministerial cause of their institution. By this we mean that Christ called into play His human nature, His mind, will, voice, when He instituted the sacraments.

4. In perpetuity. The sacraments are to last until the end of the world.

5. To signify. This phrase simply makes explicit that the sacraments are theoretical signs as previously explained.

6. To produce. This phrase emphasizes the fact that the sacraments are also practical signs.

7. Sanctifying grace. All sacraments confer sanctifying grace, a share in God's own life. Although each sacrament signifies other effects proper to itself, all sacraments produce grace when duly received. When we see a baby being baptized, we know at once that the baby is receiving sanctifying grace. The same holds true for the rest of the sacraments.

Adversaries. All Protestants, except some High Church Anglicans, deny that sacraments produce grace. They believe that sacraments were intended to excite confidence in God, or that they merely signify that a person belongs to the Christian religion.

Dogmatic Note

This Conclusion, considered substantially, is part of our Catholic faith and could be included in the "Credo." God Himself, therefore, revealed in the deposit of faith the true nature of a sacrament.

This Conclusion could be proved also from Scripture and tradition, but since these proofs will be introduced when we treat of each sacrament, we need not develop them here. For the present, the important thing is to learn the nature of a sacrament. This knowledge is basic for the entire course that follows.

*

Conclusion 2. There are exactly seven sacraments.

Introduction. Having determined the nature of a sacrament, we now logically inquire how many sacraments there are. Protestants in general admit only two sacraments, baptism and the Lord's supper, but since their idea of a sacrament is false, they do as a matter of fact deny them all.

Explanation of Terms

1. Seven. This is the only term that needs explanation. There could be seven sacraments without their being counted. This was the case up to the twelfth century. Although the sacraments were in daily use from the very foundation of Christianity, systematic theological treatises did not appear until the twelfth century. As a result, the precise definition of a sacrament was not known until that century.

It is impossible to count things until we have an accurate notion of the things to be counted. Suppose, for instance, that we were to ask how many methods of teaching there are. We cannot answer because the precise meaning of "methods of teaching" is not determined.

We can also be using things every day without ever counting them. For example, if some one were to ask you how many articles of clothing you are wearing, you would have to stop and count them. Yet, you have been wearing approximately the same number for years, putting them on and taking them off every day. But you never counted them.

Once the accurate definition of a sacrament was generally accepted, it was easy to determine the number of sacraments and the entire Church accepted the number seven without hesitation.

Adversaries. The Protestant dissenters, Luther, Melancthon, Zwingli, and Calvin, were the first to deny this Conclusion. For a brief digest of their opinions, read Pohle-Preuss, *The Sacraments,* I, 32, 33.

Dogmatic Note and First Proof

This is an article of divine faith. The Council of Trent (DB. 844; CT. 665) in the sixteenth century defined it as follows: "If anyone says that the sacraments of the New Law . . . are more or less than seven, namely, baptism, confirmation, Eucharist, penance, extreme unction, holy orders, and matrimony, or even that any one of these is not truly and properly a sacrament, let him be anathema."

Proof 2. From Holy Scripture. This is the second proof because the dogmatic note is always the first and best proof in theology when the Church has made a pronouncement upon any subject. However, the Church herself, before making such pronouncements, investigates Scripture and tradition. These are the remote founts of revelation and so provide proofs for our Conclusions.

From Scripture six of the sacraments can be proved quite satisfactorily. The remaining one, matrimony, can be established with probability. Since these texts will be explained when we deal with the sacraments individually, we shall now omit this proof. It will be known when the course is finished.

Proof 3. From prescription. This is a specific kind of argument from tradition. It not only demonstrates from historical sources, such as the Fathers, theologians, and councils, that a definite teaching is of faith (this is not always accomplished by a general proof from tradition), but it also unites the testimony of historical sources with a dogmatic principle and combines the two into a syllogism, the conclusion of which is peremptory. An apt syllogism for the matter in hand may be expressed as follows:

What the Church universally and for a long time teaches as a dogma of faith, must have been revealed in the deposit of faith;

But the doctrine of seven sacraments was taught by the Church universally from the twelfth to the sixteenth century as a dogma of faith:

Therefore, the doctrine of seven sacraments must have been revealed by God in the deposit of faith.

Proof for the major. Christ promised inerrancy to the Church in matters of faith and morals. Consequently, the whole Church could never err for even an instant in regard to revealed truth. This is part of our Catholic faith and is the principle which is to be united with the historical testimony provided in the proof for the minor. We recall here that God's public revelation ceased with the death of St. John, the apostle, about the year 95.

Proof for the minor. The Councils of Lyons II (1274 A.D.) and of Florence (1439 A.D.) explicitly declare (DB. 465, 695; CT. 660, 663) that there are seven sacraments. These councils were attended by bishops and theologians from the Church at large. Besides, the Council of Lyons proposes this doctrine as a matter of faith since the doctrine is found in the "Profession of Faith of Michael Paleologus." Other councils, one general, the others local, also propose this doctrine long before the Protestant dissension.

Many individuals, both bishops and theologians, also testify to the existence of seven sacraments. For instance, St. Otto, bishop of Bamberg (d. about 1139), is reported by his biographer to have declared to his people: "Now that I am about to die, I give you the seven sacraments of the Church that were handed over to us by the Lord—those seven sacraments, therefore, which I shall name for your benefit: baptism, Eucharist, confirmation, anointing of the sick, reconciliation of the fallen, marriage and orders (PL. 173, 1360)." For additional historical evidence on this point, read Pohle-Preuss, *The Sacraments,* I, 34–37.

It should be observed that, once the fact is established that the Church universally for four centuries before Martin Luther taught the doctrine of seven sacraments as a matter of faith, we could argue from reason alone that this doctrine must have come down from the apostles.

The Catholic mentality has always cherished the traditional faith and been on the alert lest it be contaminated. So if anyone by deception or error had tried to introduce the doctrine of seven sacraments, an uproar would have been created at once. No trace of such an uproar exists. Once the precise definition of a sacrament was formulated, the Catholic world accepted without question the doctrine of seven sacraments.

Confirmation of the Conclusion. It is a striking fact that the Oriental schismatical churches, such as the Monophysites and Nestorians (fifth century), agree that Christ instituted exactly seven sacraments. They would never have accepted this teaching from the Catholic Church whose authority they denied. They found it, however, in Christian tradition which they venerate. When Protestants have on diverse occasions attempted to persuade them to change the number of the sacraments, they have always refused.

OBJECTIONS

1. Holy Scripture does not say that there are seven sacraments.

Answer. Holy Scripture contains the seven sacraments. Hence, if the sacred writers had been inspired to count them, they would have necessarily said seven.

The fact that they do not count them proves nothing. If I have seven coins in my pocket, I cannot change the number whether I count them or not, so long as exactly seven are there. Neither does Scripture say that there are three or four sacraments. How then can a Protestant defend two sacraments? Scripture nowhere says that there are two.

2. The washing of the feet of the apostles by Christ at the Last Supper is also a sacrament (John 13:14). It is a perceptible sign instituted by Christ to give grace.

Answer. This text from St. John does not prove that the washing of the feet conferred grace. This rite was performed for the personal benefit of the apostles, not to give them grace, but to teach them humility. This becomes clear from Luke 22:24: "And there was also a strife among them, which of them should seem to be greater."

3. Why do some theologians of the Middle Ages, such as St. Bernard (d. about 1153), count more or less than seven sacraments and actually write down a different number from seven?

Answer. Because the definition was not yet accurately established in their time. You must know exactly what a thing is before you can count how many things you have.

4. Christ said (John 4:23) that God should be adored in spirit and in truth. So sacraments are unnecessary.

Answer. The use of sacraments does not contradict this command. Pious interior dispositions should accompany the reception of the sacraments. In fact, sacraments foster such dispositions.

Comment 1. Were sacraments in existence before Christ's coming?

The Mosaic Law had no sacraments in the strict sense of the term as explained in Conclusion 1. However, it is proper to refer to some of the rites of that Law as sacraments in a more general sense.

They differed from our sacraments in three ways particularly. They were instituted by God alone before Christ's advent; they were temporary and were abrogated with the establishment of the Church; finally and most important, they did not actively produce sanctifying grace.

Theologians admit that circumcision was such a sacrament. Most theologians say that various other rites such as the celebration of the paschal lamb, the loaves of proposition, diverse ceremonies of purification, and some consecratory rites were also sacraments in this general meaning.

Moses lived about 1500 years before Christ. Circumcision, however, was revealed to Abraham about 400 years before Moses and so preceded the Mosaic Law. The other Hebrew rites that were sacramental pertained to the Mosaic Law.

Was there any sacrament (always understanding "sacrament" in its general meaning) in use among pagan nations from the fall of Adam down to the establishment of the Church? Yes, and it is certain in the case of infants. God established some means whereby they might be freed from original sin.

This means is often called the Sacrament of Nature. It consisted probably in some external profession of faith in the coming Redeemer and was made by parents for their infants. All infants, excepting males of the Hebrews, had to receive this sacrament in order to be freed from original sin.

We do not know whether pagan adults had any sacraments during this long period of time. They could have liberated themselves from original sin, in case it had not already been remitted by the Sacrament of Nature, by making an act of perfect contrition.

It is also disputed whether Adam and Eve had sacramental rites before their fall. The majority of theologians follow the

opinion of St. Thomas who denies that they had any sacraments.
Comment 2. Concerning the matter and form of the sacraments.

If a perfect stranger were to hand a civil official a box of candy, the meaning of the gift would not be clear. It might be a bribe, or a token of esteem, or an expression of gratitude. But the meaning of the gift does become clear if the stranger says: "This is a token of appreciation for the many favors you have done for my sister who is your secretary." These words lend definite significance to the gift. It is now a sign of gratitude.

Similarly, the mere washing of a baby's head with water does not have a precise meaning. It may be done to cool the baby, to relieve a headache, to awaken it. But if the words of baptism are pronounced, the washing gets a definite signification.

The washing with water is called the matter of the sacrament because by itself it has no precise meaning. The water itself is called the *remote* matter of baptism. The application of the water by washing is called the *proximate* matter. But the washing does not obtain a religious significance until the words, "I baptize you in the name of the Father and of the Son and of the Holy Ghost," are pronounced. These words are called the *form* of the sacrament.

The same, generally speaking, is true of the other sacraments, as will be explained when we deal with them individually. The matter is always undetermined in meaning, but this indetermination is removed by the form, the words pronounced by the minister.

It is important to know the matter and form of each sacrament. If they are correctly united together with the requisite intention, the sacrament is valid, i.e., it has the power to produce grace in a disposed person. If they are absent, no sacrament has been administered.

All other ceremonies and words may happen to be omitted, but their omission cannot make a sacrament invalid. It would be illicit, i.e., sinful, for the minister to omit the accidental rites under ordinary circumstances, but the sacrament would be able to produce grace so long as the matter and form were properly placed.

Since sacraments are composed of words joined to things or actions, it follows that the sacraments are not entities of the same kind as trees or any other unified material thing. Words may be contemporaneous with things or actions, but they cannot be united with them physically. Consequently, we call the sacraments, not physical, but moral or intentional entities.

It is the constant Catholic teaching, though not of faith, that sacraments come into existence by the placing of their matter and form. The Council of Florence (DB. 695; CT. 663) in its *Decree for the Armenians* (the dogmatic value of which we shall discuss under the sacrament of orders) explicitly says this. All theologians agree. Some theologians deny that matter and form actually constitute the sacraments of penance and the Eucharist, but they, too, concede that without matter and form these sacraments could not come into existence.

When all seven sacraments are to be enumerated at one time, either orally or in writing, they should be arranged as follows: baptism, confirmation, Eucharist, penance, extreme unction, holy orders, matrimony. The Council of Trent (DB. 844; CT. 665), theologians, and catechisms follow this order. To follow a different order without some special reason indicates one not versed in technical theology.

*

Conclusion 3. The sacraments confer sanctifying grace, not merely acts of confidence in God; they confer their grace *ex opere operato;* furthermore, they operate as instrumental causes in producing grace.

Introduction. Having considered the nature and the number of the sacraments, we begin in this Conclusion to treat of their effects. This is a matter of great consequence.

The first part of the Conclusion asserts the fact that the primary effect of the sacraments is to confer sanctifying grace. The second part explains the manner in which the sacraments produce grace. The third part clarifies further the manner of their operation.

Explanation of Terms

1. Sacraments. The definition has been given in Conclusion 1.

2. Sanctifying grace. It is a supernatural quality of a physical kind. It is just as real as the light of the sun or the hardness of metal, but since it is spiritual, it has no parts. It is created by God and is infused into the soul. It may be continually increased. It is a share in God's own life and makes its recipient an adopted child of God with a title to everlasting happiness in the beatific vision.

3. Acts of confidence in God. According to Luther a sacrament, such as baptism when conferred upon an adult particularly, would be likely to stir up in his soul and in the souls of the onlookers feelings of piety and of trust in God. These feelings of confidence were in his opinion the primary effect of the sacrament.

Catholics do not deny that this effect may follow from the conferring of a sacrament, but they maintain that it is not the primary effect. Sacraments confer grace. All other effects are secondary.

4. Ex opere operato. We all know how an automatic gun operates. Pull the trigger once and the gun will continue to fire its shells until the magazine is empty. The gun contains a mechanical device so that the hunter does not have to pull the trigger more than once. After that the gun works by itself.

Somewhat similarly, when we say that the sacraments operate ex opere operato, we mean that the sacramental rites of themselves contain the power to confer grace independently of the meritorious acts of the recipient. The only requirement for the recipient is a disposition of soul, i.e., he must be in a definite spiritual condition in order to obtain grace from the sacrament. Fire has the power to burn, but it will not burn soggy wood because the wood has not the right disposition or quality. In a Comment following this Conclusion we shall explain the dispositions necessary for the various sacraments.

It is important here to note the difference between these dispositions in general and meritorious acts. The latter are always positive acts; they are elicited at the time the good work, e.g., the saying of the "Hail Mary," is performed; they are causes of the increase of grace and so are said to produce grace "*ex opere operantis,*" i.e., owing to the efforts of the agent.

On the other hand, the dispositions for a sacrament need not always be positive acts; they may precede the reception of the sacrament; they are not causes, but mere conditions which make it possible for the sacrament by its own efficacy to produce grace.

In the case of merit, the subjective acts of the agent are the cause of grace, whereas the good work performed (visiting a church, giving an alms, saying a prayer) is only a condition or occasion of the grace received. But when a sacrament is administered, the sacrament itself is the cause of grace. The subjective acts of the recipient are simply a condition which permits the sacrament either to cause grace if it is absent, or to cause its increase.

5. Instrumental causes. These are a species of efficient causes. An efficient cause is one that by its own inherent action brings another thing into existence. Thus the sun is an efficient cause of the growth of plant life, though not the only one. Wind is a cause of erosion. A writer is the efficient cause of his story.

An efficient cause is the *principal* efficient cause if it is not subordinated to any other efficient cause in producing the effect. Thus the writer is the principal cause of his story.

But the story must be put on paper. To do this the author uses a typewriter or pen or pencil. These are *instrumental* efficient causes. They truly act, but they do so under the guidance of the principal cause. Yet, their action leaves a mark on the effect produced. If the author's penpoint is dull, dullness will show up in the writing. If his typewriter does not space properly, this will be revealed in the finished composition. But the pen and typewriter could not move at all unless they were manipulated by the principal cause, the author.

The sacraments are instrumental causes of grace. They are like the pen and the typewriter. God is the principal cause of grace, but He uses the sacraments as His instruments to produce it.

Sacraments, therefore, are not merely conditions or occasions of grace. A *condition* is necessary either in order that a cause may operate at all (necessary condition), or in order that it may produce its full effect (simple condition). But no condition actively participates in producing an effect. A modicum of dryness is a necessary condition in wood in order that fire, the cause, may burn it. Light comes into a home through the windows, but the windows do not cause the light. The sun does that. The windows are conditions without which the light cannot enter. We repeat again: Sacraments are not conditions, but causes of grace.

An *occasion* is not required at all for a cause to operate. We may have a banquet at Christmas, but Christmas does not cause the banquet. We might postpone the banquet until the day after Christmas. Christmas, however, is a fitting occasion on which to have a banquet. If sacraments are not merely conditions of grace, much less are they merely occasions for its reception.

The Conclusion is divided into three parts.

1. The sacraments confer sanctifying grace, not merely acts of confidence in God.

2. They confer their grace *ex opere operato.*

3. They operate as instrumental causes in producing grace.

It should be observed that the second and third parts are distinct. The *ex opere operato* production of grace does not mean a causing of grace. Circumcision gave sanctifying grace *ex opere operato.* When God saw this rite performed, He always conferred grace, but circumcision did not cause the grace. It was simply a necessary condition without which grace was not obtained by an infant of the male sex.

Adversaries. Luther thought that the primary purpose of the sacraments was to produce filial trust in God in all recipients. Calvin believed that this trust would be produced in the predestined only. According to Zwingli the sacraments produce nothing. They are merely external signs like badges whereby a person acknowledges his membership in the Christian fraternity. Since these men reject the first part of the Conclusion, they necessarily reject the second and third parts.

Dogmatic Note

Part 1. This is an article of divine faith from the Council of Trent (DB. 848; CT. 669): "If anyone says that these sacraments were instituted for the sake of nourishing faith alone, let him be anathema." This declaration condemns the general Protestant opinion.

But the council (DB. 849; CT. 670) also positively states that the sacraments produce grace: "If anyone says that the sacraments of the New Law . . . do not confer grace itself on those who do not place an obstacle thereunto . . . let him be anathema."

Part 2. This, too, is an article of divine faith since Trent (DB. 851; CT. 672) declares: "If anyone says that by the said sacraments of the New Law grace is not conferred *ex opere operato* . . . let him be anathema."

Part 3. This is certain. Trent affirms that the sacraments "contain" (DB. 849; CT. 670), "confer" (DB. 849; CT. 670), and "give" (DB. 850; CT. 671) grace. Although the words "confer" and "give" might possibly refer to conditions only, the word "contain" necessarily denotes causality. We cannot say that a mere condition contains an effect. A condition is extrinsic to the cause, the container.

Some prominent theologians who antedated Trent held that the sacraments were merely conditions for obtaining grace. It is certain that the council did not wish to condemn this opinion as heretical. However, the meaning of the council is so obvious that all theologians now admit that sacraments are genuine instrumental causes of grace.

Proof 2. From Holy Scripture (II Tim. 1:6): "For which cause I admonish thee that thou stir up the grace of God which is in thee by the imposition of my hands." By these words St. Paul reminds St. Timothy that he had received the sacrament of orders from Paul.

We shall prove the three parts of the Conclusion from this text. The proof is dogmatically certain; apologetically probable.

Part 1. The sacraments produce sanctifying grace, not merely acts of confidence in God.

The sacramental rite mentioned is an "imposition of hands." The effect of this rite is "grace." St. Paul never uses the word "grace" to mean acts of faith or of some other virtue. Such acts, therefore, are not the effect of the sacrament of orders.

"Grace" according to St. Paul means either sanctifying grace or a charismatic gift. In our text it cannot mean a charismatic gift because the "grace" conferred on Timothy depends for its exercise upon his free will, whereas charismatic gifts were inspired by the Holy Ghost independently of one's free will. It would be useless for St. Paul to counsel Timothy to "stir up" a charismatic gift. "Grace," therefore, means sanctifying grace.

Part 2. The sacraments confer their grace *ex opere operato.*

This follows from the fact that the "grace" given by the imposition of hands is not attributed by St. Paul to his own merits or to the merits of Timothy, but to the imposition itself. Nor does the exercise of any virtue come between the imposition and the grace. Hands were imposed. Grace followed *ex opere operato,* i.e., spontaneously.

Part 3. The sacraments are instrumental causes in producing grace.

The exegetes tell us that the preposition "through," when found in Scripture within a context requiring the meaning of instrumentality, generally signifies true causality. Since, however, exceptions occur to this general rule, we prefer to argue from a different text.

The causality of baptism is indicated quite clearly from the following sentence (John 3:5): "Unless a man is born again of water and the Holy Ghost, he cannot enter into the kingdom of heaven."

In this text the Holy Ghost is certainly a cause, and the principal cause of supernatural regeneration, i.e., of the infusion of sanctifying grace. Hence "water," i.e., baptism, should also be a true cause of grace, though an instrumental one, by reason of the co-ordination of the prepositional phrase. It would be an anomalous use of language to link a principal cause with a mere condition after the same preposition to denote the production of an effect.

Proof 3. From the Church's practice of baptizing infants. No acts of confidence in God can be aroused in an infant. Yet, the Church gives it baptism; teaches, in fact, that baptism is necessary for its salvation.

Neither can an infant possess any merits since it has not the use of reason and will. Accordingly, for infants, baptism must function *ex opere operato.* However, the causality of baptism cannot be proved from this practice.

Proof 4. From the Fathers. St. John Chrysostom says: "What the mother is to the embryo, water (baptism) is to one of the faithful, for by water the faithful is fashioned and formed. . . . Water produces rational souls that bear the Holy Spirit" (*In Joan. hom.* 26, 1; PG. 59, 153).

St. Augustine expresses the *ex opere operato* action of baptism lucidly when he declares: "Baptism gets its value, not from the merits of those by whom it is administered nor of those to whom it is administered, but from its own holiness and truthfulness through Him (Christ) who instituted it . . ." (*Contra Crescon.* 1. 4, c. 16, n. 19; PL. 43, 559).

Objections

1. It is a kind of magic to believe that a simple external rite can produce a wonderful effect like sanctifying grace.

Answer. Magic means to procure an extraordinary effect beyond man's power by invoking some creature as though it were God.

Catholics do not invoke the sacraments as though they were principal causes of grace. They are but instruments of God and were instituted by God to give grace.

If Moses had believed that he could obtain water from the rock simply by striking it with his wand, he would have been guilty of superstition. But after God had promised to work this miracle through the striking of the wand, there was no superstition. The wand was merely the instrument which God used to supply water. Moses really prayed to God when he applied the wand. He did not invoke the wand itself. The same is true of the sacraments.

2. How can there be any proportion between a natural rite like a sacrament and a supernatural effect like grace?

Answer. The sacrament is merely an instrument. God, if He wishes, can communicate a supernatural efficacy to what looks like a natural rite. That He has done so is clear from revelation as we have explained in the Conclusion.

3. Salvation depends upon faith alone. Sacraments, therefore, should produce acts of faith.

Answer. St. James (2:17) says: "Faith without works is dead." Hence salvation does not depend on faith alone, not even on supernatural faith.

Much less does it depend upon mere confidence in God, Luther's idea of faith. Protestants have so revolted against this teaching of Luther that nowadays many of them say the exact opposite: "It does not matter about your faith: what you do is the important thing."

4. Christ usually demanded some good internal or external work before He performed miracles. Yet you say that the sacraments produce grace without any such works.

Answer. We do not say this. The adult recipient of a sacrament must always have a good intention, without which no sacrament can exist. He must also have a good disposition in order to receive any grace from a sacrament.

Only babies can receive a sacrament without supplying a good disposition. They are naturally incapable of supplying one.

5. Since sacraments of the living require grace before they are received, how can they produce grace?

Answer. These sacraments intensify or increase the grace already present in the soul.

Comment 1. Further explanation of the manner in which sacraments confer grace *ex opere operato.*

The following items are of exceptional importance and require reflection.

1. If an adult recipient has no disposition whatever, it is certain that he receives no grace at the time the sacrament is administered. The sacrament will be valid if matter and form are properly placed and if the necessary intention is present, but no grace will result unless the recipient has some kind of a disposition. The only exception to this law is infant baptism.

2. The state of sanctifying grace is the necessary or indispensable disposition required to obtain more grace from the sacraments of the living (confirmation, Eucharist, extreme unction, orders, and matrimony). For adult baptism acts of sorrow for sin, faith, and hope are the necessary disposition.

3. This necessary disposition can be improved by an accidental or active disposition so that a sacrament can bestow more grace *ex opere operato* than it would if the disposition were merely the essential or necessary one.

Suppose that a Catholic prays in order to prepare for Communion. These prayers improve his necessary disposition so that the sacrament gives him more grace *ex opere operato* than if he did not so prepare.

The accidental or active disposition always consists of acts of virtue made before the sacrament's reception and directed to it. Hence any prayers, or acts of mortification such as fasting and rising early, enter into the active disposition and gain more grace *ex opere operato* from Communion. The drier wood is, the more easily it burns. The better a person prepares to receive a sacrament, the more grace he obtains from it.

4. Sacraments do not give more grace simply because one recipient, when receiving a sacrament, happens to have more sanctifying grace than another recipient. In other words, the intensity or degree of sanctifying grace does not by itself improve one's active disposition. A person with thirty degrees of sanctifying grace will obtain no more grace from the same sacrament than a person with two degrees. The one who has the better active disposition will receive more grace. This is a highly probable opinion.

It is possible, of course, that a person having more sanctifying grace will thereby be enabled to prepare better for a sacrament's reception. In this case, a higher degree of grace indirectly enables a person to obtain more grace *ex opere operato* from a sacrament. But the general principle remains true. The active disposition is improved only by acts of virtue made beforehand and with a view to the sacrament's reception.

5. The same sacrament has in itself an equal power to give grace whenever and wherever it is administered. Confirmation, whether administered in New York or Honolulu, to a baby or to an adult, always has in itself the same capacity to produce grace. A difference of active dispositions is the only condition which enables the sacrament to produce more or less grace.

6. It follows, therefore, that when dispositions are exactly the same, the same degree of grace is bestowed by the same sacrament. If two babies are baptized, they both receive the same degree of grace.

In the case of adults, no two active dispositions are likely to be the same and so the degree of grace conferred will vary with each person. But if the dispositions did happen to be identical, the sacrament would give an identical degree of grace to each recipient.

7. It is an article of faith (DB. 846; CT. 667) that the seven sacraments are not equal in dignity. The Eucharist is the most noble because it contains Christ Himself. It is difficult to arrange the rest of the sacraments in order of dignity. But it would be clear, for instance, that confirmation would be of greater dignity than penance, which is primarily a cure for spiritual sickness.

8. It is probable that the more noble sacraments confer more grace *ex opere operato* than the less noble, provided that the dispositions of the recipient are the same. Hence Holy Communion probably gives more grace than any other sacrament. However, a person who prepares devoutly for confirmation may obtain more grace from this sacrament than from a poorly prepared Communion. His active dispositions make the difference.

9. It is important to remember that one who devoutly receives a sacrament of the living, also obtains more sanctifying grace independently of the sacrament. He is in the state of grace and so all his acts of virtue merit more sanctifying grace whether he is going to receive a sacrament or not. He does not lose this grace by the fact that his acts of virtue are also a means of improving his active disposition so that the reception of a sacrament can give him more grace *ex opere operato*.

10. Sanctifying grace when given by a sacrament is called sacramental grace. In itself sacramental grace is more probably exactly like the sanctifying grace obtained by other means, but there is a difference in the moral order.

Sacramental grace carries with it a title to actual graces which will help the recipient to implement the purpose of each sacrament. Thus the sacramental grace of confirmation bestows a title to actual graces which will enable the recipient to be a soldier of Christ. The sacramental grace of penance gives a right to actual graces to enable the recipient to overcome sin, avoid occasions, suppress bad habits.

These actual graces continue to come after a sacrament has been received. In sacraments like baptism, confirmation, and orders they keep coming until death. In the case of matrimony, these graces keep coming until the marriage bond is dissolved by the death of one partner. The actual graces of extreme unction comfort the sick person until death comes or until the danger of death is removed. The actual graces of penance and Communion come for a comparatively short time.

From now on, whenever we use the expression "sacramental grace," we mean, not the sanctifying grace bestowed by a sacrament, but the actual graces to which every sacrament gives a title.

Although it is a more common opinion to say that this title to actual graces is attached to sanctifying grace, this opinion is not without difficulty. It means that a person who falls into mortal sin after receiving, for instance, confirmation, will receive no more actual graces from confirmation until he regains the state of grace.

This is hard to believe, especially with regard to orders and matrimony. These sacraments are primarily for the common good. Orders gives its recipient a title to actual graces which will enable him to discharge properly his sacred duties. If a priest commits mortal sin, it is difficult to understand why he should be deprived of actual graces whose help is required for the benefit of others.

Similarly, the actual graces flowing from matrimony are mainly directed to the spiritual protection and betterment of the spouses mutually, and of their children. If personal sin deprives either of the spouses of the right to the actual graces of matrimony, the innocent spouse and the children would suffer spiritual detriment.

Therefore, we prefer to say that, in the cases of orders and matrimony, their sacramental graces are attached to the character and matrimonial bond respectively. It is also probable that the sacramental graces of the rest of the sacraments are not dependent upon sanctifying grace.

Comment 2. Sometimes baptism and penance confer an increase of grace.

These two sacraments of the dead are by definition primarily intended to give grace to one who does not possess it. However, under certain circumstances they act like sacraments of the living and increase grace.

Let us suppose, for instance, that a Catholic loses sanctifying grace by committing a mortal sin. After sinning, he makes an act of perfect contrition intending to go to confession later on. His act of perfect contrition restores grace to him at once, so that, when he comes to confession, he is already in the state of grace. Since penance, like the other sacraments, always gives grace to those who are properly disposed, he must receive grace *ex opere operato* from his confession. But since he already has sanctifying grace before he confesses, penance in this case must increase that grace.

Again, many Catholics having venial sins only, go to confession. They are in the state of grace when they approach confession. Consequently, penance must give them an increase of grace.

Furthermore, many adult converts probably make an act of perfect contrition before they are baptized and so obtain the state of grace. Therefore, when they come to be baptized, they receive a higher degree of grace.

Comment 3. Sometimes the sacraments of the living confer first grace.

"First grace" is a technical phrase which means that sanctifying grace is received by one who does not possess it. The five sacraments of the living, if certain circumstances are verified, give first grace. This is unusual, since by definition these sacraments are primarily intended for those who are spiritually alive, i.e., for those who already are in the state of grace.

Nevertheless, it is certain that extreme unction at times bestows grace on one who does not have it. It is the more common opinion that confirmation, the Eucharist, orders, and matrimony do the same.

What circumstances permit these sacraments to operate in this unexpected way? Let us suppose, for example, that a man has forgotten about a mortal sin which he committed. He is now going to be confirmed. He is not in the state of grace because forgetfulness of itself does not remit sin. At the same time, he does not think that he is doing anything wrong by approaching confirmation, because his mortal sin has lapsed from his memory. He thinks he is in the state of grace, though he is not.

Before receiving confirmation, he also makes an act of imperfect contrition for all sins in general, not reflecting about any one of them in particular. This act of imperfect contrition is no obstacle to the infusion of grace by a sacrament, since it certainly suffices for baptism and penance. Hence, when the man is confirmed, he receives, not an increase of grace, but first grace.

However, this would not be true if the act of imperfect contrition were not made. God never forgives sin to one who has not at least imperfect sorrow for it. If this particular man were to approach confirmation without this sorrow, he would not commit a sacrilege because he would not be aware of any wrongdoing, but neither would he receive grace.

There are other examples which illustrate how sacraments of the living may confer first grace, but two principles must always be verified. The man must be unaware that he is doing anything wrong and he must have imperfect sorrow for his sins. A person who knows the law and deliberately receives one of these sacraments in the state of mortal sin commits a great sacrilege.

If a man realizes that he is in the state of mortal sin, he should not receive any sacrament of the living without first going to confession. However, strictly speaking, he is obliged to go to confession only when he intends to receive Holy Communion. For confirmation, extreme unction, orders, and matrimony, an act of perfect contrition would suffice. Nevertheless, we should always go to confession if we are in mortal sin and intend to receive one of these sacraments.

Comment 4. The sacraments, excepting the Eucharist and penance, revive.

Let us suppose that an adult sinner is baptized without having made an act of imperfect contrition for his sins. His baptism is valid, but he gets no grace because he has not the necessary disposition. Will he, then, be forever deprived of the sanctifying grace conferred *ex opere operato* by baptism? Will he, perhaps, obtain it at some future time? If so, what must he do in order to receive the grace later on?

It is certain that the grace flowing from baptism can come to this man after the sacrament's reception. It may be after one week or one month or after many years. The influx of baptismal grace will occur as soon as he makes the act of imperfect contrition whose absence impeded the flow of grace at the time of the actual ceremony.

However, if he commits other mortal sins after his baptism and before he makes his act of imperfect contrition, he will not receive the sanctifying grace of baptism until his act of imperfect contrition is joined with the sacrament of penance.

Of course, if such a man made an act of perfect contrition at any time, all his sins would be forgiven at once and he would receive the grace of baptism. But he would be obliged to tell the mortal sins committed after his baptism in his next confession.

Similarly, if a man is not in the state of grace when he receives confirmation, orders, extreme unction, or matrimony, he will ordinarily obtain no sanctifying grace from these sacraments.

However, it is very probable that he will obtain the grace of confirmation and orders after their reception as soon as he recovers the state of grace. These two sacraments, like baptism, are absolutely unrepeatable once they have been validly conferred. It is not likely that God will forever deprive a recipient of their grace if the disposition, missing at the time of their administration, is finally provided.

In the same way and for the same reason, it is quite probable that the sanctifying grace of extreme unction and matrimony comes later on, if a person has received them unworthily. These two sacraments are to a certain extent unrepeatable. Matrimony cannot ordinarily be repeated until dissolved by the death of one of the partners. Extreme Unction, too, cannot be repeated in the same illness or, at least, in the same crisis of the same illness. It is quite likely, therefore, that God gives the grace of these sacraments as soon as those who have received them unworthily regain the state of grace.

On the other hand, it is more probable that penance cannot confer its grace after its reception, because the acts of the penitent (confession, contrition, and willingness to make reparation) are, according to the more common opinion, required for the validity of this sacrament. If these acts or any one of them are missing, no grace can come later because the sacrament never existed.

It is also more probable that the grace of Holy Communion never revives for one who has received this sacrament unworthily. If we were to admit that its grace were restored after its reception, it would be possible for a man who made sacrilegious Communions for many years, to repent on his death bed and obtain an unusually high place in heaven. All the grace of his past sacrilegious Communions would revive and a premium would seem to be placed on sacrilege itself. For this reason, and also because this sacrament is easily repeated, its grace is not likely to be restored later if the sacrament has been unworthily received.

*

Conclusion 4. The sacraments of baptism, confirmation, and orders imprint indelible characters upon the soul. Hence these sacraments cannot be repeated if they have been validly received. Their characters depute the recipients to divine public service.

Introduction. Having considered how the sacraments produce grace, their primary effect, we now logically consider a secondary effect produced by only three of them. Just as all the sacraments impart grace *ex opere operato*, so in the same way three of them also confer characters. In this Conclusion we deal with the existence and nature of these characters and also with their effects.

Explanation of Terms

1. Characters. This word takes on a technical meaning in theology. It is derived from a Greek word and signifies a seal, or stamp, or impress. Hence we may define the word theologically as "a spiritual sign indelibly impressed upon the soul by God through the operation of three sacraments in order to depute the recipient to divine public service."

We shall now explain the elements of this definition.

Like the sacramental rites themselves, the characters also are signs. They have a fourfold signification. First, they are obligatory signs, i.e., signs of conferred powers and duties. Their recipient has a right and obligation to participate in divine public service. Second, they are distinguishing signs. By them the faithful are discerned from unbelievers, and certain ones of the faithful are distinguished from the rest of the faithful. Third, they are configurative signs, which means that those marked with the characters share in Christ's priesthood. Fourth, they are dispositive signs in so far as they testify that a person who has one or more of the characters should always remain in the state of grace.

But the characters, unlike the sacramental rites, are *spiritual* signs. This simply means that they are not perceptible to the senses.

In its nature, the character is an accident, i.e., it depends upon the soul, in which it inheres, for its existence. It is supernatural because no man has a right to it. Moreover, it has no parts as do material things. It is a reality because it exists independently of the mind.

Furthermore (and this is very important to remember), it is a *physical* reality. Not only does it exist independently of the mind, but it has an entity of its own. It truly adds something to the soul. If God were to remove it, He would have to tear something off the soul.

A man's rights to his reputation or to an inheritance are independent of the mind, but such rights are moral entities. The character is more than such rights. When God infuses it into a soul, He acts like an artist putting paint upon the canvas. The coloration is something physical.

The principal cause of the character is God Himself. The sacraments are God's instruments which produce the character *ex opere operato*. Only baptism, confirmation, and orders are such instruments.

It is an article of divine faith that the characters are impressed upon the soul. Some theologians think that they are stamped directly upon either the intellect or will, and so only indirectly upon the essence of the soul. But all agree that they are rooted in the soul either directly or indirectly.

Moreover, the characters are indelible. Once they have been infused into the soul, only God can remove them and He will not do so. It is a divinely revealed truth that the characters endure as long as we live on earth. It is absolutely certain that they last for all eternity.

Finally, the characters depute their recipients to divine public service. This service is not limited to the administration of religious rites or to their reception. The character of confirmation, for instance, authorizes a person to profess the faith bravely. But every character has a public aspect. It is not intended merely for the good of the individual. This will be further explained in a Comment following the Conclusion.

It should also be noted that baptism, confirmation, and orders produce their characters when they are received *validly*. Hence no disposition except an intention is required. Sometimes, therefore, these sacraments will impress the character without giving any grace.

Adversaries. Protestants generally have no belief in the existence of the sacramental characters.

Dogmatic Note

That baptism, confirmation, and orders imprint indelible characters upon the soul and so cannot be repeated (the first two parts of the Conclusion) is of divine faith from the Council of Trent (DB. 852; CT. 673): "If anyone says that in the three sacraments of baptism, confirmation, and orders, there is not imprinted on the soul a character, that is, a kind of spiritual and indelible sign, by reason of which they cannot be repeated, let him be anathema."

The general statement that characters depute their recipient to divine public service (third part of the Conclusion) is common and certain teaching.

Parts 1 and 2. Baptism, confirmation, and orders imprint an indelible character upon the soul and so these sacraments cannot be repeated.

Proof 2. From Holy Scripture. This is not a sure proof, but the student should look up three texts (II Cor. 1:21, 22; Eph. 1:13; 4:30) which may possibly refer to the character.

However, they do not afford us a sure proof either dogmatically, i.e., from the common interpretation of councils, Fathers, theologians, and exegetes; or apologetically, i.e., from a purely reasoned interpretation of the words. Some Fathers and many exegetes assert that these texts do refer to the character, but others deny it. Hence the following proof is important.

Proof 3. From prescription. This argument proceeds like that given to prove the number seven.

What the Church universally and for a long time teaches as a dogma of faith must have been revealed by God in the deposit of faith;

But that baptism, confirmation, and orders imprint a character upon the soul and so cannot be repeated was taught by the Church universally from the thirteenth to the sixteenth century as a dogma of faith:

Therefore, that baptism, confirmation, and orders imprint a character and so cannot be repeated must have been revealed by God in the deposit of faith.

Proof for the major. It is the same as in Conclusion 2.

Proof for the minor. Pope Innocent III in a letter (1201 A.D.) affirms the existence of the character of baptism (DB. 411; CT. 684). In the thirteenth century, St. Thomas, Scotus, Peter of Poitiers, and scholastic theologians without exception teach the threefold character. In 1439 A.D. the Council of Florence (DB. 695; CT. 663) declares: "Three of these sacraments, baptism, confirmation, and orders, imprint on the soul a character, that is, a kind of spiritual sign which distinguishes them from the other sacraments. Hence they are not repeated in the same person."

When this doctrine was challenged by the Protestant dissenters, the Council of Trent, recognizing the universal belief of previous centuries, expressly defined it as an article of faith.

It should be observed that none of the sources referred to or cited above, explicitly says that this doctrine pertains to faith. However, they do so implicitly. All of them teach explicitly that the seven sacraments were revealed by God. Since this is true, it follows that we can know the effects of sacraments by revelation only. When, therefore, we find these sources testifying to the existence and unrepeatability of the character as an effect of three sacraments, we may conclude with certainty that they considered this effect as revealed.

Proof 4. From the Fathers. St. John Chrysostom, speaking of baptism, says: "As a kind of brand is imprinted upon soldiers, so the Spirit is also imprinted upon the faithful. Accordingly, if you forsake the ranks (of the faithful), you become known to all. For the Jews, circumcision was a sign; for us, the pledge of the Spirit" (In II Cor. 3, 7; PG. 61, 418).

St. Augustine teaches almost our entire doctrine about the sacramental characters. For quotations from him and from other Fathers, cf. Pohle-Preuss, *The Sacraments,* I, 79–81.

Proof 5. From reasons of suitability. When certain men are designated for public functions of importance, they are usually endowed with some kind of insignia. Soldiers, firemen, nurses, have their own uniforms. Hence we would expect God, who deals with men according to their nature, to bestow characters on those who have a special public function to perform.

Moreover, it is customary to appoint men to office once only. Even though the office may endure for life, we do not depute the incumbent more than once—in the beginning when he first assumes the office. So God takes human nature into account when He does not permit baptism, confirmation, and orders to be repeated.

Part 3. The characters depute their recipients to divine public service.

Proof 2. From the consent of theologians. The unanimous agreement of theologians on this point is expressed in various ways. St. Thomas says that by the characters men "are deputed to Christian worship." Elsewhere he calls the characters "participations, so to speak, in the priesthood of Christ."

Characters are described by other theologians as "certain powers with regard to sacred things," "participations, as it were, in the functions of Christ." The common denominator of all the expressions used is that the characters are "special deputations to divine public service," as is stated in the wording of the Conclusion.

OBJECTIONS

1. Since characters are useless, God would not imprint them.

Answer. Any supernatural entity created by God for man is a precious adornment of the soul. We guard many heirlooms which have no practical use. The thought of supernatural gifts like sanctifying grace, the infused virtues, and the characters raises our minds lovingly to God.

2. At any rate, characters are useless as signs. God, the angels, and the blessed in heaven do not need them. Men in this world cannot see them.

Answer. It is true that God, the angels, and the blessed do not need the characters in order to know that one is specially deputed to divine public service.

But signs do not inform only. Some signs might be such

beautiful works of art that we would cherish them for their own value. Characters, like such works of art, are treasures in themselves.

Moreover, the characters are indirectly perceptible to men in this life. When we see a baby baptized, we are certain that the baby now has a character, the uniform of Christ. We can obtain the information imparted by some sign or other without seeing the sign ourselves. Someone might tell us about the sign's existence. In this case, we would perceive the sign indirectly only, but we would act as though we had seen it ourselves.

Furthermore, in the next life the characters will be directly perceptible to all and they will redound to our glory or to our shame.

3. When the Fathers speak of the "seal" or "impress" of the sacraments, they refer to the external rite, not to the character which is an effect of the rite.

Answer. Sometimes the Fathers use these words in the way mentioned, but they use them also of a special effect of the rite, i.e., of the character. We use the word "seal" in the same way. Sometimes it refers to the instrument which does the marking. At others, it refers to the marking itself.

4. If a character deputes one to God's special service, all the sacraments should bestow characters.

Answer. Even if all the sacraments did depute one to God's public service, God could permit three sacraments to give a physical character even though the others did not. Objections of this sort proceed from those who imagine that they can always fathom the infinite mind of God.

However, we find good reasons why the other four sacraments do not confer characters. Although they are in a general way a sharing in the worship of God, they do not endow their recipients with any *public* function pertaining to divine service.

Three of these four are primarily for the good of the individual. The Eucharist increases the individual's love for Christ. Penance restores the sinner to the state of grace. Extreme unction helps the individual to face the personal difficulties of serious illness.

Even matrimony has a domestic aspect only. Though parents by reason of this sacrament should train their children in God's love, this training remains within the family, whereas the characters depute one to God's service anywhere, any time, before the general public.

Comment 1. A comparison of the characters with sanctifying grace.

The two have much in common. They are both real, physical, internal, spiritual, supernatural qualities inhering in the soul. The following differences between sanctifying grace and the characters should be studied.

Sanctifying grace is a sharing in God's nature. The characters depute to divine public service. Grace, therefore, has a much greater dignity and worth than the characters.

As regards their *origin,* grace comes from all the sacraments, the characters from only three. Moreover, grace can be obtained by other means than the sacraments. But the characters come from sacraments only. Even the so-called baptisms of desire and of blood do not produce the character of baptism.

Concerning *duration,* grace can be lost by sin. The characters cannot be destroyed in any way.

With regard to the *disposition of the recipient,* grace comes to those only who have at least the necessary disposition. The characters are imprinted even if the recipient has no disposition, provided that the sacrament is valid.

Comment 2. The intrinsic nature of the characters.

The theologian, Durandus, who lived before the Council of Trent, thought that the characters were not qualities, but mere relations devoid of any physical foundation. Thus the character of baptism would merely mean that a baby is consecrated to God somewhat as a chalice is consecrated to God by the prayers of a bishop. Such a consecration is something real, i.e., independent of the mind, but it is only a moral entity.

According to Trent, however, the character is something "impressed on the soul." This evidently means that the character is something physical and a quality. It is true that a new relation begins to exist between a person who receives a character and God. But the relation does not constitute the character. The character is the foundation for the relation.

Scholastic philosophers distinguish four kinds of qualities. Under which of these to classify the character has not yet been determined by the theologians. It is better to adopt the opinion of St. Thomas who reduces the character to the species of quality called "power" because it authorizes one to perform legitimately certain public acts of divine service.

Comment 3. The specific powers conferred by the characters.

Each character bestows its own special deputation to divine public worship. The deputation conferred by the character of baptism is mainly passive. It enables a person to share publicly in the religious benefits flowing from membership in the Catholic Church. However, the deputation received by this character is active to some degree. By it a person is entitled to assist at the Mass and to associate his internal offering of the sacrifice with the priest's external offering. This will be explained more fully when we treat of the Mass.

The character of confirmation officially authorizes its recipient to profess and defend the Catholic faith publicly. Of course, one who is baptized only, may be required to profess and defend his faith publicly, sometimes even unto death. However, by the character of confirmation a person is *officially* deputed to do this. All citizens should welcome the President when he visits their city. But a welcoming committee is appointed to tender an official greeting.

Finally, the character of orders empowers its recipient to perform publicly sacred rites and functions.

*

Conclusion 5. The sacraments produce grace either as physical causes, or as moral causes, or, more probably, as intentional causes.

Introduction. Although the sacraments are true causes of grace, their manner of producing it is mysterious. The sacraments appear to be a composite of purely natural elements, the saying of words and the application of some substance or other. Yet they confer grace, a supernatural effect.

How is it possible for an apparently natural cause to engender an effect out of all proportion to itself? This is the question with which we deal in this Conclusion.

Explanation by Physical Causality

This theory is defended by outstanding theologians like Cajetan, most Thomists, St. Robert Bellarmine, Suarez, Tanquerey. A general sketch of their system follows.

God uses the sacraments to cause grace in much the same way as a man uses any physical instrument to produce an effect. Whenever a physical instrument is used, it must have its share in the effect resulting. For instance, a person writing with chalk upon a blackboard is the principal cause of the writing. Nevertheless, the chalk itself has its influence though it is directed and set in motion by the person. If the chalk is blue, the writing is blue. If the chalk is blunt, it will be difficult to etch the letters plainly.

Consequently, since the sacraments are physical causes of grace, they must in some way be elevated by God in order to have a proportion between them and grace. God, therefore, transmits a transient, supernatural quality or movement to the sacraments when they are administered. In this way they are endowed with supernatural power so that they become physical instruments in the production of grace.

Explanation by Moral Causality

Eminent theologians like de Lugo, Franzelin, Pesch, the Scotists propose this theory.

According to them the sacraments do not need any supernatural elevation because they are not physical, but only moral causes of grace. Sacraments possess an intrinsic dignity since they were instituted by Christ, are administered in His name, and are channels through which the merits of His passion flow.

When God sees a sacrament conferred, He does not behold a rite composed of purely natural elements. A sacrament is like a coin made golden by Christ which stirs God, by His own free predetermination, to give grace. Or, a sacrament is like a letter written to God on the most excellent stationery, in Christ's own handwriting and with His signature, and containing an appeal for grace.

In this theory, therefore, the sacrament does not come between God and the grace. It comes before God's action by providing Him with an efficacious reason for producing grace through the sacrament.

11396755

Explanation by Intentional Causality

Some prominent theologians of more recent years, like Billot, Van Noort, Lercher, do not call upon the intrinsic dignity of the sacraments in order to explain how they confer grace. They do not deny that the sacraments have the dignity ascribed to them by those holding moral causality, but they deny that this dignity is intrinsic to the sacraments.

Nor does this theory require any physical elevation of the sacraments to explain their efficacy. Yet it succeeds in putting the sacrament between God and the grace produced and so differs, in this respect also, from moral causality.

This explanation begins by saying that the sacraments are essentially signs, i.e., they are in the intentional or moral order. This being the case, they already possess an instrumental power to produce something in the same intentional or moral order. This is precisely how God uses them.

When they are validly placed, they, under God's direction, produce, not grace itself, but a title to grace. This title is something objective, but not physical. It is in the moral order like all rights and obligations. It is produced *ex opere operato* by the sacraments.

Ordinarily, of course, grace is conferred at the same time as the title, but in the order of dependence, the title is always first. Hence if a person receives confirmation in the state of mortal sin, no grace is obtained, but the title to grace does come and it endures objectively in the person. Grace as a physical entity is produced by God alone, but the title to grace results from God's use of the sacrament as an instrument.

Brief Criticism of the Three Theories

1. *Physical causality*. This theory has the merit of guaranteeing the genuine causality of the sacraments. It fits in suitably with some patristic quotations, with various Scripture texts, with

statements of councils (DB. 849, 872; CT. 670, 709). These, however, can be made to harmonize with the other theories.

Two of the major objections to physical causality are these. First, it cannot explain how the grace of five of the sacraments revives. Physical causes operate while they exist and then only. How, then, can the sacraments be physical causes when they sometimes produce their grace long after the rite has ceased to exist?

Second, the sacraments are moral and intentional entities. Words and actions and material substances cannot be physically united. How, then, can a supernatural quality or motion be imparted by God to such a nonphysical thing?·

Moreover, the form of the sacraments does not produce its effect until its last essential word is uttered. By that time the preceding words no longer exist physically. Yet some of these words are essential to the form. How, therefore, can they operate physically when they have physically passed away?

It is difficult to find satisfactory answers to these objections.

2. *Moral causality.* This theory jars the mind because we are accustomed to think in terms of physical causality. Yet moral instrumental causality (for instance, a gift bestowed to win the favor of another) is a common fact of life.

True, in this theory God alone physically produces the grace. However, the sacrament impels, so to speak, God to produce it. Moreover, the sacrament by its very nature is ordained primarily to obtain the conferring of grace, not of anything else.

Nevertheless, two principal objections may be raised against this explanation. First, we may doubt if the sacraments possess a truly intrinsic dignity. If Christ Himself, the God-man, were personally to administer the sacraments, they would clearly be gifted with an intrinsic dignity. But the sacraments, as a matter of fact, are conferred by men even though they act as Christ's vicars.

Can a human agent transform a sacrament, of itself like a coin made of lead, into a coin of gold? This can be argued and different men would view the matter differently. If, however, intrinsic dignity is not present in the sacramental rites, they are reduced to mere conditions of grace. This would be untenable.

Second, this theory offers no basic reason why some sacraments revive if the recipient is indisposed. It is not enough to say that God's acceptance of the valid sacrament remains and, therefore, that God gives the grace later on when the obstacle to it has been removed. This does not explain why Communion does not revive even though the recipient may later on provide excellent dispositions. Why does not this sacrament remain in God's acceptance and revive?

3. *Intentional causality*. This theory is the only one that affords a satisfactory explanation for the revival of some sacraments. They revive because, when validly received, they impart an objective title to grace. Holy Communion does not revive because its title to grace is dependent upon the Real Presence. Once the species have disappeared through digestion, the Real Presence ceases and, consequently, the title to grace is lost. Hence the grace of the sacrament will never revive.

This theory also explains how a sacrament can be valid, but unfruitful. According to the other theories a sacrament like extreme unction produces nothing if the recipient is not disposed to receive grace. It is only reasonable to ask how the sacrament can be valid and yet effect nothing at all. If it is valid, it has its operative forces and must be linked with the recipient by some effect. All agree that baptism, confirmation, and orders, if valid, imprint the character even though grace is not bestowed. Accordingly the other four sacraments should produce some effect when they are valid, but unfruitful. This effect, according to this theory, is the title to grace.

Various objections have been advanced against intentional causality. First, it seems to be opposed to the Council of Trent which teaches that the sacraments produce grace directly so that nothing intervenes between the rite and grace itself.

To this we reply that Trent intended to exclude any subjective acts of virtue, such as confidence in God, as possibly coming between the rite and grace. The declarations of Trent were directed against the Protestants only. This theory inserts merely a title, something in the moral order and independent of the merits of the recipient, between the rite and grace. Consequently it has no affinity with Protestantism.

Second, this theory is new and novelties are dangerous in theology.

We answer that this theory has a basis in the teaching of some of the pre-Tridentine scholastic theologians. Furthermore, in undecided speculative problems like this new theories should be encouraged so long as they do not violate any established theological data. In no other way can theology advance.

Third, some adversaries maintain that this theory avoids the point at issue. Its very title to grace, they say, must be produced by either physical or moral causality.

We answer that intentional causality differs from the other two kinds. The sacrament as a sign is in the intentional order, the order of ideas. Hence it possesses by its nature an instrumental power to effect something in the intentional order. Such an effect is the title to grace. Nothing physical need be added to the rite. No intrinsic dignity is required in it. God alone produces the grace physically, but He uses the sacrament to impart the objective title.

For additional information about this problem, the student should read Pohle-Preuss, *The Sacraments,* I, 143–160.

*

Conclusion 6. Christ our Lord instituted all the sacraments. He did so directly. He used His human nature when He instituted them. He instituted the identical matter and form which we use today in their administration.

Introduction. In our definition of a sacrament we find the phrase "instituted by Christ Himself." We now wish to explain more fully this phrase. Since sacraments are mainly arbitrary signs, someone must have originated them. Having previously studied their material, formal, and final causes, we now investigate their efficient cause. Who brought them into being?

Explanation of Terms

1. Instituted. The institutor of the sacraments must have done three things. He must have determined their specific purposes;

He must have imparted their supernatural efficacy to them; He must have decided their matter and form, at least in a general way. Matrimony is the only sacrament whose outward rite was not established by Christ. But He did determine the specific supernatural purpose of Christian marriage and also imparted to the outward sign its supernatural efficacy.

2. Christ our Lord instituted the sacraments. This simply means that our sacraments do not owe their origin to the Jewish or to pagan religions, but to Christ Himself.

3. He did so *directly*. This refers to the time of the institution of the sacraments. Christ personally instituted them before His ascension into heaven.

We exclude the ideas that God, after our Lord's ascension, may have revealed any one of the sacraments to the apostles, or that the Church may have instituted any one of them after revelation was closed. We do not know the exact occasions on which our Lord instituted five of the sacraments, but we do know that He instituted all of them before His ascension.

4. He used His *human nature* when He instituted them. Since sacraments communicate divine life, they must have been instituted by Christ as God. Moreover, since all of God's productions proceed from the one divine nature, they must be attributed to the entire Trinity. We take this for granted. But we now assert that Christ, when He instituted the sacraments, used also His human nature, His human mind and will and even His body.

5. The identical matter and form which we use today. This fourth part of the Conclusion deals with a matter freely disputed among Catholics. We try to answer this question: How precisely did Christ decide the matter and form of each sacrament? Although the opinions of theologians vary considerably, they may be reduced to the following two general theories.

Specific institution. This is the more common opinion. It means that Christ when, for example, He instituted confirmation, told the apostles: "You are to confer a sacrament whose purpose is to bestow greater courage in professing the faith. When you administer this sacrament, I want you to impose your hand on the recipient while you anoint him with chrism. At the same time you will speak words which will express the purpose of this anointing. The words may be in any language, and they may vary in the same language, but they must always express the essential function of the sacrament."

According to this opinion, therefore, the Church in confirming has always used and will always use chrism blessed by a bishop. She is bound to do this because Christ decided the matter. The Church cannot add anything essential to the chrism; she may not abolish chrism and use some other substance. Moreover, the chrism must be applied by the hand of the minister, not by an instrument. The matter and form of the rest of the sacraments were similarly determined by Christ.

Generic institution. Reliable theologians defend this opinion. Relying on historical evidence, they think that the essential matter of some sacraments, especially of confirmation and orders, has in fact been altered by the Church. Generally admitting the specific institution of baptism and the Eucharist, they deny this kind of institution for the other sacraments.

When Christ instituted confirmation, they think that He spoke somewhat as follows: "You are to confer a sacrament whose aim is to transmit greater courage in professing the faith. You may choose any formula of words which expresses this function, and you may select any sign or matter that you wish, provided that it is symbolic of the sacrament's purpose. You might simply impose hands, or you might make the sign of the cross on the recipient's forehead, or you might anoint him with chrism or some other suitable fluid, or you might light a candle and place it in the recipient's hand. Choose any matter that you wish, but, remember, it must symbolize the effect of the sacrament."

According to this opinion, therefore, the Church would be empowered to add to or to change the matter of some sacraments since Christ Himself did not determine their matter specifically. These theologians, of course, admit the first three parts of the Conclusion, viz., that Christ instituted the sacraments, decided their purposes, and gave them their efficacy. They merely affirm that Christ could have instituted the matter of some sacraments without specifying any particular matter to be used, so long as it would harmonize with the sacrament's significance.

The four parts of the Conclusion are evident from its wording.

Dogmatic Note

Part 1. It is an article of divine faith that the sacraments do not derive from the Jewish or from pagan religions, but from Christ. The Council of Trent (DB. 844; CT. 665) declares: "If anyone says that the sacraments of the New Law were not all instituted by Christ our Lord, . . . let him be anathema."

Part 2. It is Catholic Doctrine that the Church did not institute any sacrament after the close of revelation.

It is common and certain teaching that no sacrament was revealed to the apostles after our Lord's ascension.

Part 3. Since Christ manifested all the sacraments to the apostles before His ascension, and since this manifestation necessarily required the use of His human faculties, it is certain that He used His human nature in instituting, at least generically, the outward rite and the specific purpose of each sacrament.

It is more probable (Scotus and some of his followers seem to deny it) that Christ used His human nature also when He imparted to each sacrament its supernatural efficacy.

Part 4. Specific institution is more common and more probable.

Part 1. Christ our Lord instituted all the sacraments.

Proof 2. From Holy Scripture. References are given to texts referring to each sacrament, but these texts need not be learned now.

Christ explicitly instituted baptism (Matt. 28:19), penance (John 20:23), the Eucharist (Matt. 26:26 ff.).

Christ implicitly instituted confirmation (Acts 8:12–18), extreme unction (Jas. 5:13–15), orders (II Tim. 1:6), more probably matrimony, though not as a rite (Eph. 5:32).

We can prove that Christ instituted all the sacraments from a single text of St. Paul (I Cor. 4:1): "Let a man look upon us as ministers of Christ and dispensers of the mysteries of God." This text is dogmatically certain; apologetically quite probable.

St. Paul must mean to include the sacraments in the word "mysteries," since the sacraments are the principal mysterious and sacred rites of Christianity. In their administration St. Paul declares that he is a minister of *Christ,* not of the Jewish or pagan religions. Furthermore, St. Paul had an abhorrence of pagan rites, and wrote his Epistle to the Galatians with the intention of persuading them to omit their observance of the rites of the Old Law.

Again, Christ is portrayed by St. Paul (Eph. 2:20–22) as the foundation of the Church. Since the sacraments belong to the very essence of the Church, they must have been originated by Christ, the Church's foundation.

Part 2. Christ instituted the sacraments directly.

Proof 2. From Holy Scripture. The preceding texts show that all the sacraments were revealed by God and so were not instituted by the Church after the close of revelation.

However, we cannot prove from these texts that no sacrament was revealed to the apostles after our Lord's ascension. The texts pertaining to confirmation, extreme unction, orders, and matrimony give no clue as to whether they were instituted by Christ before or after His ascension. Since it is clear from Scripture that baptism, the Eucharist, and penance were instituted before the ascension, we might argue that Christ would have instituted the other sacraments while He was on earth. But such an argument would be probable only.

Proof 3. From the Fathers. Whenever the Fathers deal with the institution of the sacraments, they attribute them to Christ, not to the Church. Referring at least to baptism, confirmation, and the Eucharist, the author (probably St. Ambrose) of the *De Sacramentis* writes: "Who but the Lord Jesus founded the sacraments?" (l. 4, c. 4, n. 13; PL. 16, 439).

St. Augustine declares: "Adam sleeps that Eve might exist; Christ dies that the Church might exist. While Adam slept, Eve was formed from his rib; when Christ was dead, his side was struck with a lance that the sacraments might flow forth to energize the Church" (*In Joan.* 9, 10; RJ. 1814).

From this general referral of the sacraments to Christ, we may infer that no sacrament was instituted by the Church after the termination of public revelation. If this had been the case, the Fathers could not simply and generally attribute the sacraments to Christ.

We may also conclude that no sacrament was revealed to the apostles after our Lord's ascension. Revelation is appropriated to the Holy Ghost, not to Christ. But the Fathers attribute the sacraments to Christ. Their more obvious meaning, therefore, is that Christ personally instituted them before His ascension.

Proof 4. From theological reasoning. It is of faith that Christ directly established the Church. Accordingly, He should have directly instituted all the sacraments, since they are essential elements of the Church.

Part 3. Christ used His human nature in imparting supernatural efficacy to the sacraments.

From the texts referred to in Part 1, it is plain that Christ instituted, at least generically, the outward rites of the sacraments. It would have been unreasonable for Him to do this without telling the apostles what these rites were intended to accomplish. Christ, therefore, used His human mind and will, and even His bodily faculties, when He established the sacramental rites and their purposes. Hence the only point to be proved is that His human nature cooperated also in the transmission of supernatural efficacy to the rites.

Proof 2. From theological reasoning. It is of faith that Christ as man merited all graces by His death. Consequently, Christ as man should have a subordinate dominion over the distribution of all grace. Since, then, the sacraments are means of distributing grace, Christ as man should have had a share in establishing their efficacy.

Moreover, it is also of faith that Christ as man founded the Church. Since sacraments belong to the essence of the Church, the supernatural power by which they confer grace should be attributed to Christ as man also.

Finally, it is likewise of faith that Christ as man is the Head of the Church which He founded. As such, He as man should direct all the activity within the Church. Part of this activity and life is concerned with the giving of grace through the sacraments. Hence Christ as man should participate in the life-giving power of the sacraments.

Part 4. Christ instituted the identical matter and form which we use today.

Proof 2. From theological reasoning. The syllogism follows.

An opinion which harmonizes better with authentic declarations of the Church and is not proved false from other sources, should be defended;

But our opinion about specific institution of the sacraments is such:

Therefore, our opinion about specific institution should be defended.

Proof for the minor. The major is evident.

1. Specific institution harmonizes better with authentic declarations of the Church.

From a negative point of view, our adversaries cannot point out a single declaration from any pope or general council which made an essential change in the matter or form of any sacrament. Yet they admit that only a pope or general council could have inaugurated such a change.

We argue positively from the following statement of the Council of Trent (DB. 931; CT. 678): "Moreover [the council] declares that the Church, in controlling the sacraments, was ever empowered to make those regulations or changes which, according to variations of circumstances, times, and places, she would judge more conducive to their veneration, *provided that their substance is kept intact.*"

If the substance of the sacraments must be kept intact, the only reason must be because Christ Himself instituted their substance. The Church must keep inviolate whatever Christ instituted.

But what does the council mean by "substance"?

It would be an arbitrary interpretation to say that this word means merely the purpose of the sacraments—that the Church cannot alter the function which each one has received from Christ. "Substance" does not mean purpose. By its very nature it refers to the internal makeup of an object. This is the scholastic meaning, and it is the meaning of the council in other passages (DB. 910; CT. 834).

Furthermore, in the sentence quoted, the council is comparing accidental rites (which she *may* change) with essential rites. Therefore, the "substance" of the sacrament refers to the rites themselves, not to their purpose.

But, perhaps, "substance" does refer to the constitution of the rites, but merely means "the substance of the rites as instituted by Christ," prescinding from whether Christ instituted them generically or specifically. In this case "substance" would only mean that something in the rites themselves, their aptitude, namely, to express symbolically the purpose of each sacrament, cannot be altered by the Church. The word might refer to the essence of the sacraments without meaning that Christ pinpointed their essential matter and form, a question from which the council might be prescinding.

Such an interpretation is hard to defend. First, it opposes the obvious meaning of "substance" which necessarily results from the combination of a *specific* matter and form.

Second, there is in the passage a decided contrast between the accidental rites which the Church may change and has often changed, and the essential rites with which the Church may not tamper. Since any accidental change must be of a specific kind, the contrast loses its force unless the essential rites are specifically determined by Christ. How could we know whether the introduction of a rite was accidental or substantial unless we already had a specifically determined essential rite to compare it with?

It is no wonder, then, that Benedict XIV (not speaking as pope) states: "Let them [those who hold generic institution] tell us where, when, by what council or pope such a change was made. The contrary seems to be evident from the Tridentine council which declares that Christ gave His Church the power to ordain or change whatsoever she might judge expedient in the dispensation of the sacraments, 'their substance remaining unchanged:' a change of matter and form would touch, not the rite and dispensation, but the substance."

A second declaration of the Church is found in a letter (December 10, 1910) of Pope Pius X (DB. 2147a): "Catholic doctrine about the most holy sacrament of the Eucharist is damaged . . . since it is manifest that the Church has no right whatever to make any innovations with regard to the substance of the sacraments."

In this statement the following points should be noted. First, the pope is speaking about the *specific* form of the Eucharist. The Church cannot alter it. With this all theologians agree. Second, the pontiff passes from the Eucharist alone to a consideration of all the sacraments. Third, he declares that the Church cannot alter the substance of any sacrament. Under "substance" he certainly includes the *forms* of the various sacraments. These forms are equated with the specific form of the Eucharist. His more obvious meaning is: Just as the specific form of the Eucharist cannot be altered by the Church, so the specific forms of the rest of the sacraments cannot be altered by her.

Moreover, "substance" evidently includes also the *matter* of the sacraments. Since, however, by "substance" he means that the specific forms of sacraments cannot be altered, he more obviously also means that the specific matters of the sacraments must remain unchanged. It would be an unaccustomed use of language to include both form and matter under the one word "substance," and at the same time to mean that the form is specified, but that the matter is vague, undetermined.

2. Specific institution is not proved false from other sources.

Solid historical proof is wanting to prove that the Church has altered the essential rites of the sacraments. Cf. Pohle-Preuss, *The Sacraments,* I, 109, 110, 293: IV, 62–67.

Proof 3. From reasons of suitability. The dignity of Christ, the Founder and Head of the Church, is enhanced if we hold the specific institution of the sacraments.

The fact that the apostles and their successors are merely the ministers of Christ (I Cor. 4:1) seems to demand that they should not alter the sacramental rites.

Since Christ instituted baptism and the Eucharist specifically, we would expect Him to have instituted the other sacraments in the same way.

When we say, as all do, that Christ is the institutor of the sacraments, the more obvious meaning is that He instituted their specific outward rites.

OBJECTIONS

All of them pertain to the fourth part alone.

1. Some essentials of the sacraments as we have them today cannot be found either in Scripture or in early writings, e.g., that the chrism of confirmation and the oil of extreme unction must be blessed by a bishop. The Church, therefore, introduced these requirements and so added to the substance of the sacraments.

Answer. Besides Scripture and written tradition, there is oral tradition. Moreover, writings about the essence of the sacraments are rare in the early Church. It is a remarkable fact that Innocent I, as long ago as the year 416, when speaking about confirmation, says that the chrism must be blessed by a bishop (DB. 98).

This objection may be classified as an argument from silence. It proves nothing unless the objector can show that some writer should have recorded all the essential constituents of the sacraments. This cannot be shown.

2. Christ did not institute the matter and form of matrimony because the matrimonial contract existed before His time.

Answer. Christ did not change the contract, but He made it sacramental. Therefore, He instituted matrimony as a sacrament.

3. The Church by her laws can make a sacrament invalid even though all its essentials are present. For instance, if a youth of fifteen goes through the matrimonial contract in the presence of a priest and two witnesses, he is not married unless he has obtained a dispensation, since by Church law he must be sixteen years old.

Answer. In this and similar cases, the Church does not alter the substance of the sacrament. Every contract requires certain fulfilled conditions before it can be made. The Church by her matrimonial impediments simply sets these preliminary conditions. She does not change the contract itself.

We find something analogous in the sacrament of penance. To act as a judge requires jurisdiction. So the Church does not change the substance of this sacrament when she declares that absolution given by a priest who has no faculties is void. Jurisdiction is a preliminary to the sacrament. Without it a priest does not have the power to confer the sacrament.

*

Conclusion 7. A minister who lacks the Catholic faith or who is a sinner can confer the sacraments validly.

Introduction. This is an astonishing statement. It explains more fully how the sacraments give grace *ex opere operato*. In Conclusion 3 we laid stress on the fact that sacraments confer grace independently of the merits of the *recipient*. Now we stress the fact that they give grace independently of the merits and, to some extent, independently of the disposition of their *minister*.

We assume various truths in this Conclusion. First, we take for granted that the minister is in this world and that he has the use of reason when he administers a sacrament. Second, we suppose (and this is most important) that the minister has the spiritual power that comes from ordination. Only matrimony can be validly and licitly administered by the laity. The laity, whether Catholic or not, can also validly baptize, but they would sin grievously if they did so outside of cases of urgent necessity. Third, we presuppose that the minister would not confer any sacrament except the Eucharist upon himself. This would be invalid. Fourth, we assume that the minister uses the correct matter and form; that he unites them properly; that he alone (not two ministers) unites them. Finally, we take for granted that the minister has the right intention. This will be explained in the following Conclusion.

If the minister has these prerequisites, his lack of the true faith or his sinful condition cannot destroy the validity of the sacraments which he administers.

Explanation of Terms

1. A minister who lacks the Catholic faith. The *act* of faith is the free, rational acceptance of all of God's revealed truths because of the authority of God revealing. As a *virtue*, faith is an infused supernatural habit which disposes a person to make the act of faith. Neither the act nor the virtue is necessary in the minister of a sacrament in order that he may confer it validly.

Ministers who would lack the Catholic faith are heretics, schismatics, orthodox Jews, all of whom have some supernatural faith, but not the entire Catholic faith; also pagans (those who have never heard about the faith or who have not heard about it sufficiently); rationalists (those who despise all supernatural faith even after it has been sufficiently proposed to them); apostates (those who once possessed the Catholic faith and have rejected it completely). All these can confer sacraments validly if the prerequisites of the Conclusion are fulfilled.

2. A minister who is a sinner. The minister does not have to be in the state of grace in order to administer a sacrament validly. In fact, he could be the greatest sinner on earth.

3. Validly. This word should be noted. It is opposed here to licitly, not to fruitfully. It means that a sinful minister, or one lacking the Catholic faith, will ordinarily commit a sin by administering a sacrament. Nevertheless, the sacrament administered by him will possess all its supernatural forces so that it will give grace to a disposed person.

The Conclusion has two parts:

1. A minister who lacks the Catholic faith can confer the sacraments validly.

2. A minister who is a sinner can do the same.

Adversaries. St. Cyprian (middle of third century) was bitterly opposed to the first part of the Conclusion. We shall say more about him in our proof from prescription.

The Donatists (fourth century) denied both parts.

Dogmatic Note

It is of faith from the Council of Trent (DB. 860; CT. 690) that a heretic can validly confer *baptism:* "If anyone says that baptism given by heretics in the name of the Father and of the Son and of the Holy Ghost, with the intention of doing what the Church does, is not a true baptism, let him be anathema."

The first part *as stated in the Conclusion* is Catholic Doctrine. If an heretical minister can baptize validly, there is no reason why he cannot confer the other sacraments, since their manner of producing grace *ex opere operato* is common to them all.

It is of faith from the constant teaching of the Church that baptism can be validly administered by those who have no supernatural faith at all. Cf. Lateran Council IV (DB. 430; CT. 659).

Since this is true of baptism, it is also true of the other sacraments for the reason explained above.

The Council of Trent (DB. 855; CT. 676) has without any distinctions defined the second part as an article of faith: "If anyone says that a minister being in mortal sin, even though he observes all the essentials which pertain to the placing or conferring of a sacrament, does not place or confer the sacrament, let him be anathema."

Part 1. A minister who lacks the Catholic faith can administer the sacraments validly.

Proof 2. From prescription. This argument proves that *heretics* can validly *baptize*. It does not prove that all those who lack the Catholic faith can validly baptize or confer the other sacraments. The syllogism follows:

A doctrine pertaining to faith and contained in a universal and long-standing custom is revealed by God in the deposit of faith;
But the doctrine that heretics can validly baptize is such:
Therefore, the doctrine that heretics can validly baptize is revealed by God in the deposit of faith.

Proof for the major. This major differs slightly from the majors which we used in our prescriptive arguments to prove the number seven and the character. In those we did not rely on any custom, but on direct assertions by councils and theologians.

However, this argument is equally valid. Practices and customs reveal beliefs even though the beliefs are not expressly declared. If a teacher repeats in class every day, this custom manifests the teacher's belief that repetition is a help to learning. If a child is obedient to his parents, this conduct manifests his belief that his parents deserve his obedience.

If a doctrine pertaining to faith is certainly contained in a universal and long-observed custom of the Church, the doctrine must have been revealed by God. Otherwise, the infallible Church would fall into error.

Proof for the minor.

1. The custom itself. During the first two centuries of the Church, converts who had been baptized by heretical ministers were not rebaptized when they entered the Church.

2. This custom was universal and of long-standing. Up to the time of Agrippinus, bishop of Carthage (about 220 A.D.), the custom of not rebaptizing heretical converts does not seem to have been questioned. But Agrippinus and his successor at Carthage, St. Cyprian (about 250 A.D.), challenged it and obtained the sanction of nearly all the bishops of North Africa. When Pope St. Stephen contradicted the claims of St. Cyprian, the latter wrote to Firmilian, bishop of Caesarea in Asia Minor, who sided with St. Cyprian.

Nevertheless, St. Cyprian was opposing the universal custom of two centuries because he admits it himself when he says about the question: "It is not to be settled by custom, but by reason" (*Epist.* 71, 1; RJ. 592a).

Pope St. Stephen (DB. 46) declares that St. Cyprian is introducing an innovation contrary to tradition.

St. Augustine (d. 430 A.D.) testifies that the early custom of not rebaptizing heretics was "most wholesome" and that "it was rather corrupted than corrected by Agrippinus" (*De bapt.* 1. 2, c. 7, n. 12; PL. 43, 133).

St. Vincent of Lerins (about 434 A.D.) states: "The antiquity was retained, the novelty was exploded" (*Commonit.* I, 6, Pl. 50, 646).

3. This custom certainly implies the conviction of the Church that heretical baptisms were valid. It is plain from Scripture and the whole of tradition that baptism was the door to the Church. By admitting without rebaptism heretical converts, the Church evidently thought that they had already passed through this door.

4. This implied teaching of the Church must have pertained to faith. Since Christ revealed the Church itself, He must have also revealed how a fundamental condition for membership in it, viz., baptism, is validly fulfilled. It would be unreasonable for anyone to found a society and not lay down the fundamental conditions for belonging to it.

Moreover, Christ revealed that the purpose of the Church is to save souls. He must, therefore, have also revealed how this purpose is to be achieved. Baptism, however, is a fundamental requisite for obtaining salvation. This sacrament is necessary with the necessity of means. God, accordingly, must have told the apostles who could be the valid ministers of this sacrament.

Furthermore, unless baptism conferred by heretical ministers is valid, the Church would positively fail in her duty to save souls. She admits heretics to full membership without rebaptizing them. She allows them to receive the rest of the sacraments and so assures them that they are being sanctified. But if their heretical baptism is invalid, no other sacrament can be received, since the character of baptism is an indispensable condition for receiving the other sacraments.

It is evident, therefore, that this doctrine about the validity of baptism when administered by heretics pertained to faith. Otherwise, the Church would have failed in her obligation to sanctify men. More than that, she would have given the impression that these converts from heresy were sanctified although they were not. Finally, some of these converts would have lost their souls (e.g., by going to confession with attrition only, and so believing that mortal sins were forgiven although they were not) and this would have happened through the Church's fault.

Since by this proof from prescription we have established that heretics can validly baptize, it follows that they can administer the other sacraments. All of them have the same objective efficacy. Since the subjective condition of heresy in the minister cannot nullify baptism, neither can it nullify the other sacraments.

However, it cannot be deduced from our argument that those who have no faith at all can validly baptize and confer the other sacramental rites. A vast difference exists between a heretic and a total unbeliever. Baptism administered by unbelievers did not enter into the dispute between St. Cyprian and St. Stephen. Unbelievers rarely conferred the sacrament. Our only proof for this point is our dogmatic note.

The second part of the Conclusion, viz., that sacraments can be validly administered by sinners, can be reasoned to from the prescriptive argument. Some of the heretical ministers of baptism were probably formal heretics and so sinners. Yet even St. Cyprian does not claim that baptism was invalid for this reason. He worried about their faith only.

Moreover, St. Cyprian certainly knew that some heretical, and also some Catholic ministers of baptism, must have been in the state of sin when they baptized. Yet he never proposes this fact as an obstacle to the validity of baptism.

Parts 1 and 2.

Proof 3. From reasons of suitability.

First, the good of the individual demands that this Conclusion be true. Christ wants peace in the Catholic heart: "My peace I leave unto you; my peace I give unto you." But the individual would have no spiritual peace if his attendance at Mass and reception of sacraments depended on the faith or state of grace of the minister. After confessing mortal sins, he could reasonably ask: "Was the confessor in the state of grace when he absolved me? If not, my sins are not forgiven." When approaching Holy Communion, he might have this worry: "Was the priest who consecrated in the state of grace and did he have faith? If not, I shall be deprived of Holy Communion."

On the other hand, the faithful do not worry about the minister's intention. To have this, the only requirement is that the minister be an honest man, and everyone is prompted to honesty and sincerity by nature itself. But it is comparatively difficult for a person to retain the state of grace. It demands a constant struggle. Only, too, by loyal correspondence with grace can anyone preserve the faith. Hence if our Conclusion were not true, the faithful would have legitimate cause for worry.

Second, the good of the Church postulates the truths enunciated in this Conclusion. Christ wants peace among the members of His mystical body (I Cor. 13). This peace would be disrupted if faith and the state of grace were necessary in the minister of sacraments. The faithful would maintain a constant surveillance over their priests and bishops. They would suspect them of wrongdoing. They would make rash judgments about them. They might even detract or slander innocent priests and bishops. This condition of affairs would be intolerable.

Third, the good of the sacraments themselves requires that our Conclusion be true. If it were not, the faithful would have less esteem for the sacraments. Their desire to receive them would be lessened. Finally, the objective efficacy of the sacraments is protected by our doctrine.

We do not deny, of course, that Christ could have made the validity of sacraments depend upon the faith and the state of grace of the minister. But once we know that He did not do this, we see excellent reasons for His decision. An additional reason is offered by St. Thomas (*Summa*, III, q. 64, aa. 5, 8).

OBJECTIONS

1. How can a minister who lacks sanctifying grace give this grace through a sacrament?

Answer. Because he does not give his own grace, but the grace of Jesus Christ.

2. How can he give the grace of Jesus Christ? He is Christ's minister and so must be linked with Christ in some way.

Answer. He must be linked with Christ by his intention, as we shall explain in the next Conclusion. He need not be joined to Christ by faith or the state of grace.

3. The sacraments were given by Christ to the Catholic Church. Only Catholics, therefore, can be ministers of sacraments.

Answer. It is true that only the Catholic Church has the power to make regulations regarding the administration of the sacraments. However, Christ Himself laid down the conditions for their valid administration and so the Church cannot alter this doctrine about the minister.

4. It is contrary to Scripture (Matt. 7:18) to say that an evil tree can produce good fruit. Consequently an evil minister cannot confer a sacrament.

Answer. The fruit produced by the minister is not his, but Christ's.

5. Did not some of the Fathers deny the first part of the Conclusion?

Answer. St. Basil and a very few other Fathers may possibly have erred in this matter. However, their statements can be interpreted in conformity with our Conclusion.

Comment 1. Some practical deductions from this Conclusion.

Fervent faith and lofty sanctity in the minister cannot increase the efficacy of the sacraments. They can do this indirectly only. People may frequent the sacraments because they have a holy pastor. Their dispositions when they receive a sacrament may be enhanced by the piety of the minister, so that more grace can be obtained. But a pious priest cannot increase the objective efficacy of a sacrament.

Personal qualifications are less necessary in the Catholic priest than in the Protestant minister. The latter has no objectively efficacious rites and so his personal talents and goodness must inspire his people to sanctity. These personal qualifications are an asset to a priest, but they are secondary.

One practical lesson flowing from this Conclusion should be remembered by the student. It makes no difference to which priest a Mass stipend is given. It makes no difference who the absolving priest is. All priests are God's instruments equally, when they confer the sacraments or offer the Mass. Some accidental circumstance may make one priest preferable to another, but it cannot in any way alter the substantial power common to all priests.

*

Conclusion 8. To confer a sacrament validly the minister must have, at the very least, both an external and an internal intention to do what the Church does.

Introduction. We are still dealing with the efficient cause of the sacraments. We have already proved that the minister does not need faith or the state of grace in order to confer a sacrament validly. We now consider a subjective act, the intention, which the minister must have lest the sacrament be nullified.

This Conclusion explains even further the *ex opere operato* efficacy of the sacraments. Although they operate independently of the merits and the faith of the minister, they do not operate independently of all subjective disposition on his part. He must have an intention. It is a constitutive element of a sacrament.

Explanation of Terms

1. To confer validly. This means to effect the sacrament so that it can confer grace on a recipient who is properly disposed. If a sacrament is conferred invalidly, it does not exist at all.

2. Must. Nothing can substitute for the minister's intention. If it is wanting, no sacrament is administered.

3. At the very least. We do not deny that the minister should try to have a more perfect intention. But he must have the intention described in the Conclusion under penalty of not giving the sacrament at all.

4. Intention. In general, it is an act of the will by which a free person aims at obtaining some good or apparent good. It differs, therefore, from *attention* which is an act of the mind by which this faculty applies itself to something.

A person has *external* attention when his mind is sufficiently applied to an action so as to do it rightly even though he may be thinking about something else during its performance. Thus a man may cut his lawn well and yet be dreaming or thinking about the golf game which he plans to play afterwards. If, on the other hand, his mind is applied solely to the cutting of the lawn to the exclusion of other thoughts, he is said to have both external and *internal* attention. The minister of a sacrament needs external attention only, but our Conclusion will say no more about the attention of the minister.

Intention, as we now understand it, is a deliberate resolve to place and administer a sacrament. This resolve may be considered from two points of view.

First, we may look upon it in itself as an act of the will having a greater or lesser vigor. From this angle, the intention can be threefold.

It can be *actual*. This means that the minister's intention exists and influences him at the very time when he is administering a sacrament. It is a *reflex* actual intention if the minister expressly says to himself: "Now I am going to give this sacrament." It is a *direct* actual intention if he simply goes ahead and administers the sacrament without forming an explicit intention in his mind. If we had to make continuous *reflex* intentions for all of our actions, we would soon become insane.

An intention can also be *virtual*. When a minister has such an intention, his resolve to confer a sacrament precedes by some time its administration. At the actual moment of administration the former resolve is no longer in the foreground of the minister's consciousness. But by some mysterious process the resolve still influences him when the time for administration arrives. The resolve perseveres even though the minister does not advert to it.

Such virtual intentions are common facts in our lives. Thus a man decides in the afternoon to attend a movie that evening. He does not advert to his intention again. He finishes his work, goes home, talks to his wife and children, reads the paper, and finally finds himself seated in the theater. His intention to go there operated subconsciously all the time that he was doing other things, and finally guided him to the theater.

It should be noted that the length of time elapsing between the making of the intention and its accomplishment is relatively un-important. The question to be asked is this: Does the previous intention really influence the person's actions now? A doctor, for instance, may form a very firm resolution when he graduates to answer all night calls during his career. He may, of course, and probably does renew this intention at times, but even if he does not, the original resolution may have been so strong that it guides his conduct years later. If this is so, he is still acting with a virtual intention.

An intention may also be *habitual*. This means that an intention to do something was actually made some time in the past. But it now no longer exists in the foreground of one's conscious-ness. Furthermore (and this is the notable difference between virtual and habitual intentions), it no longer influences a per-son's actions. Yet the person never explicitly retracted his original resolution.

Many of our resolves end up as merely habitual intentions. Perhaps we once decided to say the Rosary every day. We never retracted the resolution. Yet after some time we find that we are not saying the Rosary every day. Our past resolution ceased to influence our actions.

We have explained this division of intention for the benefit of the student. It will not enter into our Conclusion. He should, how-ever, remember that the minister of a sacrament must have either an actual or a virtual intention. For the recipient of a sacrament an habitual intention suffices ordinarily.

The second division of intention deals with the good object or the amount of the good object which a person intends. For ex-ample, when about to baptize, the minister might intend many things. He might intend the outward rite alone, or this rite as something serious, or as something sacred. He might intend to re-move original sin, or to admit one into the Church, or to give grace, or to confer the theological virtues, and so on. In this Conclusion we wish to determine just how much of a sacrament's constitution and benefits the minister is obliged to intend.

The Church declares that he must have the intention "of doing what the Church does." "Church" in this consecrated expression means the Christian church. This is objectively the Catholic Church, but the minister can be totally ignorant of the Catholic

Church. He must intend to place a Christian rite. The word "does" in the cited expression is used in place of "intends," because the minister need not intend all the effects resulting from a sacrament. The Church intends them all, but such a detailed intention is not necessary for the minister.

Therefore, the intention "of doing what the Church does" means at the very least that the minister must have an *external* intention. He has this if he intends to place the external rite, the matter and form of the sacrament, and to do so seriously.

But this is not enough for validity. The minister must have an *internal* intention also. Not only must he place the matter and form seriously, but he must also intend the outward rite as an act of Christian divine worship. This does not mean that the minister personally must *believe in* the rite or the worship. He may be a pagan doctor who baptizes babies in cases of necessity. Such a doctor must intend baptism as an act of divine worship *in the belief of Christians*. In this way he intends baptism as a sacred Christian rite even though he does not personally believe it to be such.

Adversaries. We shall say more than usual about them because their opinions in this matter help to clarify the meaning of the Conclusion.

1. Luther, Calvin. According to them a sacrament is valid even though it is placed accidentally. The minister does not need an intention of any kind, either virtual or external. If this were true, a priest might say Mass in his sleep and yet truly consecrate; or a baby would be truly baptized if its mother abstractedly recited the form of baptism while bathing it.

Luther also thought that a sacrament would be valid even if it were administered as a joke. Since any action done jokingly is nevertheless done deliberately, this idea of his differs from the preceding one. According to this second notion a baby baptized on the stage in order to ridicule Christians, would be truly baptized.

It should be observed that these false ideas of Luther follow logically from his theory that the purpose of sacraments is to excite confidence in God. A sacrament placed accidentally or jokingly might possibly excite such confidence in the recipient.

2. Catharinus and Salmeron. These prominent theologians of

the sixteenth century disagree completely with Luther. They taught that the minister must intend to place the matter and form of the sacraments seriously (external intention). They denied, however, that he had to intend them as acts of Christian divine worship. Sacraments, they said, were such acts independently of the minister's intention. Their very matter and form manifest their sacred Christian character.

3. Some followers of Catharinus claimed that a sacrament becomes an act of Christian divine worship by reason of the religious circumstances in which it is administered, i.e., by the fact that it is conferred within a church, or accompanied by sacred music, or performed by a minister wearing religious vestments, and so on. These circumstances make it unnecessary for the minister to have an internal intention.

Dogmatic Note

That the minister must have an *external* intention is of divine faith from the Council of Trent (DB. 854; CT. 675): "If anyone says that the intention of doing at least what the Church does is not required of ministers when they effect and confer the sacraments, let him be anathema."

It is certain and common teaching that the minister must have an *internal* intention also.

Part 1. The minister must have an external intention.

Proof 2. From theological reasoning. The syllogism follows:

A minister endowed with free will acts as a minister, only when he seriously intends to confer the sacramental rites;

But the minister of a sacrament is a minister endowed with free will:

Therefore, the minister of a sacrament acts as a minister, only when he seriously intends to confer the sacramental rites.

Proof for the major. If one of our U.S. ambassadors were to sign a document while walking in his sleep, he would rightly reject the validity of the document because it was signed accidentally.

Again, an ambassador may give opinions to a foreign ruler about possible trade pacts, loans, political alignments. He might do this on a hunting trip or at a banquet. Such opinions would not be official and binding unless later on he expressed them when acting seriously as ambassador. Without this intention all his acts and opinions must be referred to himself as an individual, not as an ambassador.

Proof for the minor. Since Christ instituted the sacraments, the human agent of their administration is His minister. Besides, it is evident that no human agent could, in his own name, confer a rite capable of producing sanctifying grace. It is also clear from Scripture (Matt. 28:19; John 20:21-23) that one who confers a sacrament is Christ's minister.

Part 2. The minister must have an internal intention also.

Proof 2. From theological reasoning. The syllogism follows:

If the sacramental rites cannot receive a religious specification except by the internal intention of the minister, the minister must have an internal intention;

But these rites cannot receive a religious specification except by the internal intention of the minister:

Therefore, the minister must have an internal intention also.

Proof for the major. It is evident that Christ intended His sacraments not as mere outward signs, but as a means of sanctification. They were to consecrate one to the Blessed Trinity, or to remit sins, or to lend spiritual comfort to the sick, and so on.

Proof for the minor. Though it would be gravely illicit, a priest might correctly and seriously baptize a baby while intending only to instruct seminarians. The baby would not be baptized even though the minister has an external intention.

Similarly, in a drama or play an actor might correctly and seriously (though this, too, would be grievously sinful) baptize a baby. No sacrament would be administered because the actor has an external intention only. He does not have the internal intention of sanctifying the baby.

A second proof from theological reasoning. The syllogism follows:

A minister who does not intend at least the general meaning of an action enjoined by his superior, is not truly a minister;

But the minister of a sacrament who does not have an internal intention does not intend the general meaning of the sacraments as enjoined by Christ:

Therefore, the minister of a sacrament who does not have an internal intention is not truly a minister.

Proof for the major. A delegate who is ordered by the President of the U.S. to shake hands with a foreign ruler who is the President's friend, must give a hearty handshake or he does not fulfill the President's injunction. If the delegate shakes hands listlessly, he performs the outward act of handshaking (external intention), but he has not performed it as an act of friendship (internal intention), and so has not truly been a minister of the President.

Proof for the minor. The primary purpose of our Lord in instituting the sacraments was to sanctify men, not merely to place outward rites. Hence if their minister does not intend to sanctify men (internal intention), he is not truly a minister of Christ.

Outward circumstances cannot specify the sacraments as acts of divine worship, because sometimes a sacrament can be validly conferred when all such circumstances are absent. A priest, for instance, when on his vacation and in his hunting togs, might be requested by some person to hear his confession. Since the man is seriously ill, the priest cannot get home, put on his cassock, and go to the confessional. He simply absolves the man after hearing his confession. This confession is valid, though surrounded by no sacred circumstance of any kind.

OBJECTIONS

1. To demand a minister's internal intention is apt to engender worries in our Catholic people.

Answer. As a matter of fact, our Catholic people are not worried by this teaching. All professional men have both an external and an internal intention when performing their professional functions. If I see a doctor removing tonsils, I conclude at once not only that he intends to cut out the tonsils (external intention), but also that he intends to do this as a means of healing the body (internal intention). If he has any other intention, he is a hypocrite.

Priests by their profession are obliged to place sacred rites as acts of divine worship. They are not mere functionaries engaged in religious mummery (external intention). In order not to have an internal intention, the priest would positively have to reject such an intention. Since the rites he administers have all the earmarks of acts of divine worship, he would be an archhypocrite not to intend them as such.

Finally, if a priest were to withhold his internal intention, he might be obliged to restitution under pain of eternal damnation. Priests are anxious to save their souls.

2. Sacraments are specified by their form, not by the minister's intention.

Answer. The matter of a sacrament is determined by its form so that a sacrament can exist as a unified entity. But in order that this unified entity can have a religious signification, the minister's internal intention is required.

Of course, this intention is usually expressed in the form itself, e.g., when a priest says: "I baptize thee in the name of the Father and of the Son and of the Holy Ghost." That is why a priest would have to be a hypocrite not to have an internal intention.

3. The gifts of Christ are independent of man's free will and so the minister of a sacrament does not need an intention.

Answer. This is true of gifts such as the Church and the gospels. It is not true of gifts like the sacraments where the minister's intention is required in order that the gift may exist.

4. I can see how a minister who has no internal intention commits a grave sin. But we have already proved that the sinfulness of the minister does not make a sacrament invalid.

Answer. A sacrament becomes invalid if the minister does not have an internal intention, not precisely because he is a sinner, but because he fails to place a constitutive element of the sacrament.

Comment 1. Before concluding the treatise on the sacraments in general, we shall make some observations on the requisites for valid *reception* of the sacraments. The following points should be studied.

It is certain that only a human being, and a living human being, can receive any sacrament. Angels and dead persons are excluded.

It is of faith that every person can and must receive the sacrament of baptism. This will be explained more in detail in the section on baptism.

It is Catholic doctrine that only a baptized person can receive any other sacrament validly.

It is certain that not all baptized persons can receive all the other sacraments. A woman cannot be validly ordained. An infant cannot marry, or receive extreme unction, or confess its sins.

With the exception of penance, the validity of the sacraments does not depend on the faith of the recipient. Hence a baptized Catholic who has apostatized could receive extreme unction validly, though, of course, no grace would be conferred until he made an act of faith and repented.

Penance is an exception because the acts of the penitent are either the matter itself or indispensable conditions for receiving this sacrament. One of these acts is supernatural sorrow for sin. This act presupposes supernatural faith.

It is also certain that the validity of the sacraments does not depend upon the holiness or state of grace of the recipient. This is plain with regard to baptism and penance which often suppose that the recipient is in the state of mortal sin. However, it is also true of the other sacraments, though they give no grace to a serious sinner and usually he commits a sacrilege by receiving them unworthily.

What kind of intention is required of adults in order that they can receive the sacraments validly?

First, the intention must be positive. This means that an adult cannot be opposed, or even neutral or indifferent, to a sacrament's reception. He must want it.

Second, generally speaking, the intention must be at least habitual. The reason why a habitual intention suffices for the recipient whereas a virtual intention is required of the minister is because the minister's intention enters into the sacrament as a cause. The recipient's intention is only a condition for the valid conferring of a sacrament.

However, it is certain that for the valid reception of matrimony and penance (except when the penitent is unconscious and in probable danger of death) their recipient must have a virtual intention. The contracting parties are mutual ministers of matrimony and all ministers of sacraments must have a virtual intention. In penance the sinner must make human acts without which absolution is invalid. All human acts require at least a virtual intention.

For the valid reception of orders also, some theologians demand a virtual intention. But the majority holds that an explicit habitual intention suffices. This means that the recipient must have sometime in the past made up his mind to receive the diaconate or priesthood and never retracted this resolve. Yet it is no longer operative. According to this second opinion, therefore, the ordination of an unconscious man could be valid.

Some theologians maintain that no intention of any kind is required for the valid reception of the Eucharist. They mean that a person who accidentally receives a consecrated host actually receives Christ truly present beneath it. No one would deny this. Such a person, however, would not receive Christ as the bearer of grace. Hence an altar boy who accidentally consumes a consecrated host thinking it to be unconsecrated, receives no grace *ex opere operato* from Communion even though he is properly disposed. The reception is invalid owing to lack of intention to receive the sacrament.

An implicit habitual intention suffices for the valid reception of confirmation, extreme unction, viaticum, baptism, and penance (when the penitent is unconscious and in probable danger of death and has made previously an act of attrition). For instance, an unconscious Catholic who is in danger of death may never have explicitly resolved to receive extreme unction (explicit habitual intention). However, since he has lived a Catholic life, he has revealed his *implicit* desire to receive the benefits of his Catholic religion and so can be anointed validly.

It should be noted that in practice every Catholic who is conscious has a virtual intention when he receives any sacrament. In ordinary circumstances the reception of sacraments requires deliberate human acts on the part of the recipient (to go to the Communion rail, to visit the church for confession, to come to the altar for confirmation, and so on). Such actions proceed from a virtual intention, i.e., one that is actually influencing one's conduct.

Third, the recipient's intention must be both external and internal. He must intend not only to receive the sacred rite (external intention), but also to receive it as an act of Christian worship. In this matter the intentions of the recipient and of the minister correspond. In practice the faithful always have this intention and should not worry about it.

Fourth, it is certain that infants and the perpetually insane do not need any intention to receive sacraments validly and fruitfully.

However, such persons can validly receive only baptism, confirmation, Communion, and orders. Since the making of a contract supposes the use of reason, they cannot receive matrimony. They are incapable of personal sins and so cannot be absolved. For the same reason, they cannot receive extreme unction, which removes the remains of sins. If a baby were to be ordained (which would be gravely illicit), it would have no obligation later on to observe celibacy, or to recite the divine office, or to exercise the priesthood in any way, unless it freely accepts its ordination when it comes to a mature age.

We have previously explained what is required for the *fruitful* reception of sacraments by adults. With regard to babies, it should be remembered that, once they have been baptized, they are in the state of grace and so have the indispensable condition which makes it possible for the other sacraments which they can receive, to produce grace *ex opere operato*.

Comment 2. Summary of all the requisites for the valid administration and reception of sacraments.

First, the correct matter properly applied by the minister.

Second, the correct form, pronounced by the minister and properly united with the application of the matter.

Third, a virtual and internal intention on the part of the minister when he performs the sacramental rite. This intention is a contributing cause, not only to the existence of the rite, but to its efficacy.

Fourth, an internal intention is always demanded of the recipient though, as in the case of the minister, it may precede the actual reception of the sacrament. A virtual intention is necessary for matrimony and penance. An habitual intention suffices for the other sacraments. The intention of the recipient is not a cause either of the rite or of the effects of the rite, but it is an indispensable condition for valid reception of a sacrament.

It should now be clear why sacraments are not physical entities like plants or books. Sacraments require a union of words with material elements or with actions. With such, however, words cannot be physically united.

Moreover, sacraments also require a union of the minister's intention with the outward rites, but such a union cannot be physical. Finally, the recipient's intention must also be united in some way with the sacramental rites, but an intention, an act of the will, cannot be physically united with them.

The sacraments, therefore, are not merely moral entities like the right to earn a living or the obligation to love one's parents. True enough, the sacraments bestow rights to their effects and also impose obligations, but they are not constituted by these rights or obligations. All rights and duties are objective, independent of the mind, but they are not constituted by anything external as are the sacraments. Moreover, many rights and duties exist independently of a person's intention.

The sacraments, therefore, are intentional entities, i.e., their main purpose is to signify grace, both theoretically and practically.

SECTION TWO

The Sacrament of Baptism

*

Section Two

THE SACRAMENT OF BAPTISM

IN discussing the sacraments in particular as distinguished from the sacraments in general, it is customary to treat baptism first. In the natural sphere birth precedes all the other actions of life. So, too, in the supernatural sphere, since baptism is a spiritual generation and birth, it logically precedes the other sacraments. Moreover, baptism is the door to the Church and to the rest of the sacraments and so should be treated in the first place. Finally, baptism is the most necessary sacrament. For these reasons particularly, it is always explained first in theology.

Conclusion 1. Baptism is a sacrament. Its remote matter is true, natural water. Its proximate matter is a washing either by immersion, infusion, or sprinkling. In its form the three Persons of the Blessed Trinity must be invoked individually.

Introduction. Whenever we deal with any individual sacrament, we shall prove first that it has a truly sacramental character. This is the most important knowledge to possess about a sacrament, for it establishes the fact that the rite confers grace *ex opere operato.*

It is also vital to establish the valid matter and form of each sacrament, since without these no sacrament can produce grace. In this first Conclusion, therefore, we prove the sacramental nature and the valid matter and form of baptism.

69

Explanation of Terms

1. Baptism. Etymologically it means a "washing." It is defined as the sacrament of regeneration consisting of a washing with water conjoined to an invocation of each of the three Persons of the Blessed Trinity.

2. Remote matter. Usually, as in the case of baptism, it is a substance which is applied to the recipient.

3. True, natural water. That liquid which is H_2O and which men commonly call water. It may be taken from the ocean, a cistern, a brook, a lake. It may be clear or muddy, hot or cold. But mere metaphorical water or artificial water, like "rose water," is invalid. Everybody recognizes that such a fluid is not true, natural water.

4. Proximate matter. The application of the remote matter to the recipient.

5. Washing. The water must touch the head and it must flow.

6. Immersion. The plunging of the entire body beneath the water.

7. Infusion. The pouring of water upon the head. This is the common method of baptizing in the Latin Church today.

8. Sprinkling. The casting of water from a distance so that it falls upon the head and flows. This method differs only accidentally from infusion. It is the only way in which more than one person can be baptized simultaneously by a single minister.

9. Form. It is: "I baptize thee in the name of the Father and of the Son and of the Holy Ghost." To say merely "I baptize thee in the name of the Trinity," or "in the name of Jesus," is invalid.

It should be noted that we deal with that matter and form only which are necessary for validity. Other conditions are prescribed for liceity.

Adversaries. Many Baptists and a few other Protestant sects deny the third part of the Conclusion. They believe that baptism must be administered by immersion.

Dogmatic Note

Part 1. That baptism is a sacrament is an article of faith from the Council of Trent (DB. 844; CT. 665): "If anyone says that the sacraments of the New Law . . . are more or less than seven, namely: baptism . . . let him be anathema."

Part 2. Its remote matter is true, natural water. This also is of faith from Trent (DB. 858; CT. 688): "If anyone says that true and natural water is not of necessity for baptism . . . let him be anathema."

Part 3. That the proximate matter is a washing either by immersion, infusion, or sprinkling is Catholic doctrine.

Part 4. It is common and certain teaching that the three Persons of the Trinity must be invoked individually in the form.

Part 1. Baptism is a sacrament.

Proof 2. From Holy Scripture. We simply take our definition of a sacrament and show how its elements are verified with regard to baptism.

1. A perceptible sign (Matt. 28:19): "Going, therefore, teach ye all nations: baptizing them in the name of the Father, and of the Son, and of the Holy Ghost." Since "baptizing" means a washing, we have a perceptible sign.

2. To signify grace (Acts 2:38): "Do penance, and be baptized, everyone of you in the name of Jesus Christ, for the remission of your sins." Thus speaks St. Peter to the prospective converts on Pentecost Day. Since baptism remits even mortal sins, it must signify grace in some way.

3. To confer grace *ex opere operato*. This follows from the same text because the bestowal of grace which remits sins is attributed to baptism, not to the merits of St. Peter or of the people.

4. Instituted by Christ. Christ may have instituted baptism when He spoke the words cited above from St. Matthew. If not, He by those words commanded the apostles to confer baptism and so must have previously explained and instituted it.

5. In perpetuity (Matt. 28:20): "Teaching them to observe all things whatsoever I have commanded you: and behold I am with you all days, even to the consummation of the world." One of the observances enjoined upon the apostles is the conferring of baptism.

Part 2. The remote matter of baptism is true, natural water.

Proof 2. From Holy Scripture. We read (John 3:5): "Unless a man is born again of water and the Holy Ghost, he cannot enter into the kingdom of heaven." Dogmatically, it is of faith that "water" here means true, natural water (DB. 858; CT. 688). Apologetically, it is very probable that this is its meaning. Words are to be taken literally unless we have an obvious reason for understanding them metaphorically. No such reason for understanding "water" figuratively is discernible in this text.

The following incident (Acts 8:36, 38) also proves this point: "And as they [the deacon Philip and the courtier of Queen Candace] went on their way, they came to a certain water; and the eunuch said: See, here is water: what doth hinder me from being baptized? And he commanded the chariot to stand still: and they both went down into the water, both Philip and the eunuch: and he baptized him."

The meaning of "water" is so evident in this text that it needs no explanation.

Part 3. The proximate matter is a washing either by immersion, infusion, or sprinkling.

First, there must be a washing or ablution.

Proof 2. From Holy Scripture (Matt. 28:19) as previously cited. In this text the word "baptizing" means washing. Moreover, St. Paul (Eph. 5:26) calls baptism "the laver of water." Hence the water is not applied by drinking, for instance, but by an ablution.

Second, this washing can take place by immersion.

Proof 2. From Holy Scripture (Acts 8:38): "They both went down into the water. . . ." (Cf. also Rom. 6:3 ff.)

Third, this washing can take place by infusion.

Proof 2. From Holy Scripture (Acts 2:41). St. Peter baptized three thousand persons in one day at Jerusalem where, as far as we can ascertain, no large body of water existed. However, this is not a certain argument that these baptisms took place either by infusion or sprinkling.

Again, we read (Acts 16:33) that St. Paul baptized an entire household within a dwelling, probably the prison. This argument, too, is not certain since we know that the Romans quite often constructed large pools within public edifices and aristocratic homes.

Proof 3. From the practice of the Church and the assertions of Fathers. The Church has always recognized baptism by infusion as valid.

The very ancient, anonymous document entitled the *Didache* or *Doctrine of the Twelve Apostles* (written sometime between the years 95 and 150) declares: "If thou has not . . . pour water three times on the head in the name of the Father and of the Son and of the Holy Ghost" (RJ. 4). (Other patristic statements can be found in Pohle-Preuss, *The Sacraments*, I, 218–221.)

Proof 4. From theological reasoning. Immersion could cause death in some cases, e.g., when a man is so sick that he cannot rise, when a baby is newly born, when someone is dangerously injured in an accident and so should not be moved until the doctor's arrival. Eskimos and others live in excessively cold climates and often lack the means to heat sufficient water for immersion. Then too, some localities even in our own country suffer from lack of water and are compelled to import it. Yet baptism is necessary for salvation.

This argument should be used with those non-Catholics who insist on baptism by immersion only. It rests ultimately on God's goodness and reasonableness.

Fourth, baptism can be performed by sprinkling.

This is the only method whereby several persons can be simultaneously baptized by a single action of the minister and by one utterance of the form. If it were used, the water would have to strike the head of each person and flow thereon.

Sprinkling does not differ essentially from infusion, but, in sprinkling, the water is cast from a farther distance. Since, therefore, infusion is valid, sprinkling is also valid.

Since we have already proved that infusion is valid, we have refuted the opinion which holds that only immersion is effective. It is not necessary, consequently, to offer any other positive proof for sprinkling. It is sanctioned by the constant teaching of the Church.

Part 4. In the form of baptism the three Persons of the Blessed Trinity must be invoked individually.

Proof 2. From Holy Scripture (Matt. 28:19): "Going, therefore, teach ye all nations, baptizing them in the name of the Father and of the Son and of the Holy Ghost." Dogmatically, this text is certain.

Apologetically, the text is not convincing. The words "in the name of" may mean either by the authority of the Trinity or a consecration to the Trinity. If they mean "by the authority of" the Trinity, they do not necessarily signify that the three Persons must be pronounced in the form. Nevertheless, it is difficult to find a sufficient reason why Christ mentioned all three Persons unless He wanted them named individually in the baptismal formula. He could easily have said "in the name of God," or "in the name of the Trinity." Yet He enumerates the Persons.

On the other hand, if the words "in the name of" signify a consecration to the Trinity, we have a more probable argument that the three Persons must be distinctly expressed in the form. The fundamental tenet of the Christian faith is the Trinity, three distinct Persons, yet only one God. By baptism one is consecrated not merely to God, but to God as revealed to Christians. The three Persons, then, should be individually invoked in the rite of consecration to God.

Another passage (Acts 19:2, 3) provides a very probable apologetic argument: "And he [St. Paul] said to them: Have you received the Holy Ghost since you believed? But they said: We have not so much as heard whether there be a Holy Ghost. And he said: In what then were you baptized? Who said: In John's baptism."

St. Paul is astonished that they had never heard of the Holy Ghost, precisely because they should have heard the word "Holy Ghost" pronounced when they were baptized.

It is possible that St. Paul means that they should have heard of the Holy Ghost during the instructions preceding their baptism, but this is not the more obvious meaning. He lays stress on the baptism itself: "In what then were you baptized?" On that occasion they should have heard the name of the Holy Ghost and consequently, by most probable inference, of the Father and of the Son, individually expressed.

Some apt patristic quotations for the various parts of this Conclusion are offered by Pohle-Preuss, *The Sacraments*, I, 208, 215, 216, 218–220.

OBJECTIONS

1. Scripture (Acts 2:38; 8:12; 8:16; 10:48; 19:5) speaks of baptism "in the name of Jesus Christ." So it is not necessary to enumerate the three Persons in the form.

Answer. This expression is used in the Acts to distinguish Christ's baptism from that of John the Baptist, which was still being conferred quite commonly. In the texts referred to in the objection, the words "in the name of" mean merely "by the authority of." They pertain not to the form of baptism, but to the institutors of the two different baptisms.

Nevertheless, some theologians have taught that the apostles by a special privilege did confer baptism by using the one name, "Jesus," in the form. This privilege, if it ever existed, ceased with the apostles.

2. By relinquishing immersion the Catholic Church has destroyed the significance of baptism.

Answer. We admit that immersion more perfectly symbolizes the effects of baptism. Nevertheless, both infusion and sprinkling are true washings and so they symbolize the removal of sin and the purification of the baptized.

*

Conclusion 2. Baptism effects a supernatural regeneration. It also remits all sins and all punishments due to sins. It likewise makes its recipient a subject of the Catholic Church.

Introduction. We already know that baptism gives sanctifying grace and imprints a character. We now inquire into its special effects, i.e., those that are produced by baptism alone.

No other sacrament can bring about the effects enumerated in this Conclusion. The sacrament of penance restores grace to the sinner, but it does not give grace for the first time. Penance also can remove all actual sins, but it cannot destroy original sin. It should be observed that the three special effects of baptism are produced *ex opere operato* and causally.

Explanation of Terms

1. Supernatural regeneration. By natural generation a person receives natural life and a human nature. By baptism a person receives supernatural life for the first time and a supernatural nature. Baptism is called a *re*generation because people must be generated naturally before they can be generated supernaturally; also because, if it were not for Adam's sin, men would come into this world supernaturally generated already.

The supernatural nature conferred by baptism includes sanctifying grace, the infused theological virtues together with the infused moral virtues, the gifts of the Holy Ghost, a right to those actual graces which will enable a baptized person to preserve sanctifying grace by leading a Catholic life.

This regeneration is called supernatural because we have no right to it. It is a *spiritual* regeneration because it is radically different from our physical generation by which we become members of the human family.

2. All sins and all punishments due to sins. Baptism was primarily instituted to remove original sin, but it also wipes away all actual sins, whether mortal or venial, if the recipient is sorry for them, with at least attrition. It also deletes the eternal punishment and all temporal punishment due to sins committed and forgiven. Hence those who are fruitfully baptized enter heaven at once if they die immediately after baptism.

This effect is more extensive than the first effect of supernatural regeneration. The latter necessarily destroys original sin and all mortal sins, since sanctifying grace cannot co-exist with these. But sanctifying grace is compatible with venial sins and temporal punishment and so these are not included in the first effect.

3. Subject of the Catholic Church. Even validly baptized non-Catholics are spiritual subjects of the Catholic Church, though usually they do not realize it. To become a *living* subject of the Church, baptism must be received both validly and fruitfully, i.e., with the necessary dispositions in an adult. To become simply a subject of the Church, only valid baptism is required because valid baptism imprints the character. To obtain the previous effects, baptism must be received both validly and fruitfully.

Adversaries. Protestants generally deny the entire Conclusion. They have no concept of an objective regeneration by the infusion of a physical entity, sanctifying grace. They believe that sins are merely covered over, never truly wiped away. They would as a rule admit that baptism makes one a member of the Christian community, but they deny that it makes one a subject of the Catholic Church.

Dogmatic Note

Part 1. That baptism effects a supernatural regeneration is of divine faith from the Council of Trent (DB. 791; CT. 375) which calls baptism a "regeneration," the "laver of regeneration." The Council (DB. 792; CT. 376) also calls the baptized, the "reborn."
Part 2. That baptism remits all sins and all punishments due to sins is likewise of divine faith from Trent (DB. 792; CT. 376): "If anyone denies that, by the grace of our Lord Jesus Christ which is conferred in baptism, the guilt of original sin is remitted, or even asserts that the whole of that which has the true and proper nature of sin, is not taken away . . . let him be anathema." In the same passage Trent declares that nothing can prevent the newly baptized from entering heaven. Therefore, all temporal punishment is removed by baptism.
Part 3. It is implicitly of divine faith that baptism makes its recipient a subject of the Catholic Church. The Council of Trent (DB. 895; CT. 789) asserts that the Church exercises judgment upon those only who have entered it "by the door of baptism."

Part 1. Baptism effects a supernatural regeneration.
Proof 2. From Holy Scripture. "Unless a man is born again of water and the Holy Ghost, he cannot enter into the kingdom of heaven" (John 3:5). This text is dogmatically certain because it is cited by Trent (DB. 791; CT. 375). Apologetically, it is highly probable.

An effect of baptism is to be "born again." Since there can be no birth without previous generation, baptism must be a generation. Since natural regeneration is impossible, baptism must effect some other kind of generation of a supernatural kind. Besides, St. Paul (Titus 3:5–7) calls baptism the "laver of regeneration."
Part 2. Baptism remits all sins and all punishments due to sins.

Proof 2. From Holy Scripture. That baptism remits original sin, all actual mortal and venial sins, and the eternal punishment due to sin is quite clear from the words of St. Peter (Acts 2:38): "Do penance, and be baptized every one of you in the name of Jesus Christ, for the remission of your sins."

That baptism removes all temporal punishment due to sins is indicated in two texts that are dogmatically certain.

"There is now therefore no condemnation to them that are in Christ Jesus . . ." (Rom. 8:1). If the newly baptized are subject to "no condemnation," all their temporal punishment must be forgiven since unforgiven temporal punishment condemns a person to purgatory.

St. Paul (Eph. 5:25–27) declares: "Husbands, love your wives, as Christ also loved the Church and delivered Himself up for it: that He might sanctify it, cleansing it by the laver of water in the word of life: that He might present it to Himself a glorious church, not having spot or wrinkle, or any such thing; but that it should be holy and without blemish."

If all temporal punishment were not removed by baptism, the Church would never be without disfigurement, even in its newly baptized members.

Part 3. Baptism makes its recipient a subject of the Catholic Church.

Proof 2. From Holy Scripture. "For in one Spirit were we all baptized into one body . . ." (I Cor. 12:13). That this body is the Church is clear from verses 27 and 28. Moreover, we read (Acts 2:41): "They therefore that received his word, were baptized, and there were added in that day about three thousand souls." Evidently these people who were baptized by the apostles on Pentecost Day became in some way members of the visible Christian community, the Catholic Church, by baptism.

This Conclusion could be proved from tradition as manifested in the Fathers. The first two parts are quite clear from St. John Chrysostom, for instance, when he writes about the newly baptized person: "Even though he is smeared with every human vice, if he is immersed in the pool of water, he comes forth from the divine washing more sparkling than the rays of the sun" (*Ad illum. catech.* 1, n. 3; PG. 49, 227). In the same passage he continues: ". . . it [baptism] not only remits sins and blots out crimes, but it does this in such a way as though we were generated afresh."

That baptism is an essential condition for membership in the Church is clear from St. Augustine: "When we read of anyone belonging to the heavenly kingdom in the body of Christ which is the Church, we should understand those only who have been baptized" (*Epist.* 265, n. 4; PL. 33, 1087).

OBJECTIONS

1. St. Paul says that we are buried with Christ by baptism. How, then, can baptism be a regeneration?

Answer. St. Paul in this passage (Rom. 6:2–10) does not limit himself to saying that baptism is a burial. He also says (v. 4) that baptism is a resurrection. His principal meaning in the entire passage is that the baptized man should be dead to his former sinful way of living and become alive to the Christian program of life.

2. If baptism removes original sin, why does it not remove also concupiscence, death, and suffering? Adam was exempt from these.

Answer. We do not say in the Conclusion that baptism deletes concupiscence, death, and suffering. These were preternatural gifts possessed by Adam, but God did not see fit to restore them to men once they were lost. Christ Himself suffered and died, and so it is fitting that His followers should do the same. Besides, concupiscence humbles us and constitutes a large part of our spiritual warfare. By baptism we are restored substantially to the state of innocence in which Adam was created. We do not need his preternatural gifts in order to save our souls. St. Thomas answers this objection, *Summa,* III, q. 69, a. 3.

3. I thought that faith was necessary for adults before baptism. How, then, can baptism infuse faith?

Answer. The *act* of faith must be made by adults for a fruitful baptism. The *virtue* of faith is infused by baptism.

Comment 1. Why baptism cannot be repeated.

Various reasons explain its unrepeatability. First, it is a generation, and a person can be generated but once in the same order of being. Second, it imprints a character. Third, it makes one similar to Christ in His death and resurrection. Christ, however, died but once and arose from the dead only once. Finally, baptism aims primarily at the deletion of original sin which cannot be repeated.

*

Conclusion 3. All men must be baptized in order to save their souls. However, in extraordinary circumstances baptism of love and baptism of martyrdom can substitute for baptism.

Introduction. It is already plain that baptism is more or less necessary for salvation since it removes sin, gives grace, and is required for Church membership. All these effects are necessary for salvation. In this Conclusion, however, we determine precisely how necessary baptism is for salvation.

Explanation of Terms

1. All men. Even infants are included.
2. To save their souls. Without baptism men cannot attain the beatific vision, their supernatural destiny. Unbaptized infants go to limbo where they enjoy a purely natural happiness.
3. Baptism. When we use this word without qualification, we always mean baptism by water. This is the only true baptism. It alone is a sacrament, imprints a character, and enables one to receive the other sacraments. Only baptism operates both *ex opere operato* and causally.
4. Baptism of love. It is frequently called "baptism of desire," and, sometimes, "baptism of the Spirit," or "baptism of repentance."

It consists in an act of perfect love for God or of perfect contrition for one's sins and it always includes at least an implicit desire for baptism. Pagans, for instance, who cannot receive baptism, can be saved by an act of perfect love in which they implicitly desire baptism. Their love would not be perfect unless it included this desire.

Baptism of love produces the principal effects of baptism. It regenerates a man, forgives original and mortal sins, and eternal punishment. It makes one a member of the Church in desire only. It does not necessarily remit venial sins and all temporal punishment due to sins. To accomplish this, the act of love must be of most excellent quality.

Baptism of love does not give grace *ex opere operato*. It depends entirely upon the subjective acts of the person.

5. Baptism of martyrdom. Martyrdom is the patient endurance of a lethal torture inflicted out of hatred for Christ or for the Christian faith or Christian virtue.

Since infants can become true martyrs, it is evident that they do not need any subjective disposition. They owe the grace of martyrdom to God's special providence alone.

Adults, however, must have a disposition for martyrdom.

First, they must have an intention, at least habitual, to suffer martyrdom. However, a person martyred in his sleep could be a genuine martyr if he had once resolved to suffer death for the faith and never retracted this resolve.

Second, they must have at least an implicit intention to be baptized. Whenever possible, the martyr must be baptized before martyrdom.

Third, a supernatural motive is required for martyrdom. This means that the martyr must be impelled by a motive based on faith. Ordinarily this motive will be perfect love for God. However, if this were the only motive allowable, we could hardly distinguish martyrdom from baptism of love. Hence other possible motives may direct the martyr. They might be hope of eternal reward, preservation of chastity, guarding the seal of confession, love for the faith. Even in the natural sphere, not every man, a soldier for instance, who surrenders his life for some cause or other, is actuated by perfect love for some person or cause.

Fourth, an act of supernatural faith must precede or accompany martyrdom.

Fifth, one who has committed mortal sins must be sorry for them, at least with imperfect contrition. God never forgives sins without repentance.

Finally, the martyr cannot offer even lawful resistance to his persecutor. Martyrdom is objectively an imitation of Christ's death upon the cross. Christ offered no resistance.

Martyrdom has most of the effects of baptism and remits even venial sins and all temporal punishment due to sins. But it is not a sacrament, does not imprint a character, and gives no right to receive the other sacraments.

Since martyrdom sanctifies babies, who can have no merits or disposition, it must operate *ex opere operato,* i.e., the act of enduring martyrdom must have in itself the power to produce grace and other supernatural effects. The same is true for adults also, since even without perfect love they are sanctified by martyrdom. Hence the effects of martyrdom cannot be attributed to the merits of the adult martyr.

Nevertheless, it is more likely that martyrdom is a condition or occasion of sanctification, not a true cause, since, so far as we know, only sacraments produce grace both *ex opere operato* and causally. Just as circumcision sanctified *ex opere operato,* but merely as a condition, so martyrdom of itself sanctifies, but not as an instrumental cause.

6. Must be baptized. If a thing is necessary to accomplish some objective, we cannot get along without it. But necessity admits degrees. We speak of things as being more or less necessary. With regard to baptism, it is well to distinguish necessity of *precept* and of *means.*

Necessity of precept means that something is necessary because a superior commands it. Thus attendance at Mass on Sundays and holydays is necessary because the Church has ordered it. Such a precept imposes a moral obligation and so applies to adults only. When the precept cannot be fulfilled owing to ignorance or other impossibility, the precept simply ceases. Nothing else must be done in place of the act commanded. For instance, if a Catholic does not attend Mass because he is sick in bed, he is not obliged to say the Rosary or to listen to the broadcast of a Mass. Nothing has to be done and yet the man has not sinned by missing Mass for so good a reason. Since God has commanded that all people be baptized, baptism is necessary by precept, but it is more necessary even than this.

Necessity of means signifies that some act or thing is objectively necessary as a means to obtain some purpose, which accordingly cannot be achieved without the act or thing. Thus air is necessary for human life with necessity of means. Moreover, no substitute can be found for air and so it is necessary with *absolute* necessity of means. In the supernatural order, sanctifying grace is necessary for salvation nor is there any substitute for it. Repentance is necessary for the sinner in the same way. Although baptism is necessary with necessity of means, it is not necessary with this *absolute* necessity.

An act or thing can be objectively necessary in order to attain some purpose by *hypothetical* or *relative* necessity of means also. This signifies that in extraordinary circumstances some substitute can be used in place of the ordinary act or thing. For instance, some material is needed to heat a home in cold weather. For many people the ordinary fuel is gas. But if gas cannot be obtained, coal can replace it. But for these people coal will be used only because gas is unavailable. Coal is a substitute for gas, but it will be used in extraordinary circumstances only.

Similarly, baptism is objectively required for salvation. However, in certain unusual circumstances, baptism of love or of martyrdom can substitute for it in the case of adults. Infants have but one substitute, martyrdom, and it is rare. Baptism, therefore, is necessary with hypothetical or relative necessity of means.

It should be observed that two practical norms may be followed to determine whether something is necessary by necessity of precept only or by necessity of means. First, we may ask: Is this act or thing necessary for infants also? If so, the necessity is not only of precept, but also of means. Second, we may ask ourselves: When a person cannot fulfill the act required, does the duty to perform the act completely cease, or must something else be done in its place? If the obligation to perform the act simply ceases, we have necessity of precept only. If some other act must be done in its place, we have necessity of means.

7. In extraordinary circumstances. The unusual circumstances in which baptism of love or of martyrdom can substitute for baptism are these. First, when a person, a pagan adult for instance, is ignorant of baptism or of its necessity. Second, when it is impossible for some other reason for a person to be baptized. Third, when a person, at least implicitly, desires baptism.

Adversaries. Some Protestants, Quakers for example, do not think that baptism is necessary at all. Many Protestants believe that it is necessary by necessity of precept only. Comparatively few Protestants hold that baptism is necessary with necessity of means.

Dogmatic Note

Part 1. That baptism is required by necessity of precept is an article of divine faith from the Council of Trent (DB. 796; CT. 560): "If anyone says that baptism is free, that is, not necessary for salvation, let him be anathema." This definition must mean necessity of precept at least.

Part 2. That baptism is necessary for salvation by necessity of means is implicitly of divine faith. Trent (DB. 861; CT. 691), when speaking of the necessity of baptism, includes all those who have been born. Thus infants are included, who cannot be bound by necessity of precept.

Part 3. Baptism of love can substitute for baptism in extraordinary circumstances. This is Catholic doctrine from a condemned proposition of Baius (DB. 1031): "Perfect and sincere charity . . . can exist both in catechumens and in penitents without the remission of sins." The contradictory of this proposition is true. Therefore, charity cannot exist in unbaptized catechumens without the remission of their sins.

Part 4. Baptism of martyrdom can substitute for baptism in extraordinary circumstances. This is common and certain teaching with regard to both adults and infants.

Part 1. Baptism is necessary for salvation by necessity of precept.
Proof 2. From Holy Scripture (Matt. 28:19): "Going therefore, teach ye all nations baptizing them. . . ." By these words Christ commands the apostles to baptize all men. It follows, accordingly, that all men must obey this command by receiving baptism.

Proof 3. From theological reasoning. Since baptism is required by necessity of means, we may be sure that God also commanded it.

Part 2. Baptism is necessary by necessity of means.
Proof 2. From Holy Scripture (John 3:5): "Unless a man is born again of water and the Holy Ghost, he cannot enter into the

kingdom of heaven." This text is dogmatically certain (DB. 796; CT. 560); apologetically, certain.

The word "man" does not mean an adult. In the original text, the word is "anyone." By itself this word seems to include infants. But when conjoined with "born again," it certainly includes infants. The obvious meaning is: All those who are born, must be reborn. Accordingly, the necessity of baptism must be of means.

Proof 3. From the Fathers. A very clear citation from St. Augustine will suffice: "Do not believe or say or teach that infants who die before baptism are able to obtain forgiveness of original sin . . ." (*De anima et ejus orig.* l. 3, c. 9; PL. 44, 516).

Part 3. Baptism of love can substitute for baptism in extraordinary circumstances.

Proof 2. From Holy Scripture. "And he that loves Me, shall be loved of My Father: and I will love him and will manifest Myself to him" (John 14:21). The text is dogmatically certain; apologetically, probable. Since the act of love wins God's love, it must sanctify a person. God saves those whom He loves.

It is clear from the Acts (10:44–47) that the pagan Cornelius possessed sanctifying grace before his baptism, since he had already received the Holy Ghost. Moreover, he obtained this grace by an act of perfect love more probably. He was "a religious man, and fearing God with all his house, giving much alms to the people, and always praying to God" (10:2). A man so prayerful quite likely made an act of perfect love for God and so it is probable that Cornelius received grace by the baptism of love. Yet it should be noted (vv. 47, 48) that he was subsequently baptized. His act of love was not independent of baptism. Pohle-Preuss, *The Sacraments,* I, 245–248 offers some clear quotations from the Fathers to prove this part.

Part 4. Baptism of martyrdom can substitute for baptism in extraordinary circumstances.

Proof 2. From Holy Scripture (Matt. 10:39): "He that findeth his life, shall lose it: and he that shall lose his life for Me, shall find it." The meaning of this declaration is quite plain. However, infants are not necessarily included in it. As regards adults, the text is dogmatically certain; apologetically, very probable.

Proof 3. From the Fathers. St. Augustine declares: "To all those who die confessing Christ, even though they have not received the laver of regeneration [martyrdom], will prove as effective for the remission of their sins as if they were washed in the baptismal font" (*De. Civ. Dei*, XIII, 7; PL. 41, 381). This statement applies to adults at least.

That infants, too, are sanctified by martyrdom is certain from the practice of the Church which honors them as genuine martyrs. The feast of the Holy Innocents, December 28, is one manifestation of this conviction.

The Fathers, too, testify that infants can be true martyrs. For instance, Pope St. Leo the Great (died 461 A.D.) says of the Holy Innocents: "Those whom the wicked king removed from this world, were brought to heaven by Christ, and He conferred the dignity of martyrdom on those upon whom He had not yet bestowed the redemption of His blood" (*In Epiph.* I, 3).

OBJECTIONS

1. If baptism is so necessary for salvation, all pagans must be lost.

Answer. All pagan adults receive from God enough grace to make an act of perfect love and so can be saved by the baptism of love. If they do not cooperate with this grace, they are lost, but it is their own fault. Their baptism of love includes a desire for baptism because the very act of love implies a willingness to do all that God commands them. We know that God demands baptism when it is possible.

2. It is unjust for a still-born baby to be lost without any fault of its own.

Answer. There can be no question of injustice here, since eternal life in the beatific vision is a supernatural gift. No one has a right to this gift.

3. But God wants babies saved. How can we reconcile this desire with the fact that some babies are lost through nobody's fault?

Answer. Most babies can be baptized and it is the fault of their parents or guardians if they are not. Nevertheless, some babies cannot be baptized and a mystery is involved in this fact, since it is certain that God wants conditionally their salvation.

Though theologians cannot solve this mystery perfectly, they offer solutions which indicate how God may solve it. In all cases, the blame for lack of baptism must fall upon a human will, not upon God's will. Some human being, either living or dead, either by a sinful or a nonsinful act, either a relative or a non-relative, did something which prevents this particular baby from being baptized.

If we would be merciful to unbaptized babies, we should remember that God is infinitely more merciful than we are. It is also well to recall that babies that die unbaptized suffer no natural punishment. In fact, they have a perfect natural happiness. They do not even know that they have been deprived of the beatific vision. They are in the limbo of unending natural happiness.

4. In Scripture we read of adult baptisms only. Infants, then, do not need baptism.

Answer. Scripture usually mentions the baptism of adults only. But baptism was conferred upon these adults, not because they were adults, but because they were converted as adults. St. Paul (Acts 16:33) tells about the baptism of an entire household. Infants, therefore, if there were any in this household, were probably included.

Besides, in St. Paul's mind baptism corresponds to circumcision. But we know that circumcision was conferred upon infants.

Moreover, Scripture is but a partial account of the life of Christ and the early Church. Tradition shows that infant baptism has been practised from the beginning. The text of St. John is inescapable: Whoever is born, must be reborn.

To deny the necessity of infant baptism is to acknowledge ignorance of the meaning of original sin and of Christ's redemption.

5. Christ Himself was not baptized until He was an adult.

Answer. Of course not. Baptism had not yet been instituted. But Christ was circumcised as an infant. He received later on the baptism of John the Baptist. He never received the baptism which He Himself instituted and which we have today.

6. Christ said (Matt. 19:14): "Suffer the little children, and forbid them not to come to Me: for the kingdom of heaven is for such." So babies can come to Christ without baptism.

Answer. From the context it is plain that our Lord simply wished by this verse to inculcate humility in His apostles. Those adults who have the dispositions of a child will enter into the kingdom.

7. It would seem that infants are now in a less favorable condition for obtaining salvation than they were before Christ's coming. At that time only an act of faith had to be externally manifested by parents or guardians in order to remove original sin.

Answer. First, both now and before Christ's coming infants had to be saved through the agency of others. Second, faith was required in the minister of the sacrament of nature, as it is called. But faith is not required in the minister of baptism. Third, lack of faith was widespread among Gentiles before Christ's advent so that the sacrament of nature was frequently not administered. Supernatural faith is much more common today.

Comment 1. When did the necessity of baptism for all men become sufficiently promulgated?

The Council of Trent (DB. 796; CT. 560) declares that baptism became necessary "after the promulgation of the gospel." Hence, theologians inquire when precisely the gospel was sufficiently promulgated so that baptism became necessary universally.

The New Law was promulgated on Pentecost Day and so baptism became necessary for some people on that day. However, theologians commonly teach that baptism became necessary for different races at different times. No law is binding until it is sufficiently promulgated.

It is almost certain that today the baptismal law is sufficiently promulgated all over the world. A few theologians think that even now the law has not been adequately promulgated to a few isolated peoples. This opinion has not been censured.

Nevertheless, it is worth recalling that sufficient promulgation of a law does not require that the law be brought to each individual. The individual is obliged to use ordinary diligence to become acquainted with the laws. Catholic missionaries have been at work for some time in every part of the world. Therefore, the law requiring baptism seems to be sufficiently promulgated everywhere. Cf. Pohle-Preuss, *The Sacraments,* I, 241–243.

Comment 2. The minister of baptism.

As already mentioned under the sacraments in general, anyone having a sufficient intention and placing correctly the matter and form, can baptize validly at any time and at any place. No one can validly baptize himself. Moreover, for validity the same person must both pour the water and utter the form.

As regards liceity, anyone may baptize in case of necessity. However, under ordinary circumstances the minister must have the character of orders and authorization. Hence bishops may always licitly baptize members of their dioceses. Pastors may baptize members of their parishes. Other priests besides the pastor may also licitly baptize if they obtain permission. Even deacons may be licitly delegated to confer baptism.

Under ordinary circumstances baptism should be administered solemnly, i.e., with all the rites prescribed in the Roman Ritual, and usually in a church. When the laity baptize in cases of necessity, the infant, if it survives, should be brought to the church later on so that the pastor can supply the ceremonies. Lay ministers do no more than to pour the water and pronounce the form.

Comment 3. The recipient of baptism.

Baptism is invalid unless an adult consents to receive it. Hence accusations, sometimes made, that the Church forces people to be baptized are false. God compels no one to receive His gifts.

For *fruitful* baptism an adult must make an act of at least imperfect contrition involving acts of faith and of hope.

Once a person realizes the necessity of baptism, he should not defer its reception for a long time. However, it should be deferred ordinarily until the prospective convert is sufficiently instructed in the Catholic faith.

The baptism of infants is always valid and fruitful on their part. Infants should be baptized as soon as possible after birth.

SECTION THREE

The Sacrament
of Confirmation

*

Section Three

THE SACRAMENT
OF CONFIRMATION

Conclusion 1. Confirmation is a true sacrament.

Introduction. Most non-Catholic sects have no rite that corresponds to confirmation. Lutherans do administer such a rite but they deny that it was instituted by Christ. It differs, therefore, in their opinion radically from baptism and the Lord's Supper. These were instituted by Christ, but confirmation is of purely ecclesiastical origin. We recall, too, that Protestants generally deny all the sacraments since according to them no sacrament confers grace *ex opere operato.*

Explanation of Terms

1. Confirmation. Today this is the word commonly used to designate this sacrament. However, many other names were given it in the past. Some of these are: anointing, chrism of salvation, marking, the Lord's seal, consummation, imposition of hands, sacrament of completion.

Confirmation, though a distinct sacrament from baptism, is its complement. Literally, confirmation means a "strengthening." It was administered immediately after baptism in the early Church and strengthened the supernatural life of the newly baptized.

Our definition is as follows: Confirmation is a sacrament in which a bishop, while uttering the essential words or form, imposes his hand upon the recipient and anoints his forehead with chrism in the form of a cross in order to impart to the recipient spiritual strength to profess the faith bravely. In a Comment following the Conclusion we shall explain more in detail the essential matter and form of this sacrament.

Dogmatic Note

The Conclusion is of divine faith from the Council of Trent (DB. 871; CT. 708): "If anyone says that the confirmation of those who have been baptized is an idle ceremony, and not rather a true and proper sacrament, let him be anathema." (Cf. also DB. 844; CT. 665.)

Proof 2. From Holy Scripture. Our Lord *promised* this sacrament when He said (John 7:38, 39): "He that believeth in Me, as the Scripture saith, 'From within him shall flow rivers of living water.' Now this He said of the Spirit which they should receive, who believed in Him: for as yet the Spirit was not given, because Jesus was not yet glorified." Dogmatically, it is certain that these words contain a promise of confirmation. Apologetically, all the elements of our definition of a sacrament cannot be established from these verses. Not even a perceptible sign is indicated and we cannot prove the existence of a sacrament unless we find this sign.

Hence we prove this Conclusion from the *actual conferring* of confirmation by Sts. Peter and John (Acts 8:12–18):

12 "But when they [the Samaritans] had believed Philip [the deacon] preaching of the kingdom of God, in the name of Jesus Christ they were baptized, both men and women.

13 Then Simon [Magus] himself believed also; and being baptized, he adhered to Philip. And being astonished, wondered to see the signs and exceeding great miracles which were done.

14 Now when the apostles, who were in Jerusalem, had heard that Samaria had received the word of God, they sent unto them Peter and John.

15 Who when they were come, prayed for them, that they might receive the Holy Ghost.

16 For He was not as yet come upon any of them; but they were only baptized in the name of the Lord Jesus.

17 Then they laid their hands upon them, and they received the Holy Ghost.

18 And when Simon saw that, by the imposition of hands of the apostles, the Holy Ghost was given, he offered them money."

These verses offer, dogmatically, a certain proof and, apologetically, a very probable one, that confirmation is a sacrament.

First, we have a perceptible sign. An imposition of hands is explicitly mentioned (v. 17). The apostles also prayed (v. 15). This prayer may have been internal and may have preceded the imposition of hands. However, since an imposition of hands by itself does not have a precise signification, it is likely that the apostles prayed externally and while the imposition was being made. But even without the prayer we have a clear perceptible sign in the imposition itself.

This imposition of hands cannot refer to baptism because these people were already baptized (v. 12). Besides, an imposition of hands was never a part of the baptismal rite.

Nor can this imposition of hands refer to the sacrament of orders (in which the hands of the bishop are also imposed on the candidate), because all the converted Samaritans received this particular imposition of hands. It would be absurd to say that all would be given orders. There would then be no laity in the Church. Moreover, women (vv. 14–18) received this rite, but women were never admitted to orders.

Neither can this imposition of hands refer to penance in which the bishop in the early Church touched the penitent when absolving him. It would be ridiculous to say that all these converts had fallen into mortal sin immediately after their baptism. Moreover, Sts. Peter and John did not go down to Jerusalem to absolve these people. They went because they "heard that Samaria had received the word of God" (v. 14).

Second, this imposition of hands conferred grace. This point causes some difficulty apologetically. The only effect mentioned explicitly (v. 18) is a perceptible one, the charismatic gifts like prophecy and tongues, which accompanied the sacrament in the early Church. Their mention does not necessarily exclude the conferring of sanctifying grace, but neither does it even imply the giving of this grace. We use the following proofs.

"To receive the Holy Ghost" (vv. 17, 18), as used in Scripture, always includes the reception of sanctifying grace. This is the unanimous opinion of exegetes. Therefore, this phrase should have the same meaning here.

Moreover, charismata have not been bestowed by confirmation for many centuries. Yet Christ wished this sacrament to endure for all time. It must, then, have some other effect besides the charismatic gifts. Otherwise we should be obliged to say that for many centuries this evidently important rite has effected nothing.

Again, the apostles received the equivalent of confirmation on Pentecost Day (Acts 2:1–4). But the apostles on that occasion, besides the charismata, received also an internal spiritual transformation which implies the reception of grace.

Third, this imposition of hands conferred grace *ex opere operato* because its bestowal is attributed, not to the merits of Sts. Peter and John nor to those of the Samaritans, but to the imposition itself (vv. 17, 18).

Fourth, this rite was instituted by Christ because the apostles were only "ministers of Christ and dispensers of the mysteries of God" (I Cor. 4:1).

Finally, this sacrament is to last till the end of time. It is evidently of importance. Two apostles, one of them the head of the Church, make a special journey to confer it. Moreover, since it gives grace *ex opere operato,* it is an essential element of the Church whose purpose is to sanctify men.

Proof 3. From the Fathers. St. Cyprian has a valuable comment on our Scripture passage (Acts 8:12–18). He says that what was lacking to the baptized Samaritans "was supplied by Peter and John . . . and we do the same today so that the baptized are presented to the bishops of the Church and by our [Cyprian was a bishop] prayer and imposition of hands they receive the Holy Ghost and are made perfect with the Lord's seal" (*Epist.* 73, n. 9; RJ. 595). For additional patristic quotations, cf. Pohle-Preuss, *The Sacraments,* I, 282–287.

Proof 4. From the agreement of the Oriental schismatical churches.

All the schismatical and heretical Oriental churches have the sacrament of confirmation. Since they would not have accepted it from the Catholic Church, they must believe that Christ Himself instituted it. Most of them, too, antedate the Protestant dissenters by many centuries.

Objections

1. The Samaritans already had sanctifying grace by baptism. Therefore, confirmation must have conferred the charismata only.

Answer. Confirmation increased their sanctifying grace. Just because sanctifying grace is conferred by one sacrament, it does not follow that it cannot be given by another sacrament. This objection can be reduced to absurdity. It would prove that the Eucharist, extreme unction, orders, and matrimony do not give grace either, since their recipient should be in the state of grace when he receives them.

2. Perhaps this imposition of hands by Sts. Peter and John was simply an offering of the baptized to God, not a distinct sacramental rite.

Answer. This imposition of hands conferred grace of itself *ex opere operato* (Acts 8:18). Moreover, the apostles were confronted with the enormous task of converting the whole world. Would they have made a special trip taking considerable time, to perform some merely accidental rite?

3. Does Scripture say that Christ instituted confirmation?

Answer. Not explicitly. But He must have done so. Otherwise we would not find the apostles confirming shortly after His ascension. The apostles, on their own admission, were only "dispensers of God's mysteries." We do not know for sure on which occasion our Lord instituted confirmation. He probably did so some time between His resurrection and ascension.

Comment 1. The matter and form of confirmation.

For *liceity* the entire rite as presented in the *Pontificale Romanum* must be observed. For *valid* confirmation at the present time the following points should be noted.

1. The remote matter. It is chrism, which is a mixture of olive oil and balm. It is very probable that only chrism is valid matter. The Councils of Trent (DB. 872; CT. 709) and of Florence (DB. 697; CT. 707) mention chrism, but do not define that it is the

matter of the sacrament. A few theologians think that plain olive oil without balm would be sufficient for validity.

The chrism must be previously blessed by a bishop. Pope Innocent I, as long ago as the year 416 (DB. 98), and the Council of Florence assert this requirement. However, although no certain instance can be adduced from history, it is possible that an ordinary priest could be empowered by the Holy See to bless the chrism.

2. The proximate matter. It is certain that there must be an anointing with the chrism. It is more probable (DB. 697; CT. 707) that the anointing must be made on the forehead. It is also more probable that the anointing must be made in the form of a cross.

It is likewise certain that the bishop must impose his hand on the recipient. Most theologians admit that the only imposition of the hand required is that made in the very act of anointing. It is true that at the beginning of the entire rite the bishop, having both hands extended over those to be confirmed, prays aloud for them. But this particular extension of the hands should not be considered as an essential part of the sacrament.

Since the imposition of the hand and the act of anointing coincide, confirmation would be invalid if the bishop used an instrument, as is done in baptism, to perform the anointing. He must do it with his thumb, extending his other fingers over the head of the candidate.

3. The form. The present form in the Latin Church is: "I sign thee with the sign of the cross and I anoint thee with the chrism of salvation in the name of the Father and of the Son and of the Holy Ghost."

This form has been used commonly in the Latin Church since the twelfth century. It has been used more commonly than other forms since the seventh century. That other forms have been used in the Latin Church is clear from liturgical books.

The Greek Church uses the following form: "The seal of the gift of the Holy Ghost." Pope Benedict XIV in his encyclical *Ex quo primum* (1756 A.D.) declared that Greek confirmations are valid. So this form is valid. It has been used in the Greek Church since the fourth century.

In order to determine if a form is valid, its meaning must be examined. Any language can be used and the words can vary greatly. But every valid form must express, first, the act of marking or sealing and, second, the more abundant grace of the Holy Ghost.

The second requirement is verified only implicitly in the Greek form. The baptized have already received the Holy Ghost. Hence, when they are confirmed, the expression, "the gift of the Holy Ghost," implies the *special* gift of the Holy Ghost, i.e., the more abundant grace of the Holy Ghost.

*

Conclusion 2. The effect of confirmation is to confer spiritual strength to profess the faith bravely.

Introduction. When a baby is born, it has life but it is a tender life. It can easily be snuffed out and its continuance depends on the constant ministrations of others. Gradually both body and soul of the infant develop. Its body becomes more resistant to disease. Its mind unfolds. It depends much less upon others.

Similarly, by baptism a man is born into supernatural life. He is a Christian, but not an adult Christian. He is not ready to fight like a courageous soldier against the enemies of the faith. To become a Christian soldier he needs ordinarily another sacrament, confirmation. By this sacrament he reaches spiritual manhood.

Explanation of Terms

1. Effect. We deal with the special effect of confirmation. No other sacrament can produce it. This effect is brought about by a series of actual graces. The sacrament continues to fortify our souls with these graces during our entire subsequent lives. But whether we shall benefit by them depends upon ourselves. We must cooperate with these graces or we shall always remain faint-hearted Christians.

2. Spiritual strength to profess the faith bravely. If the confirmed person uses the actual graces coming from confirmation, he will manifest a soldierly spirit in various ways.

First, *publicly*, i.e., in his relations with other people, he receives more abundant graces to endure public sufferings which come upon him by reason of his Catholic faith. Thus a candidate for election might be defeated because of his Catholic faith. Confirmation enables him to accept this misfortune with equanimity. Many theologians believe that the graces of confirmation give its recipient strength to bear even martyrdom.

In addition, the confirmed person receives more abundant graces to spread the faith to others by word and example. So confirmation is sometimes called the sacrament of Catholic Action. This is undoubtedly a part of the sacrament's effect.

Second, the graces of confirmation benefit the recipient *privately*, i.e., in his own spiritual life. The Catholic is strengthened to overcome temptations of any kind. By baptism, of course, he has sufficient strength to resist serious temptations and maintain the state of grace. But he becomes stronger in the warfare against temptations in other ways also, by prayer, penance, and the reception of confirmation.

Moreover, the graces of confirmation help a Catholic to advance in virtue. They urge him to do more than to simply observe the commandments. If he corresponds with them, they unite him more closely to Christ.

Dogmatic Note

The Conclusion, in the general way in which it is worded, is of divine faith from the constant teaching of the Church. This teaching is expressed, though not defined, in the Council of Florence (DB. 697; CT. 707): "The effect of this sacrament is that by it the Holy Ghost is given for strengthening, as He was given to the apostles on Pentecost Day, namely, that the Christian may boldly profess the name of Christ." As detailed in the explanation of terms, the Conclusion is certain.

Proof 2. From Holy Scripture. We shall first formulate a syllogism and then prove its major and minor from Scripture.

The apostles on Pentecost Day received spiritual strength to profess the faith bravely;

But by confirmation the baptized receive the same gift that the apostles received on Pentecost Day:

Therefore, by confirmation the baptized receive strength to profess their faith bravely.

Proof for the major. Before His ascension Christ had promised this strengthening to the apostles (Acts 1:8): "But you shall receive the power of the Holy Ghost coming upon you, and you shall be witnesses to Me in Jerusalem, and in all Judea, and even to the uttermost parts of the earth." Christ made a similar promise to them on another occasion (Luke 24:49): "And I send the promise of the Father upon you: but stay you in the city, till you be endued with power from on high."

Moreover, before the advent of the Holy Ghost at Pentecost, the apostles were afraid to profess their faith in Christ: "Now when it was late the same day . . . and the doors were shut, where the disciples were gathered together for fear of the Jews, Jesus came and stood in their midst . . . (John 20:19)."

However, once the Holy Ghost had descended upon them (Acts 2:1–14), they became brave in professing their faith in Christ. Peter comes out at once to deliver a sermon to the people (Acts 2:14 ff.). Subsequent chapters of the Acts reveal how brave the apostles were in testifying to their faith in Christ and in suffering for it. Their cowardice was changed into bravery *after* and *on account of* their receiving the Holy Ghost.

The very outward symbols heralding and accompanying the arrival of the Holy Ghost indicate that strength was to be imparted. The Holy Ghost was announced by a sound "as of a mighty wind" (Acts 2:2), and "parted tongues as it were of fire" came and "sat upon every one of them" (Acts 2:3). Wind and fire are two of the strongest natural forces that we perceive. It is clear, therefore, that on Pentecost Day the apostles received spiritual strength to profess their faith courageously.

Proof for the minor. We wish to show that the baptized by confirmation receive essentially the same strengthening as the apostles. We do not deny that the apostles were strengthened to a higher degree then the confirmed. Nor do we claim that the confirmed receive any charismatic gifts as did the apostles. Our proof is derived from some statements in St. Peter's sermon (Acts 2:14–39).

We recall that the miraculous events of Pentecost attracted a large crowd outside the dwelling of the apostles. They were people of many different lands and yet, owing to the charismatic gift of tongues bestowed upon the apostles, all were able to understand them. The people were astonished at this and sought an explanation. St. Peter gives it in his discourse.

We assume that the apostles had already been baptized. It is incredible that Christ would have ascended into heaven without giving them this sacrament, especially since they were going to confer baptism to others immediately after St. Peter's sermon. Besides, baptism is the door through which men enter the Church. The apostles had already been empowered to be rulers of the Church, and so must have entered it previously by baptism. This point is important because it shows that St. Peter in his sermon is not trying to explain an effect of baptism.

Verses essential to the proof.

First, verses from the initial part of the sermon (Acts 2:16–18): "But this is that which was spoken of by the prophet Joel: 'And it shall come to pass in the last days (saith the Lord), I will pour out of my Spirit upon all flesh: and your sons and daughters shall prophesy, and your young men shall see visions, and your old men shall dream dreams. And upon my servants indeed, and upon my handmaids will I pour out in those days of my Spirit, and they shall prophesy.'"

Second, St. Peter's remarks to the people after the sermon (Acts 2:38, 39): "But Peter said to them: Do penance and be baptized every one of you in the name of Jesus Christ, for the remission of your sins: and *you* shall receive the Holy Ghost. For the promise is to you, and to your children, and to all that are far off, whomsoever the Lord our God shall call."

What St. Peter tells the people might be put as follows: "You have gathered here to seek an explanation of the extraordinary events which you have witnessed, especially of our ability to speak in such a way that all of you, despite your diverse languages, are able to understand us. Some of you think that the explanation lies in our overindulgence in drink (cf. Acts 2:13). That, evidently, is an absurd explanation since no Jew is ever drunk as early as nine in the morning (Acts 2:15).

"I shall now give you the real explanation. Most of you, and all of you who are Jews, are acquainted with the inspired prophecies of Joel. He foretold many years ago what took place this morning. Through him God said that He would pour forth His Spirit upon all men, upon His servants and His handmaids. This morning He has begun to fulfill that prophecy. We apostles are the first to receive the Holy Spirit. It is because of that reception that you heard the roar of the wind, and understood us despite the wide diversity of your languages.

"But do not imagine that we are to be the sole recipients of the Spirit. You, too, can receive Him. Repent of your sins and be baptized. After that you also shall receive the gift of the Holy Ghost. That promise of Joel which I quoted to you in the beginning of my sermon is for all the servants and handmaids of the Lord. Therefore, you likewise can receive the Holy Ghost. It depends upon yourselves."

It is true that in his sermon St. Peter does not tell the people that they shall receive the Holy Ghost by confirmation. However, from following passages in the Acts it is plain that this is his meaning. St. Peter himself (Acts 8:16, 17) confers confirmation by an imposition of hands and, as a result, "they [the baptized Samaritans] received the Holy Ghost." Similarly, St. Paul (Acts 19:6) imposed hands upon the baptized Ephesians and "the Holy Ghost came upon them."

This special reception of the Holy Ghost, therefore, does not come from baptism, but from a distinct sacramental rite. The apostles themselves were confirmed directly by God without the sacramental sign. But they had been instructed previously by Christ, to transmit the Holy Ghost to others by an imposition of hands, the sacrament of confirmation.

It would be a weak objection to say that St. Peter merely wishes to explain to the crowd how the apostles received the charismatic gift of tongues. This was a marvelous, perceptible manifestation of the Holy Ghost and that is why he used it as the starting point of his sermon. It is clear from the proof of the major that the great gift received by the apostles was courage to profess their faith in Christ.

Charismatic gifts are mere accidentals. They come and go as

the Spirit wills. For many centuries they have ceased to accompany confirmation. At Pentecost the apostles received that enduring power which enabled them to labor and suffer for the gospel and to persevere until their deaths by martyrdom. By confirmation the baptized receive substantially the same abiding power to help spread the faith and to suffer for it.

Proof 3. From the Fathers. A clear quotation from St. Cyril of Jerusalem will suffice: "Just as Christ went forth after His baptism and His reception of the Holy Ghost to conquer His adversary [the devil tempting Him in the desert], so you Christians, after you have put on the complete armor of Christ by our baptism and holy anointing [confirmation], take your stand against your adversary and defeat him" (*Catech.* 21, n. 4; PG. 33, 1091).

The proofs are strengthened by a consideration of the rite of confirmation. Oil, the predominant element in the chrism, symbolizes vigorous spiritual activity. Oil was formerly used by combatants in the arena to strengthen their bodies. Moreover, the chrism is administered in the form of a cross to signify that hard things are to be endured for Christ. Then too, the chrism is applied to the forehead. The temples of the head are among the first spots of the body to reveal shame. The confirmed person should never be ashamed of his faith.

The balm mixed with the oil symbolizes the advance in virtue expected of the confirmed person. Balm is characterized by its fragrant odor. By its use we are portrayed as "the good odor of Christ" (II Cor. 2:15).

It is evident that the form of confirmation expresses the strength and power to endure and to be active for the faith.

OBJECTIONS

1. Baptism confers passive powers to receive sacred things. Orders gives active powers to administer sacred things. So these two sacraments take care of everything. No power, then, is given by confirmation.

Answer. It is true that no solid proof is available to show that confirmation empowers its recipient to receive or to confer sacred *rites*. But confirmation does give power to profess the faith bravely, a power that is not imparted by baptism or orders.

2. A person who is baptized only, may be put in circumstances

where he must profess his faith bravely. Therefore, baptism gives one sufficient grace to profess the faith in those circumstances.

Answer. The baptized person has at least remotely sufficient grace to keep out of mortal sin. Hence he has strength to profess his faith. But confirmation gives him more abundant graces which are especially ordained to help him to profess his faith.

Furthermore, confirmation is the ordinary means of obtaining this help. Therefore, if a baptized person neglects to receive confirmation, he must pray or use some other means to enable him to profess his faith. Besides, confirmation does not have a merely negative effect. It enables the recipient to assist in spreading the faith under the guidance of the hierarchy, and also to advance in virtue.

3. God never refuses sufficient grace to enable a person of good will to fulfill his duties. Therefore, the baptized person can, without the graces of confirmation, profess his faith when necessary.

Answer. God never refuses sufficient grace to those who use the ordinary means of obtaining grace. Confirmation is such an ordinary means. If a person deliberately neglects through his own fault to be confirmed, he will have to repair the loss either by being confirmed, or by obtaining more actual graces in some other way. Otherwise he will not have proximately sufficient grace to profess his faith bravely.

4. Cornelius (Acts 10:44–48) received the special gift of the Holy Ghost without confirmation.

Answer. Cornelius may have received the Holy Ghost by way of baptism only, in which case he was confirmed afterwards, though this is not mentioned in the account. At any rate, it is clear that his entire conversion was extraordinary. God wished to reveal to St. Peter that he should admit Gentiles into the Church. To bring home this lesson, He gave Cornelius the special gift of the Holy Ghost including the charismata. St. Peter then realized that he should admit Gentiles into the Church. St. Thomas answers this objection (*Summa*, III, q. 72, a. 6, ad 3).

Comment 1. The necessity of confirmation.

All baptized Catholics, even those who are on the point of death, should be confirmed. The dying person who receives confirmation will not be able to use the special actual graces of the sacrament, but he will obtain an increase of sanctifying grace and so will have a higher degree of glory in heaven. He will also possess eternally the character which marks him as a Christian soldier.

Nevertheless, it is certain that confirmation is not necessary for salvation by necessity of means. However, it is required by necessity of precept.

Does this precept bind under pain of mortal sin? Probably not, generally speaking. Hence if a Catholic neglects to receive the sacrament, even though he could do so with little inconvenience, he probably commits a venial sin only. We suppose, of course, that he has no contempt for the sacrament, since this would be seriously sinful.

Because of modern living conditions in which dangers to the faith and to virtue are so prevalent, some theologians believe that it is a mortal sin for a Catholic to neglect to receive confirmation when he can conveniently do so. No Catholic, therefore, should fail to be confirmed.

Read St. Thomas, *Summa,* III, q. 72, a. 8.

*

Conclusion 3. A bishop is the ordinary minister of confirmation. However, any priest can be the extraordinary minister of this sacrament if he receives delegation from the Holy See.

Introduction. For the valid administration of all the sacraments except baptism and matrimony, spiritual power coming from orders is required in the minister. However, a difficulty arises in the case of confirmation. In the Greek Church this sacrament is usually administered by a priest. In the Latin Church it is regularly conferred by a bishop.

Since, therefore, both bishops and priests are actually administering confirmation, this Conclusion answers the questions: Are they both on an equal footing with regard to this sacrament? If there is a difference, in what precisely does it consist? We are concerned with valid administration only. For liceity canon law lays down other requirements, whether the minister be a bishop or a priest.

Explanation of Terms

1. Bishop. One who has received the plenitude of the sacrament of orders, i.e., one who possesses the three characters conferred by the diaconate, the priesthood, and the episcopacy.

2. Priest. One who has the characters given by the diaconate and the priesthood, but not that communicated by the episcopacy. He has the sacrament of orders, but not in its fullness.

3. Ordinary minister. "Ordinary" does not mean "usual" or "frequent." Even if a priest is empowered to confer confirmation, he always remains an extraordinary minister. "Ordinary" simply means that a bishop has the power to confer confirmation by the very fact that he has been consecrated a bishop and received the episcopal character of orders. To validly administer confirmation he needs no delegation or permission from anyone.

4. Extraordinary minister. When a priest administers this sacrament, he is an extraordinary minister because the character of the priesthood does not impart sufficient power of itself to enable him to give confirmation validly. He must be delegated by the Holy See. The priest who receives delegation can confer the sacrament only according to the prescriptions specified in the official document granting him delegation. He may be limited with regard to place, to persons, and to time.

Dogmatic Note

Part 1. A bishop is the ordinary minister of confirmation. This is of faith from the Council of Trent (DB. 873; CT. 710): "If anyone says that the ordinary minister of holy confirmation is not a bishop alone, but any mere priest, let him be anathema."

Part 2. Any priest can be the extraordinary minister of this sacrament if he receives delegation from the Holy See. This is Catholic doctrine. From the canon quoted above, it is clear that the council supposes that there can also be an extraordinary minister of confirmation. Otherwise, the word "ordinary" would not be found in the canon. That this extraordinary minister is a priest is clear from the practice of the Church. No deacon or lesser cleric could be empowered by delegation to confer confirmation.

That the priest himself must obtain delegation is manifest from the practice of the Church. This delegation can be granted by the Holy See only, not by a bishop.

Part 1. A bishop is the ordinary minister of confirmation.
Proof 2. From Holy Scripture. The syllogism follows.

> *Only the apostles were ordinary ministers of confirmation;*
> *But only bishops are successors of the apostles:*
> *Therefore, only bishops are ordinary ministers of confirmation.*

Proof for the major. In the only two Scriptural passages narrating the conferring of confirmation, we find that apostles are its ministers. Sts. Peter and John (Acts 8:12–18) came from Jerusalem to give confirmation to the baptized Samaritans. As apostles, they needed no delegation (and Peter could not have received any since he was the head of the Church).

In the other passage (Acts: 19:1–6) we find St. Paul, an apostle, confirming the Ephesians.

We admit, apologetically speaking, that this proof is probable only. There may have been no priests present in Samaria and at Ephesus. Besides, we would not draw a general conclusion from two examples only. However, it is dogmatically certain from the universal agreement of the Fathers that we may conclude from these two passages that only the apostles were the ordinary ministers of confirmation.

Proof for the minor. It has been defined by the Church that only bishops are successors of the apostles by virtue of their episcopal consecration and its character.

Proof 3. From the Fathers. Commenting on Acts 8:12–18, St. Cyprian declares: "What was wanting to the baptized Samaritans was supplied by Peter and John; . . . and this is also done in our day. Those who are baptized in church are presented to the rulers of the Church [bishops], and by our [Cyprian was a bishop] prayer and imposition of hands, they receive the Holy Ghost and are perfected with the seal of the Lord" (*Epist.* 73, n. 9; PL. 3, 1115).

Pope Innocent I (died 417) says that the conferring of confirmation is an episcopal prerogative (DB. 98).

St. John Chrysostom says that Philip, the deacon, "did not confer the Holy Ghost upon the baptized [Samaritans]. He did not have the power. Only the twelve had this power. Hence it was a prerogative of the apostles. Accordingly we observe that bishops and no others do this" (*In Act., Hom.* 18, n. 3; PG. 60, 144). For some reasons of suitability, read Pohle-Preuss, *The Sacraments,* I, 309–10).

Part 2. Any priest can be the extraordinary minister of this sacrament if he receives delegation from the Holy See.

Proof 2. From the practice of the Church. Even before the schism of Photius (c. 815–97) it was customary in the Greek Church for priests who had obtained delegation from the Holy See to administer confirmation immediately after baptism. This custom still prevails among both Catholic and Schismatical Orientals and the Holy See recognizes the validity of their confirmations.

In the Latin Church the *Code of Canon Law* (Pars. 782, 783) makes provision for the conferring of confirmation by priests. Moreover, by a recent decree (AAS., October, 1946, pp. 349 ff.) certain priests are allowed to confirm regularly those who are in danger of death.

Proof 3. From theological reasoning. If priests were never permitted to administer confirmation, it could easily happen that the Catholics of an entire country would be deprived of this sacrament. Bishops are few. They could be imprisoned or exiled or put to death. In this event the people would be deprived of the graces of confirmation unless priests could be empowered to administer it.

OBJECTIONS

1. In the Oriental Churches priests are the ordinary ministers of confirmation because they give it regularly.

Answer. We have already explained this. The ordinary minister is one who confers confirmation without delegation. The Oriental priests have received delegation and so are not ordinary ministers.

2. A priest without delegation administers confirmation invalidly. A priest with delegation administers it validly. Therefore, it seems that the Church by granting or not granting delegation uses power over the substance of the sacraments. But the Church has no such power.

Answer. The Church in no way tampers with the matter and

form of confirmation. The minister of any sacrament must possess the power before he can act validly, but a priest does not have the power to confer confirmation unless he obtains it from the Holy See. The only exceptional happening here is that the Church by an act of jurisdiction (by granting delegation) actually confers a power to sanctify. That Christ must have made provision for this is clear from the practice of the Church.

3. In the ancient Church those who had been confirmed by heretical bishops were confirmed anew when they joined the Catholic Church. So even bishops are not ordinary ministers of confirmation.

Answer. Such was never the universal practice of the early Church. Just as some bishops of that time believed that baptism administered by heretics was invalid, so some also thought that confirmation conferred by such ministers was invalid. Those bishops made a mistake. Pope St. Stephen (DB. 46) expressed the true Catholic doctrine in the middle of the third century. He does not require that converted heretics be either baptized or confirmed anew. They merely receive the reconciliation of penance.

Comment 1. The recipient of confirmation.

For valid confirmation an adult needs baptism and an intention, at least habitual. Infants need baptism only.

For fruitful confirmation adults must be in the state of grace. They must have made an act of faith also.

SECTION FOUR

The Holy Eucharist

*

Section Four

THE HOLY EUCHARIST

GOD'S goodness to man reaches its culmination in the Eucharist. Not only is the Eucharist a sacrament by which we obtain sanctifying grace, but also a sacrifice by which we acknowledge God's supreme dominion over us in the most perfect way. Since, however, the existence both of the sacrament and of the sacrifice depends upon belief in Christ's Real Presence in the Eucharist, we divide this section into three main parts: first, Christ is really and truly present in the Eucharist; second, the Eucharist is a sacrament; third, the Eucharist is a sacrifice.

Part 1

THE REAL PRESENCE

Conclusion 1. Christ is truly, really, and substantially present in the Holy Eucharist.

Introduction. Although many Protestants celebrate the Lord's Supper, they, with few exceptions, do not believe that Christ is physically present in the Eucharist. We wish now to establish this truth against the Protestant dissenters.

Explanation of Terms

1. Eucharist. We define it here as the Real Presence of the body and blood of our Lord Jesus Christ beneath the appearances of bread and wine. This definition means that, not only the body and blood of Christ, but also Christ whole and entire, exactly as He is in heaven, is in the Eucharist.

We mention only the body and blood in our definition because when instituting the Eucharist our Lord said: "This is My body"; "This is My blood"; also because belief in the physical presence of our Lord's body and blood in the Eucharist is the acid test of correct faith. But since our Lord cannot be divided or suffer in any way, He must be entirely present wherever His body and blood are present.

"Eucharist" means literally "thanksgiving" and may have been so named because our Lord gave thanks before instituting it.

Other names that have been applied to the Eucharist are: sacrament of the altar, the Lord's table, synaxis (gathering), the body of Christ, the Lord's supper, eulogia (blessing).

2. Truly, really, and substantially. These three words are found in the canon of Trent which defines the Real Presence (DB. 883; CT. 728). Each word is placed against a specific adversary of the time. "Truly" is opposed to the opinion of Zwingli who held that the word "is" in the formula of consecration means "signifies." According to this meaning Christ would be only metaphorically in the Eucharist.

"Really" is a denial of the view of Oecolampadius who believed that the words of consecration merely mean: "This is a picture of My body." Such an interpretation evidently denies the Real Presence.

Finally, "substantially" aims at the error of Calvin who taught that, although Christ's physical body is not present in the Eucharist, He does impart some spiritual fruit upon those who receive the sacrament.

All three opinions coincide in so far as they admit only a metaphorical presence of our Lord in the Blessed Sacrament. They are condemned as heretical.

Martin Luther admitted the Real Presence, but with erroneous restrictions. He thought that Christ became physically present only when a group of Christians were gathered together to commemorate the Lord's supper. Even on these occasions, Christ's presence was effected, not by the words of consecration, but by a miracle occurring at the precise moment when Communion was received. Moreover, if some consecrated hosts remained after Communion, Luther thought that Christ was no longer present in them. These opinions have been condemned by Trent (DB. 886; CT. 731).

Luther also held that the Real Presence could be proved from the words of institution, but not from the promise of St. John. Here he erred again.

Dogmatic Note

This is an article of divine faith from the Council of Trent (DB. 883; CT. 728): "If anyone denies that in the sacrament of the Holy Eucharist are contained truly, really, and substantially the body and blood together with the soul and divinity of our Lord Jesus Christ, and consequently the whole Christ, . . . let him be anathema."

Proof 2. From Holy Scripture. We have three distinct proofs from the New Testament: first, the promise of the Eucharist (John 6:52–70); second, the words of institution at the Last Supper (fulfillment of the promise) in four different passages (Matt. 26:26–28; Mark 14:22–24; Luke 22:19, 20; I Cor. 11:23–26); third, a special argument from St. Paul (I Cor. 11:27, 29; 10:16). We shall develop each of these arguments separately.

1. Proof from the promise (John 6:52–70).

All Catholic exegetes and theologians admit that this promise provides a sure proof for the Real Presence. They dispute, however, how much of our Lord's sermon (vv. 26–60) pertains to the Eucharist directly. All concede that at least verses 52–59 furnish a convincing argument. It is dogmatically certain that the Real Presence is inculcated in these verses. Apologetically, our argument is certain.

It should be observed that our Lord had prepared the way for the great act of faith that He was going to require. At Cana (John 2:1–11) He had changed water into wine and thus demonstrated His power over wine. By walking on the water (John 6:16–25) He showed that He could alter an object's relationship to space. He multiplied the loaves (John 6:1–15) and so revealed His power over bread. The very people who had witnessed the multiplication of the loaves were the first from whom He exacted faith in His Real Presence.

Circumstances preliminary to the pertinent verses.

After multiplying the loaves, our Lord retired to the mountain to pray (vv. 14, 15). During the night He walked upon the water of the Lake of Galilee, overtook His disciples who had set out by boat for Capharnaum, boarded the ship, and accompanied them the rest of the voyage (vv. 16–21). The next day the people came to Capharnaum looking for Him (vv. 22–25). They sought Him mainly because they hoped that He would feed them again (v. 26). This afforded our Lord an opportunity to tell them about another kind of Bread. At first, He speaks of this Bread vaguely, but afterwards (vv. 52–59) very clearly.

Our Lord's sermon on the Eucharist (vv. 52–59).

52 ". . . the bread that I will give, is My flesh, for the life of the world.

53 The Jews therefore strove among themselves saying: How can this man give us His flesh to eat?

54 Then Jesus said to them: Amen, amen, I say unto you: Except you eat the flesh of the Son of Man, and drink His blood, you shall not have life in you.

55 He that eateth My flesh and drinketh My blood, hath everlasting life: and I will raise him up in the last day.

56 For My flesh is meat indeed: and My blood is drink indeed.

57 He that eateth My flesh, and drinketh My blood, abideth in Me and I in him.

58 As the living Father hath sent Me, and I live by the Father; so he that eateth Me, the same also shall live by Me.

59 This is the bread that came down from heaven. Not as your fathers did eat manna, and are dead. He that eateth this bread, shall live forever.

60 These things He said, teaching in the synagogue in Capharnaum.

61 Many therefore of His disciples, hearing it, said: This saying is hard, and who can hear it?

62 But Jesus, knowing in Himself that His disciples murmured at this, said to them: Doth this scandalize you?

63 If then you shall see the Son of Man ascend up where He was before?

64 It is the spirit that quickeneth: the flesh profiteth nothing. The words that I have spoken to you, are spirit and life.

65 But there are some of you that believe not. For Jesus knew from the beginning who they were that did not believe, and who he was, that would betray Him.

66 And He said: Therefore did I say to you, that no man can come to Me, unless it be given him by My Father.

67 After this many of His disciples went back; and walked no more with Him.

68 Then Jesus said to the twelve: Will you also go away?

69 And Simon Peter answered Him: Lord, to whom shall we go? Thou hast the words of eternal life.

70 And we have believed and have known that thou art the Christ, the Son of God."

Proof from the passage. We divide it into three separate arguments, of which the first is the most compelling.

Argument 1. From the reaction of some of the auditors and Christ's attitude towards their unbelief.

The reaction of some of the Jews. They had no doubt about our Lord's meaning. This is clear from their question (v. 53): "How can this man give us His flesh to eat?"

Now it is a principle of common sense that those who hear an entire sermon understand more plainly the speaker's meaning than others who read fragments of the sermon afterwards. The Jews, however, were present at our Lord's sermon. They heard it all, even those parts missing in Scripture. Yet they were convinced that our Lord meant that He would give them His own physical body to eat.

If Christ had meant only a metaphorical eating of His flesh by the stirring up of faith, the Jews would not have protested. They would have comprehended the "how" of this easily enough. But they could not understand *how* Christ could give them His physical body to eat. They were prototypes of the Rationalists who refuse to believe anything they cannot understand. The Jews had no doubt about our Lord's meaning, but not comprehending how He could accomplish such a marvel, they refused to believe it.

Our Lord's attitude to their unbelief. Christ was anxious to enroll all these Jews among His disciples. That was the only reason for His miracles and preaching. He was aware at once of their unfavorable reaction to His sermon.

Now it was His custom to correct people when they misunderstood Him (John 3:5 ff.; 4:10–15; 11:11–14; 4:32–34; Matt. 16:6–12). Moreover, it would have been easy to make the correction in this instance. He could have simply told them: "You have understood Me too literally. I do not mean that I am going to give you My physical body to eat. I mean that you are to have great faith in Me."

But what does He actually say? "Amen, amen, I say unto you: Unless you eat the flesh of the Son of Man and drink His blood, you shall not have life in you" (v. 54).

By the words "amen, amen," our Savior practically takes an oath that what He says is true. He then proceeds to reiterate in one of the most emphatic ways possible, the doctrine which He had previously inculcated. He retracted nothing. He qualified nothing. If the Jews had understood Him literally even before, they certainly realized now that He would not change His meaning despite their incredulity.

The reaction of some of the disciples. "Many therefore of His disciples, hearing it, said: This saying is hard, and who can hear it?" (v. 61).

These disciples evidently understood our Lord literally. A mere metaphorical eating of His body would not have been "hard" for them, but it was hard to believe that He could give them His own physical body to eat. As a result, "after this many of His disciples went back; and walked no more with Him" (v. 67).

Our Lord's attitude to the unbelief of these disciples. Imagine what the loss of these men meant to Christ. He had loved them in a special way. He had counted on them to become leaders in His cause. Why then did He allow them to go away?

It would have been simple for Him to tell them that He had not spoken literally. They had misunderstood Him. He had merely been postulating faith in Himself.

But what does our Lord do? He simply lets them walk away (v. 68). If they won't accept His words literally, He does not want them to stay with Him, even though He loves them tenderly. They must believe in the Real Presence.

True, our Lord gives them a hint that His doctrine does not mean the practice of cannibalism. His body as it appeared physically to them would ascend into heaven (v. 63). Eating His flesh did not mean that they would crunch His bones and swallow His flesh. He would give them His body to eat in some miraculous way. But once His love had proferred this hint of an explanation, He said no more. He meant His words literally and He demanded faith.

The reaction of St. Peter and the apostles. This is one of the most touching passages of Holy Writ. Even while some of the disciples were yet in sight, abandoning Christ because they would not take His words literally, the Savior looks lovingly at the apostles and asks: "Will you go away too?" So insistent was Christ on the literal meaning of His Eucharistic words that He was willing to give up even His chosen twelve.

St. Peter echoed the sentiments of the twelve when he replied: "Lord, to whom shall we go? Thou hast the words of eternal life. And we have believed and have known that Thou art the Christ, the Son of God" (vv. 68, 69).

What did St. Peter mean by these words? Simply this: "Lord, I cannot comprehend *how* You are going to give me Your flesh to eat and Your blood to drink. It is a complete mystery to me. But I know that You are God. Your meaning is plain. You are all-powerful and so could do anything. You could not deceive me. Consequently, even though I do not understand *how* You can do what You promise, I believe it with my whole heart and soul."

This is the simple faith so pleasing to God. This is intellectual humility. Catholics today and Catholics from the beginning have cherished this attitude of St. Peter. We believe God's word without question.

Argument 2. From the fact that it was impossible for the audience to understand our Lord's words metaphorically.

We assume here that Christ, like any speaker, wished to be understood by His hearers. Supposing, then, that His expressions were metaphorical and not literal, how would the Jews have understood them?

Even Protestant philologists admit that "to eat the flesh of some one" had but one metaphorical meaning among the Jews, namely, "to hate some one intensely."

Similarly, "to drink one's blood" had only one metaphorical meaning for the Jews, namely, "to punish some one severely."

Hence the Jews, if they had understood the words of Christ metaphorically, would have thought that He meant: "Unless you detest the Son of man and inflict severe punishment upon Him, you shall not have life in you." The absurdity of this meaning is evident. Therefore, our Lord did not speak metaphorically.

Argument 3. From various expressions in the passage.

We do not consider each of these points as certain arguments. Some have greater force than others. Taken conjointly with the preceding arguments, they confirm the meaning of the Eucharistic promise.

First, Christ says (v. 52): ". . . the bread that I will give is My flesh, for the life of the world." In previous parts of His sermon our Lord had been speaking of bread without clearly defining what He meant by it. In this verse He finally declares explicitly its meaning. It is not likely that He would do this by using a vague and unintelligible metaphor. When we wish to explain exactly the meaning of some word, we use literal language.

Second, we read (vv. 54, 55) that our Lord threatens loss of eternal life to those who do not eat His flesh and drink His blood. Now it is a principle of common sense that laws entailing severe sanctions should be expressed in plain language. Otherwise violators would hardly be culpable. Our Lord in these verses lays down a law having dire sanctions and so wished to be understood literally.

Third, Christ distinguishes (vv. 54, 55, 57) between the eating of His flesh and the drinking of His blood. It is difficult to find a reason for this distinction if He merely wished to inculcate the necessity of faith in Himself.

Fourth, our Savior compares (v. 59) the eating of His flesh with the eating of manna by the forefathers of the Jews. The consuming of manna, however, was a literal eating of that substance. Hence, according to the normal way of using language, we would expect the eating of Christ's flesh to be a literal, not a metaphorical eating.

Finally, Christ was already demanding faith in Himself. His promise, therefore, to give men His body and blood, cannot refer to this faith, since it is to be verified in the future only.

2. Proof from the words of institution (Matt. 26:26–28; Mark 14:22–24; Luke 22:19, 20; I Cor. 11:23–26).

It is dogmatically of faith (DB. 874; CT. 719) that these four passages establish the Real Presence. Apologetically, it is certain.

The words of institution.

"And whilst they were at supper, Jesus took bread, and blessed, and broke: and gave to His disciples, and said: Take ye and eat. This is My body. And taking the chalice, He gave thanks, and gave to them, saying: Drink ye all, of this. For this is My blood of the new testament, which shall be shed for many unto the remission of sins" (Matt. 26:26–28).

"And whilst they were eating, Jesus took bread; and blessing, broke, and gave to them, and said: Take ye. This is My body. And having taken the chalice, giving thanks, He gave it to them. And they all drank of it. And He said to them: This is My blood of the new testament, which shall be shed for many" (Mark 14:22–24).

"And taking bread, He gave thanks, and broke, and gave to them saying: This is My body which is given for you. Do this for a commemoration of Me. In like manner the chalice also, after He had supped, saying: This is the chalice, the new testament in My blood, which shall be shed for you" (Luke 22:19, 20).

"For I have received of the Lord that which also I delivered unto you, that the Lord Jesus, the same night in which He was betrayed, took bread, and giving thanks, broke, and said: Take ye, and eat: this is My body, which shall be delivered for you: this do for a commemoration of Me. In like manner also the chalice, after He had supped, saying: This chalice is the new testament in My blood: this do ye, as often as you shall drink, for the commemoration of Me" (I Cor. 11:23–25).

Comments on the four passages.

They are in substantial agreement. The most marked difference occurs in the words of consecration of the wine. Sts. Matthew and Mark simply say: "This is My blood." Sts. Luke and Paul say: "This is the chalice, the new testament in My blood."

In reality, all four mean the same thing. Sts. Luke and Paul use a common figure of speech called metonomy. The container, the chalice, is expressed to denote its contents, the blood. Such a figure is perfectly clear. Similarly, a man might hand some one a pocketbook saying: "This is money." Since a pocketbook is destined to contain money, his meaning is plain. The meaning, then, of Sts. Luke and Paul is: "The contents of this chalice is My blood by which the new testament is established."

This meaning is confirmed from the fact that they both have already said when referring to the bread: "This is My body." Hence the parallelism which is expected between the two formulas of consecration is verified only if the second consecration means: "This is My blood."

Moreover, it is a hermeneutical principle that obscure texts are to be explained by clearer texts if any happen to be found. In this instance, such texts are found since both Sts. Matthew and Mark record the consecration of the wine by saying simply: "This is My blood." We are, therefore, certain that the essential words of institution are: "This is My body"; "This is My blood."

The blessing mentioned by Sts. Matthew and Mark as occurring before the consecration of the bread was either the regular blessing used by the Jews or a special one instituted by our Lord Himself. It was merely a preparation for the words of consecration which alone effected the Real Presence.

The four accounts reveal a slight discrepancy regarding the time at which Christ instituted the Blessed Sacrament. Sts. Matthew and Mark say: "*While* they were at supper." Sts. Luke and Paul, on the other hand, state: "*After* He had supped." In reality, there is no discrepancy. The first two evangelists mean that the vessels and remains of the Paschal feast were still on the table, so that in a certain true sense, this feast was still going on. Sts. Luke and Paul simply mean that the Paschal feast had been already celebrated.

The words "Hoc" (This) and "Hic" (This) in the various accounts are pronouns. Our Lord did not say: "This bread is My body," or "This wine is My blood." These statements, if taken literally, are contradictions. Taken figuratively, they destroy the Real Presence. Christ deliberately used the indefinite pronoun and it may be understood either substantively or adjectively, i.e., demonstratively. If taken substantively, "this" means: "This matter which I hold in My hands," or "This matter which is in the chalice." Understood demonstratively, "this" simply points to the predicates. The demonstrative meaning is more probable and has been adopted in the Latin Vulgate translation. As far as the proof is concerned, the pronouns can be taken either way.

The words "Do this in memory of Me" are found only in Sts. Luke and Paul. The former records them once; the latter, twice. That they were known also to Sts. Matthew and Mark is evident from the fact that the Church was already celebrating the Eucharist before the gospels were written. The words mean that the apostles and their successors were empowered and obliged to consecrate bread and wine as our Lord had done. They also mean that priests are obliged to receive Holy Communion when they say Mass.

We divide the proof from the words of institution into three parts as we did in the promise of the Eucharist.

Argument 1. From the statements themselves.

First, on the supposition that our Lord really intended to give us His body and blood, He could have found no simpler way to express this intention than by using the words as recorded.

Second, assuming that Christ spoke metaphorically, we find that His words are unsuited to express any definite meaning. No one ever thought of a figurative meaning until the time of Scotus Erigena (ninth century).

Furthermore, we shall never know what our Lord meant if we interpret His words metaphorically. Almost two hundred metaphorical interpretations have been advanced. Yet, our Lord evidently meant something definite, and something very important, as is clear from the circumstances in which He acted. This message we shall never know unless we understand His words literally.

Third, the literal translation of the original Greek of the words of institution is: "This is My body, the *very one* which is being handed over for you" (Luke 22:19); "This is My blood, the *very* blood which is being shed for you" (Matt. 26:28). This translation is demanded by the repetition of the article in the Greek text. Since, therefore, our Lord's material body and blood were actually sacrificed for men, He must mean that the identical body and blood are present in the Eucharist because He identifies these with His redemptive body and blood.

Argument 2. A metaphorical interpretation of the words is impossible.

Metaphors can arise in three ways only. First, they can come from the nature of a thing. Our Lord referred to Herod as "that fox." It is the nature of a fox to be cunning. Hence it is clear when we hear Herod called a fox that he was cunning.

Second, metaphors may originate by agreement among men. Thus in the litany of Loretto we invoke Mary as "Gate of heaven" because all Catholics know that their salvation depends on Mary's intercession.

It should be observed, however, that these two sources of metaphors are usually combined. A person who cannot be trusted is called a "snake." This metaphor arises not only from the nature of a snake, but also from agreement of men, since men usually agree upon what constitutes the nature of a thing.

Third, metaphors are sometimes coined by a writer or speaker. Thus a speaker might refer to a person as a "pine tree." It is not clear from the nature of such a tree or from common agreement what this means. Therefore, the speaker must clarify the metaphor. He might mean that the person so designated is always in good health like a pine tree, which remains green all year, or that the person is imperturbable like a pine tree, which is agitated comparatively little by the wind. But the speaker must explain his meaning explicitly.

Applying these principles to the words of institution, we conclude that bread and wine are not mere figures representing the body and blood of Christ. Considering the nature of bread itself, we could not say expecting to be understood: "The bread of the soldier lay on the field," meaning that the soldier's body was there.

Second, bread is so poor a symbol for the human body that men have never agreed to use it as such.

Third, our Lord does not coin a metaphor at the Supper. He does not say: "Let us assume that this bread is My body." He gives no hint which would justify a metaphorical interpretation of His words. He simply says: "This is My body." Therefore, He must mean that His true body is present though the outward appearances of bread remain.

Argument 3. Various circumstances which confirm the proof.

The Eucharistic rite is part of Christ's legacy to mankind. It is, as it were, the last section of His will which provides mankind with a new testament or covenant (Exodus 24:8).

Now it is a fact that contracts in general, laws, and wills are expressed in plain language. Metaphors are scarcely ever used and vague metaphors are always excluded. If a husband says in his will: "I leave my automobile to my wife," no court will interpret this to mean that he simply wanted to leave a metaphorical auto or some kind of representation of an auto to his wife. Since, then, the words of the Last Supper express a part of Christ's legacy to men, they should be taken literally.

Again, when Christ instituted the Eucharist, He knew that His followers throughout subsequent ages would take His words literally. They would adore Him in the Host. Knowing this fact, Christ would have had a moral obligation to explain to the apostles that the words of institution were to be understood metaphorically. Since He gave no such explanation, the sinless Christ would have to be held responsible for the literal meaning attached to His words and for the ensuing idolatry practised by millions of Catholics down to the end of the world.

Finally, the subjective condition of the apostles was such that they must have understood the words of institution literally. First, by nature and environment the apostles were simple men. Their inclination, therefore, was to understand all language literally. This beautiful trait of their character comes often to the fore in the gospels. They are baffled by parables (Matt. 13:36; Mark 8:16); they cannot understand that Lazarus is dead when our Lord says that he is "asleep" (John 11:11–14). By reason of this simplicity, they must have received the words of institution literally. They ask no questions about their meaning, as they did on other occasions when they failed to comprehend Christ's statements.

Second, in addition to this simplicity, the apostles, by the education which they had received from Christ, were predisposed to believe anything that He said. They had been witnesses of His many miracles. St. Peter had attested for them all: "Thou art the Christ, the Son of God." The mere fact that some statement of our Lord was mysterious or involved the miraculous was no obstacle to their reception of it. Accordingly, when they heard the words of institution, they were disposed to accept them literally, and Christ was obliged to take their disposition into account.

Third, the apostles had been specially prepared to receive the doctrine of the Real Presence. They were, so to speak, waiting for it, since they had heard our Lord's promise of the Eucharist. Indeed, so plain was our Lord's promise that, when the apostles heard the words of institution, they could not have understood them except literally. To have understood them metaphorically would have been to contradict the evident literal meaning of the promise.

Our Lord had to bear in mind these subjective attitudes of His apostles at the Last Supper. He well knew their native simplicity, their general readiness to accept His words at face value, their particular willingness to believe in the Eucharist because of the antecedent promise. Under such circumstances it would have been impossible for Christ to have used obscure metaphors when speaking to them. This would have been the equivalent of deceiving them. He would have deliberately prepared them to believe in His Real Presence and then, without any hint of an explanation, deceived them by speaking metaphorically. This is opposed to the honesty, the integrity, the holiness of Christ.

3. The special proof from St. Paul (I Cor. 11:27, 29; 10:16).

It should be noted that verses 27 and 29 follow immediately after the words of institution and are, indeed, an interpretation of them. As we have seen, these words by themselves must be taken literally. Hence we know from the mere fact that St. Paul narrates them that he so understood them. But by the additional verses now to be considered, he actually reveals that this was his understanding of them. His main object is to put an end to unworthy Communions, but while doing this he makes it plain that the true body and blood of Christ are present in the Eucharist. Here again we have three distinct arguments.

Argument 1. "Therefore, whosoever shall eat this bread, or drink the chalice of the Lord unworthily, shall be guilty of the body and of the blood of the Lord" (v. 27). This text is dogmatically certain; apologetically very probable.

If the consecrated bread and wine were mere symbols of the body and blood of Christ, St. Paul could not have said that unworthy communicants are "guilty of the *body* and of the *blood* of the Lord." He could have said that they are guilty of sacrilege or of insult to the Lord, but not of His body and blood.

To illustrate by an example. A statue is a mere symbol of the President of the United States. His true body and blood are not in it. If a man were to disfigure the statue, we could say that he commits a personal offense against the President; he insults the President. However, we could not say that he is guilty of the body and blood of the President, because the President's body and blood are not in the statue. Therefore, St. Paul could not have said that unworthy communicants are "guilty of the body and of the blood of the Lord," unless the Lord's true body and blood were present under the appearances of bread and wine.

Argument 2. "For he that eateth and drinketh unworthily, eateth and drinketh judgment to himself, not discerning the body of the Lord" (v. 29). This text is dogmatically certain (DB. 880; CT. 725); apologetically very probable.

Three reasons, considered conjointly, show that this text means the Real Presence.

First, the unworthy communicant commits an extraordinary crime, one that deserves severe punishment.

Second, he merits this punishment by the very fact of his eating and drinking, "eateth and drinketh judgment to himself." If the Eucharist were a mere symbol of Christ's body and blood, it would be difficult to say that the very acts of eating and drinking could deserve severe punishment. Something extraordinary must be present in what is eaten to justify such an expression.

Third, St. Paul says that the unworthy communicant does not "discern the body and blood of the Lord." The obvious meaning of this expression is that the unworthy communicant does not perceive by faith that Christ is truly present beneath the Eucharistic appearances. If Christ were present only symbolically, there would be no need to "discern" anything. It would merely be necessary to *remember* that the bread and wine have been set aside as religious symbols.

Argument 3. "The chalice of benediction which we bless, is it not the communion of the blood of Christ? And the bread, which we break, is it not the partaking of the body of the Lord?" (10:16). This text, too, is dogmatically certain; apologetically very probable.

It is a strange fact that this verse which affords a sound proof for the Real Presence is twisted by some adversaries into an objection against it. They emphasize the word "bread." St. Paul, they say, asserts that the Eucharist is bread. Therefore, Christ Himself is not bodily present.

The falsity of this objection should be evident to the unprejudiced reader.

First, no valid reason can be given for emphasizing the word "bread." It is the last part of each sentence that obviously should be stressed.

Second, St. Paul when he says "bread" may be actually considering it before its consecration. Just as at the Last Supper our Lord "took bread and blessed it and broke it," and then consecrated it, so here St. Paul may be thinking of the unconsecrated bread which was first broken and then became Christ's body. Hence he declares that this bread is "the partaking of the body of the Lord." He does not say that the bread has become a symbol of Christ's body, but that it has become His true body.

Third, in case St. Paul is already considering the "bread" as consecrated, he can say "bread" without in any way denying the Real Presence for various reasons.

Since the outward appearances of bread remain after consecration, he might call the Host "bread" meaning only, "that which appears to be bread."

Moreover, Scripture in other passages, and even the ordinary use of language, allows us to call a transformed object by the name which it had before it was transformed. Thus, the blind man whose sight is restored by Christ is still called a blind man after he can see (John 9:17). The serpent is still called a rod because it was made from a rod (Exodus 7:12).

Furthermore, St. Paul was compelled to say "bread" because of the specification which he gives it. It is "the bread which we break." He could not possibly have said, "the body of Christ which we break." This would be false since the body of the Eucharistic Christ cannot be broken.

Again, it is noteworthy that, when circumstances permitted St. Paul to avoid using the word "wine" in the first sentence of the verse, he avoids it. He does not say "the wine which we bless," but "the chalice."

Finally, the Church herself still allows the Eucharist to be called "bread." Thus we speak of the Eucharist as "heavenly bread," or as "the bread of angels." These expressions do not deny the Real Presence.

This development of the text not only answers the objection, but also proves that this verse inculcates the Real Presence.

Proof 3. From the Fathers. Belief in the Real Presence is substantiated by a continuous tradition which can be traced to the earliest days of the Church. Included in this tradition would be the testimony of archeology, of art, of liturgical books, of local councils, of Fathers.

We shall limit our evidence to statements from some of the Fathers. It should be noted that this testimony, if we were to give it in full, would be a certain apologetic proof for the Real Presence, even if we had no Scripture proof whatever.

St. Ignatius of Antioch (died c. 117): "They [the Docetists] abstain from the Eucharist and from prayer because they do not believe that the Eucharist is the flesh of our Savior, Jesus Christ, which suffered for our sins and which the Father in His goodness restored to life" (*Ad Smyrn.* 7, 1; RJ. 64).

The Docetists were heretics who denied that Christ had a true human body and so they logically denied that Christ's true body was in the Eucharist. They are Christological rather than Eucharistic adversaries.

St. Justin Martyr (died c. 163): "We do not receive this [the Eucharist] as ordinary food or ordinary drink; but, as by the word of God, Jesus our Savior was made flesh and had both flesh and blood for our salvation, so also the food which has been blessed by the prayerful words instituted by Him, and by which our flesh and blood through assimilation are nourished, is, we are taught, both the flesh and blood of that Jesus become man" (*Apol.* 1, 66; RJ. 128).

St. Irenaeus (died c. 203). Arguing against the Gnostics who maintained that all matter was essentially evil, he says that this is impossible since wine and bread are "by the word of God changed into the Eucharist which is the body and blood of Jesus Christ" (*Adv. Haer.* V, 2, 2; RJ. 249).

Tertullian (died c. 220): "The flesh [of Christians] is nourished by the body and blood of Christ, in order that the soul, too, may be sated with God" (*De Resurr.* 8; RJ. 362).

St. Cyprian (died c. 258). He gives a reason why penitents who had committed grave crimes should be absolved and admitted to Communion when persecution is imminent: "Communion should be given by us: so that those whom we incite and exhort to battle may not through our fault be left unarmed and helpless, but fortified by the protection of the body and blood of Christ. . . ." (*Epist.* 57, 2; PL. 3, 883).

St. Cyril of Jerusalem (315–386): "Since He [Christ] has said of the bread, 'This is My body,' who shall dare doubt? Since He has said and asserted, 'This is My blood,' who shall ever doubt that it is His blood? He once changed water into wine, which is akin to blood; shall we not therefore believe when He changed wine into blood?" (*Catech.* XXII, 2; PG. 33, 1097.)

Again St. Cyril says: "Having been thus instructed and convinced that what appears to be bread is not bread, though it seems so to the taste, but the body of Christ; and what appears to be wine is not wine, though it seems so to the taste, but the blood of Christ, . . . strengthen thy heart by eating this bread as spiritual food and gladden thy soul's countenance" (*Catech.* XXII, 9; PG. 33, 1104).

St. John Chrysostom (344–97) is perhaps the outstanding Eucharistic teacher and many passages could be quoted from him. One statement will suffice: "That which is in the chalice, is the same as that which flowed from the side of Christ, and of this we are made partakers" (*In 1 Cor., Hom.* 24, 1; RJ. 1192).

Other patristic citations can be found in Pohle-Preuss, *The Sacraments,* II, 45–88; also in *The Teaching of the Catholic Church,* II, 850–857.

It should also be noted that all the liturgical books contain some prayer which invokes God to change the bread and wine into the body and blood of Christ.

The Conclusion is confirmed by the fact that all the Oriental schismatics teach the doctrine of the Real Presence.

OBJECTIONS AGAINST THE PROOF FROM THE PROMISE

1. If the words of St. John are taken literally, the people would not have understood what Christ meant.

Answer. We admit that the people could not have understood all the implications of the doctrine, but we deny that they could not have understood the simple truth that Christ was to give them His true body and blood as food. It is clear from our proof that they did grasp this truth.

2. When the expression "the bread of life" occurs (vv. 26–48), it is a metaphor signifying faith. It should retain this meaning during the rest of the sermon.

Answer. It is evident from the reactions of the auditors, as explained in our proof, that "bread" occurring after verse 52 means the true body of Christ: "How can this man give us His flesh to eat?" Neither does the metaphorical meaning of "faith" in the first section of the sermon exclude all reference to the Eucharist. Belief in the Real Presence is an important part of the faith in Christ which a person must have.

3. Christ says: "It is the spirit that quickeneth; the flesh profiteth nothing" (v. 64). In this verse "flesh" must be understood metaphorically since Christ's true flesh would certainly be of great profit. Therefore, "flesh" should be taken metaphorically in the sermon itself.

Answer. "Flesh" in this verse does not refer to the flesh of Christ. It is metaphorical and means a purely human and rationalistic outlook, as opposed to supernatural faith, which is the meaning of "spirit" in the first half of the verse. A man must have supernatural faith to accept Christ's teaching.

Moreover, in no way did our Lord retract His previous teaching, as is evident from the fact that even after the utterance of verse 64, some disciples abandoned Him.

Finally, it is impossible that our Lord should have insisted so strongly on the Real Presence, and then reversed that doctrine by the comment contained in verse 64.

4. Christ says: "He that eateth My flesh and drinketh My blood hath everlasting life" (v. 55). Yet we know that reception of the Eucharist does not infallibly guarantee eternal salvation.

Answer. Christ is speaking to adults. He commands all adults to receive the Eucharist. If they fail to do so through their own fault, they cannot be saved. If they do not receive the Eucharist because it is impossible for them to do so, they can be saved anyhow because they desire, at least implicitly, to receive Him. Infants are saved even though they never receive Holy Communion.

In so complex a process as the working out of one's salvation, we could not expect all its conditions to be found in every sentence where the subject is mentioned. For instance, Christ says: "He that believeth and is baptized shall be saved" (Mark 16:16). Does this mean that a person can be saved even though he *acts* as he pleases?

OBJECTIONS AGAINST THE PROOF FROM THE
WORDS OF INSTITUTION

1. In many passages of Scripture (Gen. 41:26; John 10:7, 15:1; Gal. 4:24; Exodus 12:11; I Cor. 10:4 and elsewhere) the word "is" means "signifies." So it can have this meaning in the words of institution.

Answer. In all those cases it is plain from the context that "is" must mean "signifies." This is not true of the words of institution.

2. The Aramaic language used by Christ had no word for "signifies."

Answer. This is false. More than forty ways of expressing "signifies" are found in that language. In fact, no language could get along without a word to denote "signifies." The idea which it represents crops up constantly, since every object in this world is a sign of something else.

3. The word "is" expresses an identity between the subject and predicate. But no identity is possible between bread and Christ's body. Therefore, "is" means "signifies."

Answer. Christ does not say: "This bread is My body," but "This is My body." The bread, when the declaration is terminated, is changed into Christ's body, as we shall show in the following Conclusion.

4. Christ said: "Do this in memory of Me." When we do something in memory of some one, we suppose that the person remembered is not present. Therefore, Christ is not present in the Eucharist.

Answer. Christ is not insisting on memory of His Person, but of His passion. The Eucharist involves the sacrifice of the Mass which is objectively a memorial of the death of Christ.

However, even if our Lord had insisted on the Eucharist as a memorial of Himself, it would not follow that He was denying the Real Presence, because He is present in the Eucharist *invisibly.* He cannot be seen or observed by any of the senses. He is present *as though* He were absent and so the sacrament can be called a memorial of Him who once walked visibly on earth.

5. If an ordinary person were to say, "This is my body," while holding a piece of bread, we would take for granted that he was

speaking metaphorically. Similarly, when the apostles heard Christ say those words over bread, they understood Him figuratively. Therefore, "is" means "signifies."

Answer. If an ordinary person were to say, "This is my body," while holding a piece of bread, we would not know what he meant unless he added an explanation. Certainly, bread is not a symbol of the human body. We would ask such a person: "What do you mean?"

The apostles do not ask this question of Christ at the Supper. Because of the preceding promise of the Eucharist, they knew His meaning. They also knew that Christ was not an ordinary person. He was the Son of God and had worked many miracles in their sight.

Moreover, on the supposition that Christ wanted to institute the Blessed Sacrament, the simplest way of doing this was by His words uttered at the Supper. Christ really explained the meaning of the words of institution before He pronounced them, i.e., when He promised to give the sacrament.

This objection is based on the false assumption that the Eucharist is impossible even to God's omnipotence.

*

Conclusion 2. Christ becomes present in the Eucharist by transubstantiation of the bread and wine into His body and blood.

Introduction. This Conclusion is of great importance because, first, it contains a truth revealed by God; second, because even those Protestants who admit the Real Presence deny transubstantiation; third, because this doctrine throws some light on two great mysteries connected with the Blessed Sacrament, viz., how Christ's body can be entirely present without occupying space, and how He can be present in thousands of tabernacles at the same time.

In the preceding Conclusion we answered the question: Is Christ truly present in the Eucharist? Now we answer this question: *How* does Christ *become* present in the Eucharist?

Explanation of Terms

Only the word "transubstantiation" needs explanation. Before elucidating it, we call the student's attention to the following important remarks.

Although the Council of Trent, when exposing the doctrine of transubstantiation, uses the terminology of scholastic philosophy, it does not define the truth of this philosophical system. There are other ways of explaining the ultimate constitution of material bodies, and a Catholic may adopt any one of them that does not conflict with the revealed truth, as we shall explain it.

The Council employs scholastic terms like substance, accidents, and conversion. Without any doubt these terms are very suited to manifest the meaning of our doctrine, and we, too, shall use them. But these terms, as used by the Council, need not be understood in their strict scholastic meaning.

Christ wanted His revealed truths, in their essential signification, to come within the intellectual compass of all men. Transubstantiation is one of these truths. If the comprehension of the essential meaning of this truth depended on an understanding of scholastic philosophy, it would be unintelligible to many.

Transubstantiation, then, is a kind of conversion. A substantial conversion takes place when one thing is changed into another. Thus, at Cana the water miraculously became wine by a substantial conversion (John 2:1–11).

Such a conversion requires three essential elements. First, there must be a substantial entity which is going to disappear. At Cana this was the water. Second, a new substantial entity must come into existence, or, at any rate, come into existence in a new way or in a new place. At Cana this was the wine. Third, an inherent connection must flourish between the entity which ceases and the new entity. The first must be ordained to become the second. The first must cease by becoming the second. The second object must come into existence by the cessation of the first object. Thus at Cana the disappearance of the water postulated the coming of the wine, and the coming of the wine was brought about by the ceasing of the water.

This inherent connection has been established ordinarily by God's natural laws. This is not true of the miracle at Cana.

Water has no intrinsic aptitude to become wine. At Cana water, and only the water contained in the six jugs, received this aptitude by a special decree of God, and this decree was limited to this one occasion.

This point is applicable to transubstantiation. Clearly, bread and wine are not ordained by natural laws to become the body and blood of Christ. This capability arises from God's special decree manifested to the apostles at the Last Supper.

From the foregoing explanation it should be clear that a conversion is not the same as creation, in which the starting point is nothing at all. Neither is it the same as annihilation, which terminates in a vacuum. Nor is it a mere succession or substitution as when a magician first shows us a dime and then, closing his hand, opens it to reveal a quarter. The dime is not ordained to become a quarter and it remains, though concealed, after the quarter appears.

Some authors demand that some element common both to the entity which ceases and to the entity which begins to exist should remain after a substantial conversion. No one denies that such a common element is found in all natural conversions, but some deny that the very concept of conversion requires it. If it is necessary, it is provided in the Eucharist by the appearances or accidents of bread and wine which remain the same both before and after transubstantiation.

Transubstantiation, therefore, may be defined as the conversion of the entire substance of bread into the substance of Christ's body and the conversion of the entire substance of wine into the substance of Christ's blood, so that only the accidents of bread and wine remain.

Explanation of This Definition

1. Conversion. The three essential elements of a substantial conversion are verified in this definition. First, the substance of bread and wine are entities which cease to exist. Second, the substance of Christ's body and blood is an entity which begins to exist in a new way, i.e., in the sacrament. Third, the coming of Christ's body is postulated by the cessation of the bread and wine because these two natural substances, when placed in definite circumstances (namely, when the words of consecration

are pronounced over them by a priest), necessarily, by Christ's special decree at the Last Supper, become His body and blood. They are ordained to this purpose.

2. Substance. If substance is considered in its strict scholastic meaning, bread is composed of more than one substance. It is heterogeneous. In clarifying the doctrine of transubstantiation we do not follow this strict scholastic meaning.

Common sense tells us that every perceptible object has, besides its outward manifestations, an underlying and permanent reality beneath it. Hence, in our definition "substance" means that whatever underlying and enduring reality subsists beneath the external appearances of bread and wine is changed into Christ's body and blood.

3. The entire substance. Transubstantiation differs from all purely natural substantial conversions. When, for instance, a caterpillar by being eaten is transformed into the substance of a bird, all the appearances or accidents of the caterpillar disappear within the body of the bird. However, something substantial (scholastic philosophy calls it the "form," i.e., the principle of an object's activity) within the caterpillar also disappears, because the source of life and activity of a bird differs radically from that of a caterpillar.

Yet it is evident that something is received by the bird from the caterpillar. This "something" cannot be the accidents of the caterpillar since these are completely transformed when assimilated. Hence it must be something substantial that passes from the caterpillar into the bird so that there is a substantial element common to both. In scholastic philosophy this is called "prime matter."

In transubstantiation, however, the *entire* underlying reality of the bread, its complete substance (whether we conceive this substance according to the scholastic explanation of matter and form or not) is converted into the body of Christ.

4. Into the substance of Christ's body. Since we already know that Christ is entirely present in the Eucharist, why do we say here, "into the substance of Christ's *body?*" Because the conversion is directed *specifically* to the coming of His body. The words of consecration expressly say: "This is My body."

Since, however, Christ is indivisible so that His body cannot be separated from His blood, His human soul, His divine nature, and His divine personality, He is wholly present in the Eucharist. But only His body becomes present as the specific termination of the conversion. His blood, soul, divinity, and personality become present by *concomitance*, i.e., by the inseparable connection which they have with His body. We say the "substance" of Christ's body because its accidents, though imperceptible, are also present by the same concomitance, not precisely because of the words of consecration.

In the second consecration the conversion terminates specifically in the presence of Christ's blood: "This is My blood." But by concomitance His body and entire Self become present.

This distinction between the effect produced by the words themselves and the effects that result by concomitance has practical consequences and should be reflected upon by the student. It explains, as we shall see later, how there is an immolation of Christ in the Mass. It also answers the question, sometimes proposed as an objection to transubstantiation: "Does bread become God?" The answer is no. Bread becomes another material substance, the body of the Second Person of the Blessed Trinity. But as a consequence of this advent of His body, He Himself becomes present in His entirety. God is in the Eucharist by concomitance.

5. So that only the accidents of bread and wine remain.

The word "accidents" simply means all the appearances of bread and wine, their size, weight, color, temperature, resistance, taste, odor, and so forth. These remain exactly the same after transubstantiation. They are often called the species.

The Conclusion has two parts: first, absolutely nothing of the substances of bread and wine remains after consecration; second, these substances cease because they are converted by transubstantiation into the body and blood of Christ.

Adversaries. Luther held that both the substance of the bread and the substance of Christ's body are present after the Real Presence has been effected.

Osiander, a disciple of Luther, thought that the substance of bread remained, but that it was assumed by Christ in a manner similar to that by which He assumed His human nature.

Durandus (before Trent) taught that part of the substance

of the bread, its "matter," remained after consecration and was vivified by the human soul of Christ. This opinion is heretical.

Other Catholic theologians of comparatively recent times have erred in explaining transubstantiation. Some of them have been condemned (DB. 1843–46; 1919–20).

Dogmatic Note

The Council of Trent (DB. 884; CT. 729) has defined both parts as articles of divine faith: "If anyone says that in the sacred and holy sacrament of the Eucharist, the substance of the bread and wine remains conjointly with the body and blood of our Lord, Jesus Christ, and denies that wonderful and singular *conversion* of the *whole* substance of the bread into the body, and of the *whole* substance of the wine into the blood—the species alone of the bread and wine remaining—which conversion the Catholic Church aptly calls transubstantiation; let him be anathema."

Proof 2 for both parts. From the words of institution in Holy Scripture.

It is dogmatically certain (DB. 877; CT. 722) that transubstantiation is implied in the words of institution. Apologetically, our proof is highly probable. The argument follows:

If at the Last Supper the words of consecration, "This is My body," necessarily meant

1. that the substance of Christ's body was present;

2. that the substance of the bread had ceased to exist;

3. that the substance of the bread was intrinsically ordained to become the body of Christ;

then transubstantiation can be deduced from these words;

But these three meanings are contained in them:

Therefore, transubstantiation can be deduced from them.

Proof for the major. If the three points indicated can be proved, we have all the essential elements of a conversion: a new entity which begins to exist in a new way; an entity which lapses from existence; an intrinsic aptitude of the entity which ceases to become the new entity.

Proof for the minor.

1. We have proved in the preceding Conclusion that the words of institution meant that Christ was truly present. His

body, therefore, began to exist in a new way, i.e., under the species of bread. We call this His sacramental presence.

2. The substance of the bread had ceased to exist. If the substance of the bread had remained after these words were uttered, our Lord could not have said simply: "This is My body."

We are so bound to our sense cognition that we naturally designate in our speech that substance whose appearances are manifested to our senses. For instance, although we know that God is substantially present in a tree, we cannot point to a tree and tell somebody: "This is God." Why? Because only the appearances of the tree are apprehended by our senses. We have no sense perception of God in the tree.

Similarly, if we know that a bird is concealed in a tree, we cannot point to the tree and tell somebody: "This is a bird." Why? Because the bird is hidden from our sense perceptions.

The only exception to this rule of speech occurs when one substance is a natural container for another. Thus we can point to a pocketbook and tell some one: "This is money." This exception is not applicable in our case because bread is not a recognized container for the human body.

Since, then, only the accidents of bread were perceptible to the apostles, our Lord would have had to say, had the substance of bread remained: "This is bread and My body is there too," or, "Here is My body." But Christ did not use any expression like these. He said simply: "This is My body." Therefore, the substance of bread had ceased to exist.

It should be noted that this argument proves that a part, at least, of the substance of bread must have disappeared. Accordingly, it is sufficient to refute the Protestant adversaries, who contend that the entire substance of the bread remained after the words of institution.

The student should remember that, since the time of our Lord's bodily resurrection, the words of consecration at the Mass necessarily involve a total cessation of the substance of the bread. At the moment of the resurrection our Lord's body became a glorified one. Since a glorified body has no vegetative functions, it could not assimilate any part of the substance of bread.

3. The substance of the bread was intrinsically ordained to become the substance of Christ's body.

Since the Protestant adversaries hold that the entire substance of the bread remains, they necessarily deny this third point. Since we have refuted their opinion above, we shall deal with this item, not apologetically, but positively.

Before developing the proof, we call attention to the following possible misconception of transubstantiation. We should not imagine that the whole substance of bread is annihilated and that Christ's body becomes present after its annihilation. This would be a mere substitution of Christ's body for the bread and so could not be a conversion.

Yet it would be easy to form this false idea. It is of faith that the entire substance of the bread ceases, and so we may be inclined to view transubstantiation as an annihilation of the substance of the bread and the subsequent coming of Christ's body.

A complete cessation of the substance of the bread occurs, but its very cessation demands the advent of Christ's body. The substance of the bread ceases, not by way of annihilation, but by being *changed* into the Lord's body.

When, for example, our Lord changed water into wine, the form or active principle of the water completely disappeared when it was succeeded by the form of the wine. The ceasing of the water's form, objectively, by God's special decree on this occasion, postulated the advent of the wine's form. We could not say that the water's form was annihilated and that, afterwards, God produced the form of the wine.

The same is true of the natural transformations in the world about us. When, for instance, a caterpillar is eaten by a bird, the process does not involve two distinct actions: one which reduces the form of the caterpillar to nothing by way of annihilation and another which produces the form of the bird. Only one action occurs. The form of the caterpillar disappears by being *converted* into the form of the bird.

What is true of only the forms in these examples, is true of the entire underlying reality (both matter and form) of the bread. Both its matter and form cease to exist, but their cessation results, not from a distinct act of annihilation, but from their conversion into the body of Christ. God is the sole principal cause of this wonderful and unique conversion.

Up to the time of the Last Supper bread had many intrinsic purposes (which it still retains) and could be converted into various objects. It could be converted into the flesh of man and of many animals. It could corrupt under diverse circumstances and become many different substances as a result. But at the Supper our Lord bestowed on bread a *new* objective destiny. From then to the end of the world it could and would under the proper circumstances become His body. Just as the ceasing of the form of bread by digestion objectively demands that it become my own body, so now the total cessation of the matter and form of bread by the words of consecration at the Mass, objectively postulates that they become the body of Christ.

Why is this true from the words of institution? Our Lord said: "This is My body." When He pronounced the word "this," He held bread in His hands. When He finished the sentence, the bread was gone and His body was present. In other words, there was a substantial identity between "this" and "body," the subject and the predicate.

As we saw in the preceding Conclusion, He could not have meant: "This bread is My body." This would be a patent contradiction. Neither could He mean that the bread was annihilated and then replaced by His body. This interpretation would deny an objective identity between the bread and His body. He says in fact: "*This* is My body," thus evidently meaning that some intrinsic and substantial connection exists between the two. The only possible connection of this kind is a conversion of the bread into His body.

Suppose, for instance, that a man were endowed with power to change a caterpillar into a bird. He shows you a caterpillar and says: "This is a bird," and the wonder takes place. It would be evident that the caterpillar had not been annihilated. Had annihilation occurred, it would have been false for the speaker to say: "*This* (referring to the caterpillar) is a bird." The identity between subject and predicate contained in his words demands that the object referred to by the subject be transformed into the object expressed by the predicate. So it is with the words of institution.

Proof 2. From the Fathers. The general idea of transubstantiation is clearly and frequently expressed by various Fathers.

For instance, that the substance of bread and wine do not remain after consecration, is clearly enunciated by St. Cyril of Jerusalem: "What seems to be bread is not bread, though it has the taste of bread, but it is the body of Christ; and what seems to be wine, is not wine, though it tastes like wine, but it is the blood of Christ" (*Cat.* 22, 9; RJ. 848).

St. Ambrose testifies that the bread and wine "are transfigured" (*transfigurantur*) into the body and blood of Christ (*De fide,* 4, 10; RJ. 1270).

St. Gregory of Nyssa says that the bread is "transmuted" (*transmutari*) (*Oratio catech.* 37; RJ. 1035). St. Cyril of Jerusalem uses the same word when speaking of the wine (*Cat.* 22, 2; RJ. 844). St. John Chrysostom declares that the bread and wine are "transformed" (*transformari*) (*De prod. Judae,* Hom. 1, 6; RJ. 1157); St. Cyril of Alexandria says that they "are led across" (*traduci*) (*In Mt.* 26, 27; RJ. 2101).

Moreover, the comparisons used by some of the Fathers show that they held transubstantiation. They compare the Eucharistic change with the conversion of food into the human body, with the conversion of water into wine at Cana, with the conversion of the rod into a serpent.

St. Thomas expresses the universal teaching of the theologians when he writes: "The whole substance of the bread is changed into the whole substance of the body of Christ, and the whole substance of the wine is converted into the whole substance of the blood of Christ. Hence this conversion is not according to the form, but according to the substance" (*Summa,* III, q. 75, a. 4).

The Conclusion is confirmed by the fact that the Oriental schismatics also admit transubstantiation.

Comment 1. A further explanation of transubstantiation.

It is perfectly legitimate for theologians to delve more deeply into this mystery by attempting to expose with greater precision the action wrought by God when transubstantiation takes place. Different opinions are held.

Some say that Christ's coming can be explained more exactly by a process called "adduction." Others resort to what they call "production." All admit that Christ does not move locally from heaven to the altar.

Since both these explanations are vague and unsatisfactory, we believe that it is better to join a third group of theologians who rest satisfied with transubstantiation alone. As Fr. Van Noort says: ". . . since the ways so far attempted [to analyze transubstantiation more accurately], namely, those of adduction and production, seem rather to corrupt the true idea of conversion than to illustrate its true nature more in detail, it is better to accept the fact without further explanation. Nor is it surprising that a more detailed analysis of transubstantiation, since it is a mystery, should be unobtained" (*De Sacramentis,* I, n. 348).

We simply affirm that in effecting transubstantiation God acts, not twice, but once. He does not first annihilate the substance of bread and then by a distinct action bring about the Real Presence. Furthermore, God's single action affects only the substance of bread and wine, not Christ, since He could not be the recipient of such an action. By reason alone we can merely indicate that no rational objection can prove that the ineffable mystery of transubstantiation is impossible or contradictory.

Comment 2. The accidents of bread and wine.

In the Eucharist all the physical accidents or appearances of bread and wine remain. This is of faith from Trent (DB. 884; CT. 729): ". . . only the accidents of bread and wine remaining." It is also evident from experience.

These accidents or appearances or species have objective reality after transubstantiation. This statement contradicts Descartes who said that they remained only in the sense that God arouses within us the same subjective sensations after transubstantiation.

It is Catholic doctrine that these accidents retain their objective reality. Trent necessarily meant this when it defined that the accidents remain, because the theory that accidents might be purely subjective sensations was unknown to the bishops of the council.

Again, if these accidents are not objective, we have no perceptible sign for this sacrament.

Furthermore, to deny the objectivity of these accidents is to say implicitly that God leads us into error about them, an error which we cannot correct either by faith or reason.

Finally, it is evident that the sacrament has relationships to space. It is carried in processions; it is in the tabernacle. But Christ Himself, as He is present in the sacrament, has no relationship to space. Only the accidents provide this relationship. As a result, if the objective reality of the accidents is denied, Christ's true presence in the sacrament cannot be maintained.

It makes no difference whether a philosopher holds that some sensations like color are present in their substance formally (just as we perceive them) or only fundamentally. In either case these sensations proceed from objective realities which are distinct from their substance.

A few minor theologians thought that the Eucharistic accidents have objective reality only in the sense that God conserves the same undulations of the air or ether which before transubstantiation proceeded from the bread and wine. In this opinion something objective does remain.

However, it is Catholic doctrine that the same *numerical* accidents remain objectively after transubstantiation. Evidently, the fathers of Trent had in mind no such bizarre explanation of the Eucharistic appearances when they defined that only the accidents of bread and wine remain.

Moreover, the whole of tradition teaches that something is left from the bread and wine, not just some of the *effects* produced by their accidents. For more information about this, consult Pohle-Preuss, *The Sacraments*, II, 150, 151.

After transubstantiation the accidents of bread and wine do not inhere in any subject or substance whatever. This, too, is Catholic doctrine. The Council of Constance (DB. 582) condemned the following proposition of John Wiclif: "The accidents of bread do not remain without a subject in this sacrament."

Fr. Palmieri thought that the ether, which before transubstantiation permeated the atoms of bread and wine, remains afterwards to support the Eucharistic accidents. This opinion can hardly be reconciled with the condemned proposition quoted above and with the definition of Trent which states that nothing of the bread and wine remains except the appearances.

Theologians commonly teach that the Eucharistic accidents are supported by God's omnipotence. It is preferable to say with St. Thomas that the quantity of the bread and wine is sustained immediately by God's power, whereas the other accidents are sustained by Him only mediately, i.e., by the medium of the quantity, which is the substratum of all other accidents.

The Eucharistic accidents can produce all the effects, both mental and ontological, which they were able to produce before transubstantiation. They are subject to the same physical changes; they can by their action produce the same physical effects; they can excite the same subjective images and ideas. This is common and certain teaching.

When the Eucharistic appearances are corrupted, it is certain that Christ ceases to be present beneath them. When corruption occurs, the new set of appearances (no longer of bread and wine, but of vinegar or something else) are not supported by God without a substance. He supplies them with that substance which they would ordinarily receive by natural law. Thus when consecrated wine corrupts into vinegar, the accidents of vinegar are actually inhering in the substance of vinegar which God has produced for them. This is the more probable explanation.

It follows, therefore, that the Eucharistic accidents can undergo all the *substantial* changes which unconsecrated bread and wine can undergo. Thus although only the appearances of bread remain after consecration, they are transformed by nutrition into the body of the communicant in the same way as if they had never been consecrated. It is, then, more probable that God endows the quantity of the bread, since it is the substratum of all other accidents, with the potentialities of the substance of bread.

All theologians admit a union of some kind between the body of Christ and the Eucharistic accidents. Wherever the consecrated appearances are to be found, Christ is present beneath them. Wherever Christ is bodily present in this world, the Eucharistic accidents must be found. Therefore, the two are evidently inseparable and so must be united in some way.

Nevertheless, it is certain that the accidents do not inhere in the body of Christ as they formerly did in the substance of bread and wine. In the Eucharist the body of the Lord possesses its own accidents, and no substance can have two sets of accidents actually inhering in it.

Besides, it would be impossible for the glorified body of Christ to be acted upon in such a way by the accidents of bread and wine.

Furthermore, if the accidents of bread inhered in Christ's body, we would have to say that Christ's body in the Eucharist is round or white, because the Host is round or white.

Finally, since Christ is present in the Eucharist without any direct relationship to space or to an extended object, His body cannot be physically united with the accidents of bread and wine.

But although no intrinsic physical union exists between Christ's body and the accidents of bread and wine, some most intimate bond must exist between them. So close is this bond that the Eucharistic species are worthy of divine cult, not by themselves, but precisely because of their close union with the Second Person of the Blessed Trinity.

Theologians differ in explaining the nature of this union between Christ's body and the accidents. All concede that it is a singular union, mysterious, not physical, yet most intimate. It could be that Christ's body as God's instrument imparts by purely efficient causality a physical influx which sustains the accidents. This would not imply any physical union, since cause and effect remain physically distinct.

It could be held, but seems insufficient, to say that there is merely an external union between the accidents and Christ's body, like, for instance, the union between a man's body and his clothing.

We cannot expect to find any close analogy from the various kinds of union which come within our experience. Christ's Eucharistic body is the only material thing in this world that has no contact with another material thing. He is present throughout the consecrated accidents somewhat as water is diffused throughout a sponge. However, even this example is misleading because there is a physical union between the water and the sponge. Moreover, by pressure water and sponge can be separated again, both retaining their natures, whereas only the corruption of the accidents can separate Christ from them. (Cf. Pohle-Preuss, *The Sacraments*, II, 158 ff.)

OBJECTIONS

1. Transubstantiation is not necessary to explain the words of institution. Christ merely meant that His body was contained in the bread, just as a person handing over his pocketbook might say: "This is money." He would simply mean that his money was inside the pocketbook.

Answer. The reason why a person can say, "This is money," when he hands over his pocketbook is that this object is known by everybody to be a container for money. But bread, neither by its own aptitude nor by usage, is a container for the human body. Hence Christ could not have meant that His body was contained in the substance of bread. If He had meant this, He would have had to give an explanation to the apostles. No explanation is found in Scripture.

2. If only the appearances of bread and wine remain after consecration, we are led into error since our apprehension of these appearances induces us to conclude that the substances of bread and wine are also present.

Answer. We would be led into error if we did not know on the word of God that the substances of bread and wine are no longer present. Since faith teaches us that the conclusion which we would ordinarily draw from our sensations is false, we are not led into any error.

3. Chemical analysis reveals that the same elements of bread are present after consecration. Therefore, no transubstantiation takes place.

Answer. Chemistry deals only with the *accidental* qualities of material things. Substance is beyond the reach of microscopes and test tubes. It is a reality which reason forces every man to admit.

*

Conclusion 3. Christ is present in his entirety beneath either of the sacramental species. He is present in His entirety in every portion of either species after it is divided. He is present in His entirety in every spot of either species even before it is divided.

Introduction. We have answered the questions: "Is Christ truly present in the Eucharist?" and "How does Christ *become* present in the Eucharist?" We now ask: "How *is* Christ present in the Eucharist?" Our answer is contained in the three parts as expressed in this Conclusion.

While studying this matter particularly, the student is cautioned not to be misled by his imagination. He will be inclined by his natural experience to picture Christ to himself as visibly extended like other material objects. This would be an erroneous procedure. The student here must use his reason enlightened by faith.

Explanation of Terms

1. Christ is present in His entirety. This has the same meaning in the three parts of the Conclusion. In a summary way we may say that it means that the same Christ numerically, now truly present in heaven, is also present in the Blessed Sacrament. There are not two Christs, one in heaven, the other in the sacrament. There are two *presences* of the same identical Christ. This is a basic principle of Eucharistic theology about which the student should reflect, since we have no analogy for it in the world about us.

More specifically, we repeat what we said in treating of the Real Presence. Christ is present in the Eucharist with His divine nature and His human nature. He has His human soul with all its faculties, His human body with its blood, with its entire quantity, with all its organs arranged harmoniously, with all those accidents which lend any intrinsic perfection to the body.

It should be noted particularly that our Lord's body in the Eucharist has its entire quantity. In heaven this quantity is in space and so is measured by whatever physical entities surround it. In the sacrament Christ's body has its natural size, but it is not measured by any object around it, not even by the species of bread and wine. That is why the actual size of Christ's body is not discernible in the Eucharist. More will be said about this when we answer the objections.

2. Under either species. Christ is wholly present under either the consecrated species of bread or the consecrated species of wine. We have explained in the preceding Conclusion that in the first consecration His body alone becomes present by the explicit declaration of the words. He becomes entirely present by concomitance. In the second consecration the blood only becomes present by the explicit declaration of the words, but by concomitance He becomes entirely present. This distinction between the explicit declaration of the words and concomitance is validated by the Council of Trent (DB. 876; CT. 721) and has the practical consequences which we mentioned under transubstantiation.

It should also be observed that by circumincession and immensity the Father and the Holy Ghost are also present in the Eucharist together with the Son. But only the Son has a human nature and that nature is wholly present in the sacrament.

3. Christ is present in His entirety in every portion of either species after it is divided. Catholics know that when a priest divides a consecrated Host, each person who receives a part actually receives Communion. They also know that Christ is not lessened or maimed in any way by this division of the Host. The entire Christ is present in every separated part. Furthermore, if the consecrated wine is divided, Christ is wholly present in every distinguishable drop of it.

4. Christ is present in His entirety in every spot of either species even before it is divided. This means that we can look at any spot of an undivided Host or of the consecrated, but unseparated, wine and say: "Christ is wholly present in that spot." The same numerical Christ is entirely present in every single spot of the undivided Host.

This does not mean that we can say that Christ is present a hundred or a thousand times in a Host before it is divided. No, there is only *one* actual presence. Things can be counted only after they are separated. Thus I cannot count the number of slices in a loaf of bread until the bread is actually sliced. Yet while looking at a loaf of bread or at any spot of it, I can truly say: "This is bread." Moreover, the entire substance of bread is present in every spot of the loaf. Each spot is actually bread.

Just as I can look at any spot of the air surrounding me and say: "This is air," so I can look at any spot of the consecrated bread and wine and say: "Christ is there in His entirety." It is plain, therefore, that Christ is present in the consecrated bread and wine according to the manner of any natural substance which, wherever it is, is there wholly.

Sometimes we read that Christ is present in the Eucharist "according to the manner of a spirit." We do not like this expression as much as "according to the manner of a substance." It is true of my soul (a spirit) that it is present in its entirety in my whole body and in every spot of it. The same is true of Christ in the Eucharist. But the expression, "according to the manner of a spirit," might engender the false idea that Christ's quantitative body is not present in the Blessed Sacrament.

The three parts are clear from the wording of the Conclusion.

Adversaries. Those who deny the Real Presence deny the entire Conclusion. Orthodox Lutherans who still believe in the Real Presence when Communion is received, think that only Christ's body is present beneath the appearances of bread, only His blood beneath the appearances of wine. This is heretical.

Dogmatic Note

The first part is of divine faith from Trent (DB. 885; CT. 730): "If anyone denies that in the venerable sacrament of the Eucharist the whole Christ is contained under each species and under every part of each species when separated, let him be anathema."

The second part is also of faith and is contained in the same quotation: "under every part of each species when separated."

The last part is Catholic doctrine. It can be deduced from the fact that Trent (DB. 876; CT. 721), without distinguishing whether the consecrated appearances have been actually divided or not, says simply: "The entire, intact Christ exists beneath the species of bread and beneath any part of that species; the entire Christ likewise, beneath the species of wine and beneath its parts."

Part 1. Christ is present in His entirety beneath either of the sacramental species.

Proof 2. From Holy Scripture. In His promise of the Eucharist our Lord says (John 6:58): "He that eateth Me, the same shall live by Me." This text is dogmatically certain; apologetically very probable.

The word "eateth" can refer to only one species, that of bread. Yet Christ says "Me," i.e., His whole Self. Therefore, He must be entirely present under this one species.

The words of institution also provide a dogmatically certain, apologetically probable proof. When Christ consecrated the wine at the Supper (and the same would hold true for the bread), only the one species was present after consecration. Yet Christ must have been entirely present under this one species because, if His blood alone were present, it would have been separated from His body while He stood before His apostles.

At the consecration of the Mass, as distinguished from that of the Supper, Christ must become present in His entirety beneath either species because since His resurrection "Christ can die no more." But He would die if His body alone became present under the species of bread, and if His blood alone became present under the species of wine. The Church has defined (DB. 148; CT. 414) that the hypostatic union is absolutely indissoluble.

Part 2. Christ is present in His entirety in every portion of either species after it is divided.

Proof 2. From the words of institution (Mark 14:23): "And having taken the chalice, giving thanks, He gave it to them. And they all drank of it."

Only one species comes into consideration, that of the wine. This was in one mass when Christ consecrated it. But the chalice was passed around to each apostle, and so each one received only a portion of the consecrated wine. Yet Christ evidently intended to give Communion to each one. Therefore, He was present in each divided portion of the consecrated wine. Moreover, He was wholly present in each portion because at the Supper He was intact, one Person with His two natures. Hence, when receiving a portion of the wine, each apostle received the entire Christ or He did not receive Christ at all.

The reason why we have used the species of wine instead of that of bread is that we are not sure from the Scriptural account whether the bread was consecrated before it was divided or afterwards. If it was divided beforehand, we could not prove this part from the first consecration.

Proof 3. From the practice of the Church. It sometimes happens that a priest must divide a Host in order to be able to give Communion to everybody. This shows that the Church recognizes that Christ is present in every particle of a divided Host. The faith of the people manifests the same belief.

Proof 4. From theological reasoning. The argument follows. For the sake of brevity we shall speak of the species of bread alone.

If the substance of Christ's body is present beneath the accidents of the consecrated bread in the way that the substance of bread was present beneath these accidents before consecration, then Christ is entirely present in every particle of a divided Host;

But the substance of Christ's body is present beneath the accidents of the consecrated bread in the way that the substance of bread was present beneath them before consecration:

Therefore, Christ is entirely present in every particle of a divided Host.

Proof for the major. Every particle of a divided, unconsecrated piece of bread contains the entire substance of bread. Hence, if the substance of Christ's body, and so the entire Christ, replaces the substance of the bread, every particle separated from a consecrated Host must contain the entire Christ.

Proof for the minor. It follows from the fact of transubstantiation. The entire substance of bread is changed into the substance of Christ's body.

Part 3. Christ is present in His entirety in every spot of either species before it is divided.

Proof 2. From theological reasoning. The syllogism would be formulated as above, except for the last part of the major premise and for the conclusion. This is the gist of the argument. Just as the substance of bread was present in every spot of an unconsecrated host before any division of it, so Christ must be entirely present in every spot of a consecrated Host before its division. The substance of Christ's body succeeds the substance of bread.

Moreover, only the words of consecration can effect the Real Presence. The mere act of dividing a Host cannot do so. Yet when a Host is divided, the words of consecration are not uttered over each particle. Consequently, unless Christ is entirely present in every spot of an undivided Host, He cannot be entirely present in every particle of a divided one. But He is entirely present in every particle of a divided Host, as we proved previously. Therefore, He is entirely present in every spot of an undivided Host.

OBJECTIONS

The mystery of the Eucharist is to be accepted with a child-like faith. Since, however, it is certain that no contradiction can exist between faith and reason, we must apply our minds as far as possible to remove any apparent contradictions between them. Probably no stronger rational objections can be advanced against any mystery of our faith than those proposed against this Conclusion.

It is important to remember the attitude of mind which we should retain while discussing these objections. It is certain that the mystery of the Eucharist is beyond the explanatory powers of our intellect. We accept this mystery, not because we understand it, but because God has revealed it.

When confronted by rational objections, we do not profess to give positive answers, i.e., we do not attempt to say: "We can show you *why* there is no contradiction." All that we can say to an objector is: "Your arguments do not prove that there is a contradiction." In short, we can only parry the thrusts of the adversaries. If no contradiction can be proved, we know for sure that there is none, even though we cannot positively explain why this is so. Three apparent contradictions are advanced against our doctrine.

1. In the Eucharist it is of faith that the appearances of bread and wine remain after transubstantiation. Now these appearances are accidents, and accidents of their very nature demand that they inhere in a substance. As a matter of fact, however, the Eucharistic accidents do not inhere in any substance: not in the body of Christ which has its own accidents; not in the bread because its substance has been totally changed. Therefore, we find a philosophical impossibility in the doctrine of the Eucharist— accidents supported by themselves.

Answer. Accidents do not necessarily have *actual* inhesion in some substance, but by their very nature they *should* inhere in one. Hence it is only by a miracle that they can exist independently of the substance to which they belong. God works this miracle in the Blessed Sacrament.

If God by a creative act enables accidents to inhere in the substance of bread, can He not do by His own power what He would ordinarily do through the agency of substance? In the Eucharist God sustains the accidents by His omnipotence. It cannot be shown that it is impossible for Him to do this. Hence no contradiction can be proved.

2. According to Catholic belief the entire body of Christ is present in the Eucharist, just as that body exists wholly in heaven. But the entire body of Christ cannot be contained in a small particle like the Host; much less can that body be contained in every single spot of a Host. In the latter case, the body of Christ would have no extension whatever. It is, then, a contradiction to say that the adult body of Christ has its entire extension in the Eucharist when such extension is opposed to the evidence of the senses.

Answer. The entire body of Christ is present in the Eucharist. It has its substance and its accidents, and all parts of the body are harmoniously arranged just as they are in Christ's heavenly body. Among the accidents of Christ's body is that of quantity. The body of Christ in the Eucharist has its entire quantity and, therefore, its entire extension.

Now ordinarily when a body exists in this world it must occupy a commensurate part of space. To occupy a commensurate part of space simply means to be measured by another extended object. Thus we find that every quantitative body in the world is measured by some other quantitative body or bodies which surround it. The swimmer is completely measured by the water when he dives beneath the waves. The pedestrian is completely measured by air when he walks. It is, then, a *physical* law that extended bodies should be measured by other extended things. But is this physical law so binding that God could not produce a material body in this world which would not be measured by another material thing?

This is precisely what the adversaries must prove. But it cannot be proved. Suppose that God were to create a material thing but keep it sequestered from every other material thing in the world, so that it would not come in contact with air or water or heat or anything else. Is this impossible for God? It would merely mean that this particular object is exempted from the *natural* law which requires that all material things be commensurate with the other material things which envelop them. It cannot be shown to be beyond God's omnipotence to do this.

This is what He does do in the Blessed Sacrament. The entire material body of Christ is present in every spot of each consecrated Host, but this body is miraculously kept from occupying space, i.e., from being bounded by any other material thing. Suppose, for instance, that God had decreed to create one material thing only, a star. No ether, no atmosphere, no air, no other star or other extended object would be in existence. The star could not be measured by any other thing. It would not be in space, consequently, and yet it would have its entire extension. A human eye could never know its size because the eye would have no external ruler by which it could be measured.

It is somewhat like this that Christ's body is present in the Blessed Sacrament. It is there in its entirety, but it does not have *local* extension, i.e., it is not in contact with any other material thing, not even with the accidents of bread and wine. This is a great mystery, an act of God's omnipotence, but it cannot be proved to be impossible.

3. Catholics believe that the entire body of Christ is present in every consecrated Host anywhere in the world. It is everywhere numerically the same body of Christ. The presence of Christ is multiplied, but Christ's body is not. This involves a contradiction. No human body can be in two places, let alone thousands of places, at the same time. It is against reason to say that the body of Christ, numerically the same, is present under accidents of bread which are not numerically the same; that the body of Christ is moving in one place during a procession, but stationary in another where it is in the tabernacle; that Christ has sensations in heaven, but does not have them in the Eucharist.

Answer. When a material body is present in the ordinary way, it has what we call *circumscriptive* presence. This merely means that it is contained and measured by other material bodies. To say that the same numerical body can be in two places simultaneously by such circumscriptive presence is probably a contradiction.

We mean by this that not only would such bilocation be against natural law, but also that it would be impossible even for God to produce such a presence in two or more places. If such multilocation were possible, we should have to admit that the same man could be sick in London and healthy in New York, struck by an auto in Paris and walking safely in Chicago. This seems to involve contradictions beyond even God's power to reconcile.

However, we do not hold that Christ in the Eucharist has this circumscriptive multilocation. Christ is circumscriptively present in heaven only. There His body occupies space and is bounded by whatever circumambient materials are present. But in the Eucharist the body of Christ is not bounded by any other material thing, as we have explained. Hence the contradictions involved in the case of the ordinary person whose presence would be multiplied are avoided.

Accordingly, it cannot be shown to be impossible for God to multiply Christ's presence provided that the various presences are not circumscriptive.

It is not true to allege that Christ is moving in one Host and stationary in another. Moving means to pass through space. But Christ in the Eucharist is independent of space. Only the species can be affected by the objects surrounding them. In one place where there is a procession, the species or accidents are moving; in another where Christ is in the tabernacle, the species are not moving. But there are *two numerically distinct* sets of accidents.

Neither is it true to say that Christ has sensations in heaven, but none in the Eucharist. Christ has the identical sensations in every Host which He has in heaven. He acquires no new sensations in the Blessed Sacrament. To acquire a sensation supposes that a person is in contact with other material things, but Christ in the Eucharist has no such contact.

Comment 1. Correct ways of speaking about the Blessed Sacrament.

It is permissible to say that the body of Christ is *on* the altar, *in* the tabernacle, received *in* the mouth and so on. These expressions do not necessarily imply a physical contact between Christ's body and other extended objects.

Although it is permitted by usage to say that Christ's body *lies* on the altar, is *touched,* is *seen,* is *placed on the throne,* is *raised aloft,* is *carried in procession,* and so on, it should be remembered that these expressions are not perfectly accurate since they connote a physical contact between Christ's body and other extended objects. Strictly speaking, only the accidents of bread lie on the altar, are touched, and so forth.

It is also allowable to say that Christ's body is *broken,* is *eaten;* that His blood is *poured out.* Here again, we remember that these expressions apply properly to the accidents alone, but precisely in so far as they are the perceptible signs of the sacrament. Our Lord Himself used the expressions "eat My flesh" and "blood which is being shed for you."

Language is constructed from our experience of things as our senses reveal them. To communicate with others we are compelled to use language in this way. We could not expect a special vocabulary to express to people our Lord's singular manner of presence in the Eucharist. Hence when our Lord said that we should "eat His flesh," He used a phrase which others would understand, though, strictly speaking, only the accidents of bread are eaten. He meant that His body and blood would be truly present in the mouths and stomachs of communicants. This is "eating," though not in the strict sense of the term.

It may never be said that Christ's Eucharistic body is *round* or *cold* or *white,* because these expressions are referable to the accidents only.

Comment 2. Desecration of the Blessed Sacrament.

Since our Lord has no physical contact with any extended object, it is evident that He cannot be physically injured in the Blessed Sacrament. He is God. He retains His divine dignity in the Eucharist, and so no creature can physically assail Him by sword or fire or any other form of desecration.

Nevertheless, we are rightly indignant when the Blessed Sacrament is profaned. Sacrilege is irreverential treatment of something sacred. It is hard to imagine a greater sacrilege than one which vilifies the sacrament in which Christ is truly present.

Part 2

THE EUCHARIST AS A SACRAMENT

IN considering the sacrament of the Eucharist, we follow the same general order of treatment as in the other sacraments. First, we prove the existence of the sacrament; then, its matter and form; next, its special effects; finally, its minister, subject, and necessity.

*

Conclusion 4. The Eucharist is a true sacrament. One of its properties is that of relative permanency. This sacrament is to be adored with the same kind of adoration that is rendered to God alone.

Introduction. Since almost all Protestants deny the sacramental nature of the Eucharist, it is important to prove this point. It is also of some consequence to establish in the very beginning that the Eucharist is endowed with a property, relative permanency, which is not shared by any other sacrament. It is likewise important to learn from the outset that the Eucharist merits divine adoration, though this is but a corollary flowing from the first two parts of the Conclusion.

Explanation of Terms

1. The Eucharist. It is the sacrament of the body and blood of Christ contained beneath the appearances of bread and wine for the purpose of providing men with spiritual food. This is the customary definition, but we remind the student that Christ is present in His entirety under either the accidents of bread or those of wine.

Therefore, this sacrament does not consist of the perceptible appearances only, nor of the invisible Christ only, but of the entire Christ precisely as He is beneath the outward appearances. Without the consecrated accidents of bread and wine, we would have no perceptible sign, and so no sacrament. Without Christ's presence, we would have no cause of grace, and so no sacrament. Christ as God, together with the Father and the Holy Ghost, is the principal cause of the grace conferred by the reception of the Eucharist. Christ as man is the instrumental cause of this grace.

2. Relative permanency. All the sacraments except the Eucharist are essentially completed in a very short time. They have lasting effects, but they themselves, i.e., their outward rites, are quickly dispatched. They cease as soon as their matter and form are applied to the recipient.

This is not true of the Eucharist. This sacrament comes into existence only after the proper form has been pronounced over the proper matter. Once come into existence, however, the Eucharist abides until the appearances of bread and wine are corrupted. Hence the duration of the sacrament is relative to the length of time that the species persist. This period of time will evidently vary according to circumstances such as climate, whether the Host is received in Communion, or perhaps consumed by fire, and so on. In the rest of the sacraments the form, as their active principle, enters into their very constitution. But in the Eucharist the form or words of consecration are the *efficient* cause of the sacrament.

This is an important point which requires the student's reflection. From it we draw two conclusions. First, the consecration during Mass is not the sacrament of the Eucharist, but the *cause* of the sacrament. The sacrament is permanently present

In the tabernacles of our churches. Second, the reception of Communion is not the sacrament, but a *condition* required in order to obtain grace from the already existing sacrament.

3. The same kind of adoration that is rendered to God alone. It is called latreutic cult or divine adoration. By it we acknowledge God's infinite excellence and supreme power and our own complete subjection to Him. We offer this divine adoration by internal acts of mind and will, and also by external actions like prostration or genuflection. Men are obliged to foster the internal spirit of total subjection to the Blessed Sacrament and to express this spirit outwardly on some occasions.

Adversaries. All three parts of the Conclusion are rejected by those who deny the Real Presence. Even those Lutherans who admit the Real Presence deny that this Presence is relatively permanent. They say that the sacrament cannot be reserved in the tabernacle because Christ is present at only the actual instant of Communion.

Dogmatic Note

The first part, that the Eucharist is a sacrament, is of divine faith from the Council of Trent (DB. 844; CT. 665): "If anyone says that the sacraments of the New Law . . . are more or less than seven, namely: baptism, confirmation, the Eucharist, . . . let him be anathema."

The relative permanency of the Eucharist is also of faith from Trent (DB. 886; CT. 731) when it declares against Luther that the Real Presence cannot be limited to only the instant of Communion: "If anyone says that, after the consecration is completed, the body and blood of our Lord Jesus Christ are not in the admirable sacrament of the Eucharist, but are there only during its use while being received, and not either before or after; and that in the Hosts or consecrated particles which are reserved or which remain after Communion, the true body of our Lord does not remain: let him be anathema." From this definition it is likewise of faith that the sacrament exists as soon as the words of consecration are pronounced. It is Catholic doctrine that the sacrament endures until the sacred species are corrupted.

It is also of divine faith from Trent (DB. 888; CT. 733) that the Eucharist deserves latreutic or divine cult: "If anyone says that in the holy sacrament of the Eucharist Christ, the only-begotten Son of God, is not to be adored with the worship, even external, of latria, and is, consequently, neither to be venerated with special festive solemnity, nor to be solemnly carried in processions, . . . and that the adorers thereof are idolaters: let him be anathema."

Part 1. The Eucharist is a sacrament.

Proof 2. From Holy Scripture. By combining the words of the promise with the words of institution, we find that the essential elements of a sacrament are found in the Eucharist.

When Christ uttered the words of consecration, He became truly present under the appearances of bread and wine which still remained. These appearances were perceptible and remained so, just as they do today at the consecration in the Mass. We find, then, a perceptible sign, the first essential requirement for any sacrament.

During His promise of the Eucharist our Lord said (John 6:56): "My flesh is meat indeed and My blood is drink indeed." The Eucharist is, therefore, spiritual food, which is sanctifying grace.

Moreover, Christ also said (John 6:59): "He that eateth this bread shall live forever." The reception of Communion confers a right to heaven. However, only sanctifying grace gives this right and so the Eucharist must produce grace.

Again, our Lord declared (John 6:57): "He that eateth My flesh and drinketh My blood, abideth in Me and I in him." The Eucharist, consequently, effects permanent love for Christ in the soul of the recipient. However, permanent love or the virtue of charity is inseparably connected with sanctifying grace.

Then, too, this grace is conferred *ex opere operato* because it is attributed to the very reception of Communion, not to the merits as such of the recipient.

The Eucharist, therefore, since it bestows sanctifying grace *ex opere operato*, fulfills a second indispensable requirement for a sacrament.

It is also clear that the Eucharist was instituted by Christ in perpetuity. He said at the Last Supper: "Do this in memory of Me." Since Christ wanted the apostles to have successors until the end of the world, He also wanted the Eucharist to remain until the end of time.

Moreover, the Eucharist is a source of sanctifying grace and so is an essential part of the Church, which is itself perennial.

Finally, the Eucharist is the only sacrifice which is acceptable to God and so it must remain in perpetuity, because man by his nature requires a sacrifice.

Part 2. The Eucharist has the property of relative permanency.

Proof 2. From the words of institution. When Christ said: "This is My body," "This is My blood," He meant that beneath the appearances of bread and wine He was truly present. Since He Himself attached no condition of time or of any other kind to His words, He must have meant that He is present as long as the appearances remain, because there is an intimate union between Himself and the consecrated accidents.

Moreover, in the promise our Lord said (John 6:56): "My flesh is meat indeed and My blood is drink indeed." The Eucharist is compared with natural food and drink, which possess relative permanency, i.e., they remain until they are corrupted. The spiritual food of the Eucharist, therefore, has also a relative permanency.

Proof 3. From the Fathers. We quote only St. Cyril of Alexandria who says: "I hear that there are others who assert that the Eulogium [the Eucharist] profits nothing for sanctification if a portion of it is left over for the following day. But those who say this speak foolishly; for neither is Christ altered, nor His sacred body changed, but the energy of the blessing [the consecration], as well as the life-giving grace, remain permanently therein" (*Epist. 83 ad Colosyrium;* RJ. 2139).

Part 3. The Eucharist is to be adored with latreutic cult.

Proof 2. From the practice of the Church. The Church has instituted the feast of Corpus Christi; she approves the devotion of the Forty Hours, the Holy Hour, and she recommends public processions of the Blessed Sacrament at various times. The faithful adore the sacrament on these occasions and on many others, e.g., during benediction of the Blessed Sacrament.

Proof 3. From theological reasoning. Since Christ, true God, is present in the Eucharist, and since the Eucharist is relatively permanent, it follows as a corollary that latreutic or divine worship is to be offered the Blessed Sacrament.

OBJECTIONS

1. Every sacrament must be by definition a perceptible sign. But Christ cannot be apprehended by the senses in the Eucharist. Therefore the Eucharist is not a sacrament.

Answer. The sacrament of the Eucharist is composed of Christ truly present and the consecrated species of bread and wine. It is true that Christ Himself is not perceived by the senses, but the species are perceived. The entire sacramental rite does not necessarily come within the scope of the senses.

2. A sacrament must be a sign which signifies and confers grace. The Eucharist, however, since it is a permanent sacrament, does not as such confer grace. The sacrament remains on the altar.

Answer. All sacraments except the Eucharist signify and confer grace at the same time, because they come into existence and are applied to the recipient at the same time. They cannot exist before their application.

However, the Eucharist exists before being received in Communion. Reception is a condition for receiving grace *ex opere operato* from this sacrament. The Eucharist before being received is a theoretical sign of grace; when received it becomes a practical sign and confers grace in the same way as the rest of the sacraments.

3. In ancient times particles of the Eucharist which remained after Communion were either burned or given to children as food. Therefore the Eucharist is not a permanent sacrament and should not be reserved in the tabernacle.

Answer. When we say that the Eucharist is a permanent sacrament, we mean that Christ remains present until the species of bread and wine disappear by substantial alteration. This was true even when the sacrament was burned or given to children. Christ was present in the particles until they were burned or consumed.

As regards reservation of the Blessed Sacrament after the termination of Mass, it would have been imprudent in the early centuries of the Church to reserve the sacrament in some localities. Persecutions were raging and so the sacrament would have been in danger of profanation. Even today the Eucharist is not reserved in some isolated chapels because of the danger of desecration.

Comment 1. Is the Eucharist one or two sacraments?

This question arises because Christ is wholly present under the appearances either of bread or of wine. As a result, we have two distinct perceptible signs and two distinct presences of Christ, so that we seem to have two sacraments.

We recall, however, that it is of faith that there are only seven sacraments. Hence the Eucharist must be only one sacrament, at least generically. It would be permitted to hold that this one sacrament contains two species or kinds.

However, if we remember that this sacrament is composed not only of the accidents, but also of Christ wholly present beneath them; and that *numerically the same Christ* is present under either set of accidents, we can understand why many theologians prefer to say that the Eucharist is specifically one sacrament.

From the viewpoint of signification, a unity undoubtedly arises from the distinct accidents of bread and wine. A meal is symbolized not by food alone, but by food and drink. Consequently, the Eucharistic accidents taken together perfectly symbolize the spiritual refreshment obtained from reception of Communion.

Nevertheless, it should be noted that either the appearances of bread alone or of wine alone do symbolize spiritual nourishment, though less perfectly than the two together. Hence the symbolism of the sacrament is not lost by receiving Communion under only the appearances of bread.

Concerning the amount of grace bestowed by the sacrament, it should be held that one species can confer as much grace as the two species. Accordingly, Catholics today lose none of this precious gift by being obliged to communicate under one species only.

*

Conclusion 5. In order that the Eucharist can come into being, bread made from wheat flour and wine made from grapes must be used as the remote matter. The words which must be pronounced (the form) over this matter are: "This is My body," and either: "This is My blood," or "This is the chalice of My blood."

Introduction. We deal with the matter and form which are required for validity only. Various other prescriptions are laid down for liceity. But if the conditions, as stated in the Conclusion, are fulfilled by a priest having a right intention, the Eucharistic sacrament and sacrifice will exist, even though the priest may have sinned grievously by omitting other requirements.

It should be observed that the Eucharist, because it is a permanent sacrament, also has a matter and form *after* the sacrament has been produced. This is called the matter and form of the Eucharist "in its actual existence." In this case the matter is Christ entirely present together with the consecrated species of either bread or wine. The form consists of the words of consecration, but only in so far as they continue morally to effect their signification.

We are not concerned here with this matter and form, but only with that matter and form which are necessary for the Eucharist to come into being, with the Eucharist "in its becoming."

Explanation of Terms

1. The remote matter is bread made from wheat flour. Hence bread made from barley or rye flour, or from flour of any other grain which men do not commonly consider wheat flour, would be invalid. The wheat flour would still be valid if only a very small amount of some other substance were mixed with it, but the addition would be sinful. The wheat flour is mixed with natural water and then cooked until it becomes a solid mass.

2. The remote matter is wine made from grapes. The wine cannot be obtained from fruits, berries, herbs, or from anything else except grapes. Moreover, the wine must not be made artificially, but pressed out of the grapes. Unfermented wine would be valid, but illicit. The grapes, too, must be ripe and the wine

must be in a liquid state. Wine corrupts into vinegar, and rather quickly in hot climates. Vinegar, of course, would be invalid.

3. Form. Since two separate substances, bread and wine, are the matter of the Eucharist, there are also two verbal formulae to be pronounced. "This is My body" must be uttered over the bread, and either "This is My blood," or "This is the chalice of My blood," over the wine. The two possible valid forms for the consecration of the wine have the same meaning. In the Mass, however, the second of the two is prescribed under penalty of grave sin.

The forms must be pronounced with the lips, not recited mentally only. Furthermore, the priest must intend to say them in Christ's name. When the priest says "*My* body," "*My* blood," he is actually impersonating Christ.

The Conclusion is divided into four parts.

1. The remote matter consists of bread made of wheat flour and of wine pressed from grapes.

2. No forms are valid which omit either "This is My body," or "This is the chalice of My blood."

3. These two forms by themselves suffice without the epiclesis.

4. In the second consecration the words "This is the chalice of My blood" suffice without the addition of any of the other words prescribed in the missal. These added words are, "the new and everlasting testament, the mystery of faith, which [blood] will be shed for you and for many unto the remission of sins."

Adversaries. The first part is challenged by some of the Greek schismatics who admit that wheat bread is the matter of the sacrament, but assert that for validity it must be leavened bread. This is an heretical opinion (DB. 692). The bread can be either leavened or unleavened, so far as validity goes.

A few theologians rejected the second part by holding that the Eucharist came into being when the priest said the short prayer beginning with the words "Quam oblationem." This prayer is found in the Roman missal shortly before the words of consecration and corresponds in meaning with the epiclesis.

Since the seventeenth century some schismatical Greeks have taught that consecration is effected solely by the prayer called the epiclesis. This prayer is not found in the Roman missal. It occurs in various liturgies usually after, sometimes before the words of consecration, and is an appeal to the Holy Ghost to effect the Real Presence.

The third part is denied by other Greek schismatics who maintain that both the words of consecration and the epiclesis are necessary for validity.

As regards the fourth part, all theologians agree that for the first consecration the words, "This is My body," are sufficient. However, for the second consecration some excellent theologians believe that some of the following words in the missal must be added to "This is the chalice of My blood." They do not require all the additional words, but most of them, namely, "the new testament, which [blood] will be shed for many unto the remission of sins."

Dogmatic Note

It is of faith that bread and wine are the remote matter of the Eucharist (DB. 424, 430; CT. 658, 659).

It is Catholic doctrine that only wheat bread and natural wine pressed from grapes is valid remote matter.

It is definable, though not actually defined, teaching that the words, "This is My body," "This is the chalice of My blood," must be included in any valid forms of the Eucharist (DB. 876, 698; CT. 721, 717). It cannot, therefore, be held that the "Quam oblationem" or the epiclesis by themselves effect the consecration.

That the words of consecration alone suffice for the form without the addition of the epiclesis is Catholic doctrine (DB. 2147a).

It is also Catholic doctrine that the words, "This is My body," suffice for the consecration of the bread. The particle "for" (*enim*) is not required for validity.

The more probable opinion is that the words, "This is the chalice of My blood," suffice without any of the following words.

Part 1. The remote matter of the Eucharist is wheat bread and wine pressed from grapes.

Proof 2. From the account of the Last Supper in Holy Scripture. The argument follows in form.

The matter consecrated by Christ at the Supper is the valid matter of the Eucharist;

But wheat bread and wine pressed from grapes were the matter consecrated by Christ at the Supper:

Therefore, wheat bread and wine pressed from grapes are the valid matter of the Eucharist.

Proof for the major. The Mass is a repetition of the Supper. This is evident from the double consecration, and also from the fact that nowhere else is Christ's command, "Do this in memory of Me," carried out. However, Christ's command would not be fulfilled if substances differing from those which He consecrated were used in the Mass. "Do *this*" must include the substances to be consecrated as well as the words to be pronounced.

Proof for the minor. At the Supper Christ consecrated wheat bread. The word "bread" (*artos*) occurs in all four accounts of the institution of the Eucharist. When used without a qualifying adjective, this word in Scripture means wheat bread. Moreover, we know that the Jews were accustomed to use wheat bread when they celebrated the Pasch. Even today, when we say simply "bread," we mean wheat bread. If it is any other kind, we qualify bread by saying "rye bread" or "barley bread."

It is also clear that at the Supper Christ consecrated wine pressed from grapes because He said (Luke 22:18; Mark 14:25; Matt. 26:29): "I shall not drink henceforth of this fruit of the vine. . . ."

The tradition that only wheat bread and wine pressed from grapes are valid matter for the Eucharist is constant and reverts to the earliest days of the Church. This tradition is voiced in the *Code of Canon Law* (Par. 815; 1, 2).

Part 2. The words of consecration cannot be omitted in a valid form of the Eucharist.

Proof 2. From the accounts of the Last Supper in Holy Scripture. We justifiably assume that the sacred writers give us all the essentials of the Supper. They would have written irrationally had they quoted Christ's command: "Do this in memory of Me," expressed at a solemn moment and evidently in a matter of supreme importance, and yet have left out something essential. This supposed, we argue as follows:

The only words uttered by Christ before He said: "Do this in memory of Me," are the words of consecration. Therefore, these words cannot be omitted in a valid form of the Eucharist.

The sacred writers do not mention the "Quam oblationem," which is of ecclesiastical origin. Neither do they mention any epiclesis. Hence, neither of these prayers by themselves could be the form of the Eucharist.

Part 3. The words of consecration alone suffice for the valid form of the Eucharist.

This part is clear from the preceding proof. Since neither the "Quam oblationem" nor the epiclesis were uttered by Christ at the Supper, they cannot be necessary even to round out or complete the form. They were never commanded by Christ. However, besides this Scripture proof, we can argue theologically as follows:

The words which signify what is done in the Eucharist are its form;

But the words of consecration alone signify what is done in the Eucharist:

Therefore, these words alone are its form.

Proof for the major. The form of every sacrament must express what the sacrament accomplishes.

Proof for the minor. The words of consecration by themselves signify, as we have previously proved, that Christ is truly present beneath the accidents of bread and wine.

Part 4. The words, "This is the chalice of My blood," suffice for validity without any of the additional words found in the Roman missal.

Proof 2. From the words of institution in Holy Scripture.

Only the words, "This is the chalice of My blood," together with "of the New Testament," or "the New Testament," are common to all four of the sacred writers. The adversaries do not admit that the addition of "of the New Testament," or "the New Testament," would suffice for validity. They emphasize particularly the need for the words: "which will be shed for the remission of sins."

As we said before, it would have been incongruous for any one of the evangelists to leave out anything that was absolutely necessary to fulfill Christ's command: "Do this in memory of Me." St. Paul narrates this command, yet adds only the words, "New Testament," to, "This is the chalice, [the New Testament] in My blood." Therefore, the other words are not essential to the form of the Eucharist.

Proof 3. From theological reasoning. The words, "This is the chalice of My blood," suffice by themselves to signify that Christ is truly present under the appearances of wine. Hence, no other words are necessary.

OBJECTIONS

1. The remote matter of a sacrament, in order to become the proximate matter, must be applied to the recipient. But in the Eucharist the bread and wine are not applied to anyone.

Answer. It is not of the very concept of remote matter that it should be applied to the recipient. It is true, of course, that in the other sacraments, since they are transient, not permanent, their material substance or remote matter, if they have one, is applied. But in the Eucharist the remote matter becomes proximate when it is subjected to the words of consecration.

2. Some of the Fathers say that the Eucharist is brought into existence by the epiclesis. Therefore, this prayer is part of the form.

Answer. These Fathers do not use the word "epiclesis" in the restricted meaning of a special prayer following the words of consecration. By it they sometimes mean the entire liturgical rite without determining which words constitute the form. At other times they use it to denote the words of consecration themselves. During the first three centuries of the Church no trace is found of the epiclesis as a special prayer.

Comment 1. The additional words in the second consecration.

The main reason why some theologians say that the other words must be added to "This is the chalice of My blood" is the fact that the Eucharist is a sacrifice as well as a sacrament. They do not believe that the outward sacrificial oblation or offering, which is absolutely required in order to have a genuine sacrifice, is sufficiently manifest without the additional words.

This opinion is worth remembering. It has probability and we shall refer to it again when we treat of the Mass. The added words do make it clear that the sacrifice is offered to God.

The words "mystery of faith" (*mysterium fidei*) uttered by the priest are not found in Scripture nor in any but the Roman rite.

All admit that they are not part of the form. Since in ancient times the altar was veiled from the beginning of the canon up to the communion, it is possible that the deacon spoke these words aloud to let the people know that the consecration, the mystery of faith, was completed.

Neither is the word "aeterni" (eternal) found in Scripture, though it occurs in diverse liturgies. All admit that it, too, is not a part of the form. It may have been borrowed from Scripture, "in the blood of the *eternal* testament" (Heb. 13:20).

Comment 2. Reasons why water is mixed with the wine at the offertory.

The reasons why some drops of water are mixed with the wine are given by the Councils of Trent and Florence (DB. 945, 698; CT. 754, 717). First, it is likely that Christ, in accordance with Jewish custom, mixed water with the wine at the Supper. Second, the water symbolizes the faithful, who by Holy Communion become united with Christ who is symbolized by the wine. Third, both water and blood flowed from the side of Christ pierced by the lance. A fourth reason sometimes mentioned by theologians is that the water symbolizes the human nature of Christ and so the hypostatic union is pictured by the mixture of water and wine.

As we saw when dealing with transubstantiation, whatever underlying realities are contained beneath the appearances of bread and wine are converted into Christ's body and blood. It should be held, therefore, that, since there has been a real mixture of the small quantity of water with the wine, the underlying reality of this added water enters into the transubstantiation. All wine is composed mostly of water.

*

Conclusion 6. Holy Communion produces in the recipient a special union of his body and soul with Christ.

Introduction. The Council of Trent defined (DB. 887, 893; CT. 732, 738) that the Eucharist is a sacrament of the living. As such, it confers second grace, i.e., it increases sanctifying grace.

But the bestowal of grace is an effect common to all the sacraments. Here we treat of the special effect of Communion. We ask: "What effect results from the Eucharist which does not result from any other sacrament, at least in the same way?"

Explanation of Terms

1. Union with Christ. This union of the communicant with Christ is entirely in the moral order. Christ, though physically present in the communicant, is not physically united with Him. Only the consecrated species, since they alone can come in contact with other material things, are physically united with the communicant.

Communion, therefore, aims specifically at producing a likeness to Christ in the communicant. His acts of mind and will, as a consequence of Communion, should become more conformable to the acts of Christ's mind and will. His body, too, should become more like Christ's sacred body. Such likenesses evince a moral, not a physical union.

2. A special union of the soul with Christ. This is the primary purpose of the sacrament, the chief result that Christ intended from its reception. Of course, all sacraments foster union with Christ by conferring sanctifying grace, the infused virtues, the gifts of the Holy Ghost, and a right to actual graces which inspire recipients to make diverse acts of virtue.

However, Communion produces a *special* union with Christ because, first, it probably has more efficacy to bestow grace than the other sacraments; second, (and this is the point we now emphasize) because Communion confers *ex opere operato* actual graces which, considered in their totality, are superior to those emanating from other sacraments. This superiority consists in the fact that the actual graces issuing from Communion prompt the recipient to makes acts of *love* (the supreme act of virtue) for God and for his neighbor.

We do not say that other sacraments never confer an actual grace which inspires love for God, but we do say that no other sacrament confers such graces so abundantly as the Eucharist.

Neither do we mean that every actual grace proceeding from Communion activates love *directly*. Many of its graces do this, but some of them may incite the recipient to make acts of the other virtues like humility, fortitude, conformity to God's will and so on. But even when acts of other virtues are prompted by Communion, they are basically motivated by love.

Other sacraments give actual graces which inspire a person to do Christ's will in certain circumstances. Confirmation, for instance, pours out its graces when circumstances arise which make it difficult for a person to profess his faith bravely. But the graces of Communion inspire one to live for Christ *habitually*. They intensify his spiritual life so that he thinks like Christ, acts like Christ, desires what Christ desired, and all this as an habitual state. No other sacrament aims directly at these effects. Other sacraments have love for God and the neighbor as their *ultimate* aim. But this is the *proximate* aim of Communion, and to achieve it, the Eucharist confers more abundant actual graces, and graces specifically ordained to elicit acts of love.

It is important to note that to obtain this effect the communicant must cooperate with these graces. Hence the importance of making a thanksgiving after Communion, because it is at this time that the actual graces are conferred. Without this cooperation and thanksgiving, a person might receive Communion often and yet make little progress in love for God and his neighbor.

3. Special union of the body with Christ. This is a secondary effect of Communion. As such, it is conferred only with relation to the primary effect, i.e., either to make possible the obtaining of the primary effect, or as a consequence of it.

The effect, then, of Communion on the body is twofold. First, it curbs or mitigates all disordered passions, especially the passion which incites to impurity. Second, it confers a new title to a glorious resurrection of the body. We shall briefly explain the meaning of these effects and how they are accomplished by the sacrament.

First, Communion actually checks the unruly impulses of concupiscence. This does not mean that a man, no matter how often he receives Communion, will ever be completely free from the incitements to sin arising from the body. The gift of integrity, which Adam possessed before his fall, will never be restored to us.

Neither does this effect mean that a man, after receiving Communion even many times, will necessarily experience less violent disturbances of his passions. These disturbances often depend on circumstances, both external and internal to the body. It would be a miracle for a man not to experience vile temptations when he finds himself in unaccustomed and highly provocative circumstances. Sacraments do not ordinarily work miracles.

Our meaning is, therefore, that, no matter how strongly a man may feel sense appetites contrary to reason, he is always in a better condition—the appetites are always less impelling—than he would have been if he had not received Communion. By reason of Communion the motions of concupiscence, whether they incite to anger, to lust, to greed, or to any other disordered passion, are checked to a greater or lesser extent. The habitual sinner, therefore, should go to Communion often, provided that he first goes to confession if he is in the state of mortal sin. This lessening of concupiscence is a special effect of Communion, because no other sacrament produces it to the same degree.

Theologians differ in explaining how this effect is wrought. It is more probable, and seems to be the opinion of St. Thomas, that it is effected indirectly. This means that the communicant, provided that he makes a thanksgiving and so cooperates with the actual graces inducing him to love God more fervently, will experience a psychological reaction of his subjective acts of virtue upon his body. Just as a man who deliberately fosters feelings of hatred toward another will find by psychological necessity that these feelings are still further inflamed, so the person who makes the acts of virtue prompted by the graces of Communion will find that sinful tendencies are lessened.

This effect is supernatural in so far as it is owing to the supernatural graces issuing from Communion. It is natural in so far as man is a unit and so cannot prevent bodily reactions to his voluntary mental states.

It might be difficult to see why this mitigation of concupiscence, explained in this way, is a *special* effect of Communion. Even when a person prays or makes spiritual reading or cooperates with the graces flowing from other sacraments, some cooling of unruly desires should result. This is true, but Communion lessens these desires in a *noteworthy* degree because of the abundant graces which it confers and because of the quality of love for God by which its graces are characterized. Therefore, the lessening of concupiscence is a special, though secondary, effect of Communion.

Since this matter is of great practical consequence, we shall explain briefly a few other opinions about it. Suarez is not completely satisfied with the preceding explanation. He, too, thinks that the bodily effect is produced indirectly by the intimate connection of soul and body. But he believes that the graces of Communion, though they tend mainly to excite acts of love for God, are also endowed with a secondary quality aimed at lessening concupiscence. When, accordingly, a communicant cooperates with these graces, a necessary reaction follows upon his bodily passions. But this reaction is not solely natural and psychological, as in the preceding opinion. It is facilitated and strengthened by the very fact that the graces are destined to produce this secondary effect.

Other authors, while not denying the first explanation of St. Thomas, add to it in a different way from Suarez. They believe that God adopts a special providence over those who receive Communion. He protects them from many temptations to which they would otherwise be exposed. This special protection would not be a *causal* effect of Communion, but Communion would be a *condition* without which God would not grant the special protection.

Finally, a few authors hold that Communion weakens the ill-regulated movements of bodily passions immediately and causally, though in a mysterious manner. This opinion may be held, but it very probably does not apply to all communicants and so is not an *ex opere operato* effect of Communion. God might do this favor for some, but it is not to be expected by the average person.

Communion also bestows a title to a glorious resurrection of the body. It should be remembered, however, that a man's body will rise in glory if he dies in the state of grace, even though he has never received Communion. Hence the possession of sanctifying grace at the instant of death is the basic and all-important title to the body's glorious resurrection.

Yet, Communion confers an *additional* right to this resurrection. Just as we want the homes of famous people to be preserved, so Christ wants those bodies in which He has dwelt by Communion to rise again gloriously. Although Communion bestows this right, it does not insert any kind of a physical quality into the body by which, as an instrumental cause, the glorious resurrection will be accomplished.

The Conclusion, then, has three parts. First, Communion produces an active love for God and the neighbor; second, Communion mitigates evil passions; third, it gives an additional right to a glorious resurrection of the body.

Adversaries. Luther thought that the principal purpose of Communion was to conceal mortal sins by exciting confidence in God. This idea was condemned by Trent (DB. 887; CT. 732).

Dogmatic Note

It is Catholic doctrine that active love for God is the primary fruit of Communion. This is indicated by Trent (DB. 875; CT. 720) when it declares that by this sacrament "are nourished and strengthened those living with the life of Him who said: 'He that eateth Me, the same shall live by Me.'"

That brotherly love is fostered by Communion is also Catholic doctrine from Trent (DB. 875; CT. 720) which states that this sacrament "is the symbol of that one body of which He Himself is the Head and to which He wanted us, as members, to be united by the closest bonds of faith, hope, and charity, so that 'we would all say the same thing and that there would be no divisions amongst us.'"

It is likewise Catholic doctrine that a mitigation of concupiscence results from Communion. Trent (DB. 875; CT. 720) says that this sacrament is an antidote "by which we are preserved from mortal sins." Since mortal sins are the consequence of yielding to disordered passions, Communion must have a beneficial effect upon these passions, which are of bodily origin.

The decree about daily Communion, which was approved by Pius X, also declares (DB. 1981) that from Communion the faithful "derive strength to check passion."

It is also Catholic doctrine that Communion gives a title to a glorious resurrection of the body. This is indicated by Trent (DB. 875; CT. 720) when it says that Christ wanted Communion to be "a pledge of our glory and everlasting happiness."

Part 1. Communion produces an active love for Christ.

Proof 2. From Holy Scripture (John 6:58): "He that eateth Me, the same will live by Me." This text is dogmatically certain (DB. 875; CT. 720), apologetically certain.

To live means to be active. The husband who loves his wife "lives" by her, i.e., he is inspired by her to perform many actions. Similarly, by Communion a person "lives" by Christ, i.e., is inspired to think and act for Christ. This evidently signifies more than habitual charity, which does not necessarily result in activity for the loved one.

Again, we read (John 6:57): "He that eateth My flesh and drinketh My blood, abideth in Me and I in him." Communion, therefore, produces a most intimate union between Christ and the communicant. Just as intimate human friendship engenders acts of love, so, too, intimate union with Christ must engender acts of love for Him.

Proof 3. From theological reasoning. The Eucharist is food. Just as natural food promptly invigorates the depleted energies of a hungry man, so Communion bestows, not merely a passive, but an active love for Christ.

But Communion also produces an active love for one's *fellowmen.* This is stated by St. Paul (I Cor. 10:17): "For we, being many, are one bread, one body, all who partake of one Bread."

Then, too, since active love for Christ includes a gradual adoption of the attitudes and desires of Christ, Communion must effect an active love for other men, because Christ's attitude towards them is one of active love.

Moreover, each Host, though composed of diverse grains of wheat, is a unit. Hence the consecrated Host symbolizes the unity which should flourish among the diverse people who receive Communion.

Finally, at the Supper our Lord instituted Communion after the manner of a common meal. All the apostles partook of the sacrament. However, a common repast should foster active charity among the partakers because all have their life forces nourished by specifically the same food. Those who partake of the Eucharistic banquet have their spiritual life nourished by the same food numerically, i.e., by the identical Christ.

Part 2. Communion produces a mitigation of disorderly passions.

Proof 2. From the Fathers. St. Cyril of Alexandria says: "Christ, present within us, lulls the law of the flesh that rages in our bodily members; He arouses our affection for God; He mortifies our emotional conflicts" (*In Joan.* l. 4, c. 2; PG. 73, 586).

St. John Chrysostom declares: "This blood [Communion], worthily received, drives the demons far away. . . . The demons, indeed, flee when they behold the blood of the Lord" (*In Joan.* Hom. 46, n. 3; PG. 59, 261).

Proof 3. From theological reasoning. Since Communion produces acts of divine love in the cooperating recipient, and since the acts of man's will necessarily redound upon his body, it follows that Communion must lessen concupiscence to some extent.

It should also be noted that the Catechism of the Council of Trent, which has a special dogmatic value inasmuch as it was composed at the request of the council and by theologians who were present at the council, declares that the Eucharist "necessarily curbs the heat of concupiscence" (Part 2, c. 4, q. 51).

Part 3. Communion produces a title to the body's glorious resurrection.

Proof 2. From Holy Scripture (John 6:55): "He who eateth My flesh and drinketh My blood, hath everlasting life and I shall raise him up on the last day." This text is dogmatically certain, apologetically certain.

These words necessarily refer to the body's resurrection because the souls of the just will enter heaven immediately after death.

Proof 3. From the Fathers. St. Irenaeus testifies: "Just as earthly bread, once it receives the prayer to God [the words of consecration], is no longer ordinary bread, but the Eucharist which is composed of two elements, one heavenly, the other earthly, so too our bodies when they receive the Eucharist are no longer corruptible since they possess the hope of resurrection" (*Adv. Haer.* 4, 18; RJ. 234).

St. Gregory of Nyssa declares that "by union with the Immortal One, even a human being becomes a sharer in incorruption" (*Orat. Catech.* 37; RJ. 1035).

St. Cyril of Alexandria says: "The holy body of Christ, therefore, gives life to those in whom He has been present and preserves them unto incorruption. . . ." (*In Joan.* 3, 6; PG. 73, 519).

OBJECTIONS

1. Some people who receive Communion are no more fervent afterwards than before. Therefore, the Eucharist does not produce love for Christ.

Answer. The Eucharist does not produce love unless the communicant cooperates with the actual graces which are conferred upon him.

Furthermore, it is very difficult to judge whether a person's charity has been advanced or not. We are easily deceived in such matters.

Besides, so far as we can know, some sinner might be much more of a sinner if he refrained from Communion. It is a fact of experience that frequent communicants do avoid serious sin. It is also a fact that persistent sinners are apt to quit going to Communion.

2. On Ash Wednesday we read in the third postcommunion prayer: "May this sacrament [the Eucharist] . . . be for the faithful, living and dead, the remission of all their sins." So the Eucharist remits even mortal sins.

Answer. We learn the meaning of liturgical prayers by recourse to dogmatic theology. It is of faith that a person should be in the state of grace before receiving Communion. Hence a sinner adds the sin of sacrilege to his other sins by receiving Communion unworthily.

In the cited prayer, "sacramentum" has a broad meaning and refers directly to the sacrifice of the Mass. By this sacrifice the greatest sinner obtains actual graces so that he can repent. But even if he accepts these graces and is truly sorry for his sins, he must go to confession before receiving Communion.

3. St. John says (6:55): "He that eateth My flesh and drinketh My blood, hath everlasting life." Accordingly, the Eucharist remits mortal sins.

Answer. Our Lord means: "He that *worthily* receives Communion has everlasting life if he dies in the state of grace." How could a sinner, who is an enemy of Christ, benefit by Communion unless he repents of his sins? Without repentance Communion increases the sinfulness of the recipient.

4. All the sacraments produce a union of the soul with Christ. Therefore, this is not a special effect of Communion.

Answer. All the sacraments produce a more proximate union with Christ when they are received with the proper dispositions. But no other sacrament except the Eucharist has the promotion of love as its primary and immediate purpose. Confirmation, for example, confers actual graces which incite a person to fortitude in professing the faith. If the recipient cooperates with these graces, he will have, first of all, courage; secondarily, he will be closer to Christ.

But if a man cooperates with the actual graces coming from Communion, he will by that very fact advance in love for Christ. The graces are primarily destined to produce this effect. This is not true of any other sacrament.

Of course, all the sacraments either give or increase the *virtue* of charity at the very time at which they bestow their grace. This is a general effect of all the sacraments.

Comment 1. Other effects of Holy Communion.

It is of faith that Communion remits the *personal* guilt of venial sins, for Trent (DB. 875; CT. 720) declares that by it "we are freed from daily faults." This being the case, Communion must also take away at least part of the temporal punishment due to such forgiven sins, since the personal guilt of sins is never removed without an accompanying remission of some of the temporal debt.

It is a more probable opinion that Communion remits these sins *ex opere operato,* i.e., at the very instant of its reception and by its own instrumental power. However, to obtain this effect, the communicant must have a disposition. He must have revoked his venial sins and removed any deliberate attachment to them.

Some theologians think that venial sins are forgiven only indirectly, i.e., by cooperating with the actual graces flowing from the sacrament after its reception.

It is more likely that temporal punishment remaining from past forgiven mortal sins, and whatever punishment may still be left from remitted venial sins, are canceled by Communion only indirectly, by cooperation with the actual graces bestowed by the sacrament.

Comment 2. Concerning the time when the graces of Communion are produced.

It is certain that sanctifying grace is increased *ex opere operato* proportionately to the recipient's disposition at the very moment when Communion is received.

Theologians dispute whether this grace is further increased *ex opere operato* if the communicant makes acts of virtue during the time that Christ is present within him. All admit that sanctifying grace is increased *ex opere operantis* by the acts of virtue made during thanksgiving.

All agree that the actual graces which flow spontaneously from the sacrament come at the moment of reception and as long as Christ remains present in the recipient.

More probably, these graces cease with the disappearance of the sacrament, because the Real Presence is the title to these graces. Once the species are altered by digestion, the graces come no more.

Comment 3. What it means to offer Communion for another.

We speak of offering Communion for other *living* persons only. Minor divergences would have to be mentioned if we wished to speak of offering Communion for the dead.

The principal effects of the sacrament cannot be transferred to anyone else. Therefore, the sanctifying grace, the growth in love for God and one's neighbor, the lessening of passion, the right to a glorious resurrection, and the forgiveness of venial sins cannot be relinquished in favor of another person.

However, we can offer for others the satisfactory value of our preparation for and thanksgiving after Communion. We mean by this that we can confidently beg God to remit the temporal punishment of another rather than our own. To obtain this effect, the other person must be in the state of grace.

We can also confidently beseech God to transfer to others the impetratory value of our Communions. By "impetratory" we mean the pleading or intercessory efficacy of our preparation and thanksgiving. We can, then, hope to obtain special spiritual and temporal favors for others, if these favors are conducive to their salvation.

It should be noted, too, that the satisfactory and impetratory value of prayers said *after* Communion has a singular efficacy.

because the graces of Communion are of exceptional abundance and quality.

We cannot give to another *living* person any indulgences which may be attached to the reception of Communion.

Comment 4. The obligation to receive Holy Communion.

Frequent, even daily Communion, is to be recommended to all Catholics. They must be in the state of grace, have a right intention, and observe the prescribed fast. The fast involves complete abstinence from *solid* food and *alcoholic* drinks for three hours before the time of receiving Communion, and from *nonalcoholic* drinks, water excepted, for one hour before Communion. A preparation should be made before the reception of this Sacrament and a thanksgiving of about fifteen minutes should follow it.

Yet, Holy Communion is not necessary for salvation by necessity of means. Hence, baptized infants who die before attaining the use of reason are saved. Adults, too, can be saved without ever having received Communion. Communion is a tremendous help to final perseverance, but it cannot be proved that this help is so necessary that it cannot be supplied by other means.

However, the Church commands under pain of mortal sin that Catholics receive Communion once a year during the Paschal time. Theologians teach that Catholics are seriously obliged to receive Viaticum when they are in danger of death.

Comment 5. The minister and recipient of the Eucharist.

Only a priest can consecrate the Eucharist. This is of faith from the Fourth Lateran Council (DB. 430; CT. 659): "No one can effect this sacrament except a duly ordained priest. . . ." A priest, too, is the ordinary dispenser of Holy Communion, but sometimes a deacon may be delegated to do this.

Every baptized person, and only baptized persons, may receive Communion validly. Baptized infants may receive Communion both validly and fruitfully, though the Western Church now forbids the giving of Communion to infants.

We recall again that a person conscious of mortal sin must go to confession before receiving Communion. An act of perfect contrition does not suffice.

Part 3

THE EUCHARIST AS A SACRIFICE

THIS is one of the most beautiful and most important treatises in the whole of theology. Hence the student should ponder it prayerfully.

We could be quite sure *a priori* that a public sacrifice was revealed to the Catholic Church. God's revelation harmonizes with man's natural aspirations. Sacrifice, however, is natural to man as we know from the fact that throughout history he has offered it.

Moreover, the New Law is the fulfillment and perfection of the Old. Since, then, the Old Law had genuine public sacrifices, so, too, should the New. Otherwise the New Law would be less perfect than the Old, since by its very nature sacrifice is the most exalted way of adoring God.

*

Conclusion 7. Holy Scripture teaches that the Mass is a genuine sacrifice.

Introduction. The Eucharist is superior to the rest of the sacraments, because it contains Christ Himself, because it has a nobler specific effect, and also because it probably confers more sanctifying grace than the others.

We now consider another way in which the Eucharist not only surpasses the other sacraments, but also all other acts of divine worship. For the celebration of the Eucharist is necessarily a sacrifice. As such, the Eucharist is the focal point of the Catholic religion.

Apologetically, it is important to prove from Scripture that the Mass is a true sacrifice, since Protestants, excepting the Ritualists, reject this truth. Nor have the various sects introduced any new form of sacrifice. According to them Christ's one and only sacrifice was offered on Calvary.

Explanation of Terms

1. Holy Scripture. Our proofs will be derived from both the Old and New Testaments.

2. Mass. Etymologically, the word is popularly explained today as coming from the expression, "Ite, Missa est," which the priest proclaims before the last gospel. More technically, the word probably designated that important part of the Mass which came after the offertory (when in early days the catechumens were dismissed) and before the last gospel (when the faithful were told to disperse). Hence "Mass" would be derived from the Latin word "missio," a sending, or from "dimissio," a sending away. Other explanations are given, but the matter is of little consequence.

Descriptively, the Mass is a liturgical ceremony in which is offered to God the unbloody sacrifice of the body and blood of Christ under the appearances of bread and wine.

3. A genuine sacrifice. This simply means that the elements of a sacrifice, to be explained below, are verified in the Mass. The Mass is not a mere theatrical representation of Calvary, like a passion play. Neither is it merely a sacrifice in the broad sense, as when we say that an act of mortification or of prayer is a sacrifice.

4. Sacrifice. We speak only of a public, social, liturgical sacrifice. It is an action by which a material thing which has been in some way destroyed, is offered by a priest to God alone, in order to acknowledge God's supreme dominion.

The object presented to God, its manner of destruction, and the way it is to be offered to God must all conform to the norms which God Himself has established. By the entire action man recognizes God's supreme dominion over himself and his own total dependence upon God.

We shall now explain at some length the essential nature and signification of sacrifice in general. Since by its very nature a sacrifice is an external rite, we shall first analyze the essentials of this rite. Afterwards, we shall explain its signification or symbolism.

The essentials of the external rite of sacrifice.

Its most important element is the outward offering or presentation of the destroyed object to God. This is called the "form" of a sacrifice by analogy with the "form" of a sacrament. Hence, just as happens in the case of the sacraments, the offering of the sacrifice gives meaning to the rest of the action.

An animal may be slain for many purposes—for food, because the animal is sick, because it may spread infection, and so on. But if a priest offers the slain animal to God, we know that a religious rite, a sacrifice, is taking place.

Every sacrifice is primarily constituted by such an offering to God, but not every offering of something to God is a sacrifice. An act of mortification or of prayer is an offering to God, but not a sacrifice.

It should be noted, too, that this offering to God must be perceptible to the senses, i.e., it must be *outwardly* evident that the destroyed object is being presented to God. This will be realized either by the words which the priest says or by his actions considered in all their circumstances.

The object offered to God must be a material thing. This thing can be called the "remote matter" of a sacrifice somewhat as water is the remote matter of baptism. The words "victim" and "host" are often used to designate this object.

It must be chosen by God and, besides being a corporeal substance, it must be something of value. Often, too, under the Old Law the object to be offered, such as animals, grains, fruits, bread, wine, and so forth, was intimately connected with the support of man's natural life.

We say, too, though some theologians deny it, that the material object offered in sacrifice must be *in some way* destroyed. This destruction is the "proximate matter" (like the washing in baptism) of a sacrifice and so is an indispensable element of it. This destruction is often called the immolation or mactation of the object.

Strictly speaking, man cannot destroy any material thing. The most that he can do is to change it by placing it in definite circumstances.

Such a change, when it involves what is commonly called destruction, can be done by more direct and less direct means. Thus the physical destruction of an animal might be accomplished by fire or, much more slowly, by starvation. Wine could be destroyed by exposing it to great heat for a short time or by pouring it out on the ground. Such destructions would be physical and any of them would be sufficient for a sacrifice.

However, another kind of destruction suffices for the sacrifice of the Mass. It is called mystical or symbolical and we shall explain it in detail later on. It is objective, independent of the mind, though the Victim is in no wise physically altered. Hence it is well for the student to know from the beginning that the destruction which occurs at the double consecration of the Mass is unique. No parallel for it can be found in the Old Testament or anywhere else.

We place the element of destruction in our definition of sacrifice because we are convinced that this definition is to be derived *a posteriori,* not *a priori,* and from the Old Testament alone, not from pagan sacrifices. In these we would expect to find imperfections since the people who offered them had drifted away from God's revelation.

If, however, we find a destruction of the victim in all the sacrifices revealed by God in the Old Testament, we can be sure that destruction of some kind is an indispensable element of every genuine sacrifice. We do not say that under the Old Law the victim, when it was composed of more than one inanimate object, had to be destroyed entirely. It usually was, but in the case of the loaves of proposition, only the incense, which conjointly with the loaves constituted the victim, was destroyed by burning. Again, in the sacrifice of barley meal (Numbers 5:26) only a handful of it was burned upon the altar. Animals were, of course, totally destroyed, put to death.

The reasons why the majority of theologians hold that destruction is required for a sacrifice are in our opinion convincing. Not only does God's revelation in the Old Law teach it, but without it man's *total* dependence upon God is not symbolized by the rite. Furthermore, Calvary, the most perfect sacrifice ever offered, had, as an essential constituent, the voluntary acceptance of death by our Savior.

Nevertheless, we shall briefly outline a few different opinions which may be held. It is paramount to remember here that theologians first began to explain *how* the Mass is a sacrifice after the original Protestant dissenters denied it to be such. The big hurdle for the theologians was the element of destruction, since it is of faith that Christ does not die again at Mass.

The basic reason, therefore, why some theologians modify the concept of sacrifice is that Christ is not slain again in the Mass, which is, nevertheless, a genuine sacrifice. We do not believe that the concept of sacrifice, so clearly revealed by God in the Old Testament, should be changed essentially. The explanation of the Mass, which we shall present farther on, requires only an accidental modification of the concept of sacrifice.

A few theologians have omitted all notion of destruction or even of change of the victim in their definition of sacrifice. For them, a sacrifice is merely an effective or pragmatic presentation of a worthy object to God. This opinion is so opposed to the Old Testament and to tradition that we do not believe that it merits serious consideration.

Another small group of theologians thinks that only a moral change of some kind is required in the victim. Thus if the victim is blessed by a priest, we would have a true sacrifice provided that he offered to God the victim so blessed.

This opinion adds very little if anything to the preceding one. The mere offering of a thing to someone else makes a moral change in it. Before I offer it, it belongs to me; after I offer it and it is accepted, it belongs to another. This is a moral change affecting the object because of its change of ownership. Hence a mere external blessing seems to add nothing to a mere offering, and so this view seems to coincide with the preceding one.

Other theologians believe that it is not precisely the destruction of the victim, but its change into something better that constitutes the proximate matter of a sacrifice. Speaking of the sacrifice of incense in the Old Law, they would say that it was not precisely the burning of the incense which constituted the sacrifice, but the transformation of the burnt incense into something better, i.e., a sweet fragrance.

We doubt if it is a change for the better to transform a lasting material entity such as incense into a mere passing vapor pleasing for a brief time to the sense of smell.

Moreover, changing a thing into something better is not a sign of man's total dependence upon God.

Finally, this theory not only fails to explain the Mass, but actually leads one into error about it. The Council of Trent (DB. 940; CT. 749) has defined that Christ Himself is the Victim in the Mass. But according to this theory, both the bread and wine (which are to be changed into something better—Christ Himself) and Christ as man would be the victim of the sacrifice.

Every sacrifice must conform to the norms established by God. This means, first of all, that the entire liturgical rite—victim, destruction, external offering—must be done in the way that God prescribed under pain of invalidity. If God enjoined certain accidental rites also, these too must be observed under penalty of committing sin.

Secondly, the minister of a sacrifice must be officially deputed to offer it. No man can take upon himself the right to act in the name of society. Hence only a duly ordained priest can offer sacrifice. The immolation of the victim might be accomplished by others, but a priest alone can present the immolated victim to God. The external offering is the distinctive priestly act.

Since, however, the priest acts in the name of a group, the members of the group should join internally in the outward offering made by the priest alone. Hence the people also offer, but only indirectly, i.e., through the priest. The people should also foster the same internal dispositions expected of the priest.

Speaking of the Mass, we must be careful to distinguish the various meanings of the expression "to offer the Mass." It is of faith that the priest alone can offer the Mass, in the sense that he alone can outwardly present the Victim to God for the people. It is his unique privilege to place the visible offering which is the "form" of the sacrifice, i.e., which truly constitutes it as an outward religious rite. Sometimes, therefore, when we say that "the people offer the Mass," we mean that they internally join in with the outward offering made by the priest alone.

At other times, "the people offer the Mass" simply means that they offer themselves to God. This offering does not refer to the rite of the Mass, but to its signification only. The rite is composed of the offering of Christ to the Father, not of the offering to Him of the priest or people. Since, however, every sacrifice signifies that all who share either directly or indirectly in the presentation of Christ to the Father, should offer themselves to God, the people may be said to offer the Mass directly. But this use of the expression is misleading and should be avoided.

Finally, sometimes when we say that we "offer the Mass" for other people or for some other intention, we merely mean that we wish to apply the fruits of the Mass for those people or for that intention.

It is, then, important to be accurate in the use of the term "offer." It is not enough to say that only a priest can effect the Real Presence by transubstantiation. It is also of faith that only he can offer Christ liturgically to God.

Signification of the outward rite of sacrifice.

So far we have spoken of the liturgical rite of sacrifice, what it consists of in the perceptible objective order. But a sacrifice is a sign of something else. It also has a meaning. It betokens something in the intellectual order. This is the point we now consider.

In our definition we said that a sacrifice has as its purpose to acknowledge God's supreme dominion and man's total dependence on God. This is the principal function and so the principal meaning of sacrifice. Although it has other purposes, recognition of God's sovereign sway over man is always its main purpose.

All agree that sacrifice also aims at offering thanks to God, at making reparation for our sins, and at obtaining favors. These ideas are expressed by the words, thanksgiving, reparation or satisfaction, and impetration.

These three secondary objectives of sacrifice are implicitly contained in its main objective. If we truly recognize our absolute, unqualified dependence upon God, we necessarily imply that we acknowledge everything that we have to be His gift, and so we are implicitly grateful. Similarly, if we profess our complete dependence upon God, we implicitly tell Him that we are sorry for our sins, since by sin we act as our own masters and so do not recognize our complete subjection to God. Finally, when we signify by sacrifice that God is our absolute Ruler, we implicitly tell him that if any benefit is ever going to come to us, it will have to be through His munificence, and so we implicitly ask favors from Him.

The primary purpose of sacrifice, then, is to adore God with that type of adoration that can be offered to no one else. Consequently, sacrifice cannot be offered to a saint or angel, but to God only. We are not completely dependent on anyone except God Himself.

But the question arises: "How does the dramatic action of sacrifice signify God's absolute dominion over man and man's total dependence upon Him?"

To answer this question it is basic to remember that the victim offered to God *represents* both the priest and all the people for whom the priest offers the sacrifice. Since we may not take our own lives, we choose under God's direction some object which we are permitted to destroy and use it in our stead. By destroying this object we tell God by action that we ourselves are nothing, that we ought to be destroyed, that He is our absolute Master and that we are His mere creatures, absolutely nothing of ourselves. It is, therefore, plain how the destruction of an object which represents ourselves, dramatically portrays God's supreme sway over us and our literal nothingness in His sight.

Nevertheless, the offering or presentation to God remains the most important element of sacrifice. If an object representing ourselves were simply to be destroyed, this action could have diverse meanings. It might mean that we were subjecting ourselves totally to the sun or to the devil or to the state, depending on the recipient to whom it was directed. But when a priest offers and directs the destroyed object to God alone, we acknowledge our unqualified dependence on Him alone.

It follows, therefore, that the outward rite of sacrifice demands certain interior dispositions from all who offer the sacrifice either directly or indirectly. Without them the sacrifice is a hollow ceremony. What dispositions, then, should be fostered?

First and most important, all should make acts of the most

profound reverence, for "the fear of the Lord is the beginning of wisdom." This reverence is symbolized by the destruction of the victim.

Second, all should make acts of love for God because sacrifice is, secondarily, an attempt of the creature to express his desire for union with Him. This is symbolized by the destroyed object which is tendered to God. It is the equivalent of saying: "I want to lay down my life for You." This is love in the highest degree.

Acts of thanksgiving, of sorrow for sin, of petition for both spiritual and temporal favors should also be made. They are symbolized by the object, of which we divest ourselves in order to glorify God. Men give gifts to one another for the same reasons; sometimes, to say "Thank you"; sometimes, to make amends for an offense; at other times, to obtain some benefit.

Adversaries. All Protestants, excepting some of the Ritualists or High Church Anglicans, deny that the Mass is a sacrifice. Of course, even the Ritualists do not have the Mass since their orders are invalid.

Dogmatic Note

The genuine sacrificial nature of the Mass has been defined as an article of faith by the Council of Trent (DB. 948; CT. 756): "If anyone says that in the Mass a true and proper sacrifice is not offered to God, or that to be offered is nothing else but that Christ is given us to be eaten, let him be anathema."

It is also of faith from Trent (DB. 938, 949; CT. 747, 757) that the Mass can be proved to be a true sacrifice from the words of institution.

That the sacrificial character of the Mass can be proved from the prophecy of Malachi in the Old Testament is certain from Trent (DB. 939; CT. 748).

Proof 2. From the prophecy of Malachi (Mal. 1:10, 11). The context (vv. 7–14) should also be read.

"I have no pleasure in you [the Jewish priests], says the Lord God of hosts, and I shall not accept a gift from your hands. But from the rising of the sun to the going down thereof, great is My name among the Gentiles: and in every place there is offered sacrifice and a clean oblation to the honor of My name, for My name is great among the Gentiles, saith the Lord God of hosts." The argument follows in form.

The clean, religious rite, universal in time and place, which was predicted by Malachi for the Messianic kingdom, is a genuine sacrifice;

But the Mass is the only clean, religious rite, universal in time and place, which is found in the Messianic kingdom:

Therefore, the Mass is a genuine sacrifice.

Proof for the major.

First, it is evident that a religious rite is dealt with because the prophet is speaking of God's worship.

Second, this religious rite will be clean. The rejected sacrifice of "polluted bread" is to be supplanted by a "clean oblation." The word "clean" is clearly contrasted with "polluted." Hence it will be impossible for the predicted sacrifice to be rejected by God by reason of any stain in the gift or victim.

Again, God rejects the sacrifice of the Hebrew priests, not only because the victim is contaminated, but also because of the negligence of the priests, who presumed to offer such an unworthy gift to God. But the "clean oblation" foretold by Malachi will never be rejected owing to such negligence.

Third, the predicted rite will be universal in place and time. It will be offered "in every place" and "from the rising of the sun to its going down," i.e., it will encompass the entire globe as does the sun. It will be, in short, "everywhere under the sun." The expression "from the rising of the sun to the going down thereof" refers secondarily to universality of time.

Fourth, the prophecy pertains to the future and to the Messianic kingdom because the predicted rite will be "in every place" and everywhere under the sun. This universality of religious cult is a distinctive feature of the Messianic kingdom in all the prophets. There was no such universality until Christ's coming. Besides, although scattered communities of Jews flourished in many places, the Jews could not have been said to be everywhere. Finally, the prophet explicity announces the termination of the Jewish sacrifices: "I shall not receive a gift from your hands."

Fifth, the predicted religious rite will be a genuine sacrifice. It is certain that the sacrifices which were abrogated were genuine sacrifices. The context refers expressly to the abrogation of the sacrifice of bread. This was a true, liturgical sacrifice. It had (v. 7) a victim (bread); a destruction of the bread (v. 12); a priest as offerer (v. 7). But the predicted sacrifice is represented as the *successor* and *substitute* for this sacrifice and for all other sacrifices of the Old Law: "I shall not receive a gift from your hands." Therefore, the predicted sacrifice must also be a genuine, liturgical sacrifice.

Moreover, such a solemn prophecy, if it referred only to sacrifice improperly so called, would be an anomaly. Such interior sacrifices of prayer and penance are always necessary.

Then, too, the Hebrew word (*mincha*), which is the subject of the sentence in verse 11 and means a "clean oblation," is used about 154 times in the Old Testament and always signifies a genuine sacrifice. Hence the Hebrew verbs for sacrifice (*muktar*) and offer (*muggash*) must take the meaning of *mincha,* since this word is their subject and can never designate any but a genuine sacrifice.

Proof for the minor.

It is evident that the Mass is a religious rite.

Second, the Mass is a "clean oblation." If corrupted bread were used at Mass, no sacrifice would take place because transubstantiation demands incorrupt bread.

Moreover, the Mass is "clean" on the part of the offerers. No subjective sinfulness of the priest offering Mass can taint the sacrifice. All that is required is that he say the words of consecration over the bread and wine and that he have a general intention to say Mass. If he does this, the Mass is offered and is "clean," whatever the shortcomings of the minister. If he does not do this, no Mass is offered. Hence the "cleanness" of the Mass cannot be prevented by the unworthiness of the priest.

Third, the Mass is universal in time, absolutely so. It is being celebrated somewhere in the world at every moment of the day. It is also relatively universal in place. No hemisphere, no continent, no country of any size is found where this "clean oblation" does not ascend to God's throne.

Fourth, it is plain that the Mass is in the Messianic kingdom.

Since, therefore, all the qualities required for the clean oblation of Malachi are verified in the Mass, it must be a genuine sacrifice.

It should be noted that tradition, beginning with the *Didache* (written sometime between 90–150) is unanimous in viewing the Mass as the fulfillment of the prophecy of Malachi. Adversaries, therefore, who say that the prophecy was fulfilled only by the sacrifice of Calvary, are opposed to a continuous tradition. Moreover, the sacrifice of the cross was offered in one place, not everywhere; only once, not continuously. So the prophecy by its very nature is not directly applicable to Calvary.

Also in the Old Testament it is dogmatically certain (DB. 938; CT. 747) and apologetically probable that the Mass can be proved to be a genuine sacrifice from the story of Melchisedech (Gen. 14:18) conjoined with Ps. 109:4 and Heb. 7:11. This proof is developed in Pohle-Preuss, *The Sacraments,* II, 301 ff.

Proof 3. From the words of institution in the New Testament. The argument follows in form.

The Last Supper was a genuine sacrifice;
But the Mass is a repetition of the Supper:
Therefore, the Mass is a genuine sacrifice.

Proof for the major. Christ said: "This is My body which is given over for you"; "This is My blood which is being shed for you." Everybody, Catholic and non-Catholic, admits that these expressions are sacrificial. But a dispute arises about the time to which they refer. Some non-Catholics say that they pertain to the future and so directly and exclusively to the sacrifice of the cross. Catholics maintain that they refer to the Supper itself, and, consequently, the Supper itself was a total or at least a partial sacrifice.

There are two main reasons why these expressions should refer directly to the Supper. First, the phrases, "which is given over for you," and, "which is being shed for you," are rendered by participles in the Greek text. These participles are in the present tense. But in Greek, present participles when linked to the subject of a sentence by the verb "is," can never denote future time. Hence in our texts they do not refer directly to the cross.

Second, the form for the consecration of the wine as given by St. Luke (22:20) demands present time. A literal translation of the Greek would be: "This is the chalice, the New Testament in My blood, which *chalice* [not blood] is being shed for you."

In other words, St. Luke says that Christ's blood, *precisely as it is in the chalice,* is being shed. Such an expression refers directly to the Supper. Christ's blood, as it was in His *body,* was shed on Calvary; not as it was in the chalice.

Proof for the minor. Christ's command at the Supper: "Do this in memory of Me," a command which must be fulfilled, is not carried out in any religious rite except the Mass.

Moreover, an examination of the double consecration of the Mass reveals that the Supper is repeated here. Bread and wine are used. Over them the words of Christ at the Supper are repeated by the priest.

It is dogmatically certain (DB. 939; CT. 748) that the genuine sacrificial nature of the Mass can also be proved from I Cor. 10:21. Most exegetes offer another proof from Heb. 13:10.

OBJECTIONS

1. St. Paul (Heb. 10:14) teaches that there is only one sacrifice for Christians, that of Calvary.

Answer. We admit that St. Paul teaches that there is but one *absolute* sacrifice. The Mass derives all its efficacy from Calvary and by its very nature is an unbloody repetition of Calvary. If Christ had not died upon the cross, we could not have the Mass. Hence the Mass, though it contains all the elements of a true sacrifice, is necessarily related to the cross. St. Paul himself teaches that the Mass is a genuine sacrifice (I Cor. 10:20, 21; Heb. 13:10).

2. Christ's blood is not shed in the Mass and so it cannot be a true sacrifice.

Answer. It is of faith that Christ does not die again in the Mass. But He is mystically slain again in each Mass as we have already mentioned, and as we shall explain more fully in a following Conclusion.

This objection assumes that a true sacrifice must have a physical shedding of blood. We deny this assumption. It is a fact that animals, when sacrificed in the Old Law, were slain. Christ, too, was put to death on Calvary. But the destruction in the Mass is unique. Yet Scripture teaches both that it is a sacrifice and that Christ cannot suffer in His glorified condition.

3. St. Paul (Heb. 7:23, 24) says that besides Christ there is

no other priest in the New Law. Therefore, the Mass is not a sacrifice.

Answer. St. Paul means that no other priest can equal Christ in dignity. He does not mean that there cannot be other priests who offer sacrifice in Christ's name. It is of faith that Christ is the principal offerer of the Mass. Yet the ordained priest truly performs the liturgical rite and so offers sacrifice, but dependently on Christ.

4. Malachi does not say that sacrifice *will be offered,* but that it *is being offered.* So he cannot be referring to the Mass.

Answer. Present participles of the Hebrew language denote a permanent state and can refer to the future. We have shown in our proof that in the prophecy of Malachi these participles must refer to the future, to the Messianic kingdom. The prophet uses the present because he sees the future as though it were already actuated, and because he is certain that the prophecy will be realized.

5. At the Last Supper Christ said (according to the Vulgate translation): "This is My blood which *will be* shed" (Matt. 26:28). Hence Christ is referring to the cross only, not to the Supper.

Answer. We admit that the Vulgate reads, "will be shed." However, the oldest manuscript which we have uses the present time, "is being shed."

Since the Supper was necessarily related to Calvary, it does not militate against our Conclusion *if* the words of consecration were expressed in future time. The future time would refer directly to Calvary, indirectly to the Supper. Present time would refer directly to the Supper, indirectly to Calvary. The Supper was a sacrifice, but it was inextricably linked with the cross.

6. Some of the Fathers, especially earlier ones, say that the prayers of the priest and people are the sacrifice. So the Mass is not a genuine sacrifice.

Answer. None of the Fathers even attempts to give an explanation of the Mass. When some of them, St. Justin for example, say that the prayers are the sacrifice, they mean that the true sacrifice of the Mass has little value for those sharing in it unless they have inward devotion. Their internal dispositions should correspond with the external, liturgical sacrifice which the priest offers for them.

7. Some Fathers, many theologians, popes themselves, say that the faithful are immolated in the Mass. Therefore, the Mass is not a true sacrifice in which Christ is immolated.

Answer. It is permissible to say that the faithful are immolated in the Mass. Christ Himself is the victim of the sacrifice, and He is the only victim in the ontological order. But in the intellectual order, i.e., the order of signification, the Mass means that all who share in its offering should immolate themselves in Christ's service. This is what the Fathers, theologians, and popes mean.

Comment 1. Tradition and the sacrifice of the Mass.

In the Conclusion we proved the sacrificial nature of the Mass from the Council of Trent and from Scripture. We now offer a few quotations from the Fathers. It should be remembered that this proof by itself, if sufficiently developed, would establish the sacrificial character of the Mass.

We read in the *Didache:* "On the Lord's day come together, break bread, and perform the Eucharist, after confessing your transgressions, that your *sacrifice* may be pure. But let none who has a quarrel with his fellow join in your meeting until they be reconciled, that your *sacrifice* may not be defiled. For this is that [sacrifice] which was spoken by the Lord: 'In every place and time offer Me a clean oblation, for I am a great King, saith the Lord, and my name is wonderful among the Gentiles'" (RJ. 8).

St. Justin (died 166) in his discussion with the Jew, Trypho, declares: "Also concerning the sacrifices which you were wont to offer to Him, God says, as I have already mentioned, by the mouth of Malachi, one of the twelve [prophets]: 'My will is not in you, saith the Lord, and your sacrifices I shall not accept from your hands. Therefore, from the sun's rising unto its going down, My name is glorified among the nations, and in every place incense is offered to My name, a clean sacrifice, for great is My name among the nations, says the Lord, while you profane it.' But of the sacrifices offered to Him in every place by us, the nations—the sacrifices, that is to say, of the bread of the Eucharist, and likewise of the cup of the Eucharist—of these he foretells when he says that we glorify His name, but you profane it" (*Dial. c. Tryph.* par. 41; RJ. 135).

St. Irenaeus (died about 202) writes: "Christ saying: 'This is

My body,' . . . taught the new *sacrifice* of the New Testament which the Church, receiving it from the apostles, offers to God throughout the world" (*Adv. Haer.* IV, 17, 5; RJ. 232).

Pious Christian women are told by Tertullian (died about 215): ". . . you go abroad only for some serious reason; either because some sick person among the brethren is to be visited, or because *sacrifice* is offered, or the word of God administered" (*De Cultu Femin.* II, 11; PL. I, 1329). Reference is made to a Christian sacrifice because in the context the women are praised for not visiting the pagan temples.

St. Cyprian (died about 258) states: "For if Jesus . . . is the high priest of God the Father, and if He, in the first place, offered Himself as a sacrifice to the Father and then commanded this to be done in commemoration of Him, then, in truth, that priest truly acts as Christ's minister who imitates what Christ did. He offers a true and full sacrifice to God the Father, when he offers according as he sees Christ to have offered" (*Epist.* 63, 14; RJ. 584).

For additional quotations consult Pohle-Preuss, *The Sacraments,* II, 322 ff.

Comment 2. The Mass is not only a representation, but also a repetition or re-enactment in an unbloody manner of the sacrifice of the cross.

Trent defines (DB. 938; CT. 747) that the Mass is a representation or picturing of the cross by declaring that the sacrifice of the Supper, and, therefore, of the Mass, was such that "by it the bloody sacrifice accomplished once on the cross would be represented and its memory perpetuated until the end of time. . . ."

The same truth is clear from St. Paul (I Cor. 11:26): "For as often as you shall eat this bread, and drink the chalice, you shall show the death of the Lord until He come."

However, the Mass is more than a mere representation or portrayal of Calvary. We could say that even a passion play or a crucifix is a representation of the cross. But the Mass is, in addition, an actual repetition or renewal of Calvary in an unbloody manner.

Moreover, the Mass in an unbloody manner re-enacts Calvary objectively, essentially, intrinsically, and necessarily: objectively, i.e., in itself, not merely because it might stir up subjective recollections of Calvary with corresponding emotions; essentially, i.e., in that part of the Mass which composes its essence, the double consecration; intrinsically, i.e., from the very nature of the double consecration, not from some extrinsic element added to it; necessarily, i.e., the Mass cannot exist without this objective renewal of Calvary.

It is Catholic doctrine that the Mass is such a repetition of the cross. The fact is clear also from the words of institution. These words signify the Real Presence. Since they are sacrificial expressions, they also mean that Christ really present is offered to the Father. Since, moreover, they demand a double consecration, they provide a representation of Christ's death. Christ is not really present in a passion play or in a crucifix. Nor is he offered sacrificially in them.

It is, then, very important to explain *how* the Mass is an unbloody re-enactment of Calvary. To accomplish this we shall compare the essential components of the two sacrifices.

First, the Victim is the same in both. This Victim is Christ Himself as man. This is an article of divine faith from the Council of Trent (DB. 940; CT. 749) which declares that in the Mass "there is contained, and immolated in an unbloody manner, the same Christ who on the altar of the cross offered Himself in a bloody manner."

This point is also evident from the words of institution. By them, as we have seen, the same numerical Christ who died on Good Friday becomes present in a sacrificial rite, the Mass.

The accidents of bread and wine are in no way the victim in the Mass. They are instruments by which the sacrifice is externalized. In addition, since there are two distinct sets of accidents, they help to manifest the symbolic death at the double consecration.

Accordingly, we note a difference between the Mass and sacrifices of the Old Law. In these the victim was directly apprehended by the senses. But in the Mass, Christ by the very nature of His Eucharistic presence, unbounded as He is by any material object, cannot be directly perceived. In order, therefore, that Christ, the Victim, may be at least indirectly perceptible, the appearances of bread and wine, so intimately linked with His presence, remain.

Second, in both sacrifices the principal Offerer is the same. This is Christ Himself as man, as Trent (DB. 940; CT. 749) defines: ". . . the same One [Christ] now offering by the ministry of priests, who then on the cross offered Himself. . . ." We have, then, the same Priest on Calvary and in the Mass.

However, on the cross Christ Himself made the outward offering. In the Mass the priest alone makes it, but in so doing, he acts as Christ's vicar. Priests, therefore, are true ministers of the sacrifice because they alone make the outward offering in Christ's name and because they effect the symbolical immolation.

When an ambassador signs documents and makes official declarations, he does so only by the authority and in the person of his ruler, so that the ruler himself, in the juridical order, is the principal cause of the efficacy of the documents and declarations. Similarly, the priest at Mass is Christ's appointed ambassador so that, juridically, his offering is that of Christ Himself. So Christ Himself is the principal Offerer of the Mass. The priest is Christ's vicar, the instrumental or ministerial offerer of the sacrifice.

In making this offering, the priest acts also in the name of the people since he is their divinely appointed representative and intercessor.

Most theologians hold that Christ by a special act of His human will renews the offering of Himself at each Mass. In this way He concurs not only remotely with the external offering of the priest, His vicar, but also proximately, inasmuch as He actually makes a special internal offering of Himself when the priest effects the outward offering at the double consecration.

It should be clear now why the Mass is a re-enactment of Calvary, not merely a representation of it. Christ as man is the Victim of the Mass. This could never be said of a passion play or a crucifix. Moreover, Christ as man is the principal Offerer of the Mass. In a passion play there is an outward offering, which, however, is not made in the name of Christ, but in the name of the individual who happens to play the part of Christ. In a crucifix no offering of any kind is present since no religious rite is performed.

Noteworthy, too, is the fact that the dignity and value of a sacrifice depend much more upon the dignity and value of the victim and of the offerer than they do upon the victim's destruction, though this also is required. This becomes clearer if we recall that a sacrifice is in the genus of a gift. We judge the value of a gift by its intrinsic worth and by the dignity and love of the giver. Thus we would esteem more highly a rosary sent us personally by the Holy Father than the same kind of rosary sent us by a friend. From this we obtain some idea of the incalculable value and dignity of the Mass in which Christ as man is the Gift and also the principal Giver, whose love for God and for us is unbounded.

The Mass and the cross differ in the manner in which the Victim is destroyed or immolated. This is of faith from Trent (DB. 940; CT. 749) which states that the two sacrifices differ "only in the manner of offering." Although this expression by itself is somewhat obscure, its meaning is plain from the context, in which the council declares that the immolation on the cross was accomplished in a bloody manner (*cruente*) whereas in the Mass it is accomplished in an unbloody manner (*incruente*).

However, the symbolic and unbloody separation of the body and blood of Christ at Mass portrays or represents the bloody separation on Calvary. To effect this symbolic destruction, which will be explained more fully in a following Conclusion, the double consecration is necessary.

This particular element of the Mass is not a re-enactment of Calvary, but a representation of it. Even considered as a representation or picturing of the death on the cross, it is not so vivid as that occurring in some passion plays. As regards, then, the one element of immolation, the Mass is not a repetition, but a portrayal of Christ's bloody death. Christ does not die again at Mass.

What, therefore, is the function played by destruction in a sacrifice? Although an essential element, it is decidedly secondary. It symbolizes God's supreme dominion and man's total subjugation to God, and also man's desire for union with Him. This symbolization, it should be noted, is accomplished as effectively by a representation of death as by an actual physical death.

As a result of all the foregoing considerations, it follows that the Mass by its very nature is necessarily related to the cross.

This truth is also evident from the fact that the fruits of the Mass are derived in their entirety from Calvary. This is Catholic doctrine, and is quite clear from Trent (DB. 940; CT. 749) when it declares that "the fruits of this sacrifice, the bloody one, are abundantly received from this unbloody one [the Mass]." All spiritual gifts, whether flowing from the Mass, the sacraments, prayer, penance, or sacramentals, get their sanctifying power from the one sacrifice of Calvary.

Comment 3. Whether the Mass is specifically the same kind of sacrifice as the cross.

Nobody doubts that the destruction occurring in the Mass is specifically different from that on Calvary. Actual physical death is specifically different from a mere picturing of death. This is the chief difference between the cross and the Mass, but there are other differences also.

On Calvary the Victim was directly visible whereas in the Mass He is only indirectly perceptible by the medium of the species of bread and wine. Moreover, on Calvary Christ personally offered Himself externally to the Father. In the Mass He remains the principal Offerer, but He acts through the agency of priests who alone place the external offering.

Are these divergences sufficient to constitute a specific difference between Calvary and the Mass? In the opinion of most theologians they are, and so we would say that the Mass differs specifically from the cross.

It is certain that the Mass differs numerically from the cross. There are two genuine sacrifices, not one, though the Mass is dependent upon Calvary.

Furthermore, each Mass differs numerically from every other Mass. Each Mass by itself is one more genuine sacrifice. It is true that the Victim, Christ, is numerically the same in every Mass, but the offerings and immolations differ numerically, and so each Mass is a distinct sacrifice.

Other minor differences exist between the Mass and the cross. On the cross our Lord was still subject to suffering and death; in the Mass He comes with His glorified body which cannot suffer.

On the cross our Savior, being in the wayfaring state, merited and made satisfaction by His sacrifice; in the Mass He, now removed from this state, cannot merit or satisfy. He merely applies the merits and satisfactions which He won on Calvary.

Again, the cross took place but once, and in one place. The Mass is repeated many times daily, and everywhere.

Finally, the cross was an absolute sacrifice, not dependent in any way upon any other sacrifice. The Mass, though a genuine sacrifice, is necessarily dependent upon Calvary, both by its composition and by the fact that its efficacy is derived entirely from the cross.

But the most notable difference between the two sacrifices must be placed in the kinds of immolation. On the cross Christ shed His blood and actually died; in the Mass He dies symbolically only.

Comment 4. The relationship between the Mass and the Supper.

These two sacrifices are specifically the same. They have the same Victim, Christ as man; the same Offerer, Christ as man; the same kind of destruction, symbolical.

The following accidental differences should be noted. First, at the Supper Christ offered personally; in the Mass He offers through the agency of priests.

At the Supper Christ was still subject to suffering; in the Mass He comes with His glorified and impassible body.

By the Supper Christ merited and made satisfaction; in the Mass He does not do so.

The Supper signified Christ's actual death as a future event; in the Mass this death is signified as a past event.

*

Conclusion 8. The essence of the Mass is composed of the double consecration alone.

Introduction. Since the Mass consists of a series of actions and prayers, it is natural to inquire which of these constitute its essence. Does this essence consist of one action and prayer or of several? If several are involved, do they follow one another successively or are they separated? We answer that the entire essence is found in the double consecration alone.

Explanation of Terms

1. Essence. The essence of a thing is that which makes it what it is and without which it cannot be. Thus the essence of a man consists of the union of his body and soul. Everything else is accidental.

2. The double consecration. This comprises the saying by a priest of the words, "This is My body," and, shortly afterwards, "This is the chalice of My blood. . . ." The first words are pronounced over the bread; the second, over the wine.

Adversaries. Many and varied opinions were held formerly about the essence of the Mass. Since, however, they all have been discarded in favor of the double consecration, it would be of purely historical interest to discuss them. For further information, consult Pohle-Preuss, *The Sacraments,* II, 340 ff.

Dogmatic Note

Until recent years this was the common and certain teaching of theologians. It may now be qualified as Catholic doctrine by reason of the declarations of Pius XII in his encyclical, *Mediator Dei,* par. 92 (*Catholic Mind,* June, 1948, Vol. XLVI, n. 1026, p. 353); and in his address to a special audience of the First International Congress on Pastoral Liturgy, Part II, par. 7 (Boston *Pilot,* Oct. 6, 1956, p. 10).

Proof 2. From the words of institution in Holy Scripture. The argument follows in form.

The essence of the sacrifice of the Supper was composed of the double consecration alone;

But the essence of the sacrifice of the Mass is the same as the essence of the Supper:

Therefore, the essence of the sacrifice of the Mass is composed of the double consecration alone.

Proof for the major. According to the sacred writers, all that Christ did (and what Christ did and said is all that comes into consideration, since He performed the sacrifice) was to enact the double consecration.

Proof for the minor. All theologians admit that the Supper and the Mass are essentially the same sacrifice. Only in the Mass is the command to repeat the Supper fulfilled: "Do this in memory of Me."

All other parts of the Mass are, therefore, accidental, though some are of more importance than others and some are more intimately linked with the double consecration than others.

Proof 3. From the Council of Trent. The argument follows.

The verification of four conditions laid down by Trent constitutes the essence of the Mass;

But the double consecration by itself verifies the four conditions:

Therefore, the double consecration by itself constitutes the essence of the Mass.

Proof for the major. The Council is professedly explaining the nature of the Mass. The four conditions it sets down for the essence of the sacrifice are: first, institution by Christ, not by the Church (DB. 938; CT. 747); second, an offering made in the name of Christ (DB. 940; CT. 749); third, Christ as the Victim (DB. 940; CT. 749); fourth, an objective representation of the bloody death upon the cross (DB. 938, 940; CT. 747, 749).

Proof for the minor. These four conditions are verified in the double consecration by itself. First, by it the priest accomplishes what Christ, not the Church, commanded at the Supper. Second, the priest impersonates Christ at the double consecration. Third, Christ becomes present as Victim at this part of the Mass. Fourth, the double consecration by its nature represents Christ's death upon the cross.

It should be noted that all other parts of the Mass, such as the offertory, the elevation of the Host and chalice, the oral offering contained in the prayer "Unde et memores," the breaking of the Host, the mingling of the broken Host with the consecrated wine (all of which have been suggested by some past author or other as essential to the Mass), are excluded by the fact that they are of ecclesiastical institution only. Other objections could also be raised against them.

Some famous theologians, e.g., Sts. Alphonsus and Robert Bellarmine, held that the priest's Communion together with the double consecration constituted the essence of the Mass. They believed that the element of destruction, so necessary for the sacrifice, was to be found in the priest's Communion. This opinion can no longer be defended. It is rejected by the *magisterium* in our dogmatic note and for other reasons.

First, the priest does not receive Communion in the name of Christ, but as a private individual.

Second, it is certain that he must, at least before the second consecration, make the special intention for which he is going to offer the Mass. If his Communion were essential, he could make this intention anytime before His Communion.

Third, in all sacrifices of the Old Law in which there was any banquet or communion at all, this communion was regarded as a sharing in a sacrifice which had already been essentially completed. Hence St. Paul says (I Cor. 10:18): ". . . are not they, that eat of the sacrifices, partakers of the altar?" He means that they partake of the sacrifice which has been celebrated.

Fourth, the inspired authors do not mention Christ's receiving Communion at the Supper.

Finally, the destruction required in a sacrifice must be perceptible and connected in some way with the altar. But the cessation of Christ's presence in this particular Host takes place within the priest's body and so is not perceptible and is not closely linked with the altar.

Nevertheless, the priest's Communion under both species is obligatory and, most probably, by Christ's own command. It is necessary for the integrity of the Mass, though not for its essence. This is Catholic doctrine from *Mediator Dei*, Section II, par. 112, 115 (*Catholic Mind*, June, 1948, pp. 359, 360).

The priest's Communion also has a symbolic meaning related to the sacrifice. It is God's return-gift to the priest and signifies that the sacrifice offered by him has been accepted by God.

It would be a serious dogmatic error (DB. 944; CT. 753) to say that lay people assisting at Mass must receive Communion. Yet, it is strongly recommended that they do so if possible. Often it is impossible either because they have already assisted at a previous Mass and so are forbidden under pain of mortal sin to communicate a second time on the same day, or because they are in the state of mortal sin and cannot get to confession, or because illness, e.g., great danger of vomiting after Communion, besets them, and so on.

If the faithful cannot actually receive Communion, they should make a spiritual communion, though this, too, is merely a recommendation.

The Communion of the laity, when it takes place at the regular time during Mass, has also a symbolic meaning pertinent to the sacrifice. It signifies that the offering of *themselves* to God, which they should elicit at every Mass, has been accepted by God.

Finally, it should be remarked that the priest is commanded to receive Communion under both species. The laity by Church law are forbidden to communicate under both species.

OBJECTIONS

1. The inspired writers say that Christ "blessed" the bread. Hence some kind of blessing is necessary in the Mass in addition to the double consecration.

Answer. Not all the writers mention this blessing. Sts. Paul and Luke do not say that Christ blessed the bread. None of the four sacred authors mentions any blessing of the wine. If the blessing were essential, it would have been mentioned by all four, both for the bread and for the wine.

2. All four Scriptural accounts say that Christ "broke" the bread. Therefore, the breaking of the Host by the priest must belong to the essence of the Mass.

Answer. The bread may have been broken before the consecration, in which case the breaking was not related to the sacrificial action in which Christ alone is the Victim. If our Savior broke the Bread after consecration, He did so quite evidently in order to give Communion to the apostles.

Moreover, the breaking of the Host is not found in some liturgies in which Mass is truly celebrated.

Finally, the rubrics provide that the breaking of the Host is to be entirely omitted if, for instance, the entire Host should fall into the chalice before the priest breaks it, as actually happens occasionally. If this action were essential to the Mass, it could never be omitted.

3. The consecration brings about Christ's true presence upon the altar. Such a productive action cannot be the entire essence of the sacrifice, which requires the destruction of the Victim.

Answer. Not only does the consecration effect Christ's presence under either species, but at the same time it objectively immolates Christ symbolically. Therefore, a destruction is also found in the double consecration. This point will be explained more fully in the next Conclusion.

4. The consecration is caused by God alone, not by the priest nor even by Christ as man. Hence the elements of a sacrifice cannot be found in the double consecration alone.

Answer. Transubstantiation is caused physically by God alone as its primary efficient cause. But the sacrificial action, the mystical slaying, and the offering of Christ as man, is done primarily by Christ Himself as man and, secondarily, by the ordained priest. The latter alone makes possible the visible rite, which is indispensable for a sacrifice.

Comment 1. The Offertory of the Mass.

It is certain that the Offertory does not pertain to the essence of the Mass. The external offering which constitutes the Mass cannot be made before the Victim, Christ, becomes present. The Offertory simply presents to God the bread and wine, thus setting them apart from profane use.

The Offertory is not made in the person of Christ, but in the name of the Church, whereas the entire essence of the Mass is of divine institution (DB. 938; CT. 747).

Furthermore, the Offertory can, in some circumstances, be made mentally only (*Missale Romanum,* De defectibus, III, 4). If made mentally, it is clear that it could not constitute the outward offering which is indispensable in every Mass.

Nevertheless, the Offertory may be called an important part of the Mass. Its function is to prepare the internal dispositions of all present so that they may conform to the outward rite of the sacrifice. If a person contributes to the collection box when it is passed around at the Offertory, he is apt to develop subjective feelings of sacrifice since he gives of his money, won by hard work.

This subjective disposition forms a part of the internal spirit expected of all who assist at Mass. Hence the Offertory has a beautiful symbolic meaning.

*

Conclusion 9. The element of destruction required for the Mass is to be sought in the mystical or symbolic death of Christ which occurs at the double consecration.

Introduction. Since the essence of the Mass is found in the double consecration, we must find in this rite the three indispensable constituents of every sacrifice—victim, outward offering, destruction.

All theologians agree that the Victim and the liturgical offering are found there. All concede, too, that a symbolic death of Christ takes place at the double consecration.

Some, however, deny that it enters into the essence of the sacrifice. They believe that it is necessary, not to constitute the Mass, but to effect a commemoration of the cross. They say either that the Mass does not require any immolation or that the immolation is found under some other aspect or effect of the double consecration.

Against these theologians we now affirm that the Mass demands an immolation as one of its constitutive elements and that this immolation should be sought in the mystical death alone. In a Comment we shall deal with several different ways of explaining precisely how the symbolic death effects this immolation.

Explanation of Terms

1. The mystical or symbolic death of Christ which occurs at the double consecration.

This death is not physical, since Christ cannot suffer or die in His glorified state, but mystical or symbolical. In other words, the double consecration provides us with a perceptible picturing or representation of Christ's physical death on Calvary.

When the priest consecrates the bread saying, "This is My body," Christ becomes present in His entirety, but such is not the *impression* conveyed to us by the words themselves. They say merely that Christ's *body* is present. This is all that we *hear*.

When, immediately afterwards, the priest consecrates the wine saying, "This is the chalice of My blood . . . ," Christ becomes wholly present again, but the words by themselves give the *impression* that only His blood is present.

Moreover, each of these consecrations terminates at a distinct ontological reality. The consecration of the bread effects Christ's presence under the appearances of bread, which exist objectively. Similarly, the consecration of the wine brings about Christ's presence under the species of wine, which also have objective existence. Moreover, one set of appearances is a solid, the other is a liquid.

Consequently, the words of consecration as uttered by the priest and terminating in two really distinct sets of visible appearances, give the *impression* (and it is an impression only) that Christ's body and blood are separated, that He is, in other words, slain again, since a separation of body and blood necessarily means death.

Both the ear images and the eye images evoked by the words of consecration pronounced over their respective objects, signify by themselves (not in reality) that Christ is again put to death. This is what we mean by a mystical or symbolic destruction or immolation. Although this death does not represent a death by crucifixion (it could be any kind of violent death), yet in the Mass it necessarily refers to crucifixion because our Savior actually died in this way.

Adversaries. We shall briefly explain various solutions. They will be refuted under the objections following the Conclusion. If the student studies the ensuing theories, he will understand more clearly the meaning of our own position. He should remember that any of these theories may be held without censure.

1. Theories which require some kind of immolation in the Mass, but which seek for it, not in the symbolic death, but in some other aspect or effect of the consecration.

The first opinion is attributed to Casalius. It was adopted by such prominent theologians as Lugo, Franzelin, Hurter, Sasse, De Augustinis, Cappello, and others.

Though divergences exist among these authors, this is the general idea. Christ at the consecration of the Mass is placed in a humbled condition (*in statu decliviore*), because He becomes present under the appearances of mere food and drink. He is like a king in beggar's clothing. Besides, owing to His Eucharistic condition, He is deprived of the ordinary exercise of His senses, since the use of these postulates that their possessor be present circumscriptively. Moreover, the Eucharistic Christ freely deprives Himself of His right to manifest His glorified body.

Hence Christ is in a lowly state, which is a real, though only a moral change wrought in Him. This change, however, does not affect Christ intrinsically nor does it involve any subjective suffering. But it is sufficient to constitute an immolation in the Mass.

A second theory is doubtfully attributed to Suarez and was adopted by Arriaga, Scheeben, and Schanz.

These theologians deny that destruction as such is necessary for a sacrifice. The gift or victim must be changed into something more precious and this transformation is the proximate matter of the sacrifice. In the Mass, therefore, the consecration, precisely under the aspect of transubstantiation, is the proximate matter since by transubstantiation the bread and wine are converted into something infinitely more precious, the body and blood of Christ.

2. Theories holding that no destruction or change of any kind is necessary to make the Mass a genuine sacrifice.

The theory of Fr. de la Taille. This explanation was widely acclaimed when it was first propounded some thirty years ago, but is not accepted by many today.

Fr. de la Taille seems to define sacrifice as the liturgical offering of a gift which must be destroyed either before, or simultaneously with, or after the offering. The Last Supper and Calvary composed only one numerical sacrifice in which the Supper furnished the liturgical offering whereas the cross supplied the Victim and the voluntarily accepted immolation.

But since Good Friday Christ remains in the condition of a Victim. He is, so to speak, a perpetual Victim, even though He does not suffer any more.

The Mass is the sacrifice offered by the Church through her priests. No new destruction of any kind should be sought in the Mass because Christ comes to the altar as a perpetual Victim. Consequently, the Mass is a sacrifice by the very fact that a priest, acting in the name of Christ and of the Church, renews the liturgical offering by repeating the double consecration of the Supper.

Another opinion is attributed to the Oratorian School of the eighteenth century.

According to these theologians no perceptible sacrificial immolation is necessary in the Mass. When Christ comes down upon the altar at the consecration, He has the same internal dispositions which He had on Calvary. These dispositions are sufficient to make the Mass a sacrifice.

For additional information about various theories, consult Pohle-Preuss, *The Sacraments*, II, 349–370; 398–400.

Dogmatic Note

Today it is the more probable and more common opinion that each Mass requires its own immolation and that this is to be found in the double consecration from the viewpoint of the symbolic death which it portrays.

Proof 2. From the encyclical, *Mediator Dei*, of Pius XII. This precious document more obviously teaches that the symbolic death in the Mass is necessary, not only to recall and represent Calvary, but also to provide the destruction or immolation which constitutes the essence of the sacrifice. It does not seem that the Holy Father intended to settle this dispute among theologians and so the other proposed theories may still be defended. However, our opinion is more in conformity with the mind of the Holy Father as it is revealed in the encyclical.

He says, for instance: "Therefore, the august sacrifice of the altar is not merely a simple commemoration of the sufferings and death of Jesus Christ, but a true, genuine act of sacrificing, whereby the High Priest by an unbloody immolation accomplishes what He has already done upon the cross. . . ." (*Mediator Dei*, Sect. II, par. 68; *Catholic Mind*, June, 1948, Vol. XLVI, n. 1026, p. 346).

All theologians admit that the "commemoration of the sufferings and death of Jesus Christ" is effected in the Mass by the symbolic immolation. But the Holy Father says more than this. He declares that the unbloody immolation enters into the act of "sacrificing." Consequently, he means that the mystic death is a constitutive element of the Mass, not merely a representation of Calvary.

Again we read: "For that unbloody immolation by which, when the words of consecration are uttered, Christ becomes present upon the altar in the condition of a Victim, is accomplished by the priest alone, acting in the name of Christ, not in the name of the people" (Sect. II, par. 92; *Catholic Mind, ibid.,* p. 353).

Here the Holy Father states that the mystic death or "unbloody immolation" presents Christ to God as victimized. Hence it does not merely commemorate the cross.

Another passage is significant: "For again and again notice should be taken that the Eucharistic sacrifice by its very nature is the unbloody immolation of the divine Victim, an immolation which is made manifest in a mystic manner by the separation of the sacred species. . . ." (Sect. II, par. 115; *Catholic Mind, ibid.,* p. 360).

"Nature" is the same as essence. If, therefore, "by its very nature" the Mass is Christ's unbloody immolation, this immolation must pertain to its intrinsic nature or essence as a sacrifice. It is not an extrinsic adjunct whose presence simply commemorates the cross.

Proof 3. From the Council of Trent (DB. 940; CT. 749). The first sentence of this passage begins as follows: "And since in the divine sacrifice which is accomplished in the Mass that same Christ is present and bloodlessly immolated who on the altar of the cross offered Himself once in a bloody manner. . . ."

The Council expressly declares that an unbloody immolation occurs at Mass (*incruente immolatūr*). Moreover, since the immolations of Calvary and the Mass are compared and equivalated, the unbloody immolation of the Mass must be an essential constituent of this sacrifice just as the bloody immolation was essential to the cross.

Furthermore, directly comparing the two sacrifices, the Council states: "The Victim is one and the same; the same One who then offered Himself on the cross now offers Himself by the agency of priests; only the manner of offering is different." Immediately afterwards the Council explains the meaning of "manner of offering" when it says that the cross was a bloody offering whereas the Mass is an unbloody one.

The Council is seemingly speaking about the constitutive elements of the two sacrifices. Since the first two points mentioned (the Victim and the Offerer) are essentials of both sacrifices, it would be an unjustifiable use of language to add in the same sentence, "the manner of offering," unless this also is essential.

Besides, the "manner of offering" on the cross was an intrinsic component of this sacrifice. Consequently, the "manner of offering," the unbloody immolation or symbolic death, constitutes the Mass. Otherwise, the phrase, "manner of offering," though expressed but once, would have two diverse significations. Applied to Calvary, it would signify something essential; applied to the Mass, it would mean something extrinsic and accidental to the sacrifice as such.

Our interpretation of the two statements of the Council is the natural and obvious one. Other interpretations are possible, but not without straining the mind.

OBJECTIONS

We have already summarized under the heading, "Adversaries," the general meaning of the theories opposed to our own. We shall now present the reasons why we think that they should be rejected.

1. The opinion of Casalius and Lugo attributes a true, though merely moral, abjection induced upon Christ at the Mass. Yet it safeguards all other theological verities. It should, therefore, be accepted.

Answer. There are various reasons why this humbling of Christ at the consecration cannot provide the immolation required for the Mass.

First, such a change in our Savior does not signify God's supreme dominion and man's total subjugation to God. This signification is indispensable for a genuine sacrifice and it is realized only by a destruction, either factual or symbolic.

Second, if this theory were true, the consecration of only one species would supply the sacrificial element of the Mass.

Third, a priest could say Mass if he were to go to the altar, remove a consecrated Host from the tabernacle, and offer it to God. This is untenable.

Fourth, it does not harmonize with *Mediator Dei* and Trent, which more obviously require a symbolic death for the intrinsic constitution of the Mass.

Fifth, the main reason why Christ becomes present under the appearances of bread and wine is to enable men to receive Communion, not to glorify God by sacrifice.

2. The theory of Scheeben and Arriaga is satisfactory. The substances of bread and wine are converted into the precious body and blood of Christ.

Answer. First, according to this view, both the bread and wine together with the body and blood of Christ would be the remote matter of the sacrifice. This is directly opposed to Trent (DB. 940; CT. 749) which states that the Victim of both Calvary and the Mass is the same. In a conversion the ultimate term (the body and blood of Christ) cannot be disjoined from the initial term (the bread and wine). The conversion necessarily involves both and so the substance of bread and wine would have to be regarded as a partial victim of the Mass.

Second, to assume, as these authors do, that the proximate matter of a sacrifice consists in changing a gift into something more valuable, is without solid foundation.

Third, the consecration of only one species would be sufficient to make the Mass a sacrifice.

3. The solution of Fr. de la Taille liquidates the vexing problem. No matter what theory is adopted, the Mass remains a unique kind of sacrifice. Why not solve this uniqueness by saying that Christ, since He was physically immolated once on the cross, does not have to be immolated again in any way at the Mass?

Answer. First, tradition, contrary to de la Taille, teaches that Calvary was a complete sacrifice by itself without the Supper.

Second, this theory does not conform to the more obvious meaning of Trent as explained in our proof. It also seems hard to reconcile with another passage of the council (DB. 938; CT. 747) which declares that Christ, after celebrating the ancient Pasch, instituted the new Pasch, "Himself to be immolated by the Church through her priests beneath visible signs. . . ." There is, therefore, an immolation at Mass and an immolation which actually constitutes that sacrifice. It would not be called an immolation if it were merely an extrinsic adjunct of the Mass. Immolation is essential to sacrifice.

Third, the correct way of solving this problem may some day be defined by the Church. However, Fr. de la Taille's theory could never be defined, because he himself admits that it lapsed from tradition from the time of Trent until 1924 when his *Mysterium Fidei* appeared.

Fourth, the primary purpose of every sacrifice is to signify man's total subjection to God. This purpose is not attained unless the Mass contains its own immolation.

4. The opinion of the Oratorian School seems reasonable. Christ has at Mass the same internal dispositions which He had on the cross. These dispositions signify man's entire dependence upon God.

Answer. This theory is based on an unsubstantiated definition of sacrifice. Sacrifice is not merely the offering of a gift, but of an immolated gift.

Second, the dispositions of our Lord are internal and impervious to the senses. The Mass, however, must contain its own perceptible immolation.

Third, everyone should admit that Christ in the Mass has the same dispositions as on Calvary, since the outward rite of sacrifice signifies that the priest should have corresponding religious dispositions. These dispositions are the meaning of the Mass (the Mass in its signification), but they do not constitute it, because by its very nature it is a perceptible rite.

Comment 1. Diverse ways of explaining precisely how the symbolic death of Christ effects the immolation of the Mass.

It should be observed that any of these theories may be adopted. The more probable explanation will be given last.

1. The opinion attributed to Vasquez and adopted by others.

These men do not consider the mystical death of Christ at the double consecration as an immolation taking place here and now in each Mass, but solely as a representation of the past sacrifice of Calvary. Since the Mass is essentially a relative sacrifice, it does not need in their opinion an immolation here and now, but simply a representation which recalls the physical death of the cross.

This solution has the merit of insisting on the fact that the Mass is a relative sacrifice. However, it has serious defects.

First, in all the sacrifices of the Old Law an immolation here and now was an essential constituent. Hence, such an immolation should be verified in the Mass.

Second, this view does not correspond with the more obvious meaning of *Mediator Dei* and Trent in the passages which we have previously cited. Both the encyclical and the council seem to teach that the symbolic death is a *present,* constitutive element of the Mass.

2. The theory credited to Lessius and favored by others.

These authors insist that a physical destruction is required in every true sacrifice. They admit, of course, that no such destruction of Christ occurs in the Mass, but they add that it is only accidentally that He is not again physically slain. The words of consecration by themselves really do have the power to put Christ to death and should be conceived as really trying to do so. However, this effect is impeded by the miracle which has been worked upon Christ's body which is now glorified and so cannot suffer. Just as a martyr who survives after undergoing tortures sufficient to cause death is considered a true martyr, so a sacrifice is a genuine one even though the victim is not physically destroyed, provided that the destructive action, even though prevented accidentally, tends by its own power to terminate in physical destruction.

This theory is ingenious, but is open to serious objections.

First, an unsuccessful attempt at destruction is no destruction at all. Since these theologians deny that the symbolic death, if considered independently of its aim (physical death), suffices for the sacrifice, they really say that the Mass is a true sacrifice even though it contains no immolation at all. As a result, an essential note of sacrifice, immolation or destruction, is lacking in the Mass.

Second, it is hard to believe and cannot be proved that God conferred upon the words of consecration an inherent power which they can never carry into effect. This would seem to be an irrational procedure on God's part.

3. A very recent theory of Fr. Casel. The illustrious Fr. Doronzo of Catholic University seems to favor this explanation.

This view insists that the symbolic death portrayed by the double consecration is a practical sign. It does not merely portray, but it effects what it portrays. Hence the actual death of Christ on Calvary is, in some mysterious and supernatural way, brought to the altar. The redemptive mystery of the cross emerges into time at each Mass. Each Mass is an image containing, not merely reflecting, the exemplar, Calvary.

This theory has the merit of reminding us that the sacrifice of the Mass is a profound mystery which we shall never completely understand. It might well be that these authors are closer to the truth than all others. However, as long as we are in this world, we cannot be satisfied with hazy explanations of anything. Obscure explanations, though they may actually be closer to the truth, cannot be accepted.

This is the greatest objection to this solution. It is not clear. The same numerical historical fact, Christ's death on Calvary, cannot be reproduced anywhere. If this is true, how, then, precisely is the cross made actually present at the double consecration?

4. The more probable theory is attributed to Salmeron and Pasqualigo. It has been adopted by the majority of theologians. It is often associated with the name of Cardinal Billot. Despite minor divergences the general explanation is the same.

These authors say that the symbolic death not only recalls and represents Calvary, but also that it is an immolation here and now of Christ in every Mass. In this respect they differ from Vasquez. Rejecting also the opinion of Lessius, they do not believe that the words of consecration by themselves actually tend to a physical death of Christ.

According to these theologians the double consecration simply pictures Christ's violent death on the cross and, precisely as a picture, an outward impression, it suffices to produce a destruction which, though purely symbolic, is sufficient to make a component part of this unique sacrifice, the Mass. Christ is not conceived as first becoming present by the words of consecration and then afterwards being mystically slain by the same words. No, Christ becomes present *as though* he were slain. Nor can He come in any other way when the formulas of both consecrations are uttered. The resulting portrayal of Calvary does not merely refer to and recall that event, nor is it an action done subsequently to Christ's coming in the Mass, but it overshadows Him in His very advent to the altar. So it is an immolation taking place here and now in the Mass itself.

This mystical death does not effect a re-existence, so to speak, of the cross (opinion of Fr. Casel). Yet, the symbolic death is so intimately linked to the Eucharistic Christ that He cannot become present at the double consecration without appearing to be physically dead. Why such a purely pictorial death suffices for the Mass, we shall explain in a Comment.

Not only is this the more common opinion, but it also is more in conformity with the quotations from *Mediator Dei* and Trent which we have offered in our proofs for the Conclusion. Although these quotations were advanced simply to prove that the immolation of the Mass is to be sought in some way or other in the symbolic death, the student who ponders them will discover that they point in the direction of this theory.

OBJECTIONS TO THIS EXPLANATION

1. To make this mere picture of death a sufficient destruction for the Mass is to reduce the sacrificial action to almost nothing.

Answer. We admit that the mystic immolation is no physical death. However, it is something real, i.e., independent of the mind, not purely subjective.

Furthermore, although this death is entirely symbolic and effects neither a physical nor a moral change in the Victim, it performs its specific sacrificial function as well as a physical death.

What is the specific function of destruction in a sacrifice? Simply to dramatically acknowledge God's supreme dominion over man and man's complete subjection to God. This is accomplished as effectively by a symbolic as by a physical death, just as a mere drawing or representation of a balance or scale symbolizes justice as well as a material balance or scale.

Hence we reply to the objection: In its *entity* the symbolic immolation is almost nothing compared with a physical death, we concede; in its *signification* (and that is the purpose of immolation), we deny.

It should also be recalled here that a sacrifice gets its value and dignity principally from the object offered (the gift) and from the offerer or giver. Accordingly, the Mass derives its value as a sacrifice from the facts that Christ Himself is the gift as well as the principal Giver. The purpose of destruction is to lend its significance to sacrifice, not to enhance its value or dignity.

2. This opinion makes the Mass independent of Calvary. The Mass contains within itself all the elements of sacrifice. As a result, it is an absolute, not a relative sacrifice. This is opposed to a teaching qualified as Catholic doctrine.

Answer. The Mass is an absolute sacrifice in the sense that it contains the three essential requisites of every sacrifice, an outward offering, a victim, and a destruction of the victim.

Nevertheless, the Mass does not lose thereby its essential relationship to the cross. Since the Victim is the same in both sacrifices, the Mass is essentially related to Calvary from the viewpoint of the Victim. Again, Christ is the principal Offerer of the Mass, as He was the principal and sole Offerer on Calvary. Finally, even the mystical death in the Mass necessarily represents the cross, and so there is an essential relationship on this score also. Since, therefore, each substantial part of the Mass is ineradicably related to the cross, the Mass does not lose its relative character.

Finally, all fruits coming from the Mass were earned by Christ's bloody death and so the Mass is essentially related to Calvary in this way also.

Comment 2. Why a purely symbolic death suffices for the Mass.

In the beginning of our treatment of sacrifice, we said that all sacrifices of the Old Law had a physical destruction of the victim or gift. Furthermore, we formulated our definition of sacrifice from those sacrifices. Yet, in treating of the Mass we say that a merely symbolic destruction suffices to constitute this genuine sacrifice. It seems, consequently, that we have changed basically the definition of sacrifice.

It is true that we have altered the meaning of destruction in our explanation of the Mass. The Mass remains a unique sacrifice, no matter what theory is adopted to explain it.

But we have not removed the need of destruction from our definition of sacrifice. A symbolic destruction still remains a real destruction in the sense that it is not purely subjective, but actually takes place in the objective order. It does, of course, differ specifically from a physical death. Since, however, it cannot be described except as a destruction, our definition stands intact.

Nevertheless, we must show why such a symbolic destruction is sufficient for the Mass, although it would not have been sufficient for any sacrifices of the Old Law. In short, we must offer solid reasons why we are justified in changing the meaning of the word "destruction" in our definition of sacrifice. The student should reflect upon the following reasons.

First, all the gifts or victims of the sacrifices of the Old Law were present beneath their own accidents or appearances. Consequently, they *could* be affected by a destructive action and be physically destroyed.

In the Eucharist, however, Christ is not present beneath His own outward appearances, but under those of bread and wine. By reason of this fact no destructive agent could possibly assail Christ in the Eucharist. As a result, the kind of destruction in the Mass *must* be different from the kind in the Old Law. No victim of that time was present in the way that Christ is present in the Eucharist.

Is it better, then, to say, as some do, that no destruction of any kind is required in the Mass (a basic and unjustifiable alteration of the very definition of sacrifice), or to say that there is a real destruction (thus the definition is kept intact), but that it is of a different kind from the destructions of the Old Law?

Second, once a victim in the Old Law was destroyed by sacrifice, it simply vanished by being changed into something else, and never returned again. However, Christ, after being slain on Calvary, returned to life at His resurrection. It is this resurrected Christ who is the Victim in the Mass.

Here again we have no parallel between Christ at the Mass and any victim of the Old Testament. We should not, therefore, be surprised to find that a resurrected victim is not slain again physically in a subsequent sacrifice of the same victim.

Third, it was by His bloody death that Christ won an infinite treasury of merit and satisfaction for mankind. The Mass simply applies this merit and satisfaction; it does not increase them. Hence it cannot be said that a physical death is necessary in the Mass in order to atone for sin. All sins were atoned for on Calvary.

Finally, we mention again the important truth that man's total subjection to God is signified as effectively by a mystical death as by a physical one. Moreover, this signification is the specific function of the immolation, and it is accomplished by the symbolic death.

It is not a forceful objection to say that, this being the case, a purely symbolic death of an animal should have sufficed for a true sacrifice in the Old Law. If this had happened, there would have been no sacrifice because, not the animal itself, but its picture would have been offered to God. In the Mass, however, Christ is truly offered. Only His death is pictured.

Furthermore, since the victims of the Old Law were present under their own appearances, they *could* have been physically destroyed. Since, too, they had never previously been destroyed and afterwards been restored to their original condition, they *should* have been physically destroyed. Christ, however, at Mass does not become present under His own appearances and He comes to the altar as a resurrected Victim.

We have, then, solid reasons for maintaining that in the Mass a symbolic death of Christ is sufficient.

Comment 3. How the outward offering is found in the double consecration.

All theologians admit that the outward offering or presentation of Christ as man to the Blessed Trinity is located in the double consecration. All agree, too, that the priest alone makes this liturgical offering, which is indeed the most important constituent of the sacrifice.

These truths are enunciated in *Mediator Dei* (Sect. II, par. 92, 93; *Catholic Mind*, XLVI, n. 1026, pp. 353, 354, June, 1948). For instance, the Holy Father declares (par. 92): "But by the very fact that the priest brings the divine Victim down upon the altar, *he* presents the Same as an offering to God the Father for the glory of the Blessed Trinity and for the good of the whole Church."

Two opinions are held regarding the manner in which this outward offering is *expressed* by the double consecration. The first says that it is manifested by action, not by any words. Since the Mass is a repetition of Calvary, the priest, by the very fact that he effects the presence of Christ under the guise of death, presents Him to God. Just as Calvary was by action offered to God perceptibly, so, too, is the Mass, because it is Calvary renewed by a priest whose official function it is to offer sacrifice, and because it is enacted at the altar, which symbolizes God. According to this explanation, the outward offering is identified with the symbolic death, but under a different aspect. This opinion seems to accord better with the quotation, cited above, of the Holy Father.

However, the second opinion, which we mentioned in the Conclusion dealing with the matter and form of the Eucharist, has real probability. It holds that the liturgical offering is not sufficiently manifested unless other words, especially, "which shall be shed for the remission of sins," are added to the second consecration. If the Mass is offered "for the remission of sins," it becomes outwardly evident that the sacrifice is offered to God, since He alone can remit sins.

Comment. 4. Benefits obtained by assisting at Mass.

We have previously proved that the special effect of Communion is to produce Christlikeness in our souls and bodies. By receiving this sacrament we obtain *ex opere operato* actual graces, which, if we cooperate with them, will produce this effect.

The Mass also has special effects, but they differ from those of Communion. They correspond in a general way with the fourfold purpose to which the sacrifice is ordained, i.e., adoration, thanksgiving, reparation, impetration. The Mass confers *ex opere operato* actual graces which, supposing our cooperation, will engender these dispositions in our souls.

Moreover, the Mass can bestow on those who assist at it these actual graces in greater abundance and intensity than other private or public prayers. The Mass is not merely a prayer; nor is it merely prayer in action like a genuflection. It is prayer in action immeasurably beyond the capacity of a mere human being because it is the sacrifice of Christ Himself.

First of all, then, the actual graces of the Mass, conferred proportionately to our devotion when assisting at it, enable us to fulfill our duty and privilege of adoring God in the most perfect way. The divine Son, symbolically sacrificed again, represents me and offers to the Blessed Trinity that infinite homage of which I am by myself incapable.

Another duty incumbent on all of us is to render profound thanks to God because we owe literally everything that we have, even life itself, to Him. We can and should express our gratitude at times in our private prayers which, like all other prayers and acts of virtue, become acceptable to God because they are tendered to Him by His divine Son. But at Mass Christ personally offers thanks for us and He does so in a way most acceptable to God—by renewing His sacrifice of Calvary. Consequently, acts of thanksgiving which we make during Mass possess a singular value.

Again, common decency teaches us that we should express our sorrow and make reparation when we have deliberately insulted a fellowman. Since all of us give personal offense to God by our sins, even though they be venial only, we are prompted, and it is an obligation, to express our regrets and offer satisfaction. When, therefore, we make acts of sorrow for sin during Mass, these acts are immeasureably enhanced in value because God looks upon them as though they were made for us by His sacrificed Son.

As a result, God is propitiated in our regard. He will not miraculously prevent the penalties which by natural law ensue from sins, but He will refrain from inflicting upon us other material or spiritual punishments with which He might otherwise have visited us in this world. Even now acts of reparation elicited during Mass avert the chastisements of God.

But this is not all. It is God's general law that the temporal punishment remaining after our sins have been forgiven is to be atoned for by the pains of purgatory. We can, of course, while yet alive in this world, forestall these pains by various remedies, especially by indulgences. But if we foster a general spirit of sorrow for sin during Mass, some of our temporal punishment, and perhaps all of it, depending on our dispositions, is removed *ex opere operato*. Consequently, a spirit of compunction at Mass is a solvent for the future pains of purgatory.

The Mass, too, like Holy Communion, wins for us actual graces which, if we use them, strengthen us to overcome temptations and so to avoid sins. Indeed, if a serious sinner assists devoutly at Mass, he will receive actual graces to enable him to repent and to go to confession. This is what the Council of Trent (DB. 940; CT. 749) means when it says that the Mass "remits even enormous sins and crimes." This is one reason why the Church obliges even the worst sinners to continue their assistance at Mass.

Again, when Christ sacrifices Himself in our stead at the Mass, He petitions God to grant us spiritual and temporal favors. This plea, too, has a special efficacy. We receive some favors (a few have been mentioned above) even though we do not explicitly ask for them. However, we should form the habit of begging definite blessings for ourselves and others during Mass. We should emphasize spiritual blessings, but should not neglect to request temporal ones also. Our petitions, however, should be limited by two conditions. We want them granted provided that they will promote our spiritual welfare and are in conformity with God's general providence over our lives. The specific favors, therefore, which we ask may not be obtained, but it is certain that others, more beneficial for us, will be accorded.

It should be noted, too, that the more devoutly we assist at Mass, the more abundantly will all its blessings be conferred upon us.

Comment 5. How to assist at Mass.

It is important to remember that our outward manner of attending Mass is subordinate to the correct internal dispositions which we should foster. That external method which most readily excites these dispositions is for us the most suitable.

As regards these dispositions of soul, we may say that we should try to arouse those which our Savior Himself had on Calvary. Putting it another way, we should try to evoke those attitudes of mind and heart which our Blessed Mother possessed when she stood at the foot of the cross. Consequently, we, in the words of Pius XII, "should in a humble attitude of mind pay adoration, honor, praise and thanksgiving to the supreme majesty of God."

Besides, the meaning of the Mass expects us to develop a spirit of self-immolation. Christ upon the altar is offered and sacrificed in my stead. Hence the Mass signifies that I am dedicating myself to God and subjecting myself entirely to Him. This is my sincere desire, my ambition, even though I realize that its perfect accomplishment will be attained but gradually. Hence Mass is not ended for me when I quit the church. Its spirit of self-immolation and total dedication to God should pervade my entire life. This is what authors mean when they write that we should "live the Mass."

The internal spirit of the sacrifice can be aroused by various external methods of assisting at it. In *Mediator Dei* (*Catholic Mind*, XLVI, n. 1026, par. 105, p. 357) the Holy Father praises, first of all, the use of the Roman missal. By silently reading this, we say the same prayers as the priest at the altar, and these prayers express in diverse and charming ways the appropriate internal dispositions. The dialog low Mass and congregational singing at High Mass are also advocated by the Holy Father.

However, in order to make it perfectly clear that he wishes us to be free to adopt the outward method most suitable to ourselves, the Holy Father (*Catholic Mind, ibid.,* par. 108, p. 358) states: "Most of the faithful are unable to use the Roman missal even though it is written in the vernacular; nor are all capable of understanding correctly the liturgical rites and formulas. So varied and diverse are men's talents and characters that it is impossible for all to be moved and attracted to the same extent by community prayers, hymns, and liturgical services. Moreover, the needs and inclinations of all are not the same, nor are they always constant in the same individual. Who, then, would say, on account of such a prejudice, that all these Christians cannot participate in the Mass nor share its fruits? On the contrary, they can adopt some other method which proves easier for certain people; for instance, they can lovingly meditate on the mysteries of Jesus Christ [this seems to refer to the recitation of the Rosary] or perform other exercises of piety or recite prayers which, though they differ from the sacred rites, are still essentially in harmony with them."

Comment 6. Some differences between the Eucharist as a sacrament and as a sacrifice.

We mention three of the more important differences.

First, the Mass is transitory. It is essentially completed after the termination of the second formula of consecration. The sacrament is permanent and endures until the species are corrupted.

Second, the primary purpose of the Mass is to render adoration and glory to God. The sacrament aims primarily at the sanctification of the communicant.

Third, the Mass does not confer sanctifying grace *ex opere operato*, whereas the sacrament does.

To conclude our treatment of the Eucharist, we remind the student that it is intended not only to deepen his knowledge, but also to enhance his appreciation of both the sacrament and the sacrifice. The various Conclusions are subjects for thought, but also for prayer.

SECTION FIVE

The Sacrament of Penance

*

Section Five

THE SACRAMENT OF PENANCE

BAPTISM is "the first plank" flung to shipwrecked man to save him spiritually. If a man sins after his baptism, he has within reach "a second plank" which he can grasp to save himself again. This is the sacrament of penance.

We shall treat first of the existence, nature, and necessity of the power to forgive sins in this sacrament; second, of the acts of the penitent, contrition, confession, and willingness to make satisfaction, which compose its matter; third, of the sacrament's form; fourth, of its effects; finally, of its minister and recipient.

Conclusion 1. The apostles and their successors received from Christ the power to remit effectively all sins committed after baptism.

Introduction. This Conclusion is of the utmost importance because it is denied by non-Catholics generally. We say nothing at present about the *nature* of the power to forgive sins. Later on we shall prove that it involves the conferring of a special sacrament and the exercise of a judicial process. We simply assert the fact that Christ did empower the apostles and their successors to blot out sins in God's name.

Explanation of Terms

1. The apostles and their successors. We do not wish to specify which successors of the apostles possess this power. This point will be established in the final Conclusion. For the present it suffices to prove that this power was bestowed upon the apostles, not as private individuals, but as rulers of the Church. Accordingly, it must continue after their deaths.

2. From Christ. By His personal, direct action without any intermediary.

3. To remit sins effectively. This is the principal issue. To understand our meaning we must explain, first, the notion of sin; second, the significance of effective remission of sin. We deal directly with mortal sin only.

Mortal sin is the deliberate violation of a grave precept of God. We know these precepts either by God's direct revelation, or by natural law, or by the Church's legislation. In practice, they are proposed for our observance by the Church regardless of their source.

Every mortal sin has a twofold effect. First, by it the sinner incurs God's displeasure. This is called the personal guilt of sin. Second, the sinner becomes liable to punishments. He deserves eternal punishment because we know by God's revelation that this is the penalty which He has decreed for mortal sins. He also deserves temporal punishment because every sin disturbs to some degree the harmony of God's world.

Effective remission of sin means that the apostles and their successors were empowered as God's delegates to remove from the sinner God's displeasure, the danger of eternal damnation, and part, at least, of the temporal punishment due to sin.

Though God alone, since only He has been offended, has the right to remit sin, we say, nevertheless, that He has communicated this power to the apostles and their successors. God remains the principal agent in the forgiveness of sin, but He now acts through ministers chosen and authorized by Himself. When they forgive, He ratifies their verdict. They forgive just as truly as if God acted alone without their intervention. God virtually told the apostles and their successors: "Though I alone am offended by sin, yet I authorize you to act visibly for Me on earth.

If you forgive the sinner, I do also. I restore My friendship to him, I remove his liability to eternal punishment, and I take away at least a part of his temporal punishment."

Our meaning becomes plainer when we consider the opinions of some orthodox Protestants. According to them, sins are never really forgiven, but merely covered over, i.e., God will ignore them though they remain objectively. But even this masking of sin cannot be accomplished effectively by any intermediary. The sinner himself must do it by his own direct appeal to God. No human minister is necessary or even qualified. The most a human agent can do is to exhort the sinner to ask a quasi-forgiveness from God, or to inform him that God has granted him this quasi-forgiveness.

In such explanations it is evident that the human agent merely helps the sinner, or assures him that God has been merciful to him. The agent does not act for God by truly forgiving the sins.

4. All sins committed after baptism. Since all sins committed before baptism are remitted by this sacrament *ex opere operato,* it is plain that the present power is not concerned with them, but only with sins subsequent to baptism. Furthermore, we wish to prove that the apostles and their successors were delegated to forgive any sin, no matter how heinous.

Adversaries. Although certain heretics had from time to time tried to limit the power of the Church to forgive sins, the original Protestant dissenters, like Luther and Calvin, seem to have been the first to abolish this power altogether. Cf. Pohle-Preuss, *The Sacraments,* III, 21–23.

Dogmatic Note

It is of divine faith. After quoting the famous text from St. John's gospel, which we shall cite below, the Council of Trent (DB. 894; CT. 788) declares that the meaning of the text is very plain, and that by it "the Fathers have unanimously understood that the power to remit and retain sins . . . was communicated to the apostles and their legitimate successors." Cf. also DB. 913; CT. 802.

Proof 2. From Holy Scripture. The power to say Mass and to remit sins are the two transcendent powers of the Catholic priesthood. In His goodness God saw to it that both the promise and the actual conferring of these powers would be recorded in Scripture. We have two distinct proofs.

First, the power to forgive sins was promised to the apostles and their successors. Speaking to Peter alone, Christ says (Matt. 16:19): "And whatsoever thou shalt bind upon earth, it shall be bound also in heaven: and whatsoever thou shalt loose on earth, it shall be loosed also in heaven." Sometime later when speaking to all the apostles including Peter, Christ says (Matt. 18:18): "Amen I say to you, whatsoever you shall bind upon earth, shall be bound also in heaven: and whatsoever you shall loose upon earth, shall be loosed also in heaven."

It is dogmatically certain from Trent (DB. 902, 920; CT. 795, 809) that the second text means that Christ promised to the apostles and their successors the power to forgive sins. Apologetically, our argument is very probable. The argument follows in form.

By these words the power to remove all obstacles to eternal life was given by Christ to Peter, to all the apostles with Peter, to their successors;

But the power to forgive sins is a power to remove an obstacle to eternal life:

Therefore, the power to forgive sins was given by Christ to Peter, to the apostles with Peter, to their successors.

Proof for the major. The primary purpose of the Church is to lead men to eternal life. Whatever prevents the attainment of this purpose can be loosed by Peter and by the apostles with Peter. Moreover, God ratifies their act of loosing. Furthermore, Christ includes the successors of Peter because He addresses Peter, not as a private individual, but as the rock or foundation of the Church. He also includes the successors of the other apostles because he speaks to the apostles as rulers of the Church. In fact, they are, with Peter, the "Church" (v. 17). This point is also clear from the fact that the substantial powers conferred by Christ upon Peter and the apostles were to be transmitted to their successors (Matt. 28:20).

Proof for the minor. Mortal sin is the chief obstacle to eternal life. If the apostles had been given the power merely to declare that sins are remitted or to exhort sinners to seek a quasi-forgiveness from God, they would not truly "loose" them.

Second, Christ actually conferred the power to forgive sins on the evening of His resurrection (John 20:21-23): "He [the Lord] said therefore to them: Peace be to you. As the Father hath sent Me, I also send you. When He had said this, He breathed on them; and He said to them: Receive ye the Holy Ghost. Whose sins you shall forgive, they are forgiven them; and whose sins you shall retain, they are retained."

The Council of Trent (DB. 894, 913; CT. 788, 802) has defined that our Conclusion is contained in these verses. Apologetically, the proof is probable. We shall explain in order how the various elements of the Conclusion are exhibited in the text.

First, Christ is speaking to the apostles only. This is not perfectly clear from the text or context. The word "disciples" is used throughout (vv. 19, 20, 25, 26). This word may refer to the apostles only, but it can also include others.

Nevertheless, that only the apostles were included on this occasion may be shown with some probability from verses 24, 25 where Thomas is called "one of the twelve" and seems to be contrasted with the rest of the apostles who, notwithstanding, are called disciples in verse 25.

However, to make this point more probable apologetically, we must go outside this passage and we argue as follows. First, since the promise of this power was clearly bestowed upon the apostles alone, the actual conferring of it must have been upon them alone.

Again, in verse 21 of our text Christ says: "I also send you." We know, however, from other passages of Scripture (e.g., Matt. 28:18) that only the apostles were authorized to evangelize the world.

Furthermore, the powers to say Mass, to confirm, to ordain, to give extreme unction were bestowed upon the apostles only. Hence we may reasonably infer that the sublime power to forgive sins was also granted to them alone.

Finally, the power given in our text is judicial and so should be reserved to a limited number of men.

All these reasons taken together are sufficient to show that the power to forgive sins was not granted to all the faithful, but only to the rulers of the Church.

Second, Christ on this occasion spoke to the apostles as rulers of the Church, not as private individuals. Consequently, the power did not cease with their deaths, but was handed down to their successors.

This is clear for three reasons. First, by saying to the apostles, "As the Father hath sent Me, I also send you," Christ makes it plain that He is addressing them as officials of the Church. He speaks to them inasmuch as they are "sent," i.e., inasmuch as they are to carry out His mission as the superiors in the Church.

Again, the purpose for which this power was given, namely, to remit sins, will remain until the end of time. Christ Himself foretold that sinners would always be present within the Church (Matt. 13:47–50; 24–30). It would be peculiar reasoning to say that Christ wanted the early Christians to have their sins remitted by the apostles, but that their successors could not forgive the sins committed by Christians of the following centuries.

Finally, if this power is not perpetual, then neither should the other powers conferred upon the apostles be perpetual. The Eucharist, extreme unction, confirmation should all have ceased when the apostles died.

Third, Christ gave the power to remit sins effectively. This is the most important part of the argument. It is established as follows. First, the very expression, "to forgive sins," which is found in the text, obviously means a genuine forgiveness. But we do not forgive another person an offense, unless we truly cancel the state of unfriendliness (the personal guilt) which resulted from it. So our Lord meant that the apostles and their successors would truly remove the discord (the personal offense) between God and the sinner: ". . . they are forgiven them."

Moreover, in Scripture the expression, "to remit sins," means to take away their personal guilt, to remit them truly. This is evident from various texts (e.g., Mark 2:1–12).

Again, Christ said: "As the Father hath sent Me, I also send you." We know, however, that a part of the mission of Christ as man was to remit sins effectively, as is clear from Mark 2:1–12. Since He transmits to the apostles His own power, they, too, should remit sins in very truth.

Besides, our Lord breathed upon the apostles and said: "Receive ye the Holy Ghost." This statement indicates that they are to blot out sins effectively because they receive the power of the Holy Ghost who is God. They are to be the agents of God.

Finally, this solemn passage would be meaningless if the apostles were merely designated to inform the sinner that God would mask his sins, or to preach to sinners in order to enliven their confidence in God's mercy. The apostles had previously received the faculty to preach, and they would have needed a special revelation (nowhere promised in Scripture) to know that God was ignoring the offenses of a sinner.

Fourth, the text refers to postbaptismal sins for these reasons. First, baptism could be conferred only once, whereas the power granted in this passage is not so restricted. It is indefinite: "Whose sins you shall forgive." Therefore, it can be exercised repeatedly.

Besides, baptism is a mere washing in the name of the Blessed Trinity. But the power here given is judicial, as we shall prove later, and so the rite is entirely different from that of baptism.

Furthermore, judicial power can be exercised upon those only who are already subjects of a society. But it is by baptism that people become subjects of the Catholic Church. Hence this power is to be wielded over those who have already been baptized.

Fifth, the text includes any kind of postbaptismal sin, regardless of its enormity, because "sins" in the text are in no way restricted.

Proof 3. From the Fathers. St. Cyprian made the following celebrated statement: "May each one individually, beloved brethren, heed my request to confess his sins, while he who has sinned still remains in this world, while his confession can be accepted, while penance and *absolution granted by the priest* are acceptable to the Lord" (*De Lapsis,* 29; PL. IV, 488).

In the *Constitutiones Apostolorum* ("Apostolic Constitutions"), which was written sometime between 350–400, we find the following prayer occurring at the consecration of a bishop: "Grant him, almighty God, through Christ, a sharing in the Holy Spirit so that he may have the power to remit sins as You have commanded, to confer orders in accordance with Your precept, to loose all bonds in conformity with the power which You gave to the apostles" (Bk. 8, Chap. 5, n. 7; RJ. 1234).

St. Pacian (fourth century), answering the objection that God alone can remit sins, declares: "True enough, but what He does through His priests, is an exercise of His own power. What else does He mean when He says to His apostles: 'Whatsoever you bind upon earth. . . .'? Why did He say this if priests are not permitted to bind or loose men?" (*Epist.* 1, 6; PL. XIII, 1057).

For additional quotations consult Pohle-Preuss, *The Sacraments,* III, 26–34.

Proof 4. From reasons of suitability. These, of course, are not offered as solid proofs, but they throw light on the reasons why God conferred on mere men the tremendous power to forgive or to retain sins in His name.

First, by sin a man subjects himself to some creature or other. To obtain forgiveness, therefore, it seems reasonable to expect that God would wish the sinner to subject himself to another creature, namely, a confessor.

Again, since God bestowed upon the Church the powers of giving, conserving, and increasing our supernatural life, it seems reasonable to expect that He would give her also the power to restore this life if it is lost by sin.

Besides, it seems to be consonant with God's mercy that He would have established a means of forgiveness which would give visible assurance to sorrowful sinners that they are forgiven. No such assurance would be had if a sinner could only appeal directly to God.

OBJECTIONS

1. Christ would not have instituted a power which incites people to sin. But that is what happens if Christ gave men the power to remit sin. The Catholic who is tempted to sin says to himself: "I may as well commit the sin. I can go to confession in a few days and have it forgiven."

Answer. This is a quite common objection among non-Catholics, especially Protestants. It proceeds largely from lack of knowledge about the nature of the sacrament.

First, this sacrament is effective for only those sinners who are truly repentant and who are determined not to sin again. This resolution, fortified as it is by many actual graces flowing from the sacrament, prevents the commission of many sins. Hence the sacrament does not induce to sin, but helps to avoid it.

Then, too, a man must humble himself in order to go to confession, if he is guilty of serious sins. Such humility is a help for the avoidance of future sins.

Besides, the Catholic way of remitting sins is certainly much more difficult than the orthodox Protestant way. According to some Protestants sins are masked from God's sight by acts of confidence privately expressed to God. No confession, no satisfaction are required. It probably would be true to say that this manner of covering sins really does incite a person to commit future sins.

Again, what would these objectors recommend to the sinner? Would they tell him that he cannot be forgiven at all and so lead him to despair? Any power is open to abuse, but the power to remit sins, which has been given to priests by Christ Himself, is less open to it than most other powers.

Finally, it is a fact of experience that penitents gradually overcome their sins by frequent recourse to the sacrament. Sinners who continue in their bad habits and make no sincere repentance usually quit going to confession entirely. This is a fact and it proves that the sacrament of penance is a deterrent to sin.

2. In Matt. 18:15–18 there is question only of faults against fraternal charity. These faults are sins, but the text does not view them as such. It is concerned with only the external harmony of members of the Church, not with the reconciliation of sinners with God.

Answer. It is true that the power to forgive sins which was conferred upon the apostles in this passage was occasioned by our Lord's instruction about fraternal correction. But this instruction was merely an *occasion* for teaching the doctrine of remission of sins by the apostles. In verse 18 Christ declares that whatever the apostles loose upon earth is loosed in heaven also. "Whatever" certainly includes sins precisely as offenses against God, because sins are the most formidable obstacle to salvation. Furthermore, these sins are remitted by God also, since they are "loosed in heaven."

3. In the same passage of St. Matthew the word, "church," simply means the community of the faithful. Hence no special power is granted to the apostles only.

Answer. One might conclude from the general progression of the verses that the "church" means the entire community of believers. First, an offended person is to admonish the offender privately (v. 15). If this fails, he is to give the admonition in the presence of "one or two more" (v. 16). If this correction is unsuccessful, he is to "tell the church" (v. 17).

However, if we connect verse 17 with 18, we see at once that the "church" does not mean the entire community, but the apostles only. "Church" is explained in verse 18 when Christ says: "Whatever *you* bind. . . ." *You* means the apostles alone because Christ is speaking to them only. Although St. Matthew (18:1) mentions merely the "disciples," the parallel passage of St. Mark (9:34) reveals that Christ was addressing the apostles alone: ". . . He called the *twelve*."

It should also be noted that in practice it would be almost impossible for corrections to be administered by the entire community. Frictions, more or less serious, are daily occurrences among the faithful. The community would be constantly busy trying to settle disputes. Consequently, even those non-Catholics who hold that "church" means the whole body of believers do not try to carry out our Lord's command and so fail to live up to their interpretation of Scripture.

4. The text from John 20:23 is referred by some of the Fathers to baptism. Therefore, it does not pertain to the remission of post-baptismal sins.

Answer. Most of the Fathers do not even mention baptism when they interpret this text. They refer it to the forgiveness of sins committed after baptism.

A few do say that the text pertains to baptism, but they do not deny that it also refers to penance. It is not an error to say that the text can be interpreted secondarily about baptism. Sins are remitted by baptism, but only those committed before it is received.

5. St. John's words simply mean that the apostles are to preach God's revelation and so stir up confidence in their hearers, who will then have their sins removed.

Answer. This interpretation is so opposed to the plain meaning of the text that it does not even deserve an answer. If we begin to interpret Scripture so arbitrarily, it will have no meaning at all.

6. We read (Matt. 12:32: ". . . he that shall speak against the Holy Ghost, it shall not be forgiven him, neither in this world,

nor in the world to come." According to this the apostles were not empowered to forgive all kinds of sins.

Answer. The entire context beginning from verse 22 should be read. Christ is not denying that any sin, no matter how objectively heinous, can be forgiven. From the context he evidently means that the subjective dispositions of some sinners are so unfavorable that they will not repent and seek forgiveness from God's ministers. No sin is forgiven unless the sinner is truly sorry. The priest can absolve from any kind of sin when the penitent has contrition.

7. Various texts (Heb. 6:4–6; 10:26; I John 5:16) show that some sins cannot be forgiven.

Answer. These texts merely mean that certain most grievous sins cannot be forgiven because of the faulty dispositions of the sinner. They do not deny that the apostles had the power to forgive them.

*

Conclusion 2. The efficacious forgiveness of sins which Christ instituted involves the exercise of judicial power.

Introduction. We have just proved that the apostles and their successors have been empowered to effectively forgive sins. So far, however, we have said nothing about the nature of this power and the manner in which it is to be exercised. We shall explain this in the present and the following Conclusions. At present we wish primarily to exclude the notion that our Lord wanted postbaptismal sins remitted in the same way that sins are forgiven by baptism.

To obtain forgiveness by baptism, an adult must have attrition and at least implicit faith and hope. But he has no obligation to tell his sins, no matter how many or how serious they may be. If, however, we show that our Lord instituted penance as a judicial process, it follows that the sinner who approaches this sacrament must also make a confession of his sins. Hence forgiveness by penance is more burdensome for the sinner than forgiveness by baptism.

Explanation of Terms

1. Judicial power. We are all acquainted in a general way with a judicial process. It means that someone is accused of violating a law. He is apprehended and brought to trial. Evidence is accumulated for and against him, usually through the testimony of other people and sometimes of his own. After weighing the evidence, the judge pronounces a verdict of guilty or not guilty.

Judicial power, therefore, is a public and two-edged power to pass a binding sentence upon an accused person. In exercising his power the judge is obliged to keep within the confines of law imposed upon him by the higher authority in whose name he judges, and also to weigh the circumstances and the degree of responsibility of the accused person. We shall now explain in greater detail our definition of judicial power.

First, it is a public power. The judge does not act in a personal capacity, but as the authorized representative of society. He may, for instance, have certain personal knowledge that an accused person is guilty of the alleged crime, but he may not use this knowledge. He is limited to the use of knowledge which he acquires in his official capacity.

Second, it is a two-edged power. This means that the verdict of the judge can be either of two possibilities. He may acquit or condemn. It should be noted, too, that either of these verdicts is of a positive nature. The judge may express himself in a negative way when an accused person is acquitted, by saying, "Not guilty," but this actually means: "I free you from the charge." A positive effect results because the accused person escapes any penalty and must be legally considered as innocent.

Moreover, judicial power involves the passing of a binding sentence. The judge is not merely an arbitrator, or an adviser, or a conciliator, whose recommendations may be ignored. No, a judge effectually settles the case. If an appeal is made to a higher court, the sentence of the lower court binds until the future verdict is rendered.

Again, the person hailed into court must be accused of the violation of some law. It does not follow that the person is guilty. Accused, yes, but perhaps innocent.

Furthermore, the judge is restricted in exercising his power by the regulations of the society for which he acts. Many restrictions are imposed, especially in criminal courts. Definite procedures must be adopted, prescribed ways of obtaining testimony observed, and defined penalties inflicted if the accused is found guilty. If the judge fails to conform to these regulations, his verdict is invalid. He has acted in a personal capacity, not as a representative of the society.

Finally, the judge must take into account all the circumstances, especially the degree of responsibility of the accused. This is required by natural law. Murder committed by a drunken man is not as culpable as murder committed by one whose reason is functioning clearly. By weighing all the circumstances the judge is helped to determine the degree of responsibility and so to pronounce a just sentence.

The Conclusion, therefore, means that the priest is truly a judge when he deals with sinners in the sacrament of penance. Yet, as we shall explain in a Comment, striking differences exist between the confessor and the judge in our secular, criminal courts.

Adversaries. Since Protestants in general deny the existence of the sacrament of penance, they reject this Conclusion also.

Dogmatic Note

This teaching is of divine faith from the Council of Trent (DB. 919; CT. 808): "If anyone says that the sacramental absolution of the priest is not a judicial act . . . let him be anathema." Cf. also DB. 895, 899, 902; CT. 789, 793, 795.

Proof 2. From Holy Scripture (John 20:21–23). These verses were quoted in the preceding Conclusion. It is dogmatically certain, apologetically very probable, that the essential elements of judicial power are contained in this passage. We shall now show how these elements, as they are expressed in our definition of judicial power, are found in these verses.

First, they signify that a *public* power is conferred. We have already treated of this in the preceding Conclusion. We recall that our Lord speaks to the apostles as rulers of the Church: "As the Father hath sent Me, I also send you." Besides, since the power is to endure permanently, it must have been given to the society, not to individuals in the society. Individuals die after comparatively few years, but societies remain. The apostles, therefore, did not as individuals or as private persons receive delegated power to forgive sins.

Second, the power granted is *two-edged*. Our Lord gave the apostles the faculty either to forgive or to retain sins. It is evident that the forgiving of sins is an act of positive power since it brings about renewed friendship with God, infuses grace, and liberates from the liability to eternal punishment.

It is more difficult to show that our Lord bestowed a positive power when He told the apostles that they could retain sins. To be such, this retention must produce some positive effect. It cannot be merely a refusal to use the power to forgive. Both acquittal and condemnation must be positive in order to have true judicial power.

That our Lord meant the power of retaining sins to be a positive power can be proved as follows.

First, the Greek word used in the original text is "kratein." This word signifies a positive exercise of power.

Again, the best apologetic proof is derived from a comparison of St. John's text with the parallel text of St. Matthew (18:18): "Whatsoever you shall bind upon earth, shall be bound also in heaven; and whatsoever you shall loose upon earth, shall be loosed also in heaven."

In St. John "forgive" is equated with "loose" in St. Matthew. So, too, is "retain" in St. John equated with "bind" in St. Matthew. However, the word, "bind," whether taken literally or metaphorically, means that a positive effect is accomplished. It demands that the binder actually do something to the person or thing to be bound. Since, therefore, "retain" in St. John is the equivalent of "bind" in St. Matthew, "retain" must signify a positive exercise of power.

Third, the apostles are to remit sins *effectively*. This is true because our Lord attaches no condition to His statements: ". . . they [sins] are forgiven them"; ". . . they [sins] are retained."

Moreover, the apostles are sent with the same power which Christ Himself had: "As the Father hath sent Me, I also send you." But Christ efficaciously remitted sins.

Finally, according to St. Matthew (18:18) the verdict of the apostles, whether it be to bind or to loose, is ratified in heaven, i.e., by God Himself.

Fourth, in dealing with sinners the apostles must keep within the confines of law imposed by Christ. This is true because they are to act in God's name. Their power is from the Holy Ghost. Hence, as will be proved in detail in subsequent Conclusions, the apostles must obtain a confession from the sinner, be certain that he is repentant, and impose a satisfaction or penance upon him. These requirements proceed from divine law. The Church, too, may prescribe certain norms for the confessor because he acts in her name also, when he hears confessions.

Fifth, the priest must weigh the sinner's circumstances and his degree of responsibility. This is demanded by the natural law itself and so we are certain that Christ intended it when he delegated the apostles to forgive sins. Our Lord never contradicted the natural law.

Proof 3. From the Fathers. St. John Chrysostom says: "For the judge [the priest] sits upon earth; the Lord follows him; and whatever the priest judges here on earth, the Lord ratifies in heaven" (*De Verb. Is.,* Hom. 5, n. 1; PG. 56, 130).

St. Jerome is also explicit: "Bishops, having as they do the keys to the kingdom of heaven, pass judgment, so to speak, before the day of judgment" (*Epist. 14 ad Heliod.,* n. 8; PL. 22, 352).

For additional quotations confer Pohle-Preuss, *The Sacraments,* III, 69, 70.

Proof 4. From reasons of suitability. First, it is reasonable to expect that forgiveness of sins committed after baptism would be more burdensome for the sinner, because these sins are of greater guilt than those committed before baptism. By baptism a man receives actual graces which, supposing his cooperation, enable him to avoid all mortal sin. He rejects these graces when he sins after baptism.

Then, too, the obligation to confess sins is a deterrent to the commission of future sins, since confession of sins to a fellow man is difficult for human nature.

Objections

1. It is not an exercise of judicial power when a priest retains sins by refusing to baptize an applicant. But he acts in the same way when he denies absolution to a penitent. Therefore, no strictly judicial power enters into the sacrament of penance.

Answer. No society can exercise judicial power over those who are not subject to it. The unbaptized are not subjects of the Catholic Church and so the Church cannot pass strict judgment upon them. But she can and does exercise her judicial power over baptized penitents when they confess their sins.

If a man fails to obtain baptism for some reason or other, he is still bound by God's universal law, which requires that baptism be received for the remission of sins committed previously to its reception. However, when a priest refuses absolution, a penitent is bound not only by God's general law which prescribes that all postbaptismal sins be declared in the sacrament of penance, but also by a *new title,* namely, by the fact that his sins have been submitted to an authorized priest who, as God's and the Church's representative, has bound the sinner to his sins.

Furthermore, baptism cannot be a judicial act because it is possible for some of its recipients to be without any serious sins of their own. Hence baptism is not always conferred upon "accused persons," an essential element of a judicial act. Babies never have any personal sins when they are baptized. Yet they obtain grace and the minister cannot hinder it. Even some adults may come to baptism without having any grievous sins on their souls. They may not be "accused persons."

Finally, the objection makes an imperfect analogy. Refusal of absolution is not an exact parallel with refusal to baptize. Refusal to hear a person's confession is the equivalent of refusing to baptize. When a priest refuses to hear a confession, he refrains from exercising his judicial power to forgive or to retain sins. He passes no verdict at all upon the applicant. He may be so busy preparing a talk which must be delivered within half an hour that he simply cannot take time to hear a confession. He makes no judgment upon the sinner.

2. When a man is found guilty in a criminal court, he is punished according to the gravity of his crime and its circumstances.

But in the sacrament of penance the priest simply forgives the man even though he is guilty of the greatest crimes, provided, of course, that the sinner has the requisite dispositions. So the priest does not exercise genuine judicial power in the confessional.

Answer. True judicial power consists in the fact that a judge can either acquit or condemn an accused person. This power is always verified in the confessional. The priest can either absolve or condemn the sinner, though he is bound in conscience to absolve if the sinner is properly disposed.

Again, the priest is obliged to impose a penance upon the sinner. This penance is *vindictive,* i.e., to punish the offender, though it has other purposes also.

The criminal court looks to the good of society in condemning criminals. They must not be allowed to roam at large lest others be harmed. The judicial court of the sacrament looks primarily to the good of the individual.

3. But no matter how guilty a man may be, he comes forth from the sacrament liberated from his crimes if he has confessed properly. On the other hand, a robber does not come forth innocent when he is condemned by a criminal court. He is stained by his crimes and punished for them. Hence true judicial power is not exercised by priests in the confessional.

Answer. The main purpose of the sacrament is to forgive. The main purpose of the criminal court is to condemn. But in both courts the verdict can be either condemnation or acquittal, and so the essential nature of a judicial process is verified in both.

The criminal court is concerned with the external forum only, with the external administration of justice. But the sacrament deals with the internal forum, with man's relationship to God.

4. Some of the Fathers say that the confessor is a doctor or a physician. Doctors and physicians do not use judicial power.

Answer. The priest according to these Fathers is, first of all, a judge, but, secondarily, a physician. He must advise penitents in order to cure their bad habits. The priest in the confessional is judge, teacher, physician, and father.

Comment 1. The confessor has other duties besides those of a judge.

In connection with our answer to the last objection, it should be remembered that it would be a mistake to consider the confessor as a judge only. If we were to do this, confession might become repugnant.

The confessor is a teacher also. As such he should correct erroneous consciences, inculcate the true meaning of sin, offer guidance for future conduct.

The confessor is likewise a doctor or physician who should solicitously try to help the sinner to throw off the disease of sin.

But the confessor is above all a father, who during the entire confession should radiate kindness, realizing that he himself is a sinner; never acting as though he personally had been offended by the sins of the penitent.

Comment 2. Some differences between the sacramental court and a secular, criminal court.

Important differences exist between them and they should be pondered by the student.

First, the secular judge acts in the name of the state only. But the confessor acts in the name of God by the sanctifying power which he receives at ordination, and also in the name of the Church from which he obtains jurisdiction or faculties.

Again, the principal object of the secular judge is to condemn the accused person. No one would ordinarily be brought to trial unless there were some evidence against him. However, the principal object of the confessor is to forgive the accused person.

Then, too, the secular judge is bound to punish the accused if he is found guilty, whereas the confessor is bound to forgive the penitent, no matter how guilty he is, if he is properly disposed.

Moreover, the secular judge acts primarily for the good of society. The confessor acts primarily for the good of the sinner himself.

Noteworthy, too, is the fact that the secular judge, when he acquits, can make the accused *legally* just only. As a matter of fact, the accused may be guilty, but is acquitted through some defect in the evidence or the court procedure. Nevertheless, he must be regarded externally as innocent. On the other hand, the confessor actually makes the sinner innocent again. The sinner is not only to be *considered* innocent when he has the required dispositions and is absolved, but he is innocent in fact. His sins are forgiven.

Again, the secular judge obtains his evidence occasionally from the accused, but usually from other witnesses. The confessor obtains evidence from the sinner alone.

Besides, the secular judge deals with crime as an offense against the state, whereas the confessor deals with it as an offense against God, a sin.

Furthermore, the secular judge does not deal with purely internal offenses against the state, such as evil thoughts or desires against some law or other. However, the confessor must pass judgment on man's purely mental and volitional activity when it freely opposes God's laws.

The verdict of the secular judge depends solely on the answers to two questions: Did the accused really commit the crime? If he did, how responsible was he? Besides the answers to these two questions, the confessor must obtain an answer to a third: Is the sinner sorry for his sins? The secular judge is not allowed to acquit a criminal, no matter how sorry the latter may be for his crime.

Then, too, the penalty inflicted by the secular judge is primarily vindictive. The penance imposed by the confessor is primarily intended to atone for the offenses against God, and, secondarily, to cure the sinner for the future, to take away his temporal punishment, and to punish him. Consequently, a murderer whose crime has been forgiven in the sacrament may still be hanged by the state.

Lastly, the sentence of the secular judge becomes publicly known. But the sentence of the confessor, whether it be absolution or retention, is a secret which he may not under any circumstances divulge.

Comment 3. Refusing absolution.

When a confessor retains sins, he exercises his judicial power, but he does not confer the sacrament. No grace is given to the sinner.

Even when he absolves, the confessor uses his binding power because he is obliged to assign some satisfaction or penance to the sinner.

When a penitent has only venial sins to confess, the confessor cannot use his retaining power in its strict meaning. If he should refuse absolution for such sins (an impractical supposition), the sinner may obtain their remission in other ways.

If a confessor is obligated to retain mortal sins (which rarely happens), he will ordinarily tell the sinner: "I cannot give you absolution." This statement would seem to mean merely that he cannot use his power to absolve. If this were the meaning in fact, his retaining power would be purely negative, a nonuse of the power to absolve. From the nature of judicial power, however, we know that his act of retention must produce a positive effect in the sinner. What is this positive effect?

First, the sinner departs from the confessional bearing a new obligation to return to the confessional at some future time. Of course, the sinner already has this obligation by reason of the fact that mortal sins can be forgiven by confession only. But now that his case has been heard, he has an *additional* obligation to come back.

It happens quite often in other matters that a person may have a twofold obligation to perform one and the same action. For instance, a man by natural law is obliged to support his children. If he is delinquent in this, a new duty to support them may be imposed upon him by a secular judge before whom he is brought to trial. Similarly, a Catholic is obliged by general Church law to attend Mass on Sundays. A fresh obligation to do this may be imposed on him because attendance at a Sunday Mass may be given him as a penance in confession.

Second, a sinner is not refused absolution unless he lacks some essential disposition for reception of the sacrament. For example, he may be unwilling to avoid some proximate occasion of serious sin when he could easily do so. Consequently, it is doubtful if his sorrow is genuine. Now it is God's law, and natural law also, that he must avoid occasions of mortal sin when possible. But if absolution is denied him, he is obliged to avoid these occasions from an additional source, from the fact, namely, that the confessor as God's representative has imposed upon him the duty of avoiding such occasions before absolution can be granted.

Denial of absolution does, therefore, produce a positive effect in the sinner.

*

Conclusion 3. Penance is a sacrament.

Introduction. So far we have learned that the confessor efficaciously remits sin; also that this remission is not accomplished solely by him because penance is a judicial process which, as such, requires a confession from the sinner. Moreover, the sinner must have sorrow for his offenses and a resolution to avoid all future sins.

But from these truths an apparent contradiction arises. Since the sinner must confess and be sorry, it seems as though the forgiveness of his sins results from the value of his own acts so that the confessor's absolution is not truly efficacious. Accordingly, the grace infused when sins are forgiven might seem to be earned *ex opere operantis* by the penitent. If this were true, penance would not be a sacrament because every sacrament confers grace *ex opere operato*.

Explanation of Terms

Penance is a sacrament which, by means of certain acts of the penitent and by the absolution of a qualified priest, forgives post-baptismal sins.

Adversaries. Protestants in general deny that penance is a sacrament. A few Protestant ministers encourage their people to confess their sins, but with a view to consoling and advising them, not to forgiving their sins. The Ritualists or High Church Anglicans regard penance as a sacrament, but they deny its necessity for the forgiveness of mortal sins.

Dogmatic Note

This is part of our Catholic faith. The Council of Trent (DB. 911; CT. 800) declares: "If anyone says that in the Catholic Church penance is not truly and properly a sacrament, instituted by Christ our Lord for reconciling the faithful to God as often as they fall into sin after baptism, let him be anathema." The same truth is defined in DB. 844; CT. 665.

Proof 2. From Holy Scripture (John 20:21–23). Dogmatically, it is of faith from Trent (DB. 913; CT. 802) that these verses prove penance to be a sacrament. Apologetically, the proof is very probable.

We find our definition of a sacrament verified in these verses.

First, we can reason to a perceptible sign. Since penance involves a judicial process, it requires an external accusation or confession from the sinner, and also a perceptible verdict from the confessor.

Moreover, unless sinners externally reveal their sins, a confessor could never know which men were sinners, which were not.

Furthermore, unless the confessor outwardly informs a sinner that he is forgiven, a sinner could never know this fact, so important for his eternal salvation.

Finally, our Lord Himself forgave sinners in a perceptible manner (Mark 2:1-12). Since He conferred absolving power upon the apostles and their successors, we would expect them also to remit sins perceptibly.

Second, sanctifying grace is signified and conferred when a priest remits sins. When mortal sins are forgiven, grace is always infused into the soul. Accordingly, grace must be given when a priest as judge forgives sins. It should be remembered that this grace is increased when only venial sins are confessed.

Third, this grace results not only from the confession and sorrow of the penitent (*ex opere operantis*), but primarily from the priestly absolution (*ex opere operato*). This is true because we have previously seen that the words, "Whose sins you shall forgive, they are forgiven them," necessarily mean an efficacious forgiveness. Hence it is the confessor who truly remits sins when he declares: "I absolve you from your sins. . . ." This would not be so if the grace were to come solely from the acts of the penitent.

Besides, we have already proved from this same passage of St. John that penance is a judicial process. But in every such process it is the verdict of the judge which is the most efficacious element. He decides the case. He acquits or condemns and his verdict is effectual. Since, therefore, the absolving priest is a judge, it follows that his absolution is the principal factor in the forgiveness, and so in the infusion of grace which accomplishes this forgiveness.

Furthermore, it is particularly clear that grace is produced *ex opere operato* when a serious sinner comes to confession with attrition only, as often happens. Attrition (often called imperfect contrition) is not sufficient outside the sacrament to remit grave sins. But it is sufficient, as we shall prove later, in the sacrament. Since this is true, it is evident that the grace bestowed upon a serious sinner by the sacrament does not come from his attrition alone.

Fourth, penance was instituted by Christ. It was on this occasion particularly (DB. 894; CT. 788) that our Lord instituted this sacrament. The fact is evident apologetically from the words which our Lord used in the passage.

Fifth, Christ wanted this sacrament to last until the end of time. Our Lord Himself foretold (Matt. 13:41, 49) that sinners would ever be present within the Church. Hence the main purpose of the sacrament, the remission of sins, will always remain.

Moreover, it would be unreasonable to say that our Lord wished the sins of the first Christians forgiven, but not those of later Christians.

Besides, Christ addressed the apostles, as we have seen, not as individuals in a private capacity, but as rulers of the Church. Since the Church is to last until the end of the world, it will always have rulers who will possess the powers given to the apostles in the beginning.

Proof 3. From the Fathers. Since the Fathers taught that the ministers of penance truly forgive sins, as we have shown in Conclusion 1, they implicitly teach that the grace flowing from this forgiveness is owing mainly to the act of the minister, not to the acts of the penitent. We repeat here the famous quotation from St. Cyprian: "Beloved brethren, I ask each of you to confess his sins while he is still alive in this world, while his confession can be heard, while his atonement and *forgiveness granted by a* priest are acceptable to the Lord" (*De Lapsis,* 29; RJ. 553).

OBJECTIONS

1. A sacrament must have a uniform matter and form. This is not true of penance. If the priest absolves, he says: "I absolve you from your sins." If he does not absolve, he says: "I cannot give you absolution," or "I must compel you to return after you have decided to avoid that occasion of sin," or something similar. Therefore, penance has more than one form.

Answer. This difficulty falsely supposes that the sacrament is administered when a confessor retains sins. Only when sins are forgiven is the sacrament conferred.

By definition a sacrament is intended to produce grace, but no grace is produced when a confessor refuses absolution. Although the power of the keys is both a judicial and a sacramental power, the two are not coextensive. The judicial power is of wider scope than the sacramental. The one true form of the sacrament consists of the words: "I absolve you from your sins. . . ."

2. Our Lord says (John 20:21): "As the Father hath sent Me, I also send you." Now Christ was sent to forgive sins, but not by way of a sacrament. Since the apostles are sent as Christ was sent, priests should not forgive sins by conferring a sacrament.

Answer. It is evident from the text that our Lord simply means that He is bestowing on the apostles the power to forgive sins which He as man had received from the Father. He is not telling them in this verse how they will exercise this prerogative. But He does so implicitly in verse 23.

3. The apostles preached the same kind of repentance which the prophets taught in the Old Testament. But this repentance was not part of a sacrament and so penance in the New Testament is not a sacrament.

Answer. The virtue and act of repentance or contrition have always been and will always remain the same. Both the prophets and the apostles preached the same kind of virtue and the same kind of act of contrition.

But Christ told the apostles that they were to act as judges when dealing with postbaptismal sins, and so He implicitly told them that they were to place an outward sign, a verdict, which would signify and confer grace. In the Old Testament serious sins were remitted by perfect contrition only.

*

Conclusion 4. The sacrament of penance is necessary by hypothetical necessity of means in order that a man who has sinned seriously after his baptism can save his soul.

Introduction. All the sacraments are ordained to man's salvation, but they vary in the kind of necessity by which they are required for this purpose. We learned previously that baptism is necessary by hypothetical or relative necessity of means for all men, even infants, in order that they can be saved. We now say that penance is necessary by the same kind of necessity for one who has sinned mortally after baptism.

Explanation of Terms

1. The sacrament of penance. This Conclusion must be distinguished carefully from a later one which treats of the necessity of confession. We deal here, not with confession alone, but with the whole sacrament, i.e., with the absolution of the priest conjoined with the penitent's contrition, confession, and willingness to make satisfaction.

Furthermore, in the coming Conclusion we shall consider confession from the single aspect of its necessity in order to have the *sacrament.* We are now concerned with the necessity of the *whole* sacrament in its relationship to the *eternal salvation* of a baptized sinner.

2. By hypothetical necessity of means. This was explained under the necessity of baptism. The duty of the baptized sinner to receive the sacrament of penance is not only commanded by God, but it is ontologically required for salvation. For such a person the sacrament is the only ordinary means of salvation.

If, however, it is impossible for him to receive the sacrament, he can use a substitute, an extraordinary means, which must include a desire, at least implicit, of going to the sacrament.

Two of these possible substitutes are the same as in the case of baptism, namely, the act of perfect love or contrition and martyrdom. But for penance we have a third substitute, the sacrament of extreme unction. Whenever any one of these substitutes is used, the sinner must, if possible, have recourse later to the sacrament of penance.

Adversaries. All Protestants, even the Ritualists, deny the necessity of this sacrament.

Dogmatic Note

It is implicitly of divine faith from the Council of Trent (DB. 895; CT. 789): "This sacrament of penance is necessary unto salvation for those who have fallen after baptism, as baptism itself is necessary for those who have not yet been regenerated." Since the council (DB. 796; CT. 560) had previously defined implicitly that baptism is necessary for salvation by hypothetical necessity of means, it follows that penance has the same necessity.

Proof 2. From Holy Scripture (John 20:23). From these verses we form the following syllogism.

Any means of forgiveness which would make useless the priest's power to retain sins is not independent of the sacrament;

But the act of perfect contrition is a means of forgiveness which would make useless the priest's power to retain sins:

Therefore, the act of perfect contrition is not independent of the sacrament.

Proof for the major. Notice that we speak only of the power to *retain* sins. Christ bestowed this power on the apostles and their successors. It cannot, therefore, be rendered ineffectual.

Proof for the minor. This power to retain sins would be rendered useless if the act of perfect contrition were completely independent of the sacrament. Let us take a specific case. A baptized Catholic has committed murder. He now repents and wants forgiveness. Let us suppose that he is perfectly free either to make an act of perfect contrition or to go to the sacrament. He decides upon the latter. But the confessor discovers that the penitent is unwilling to make any restitution to the family of the murdered man, though he could easily do so. In this event, the confessor must refuse absolution. He binds the homicide to his sin until he is willing to make restitution.

If, however, the act of perfect contrition were entirely independent of the sacrament, the murderer could ignore the binding power of the priest. He could simply leave the confessional and make an act of perfect contrition. Thus he would make ineffectual the verdict which retained his sin.

It follows, accordingly, that once a grave sinner has had his sins retained by the refusal of absolution, he cannot obtain forgiveness by an act of perfect contrition which would not include a sincere resolve to return to the confessional. If he could, the priest's judicial act of retention would be made useless, not binding.

Since, therefore, the act of perfect contrition is not independent of the sacrament *after* a sinner has tried to obtain sacramental forgiveness and failed, it follows that the same act was not independent of the sacrament even *before* he approached it.

Common sense tells us that when we have two or more independent means of attaining some objective, we do not lose our right to use the others because one has failed. A man can go to his place of work in his own car or by taxi or by tram or by walking. If his own car breaks down, he is perfectly free to use one of the other means. But if a sinner approaches the sacrament of penance and it "breaks down" for him, he is not free to make an act of perfect contrition independent of the sacrament. Consequently, he was not free beforehand to choose either the act of perfect contrition or the sacrament. He could, of course, make an act of perfect contrition, but he is obliged to go to the sacrament later.

Proof 3. From the Fathers. One excellent quotation from St. Augustine will suffice. He says: "Let no one say: 'I do penance secretly. I deal with God. God who pardons knows that I repent interiorly.' Was it then said uselessly: 'What you loose on earth, will be loosed in heaven?' Were, therefore, the keys given to the Church in vain? Do we void the gospel? Do we void the words of Christ? Do we promise ourselves what He denies us? Are we not deceiving ourselves?" (*Sermo* 392, 3; PL. XXXIX, 1711).

Proof 4. From theological reasoning. These arguments merely corroborate our other proofs.

First, the sacrament of penance would be widely neglected if the act of perfect contrition were entirely independent of it. It is easy to speak interiorly to God about one's serious infidelities, but it is difficult to divulge them to a fellow man. Christ certainly did not want this sublime sacrament neglected.

Second, when criminals are apprehended by the state, they are not free to handle their case as they choose. They must go before the tribunal established by the state to deal with their specific crime. Similarly, Christ established but one tribunal in his state or kingdom, the Catholic Church. Therefore, sinners must appear before this tribunal.

OBJECTIONS

1. Under the Old Law sinners could be saved by making an act of perfect contrition. Now they must go to the sacrament of penance. Therefore, salvation is more difficult under the New Law.

Answer. In some ways salvation is more difficult under the New Law than under the Old. However, this is not true in the present instance. Sinners can still be saved by the act of perfect contrition. They are, of course, obliged to confess later, but if they cannot do so, they are saved anyhow. Hence the objection has no force.

In addition, it might be well to note the following observations. It is easier now to make an act of perfect contrition than it was under the Old Law. Grace is more abundant, and we always have the picture of Christ dying on the cross for our sins, a picture which makes it easy for us to be perfectly sorry for our sins.

Again, extreme unction is administered regularly today and takes away all sins if the recipient has only imperfect contrition and cannot confess. Extreme unction did not exist under the Old Law.

Besides, only imperfect contrition is required for the sacrament of penance, so that a lesser disposition is now sufficient for the remission of mortal sins.

Furthermore, the sacrament bestows many actual graces which, if he uses them, will keep the penitent from future falls. Consequently, the need of repentance is not as widespread today as it was under the Old Law.

Finally, the penitent of today has greater certitude of forgiveness when he goes to the sacrament. He does not have to be sure that he has made an act of perfect contrition. He has a reasonable assurance that he has succeeded in making an act of supernatural sorrow of some kind.

2. Confession was not so necessary in the early centuries of the Church, because at that time only bishops heard confessions. Many grave sinners must not have gone to confession at all. There were not enough ministers of the sacrament.

Answer. Bishops were proportionately much more numerous in the early days. Many tiny villages had them. On the other hand, sinners were relatively fewer owing to the intense fervor of the early Church.

Besides, at that time venial sins were not submitted to the keys. How many confessions would be eliminated today if only serious sinners went to the sacrament?

Finally, in the third century when many Catholics defected because of persecution, priests were also appointed to hear confessions. Hence we may infer that, at least in cases of necessity, they had been appointed in earlier times.

Comment 1. How Protestants can have their postbaptismal sins remitted.

They can do so by making an act of perfect love or contrition. This act, however, must include, at least implicitly, a desire to do whatever God has commanded them. Thus it includes an implicit willingness to go to the sacrament of penance.

Comment 2. The act of perfect contrition made by a Catholic sinner.

When a Catholic commits a mortal sin, he should make an act of perfect contrition as soon as possible. His sins are forgiven by this act at once, but he must tell his sins the next time that he goes to the sacrament of penance. In the meantime, he is not allowed to receive Holy Communion. To receive Communion the serious sinner is obliged under pain of mortal sin to go to the sacrament of penance beforehand.

Conclusion 5. In order to be saved a person who has committed a mortal sin must make an act of contrition.

Introduction. We now come to consider what most theologians call the matter of the sacrament of penance. This consists of the acts of contrition, confession, and satisfaction made by the penitent. We treat here of contrition, the first of these acts.

However, before we deal with the kind of contrition needed in the sacrament, it will be profitable to explain the nature and necessity of contrition in general. In this Conclusion, therefore, we are not speaking of the sacrament. We simply say that some kind of act of contrition (whether perfect or imperfect we do not determine here) must be made by every person who has sinned grievously in order to attain salvation.

Explanation of Terms

1. In order to be saved. To obtain the beatific vision, man's supernatural destiny.

2. A person who has committed a mortal sin. Hence we speak of adults only. We should not make an act of contrition for original sin. But every adult sinner of whatever race or time (no exceptions are made) must make such an act for his personal mortal sins. Otherwise he cannot be saved.

3. Must. The necessity of such an act is not only of precept, but also of means. Moreover, this necessity of means is absolute, not merely relative or hypothetical. No substitute for the act of contrition is available.

4. Act of contrition. The virtue of contrition is a permanent disposition of soul. Since the virtue is not required, we shall not explain it.

The act, then, of contrition is a free decision involving a detestation and grief for sins committed and also a determination not to sin again. This important definition will now be explained.

The act of contrition contains a *detestation* of sin. This detestation is an act of the will which aims at the past sinful thoughts, words, deeds, or omissions. In practice it means that the sinner must retract his past sins. He must say to himself: "I wish that I had not committed them."

There must also be *grief* for sins. This act of the will is directed at the state of enmity with God which results from sinful actions. Though sins may have been committed long ago, their effects remain with us until we repent. Until then, we are still at odds with God. In practice we have the necessary grief if we sincerely wish to throw off this effect which our sins have caused.

It is not required that the acts of detestation and of grief be made distinctly in the act of contrition. If a sinner really detests his sins, he implicitly grieves over them; if he truly grieves over their effects, he implicitly wishes that he had not committed them and so he detests them.

Contrition requires, too, a *determination not to sin again*. This act of the will is a resolution to avoid all mortal sins and to take the necessary means to this end. A feeling of weakness, or a realization from past experience that one is very likely to sin again, does not vitiate one's determination. If a man truly grieves over his sins, he has implicitly a resolution not to sin again. However, the sinner should make his resolution or purpose of amendment explicitly.

Four qualities must permeate the act of contrition. They must affect all three constituents of the act, the detestation, the grief, the determination not to sin again.

First, the contrition must be *internal*. This means that it must be sincere. Mere external sorrow or "crocodile tears" not based upon acts of mind and will are mere hypocrisy.

Again, contrition must be *supernatural*. It must be inspired by actual grace and based on a motive accepted by faith. We can be sure that, if our motive is based on faith, our repentance is actuated by God's grace, since God is always willing to help the sinner to return to His friendship. Only very rarely can we be certain that grace is the cause of our conscious inspirations.

A motive based on faith is founded on God's revelation. For instance, we know by faith that hell exists for the unrepentant sinner. If, therefore, a sinner repents from the motive of fear of hell, his motive is supernatural.

A motive accepted by faith can be known also by reason and yet be sufficient for contrition. For example, we can prove by reason that we must be obedient to God's commands. But we know this also by revelation and so by faith. If, then, a sinner repents because he has disobeyed God Who has revealed that all men must be obedient to Him, his contrition is supernatural.

This supernatural motive must animate the detestation, the grief, the purpose of amendment.

Though the motive must be supernatural, natural motives are not thereby excluded. Indeed, natural motives often impel the sinner to think about the waywardness of his life and so prepare the way for repentance. A drunkard, for instance, may sorrow over his sins of gluttony because by them he has lost his employment, or his money, or his reputation, or the affection of his family and friends, or because drunkenness ill becomes a rational being.

These are natural motives and by themselves never suffice to win forgiveness. But they humble a man and make him reflect, and so create a disposition of soul in which God's grace and the inspirations of faith can operate more easily.

Third, contrition must be *universal* in the sense that it must embrace all mortal sins. As regards the detestation and grief, the sinner must be sorry for every single mortal sin whatever that he has actually committed. However, concerning the purpose of amendment, he must resolve not only never again to commit the specific sins of which he has been guilty, but also never to commit any kind of mortal sin. If our home were set on fire deliberately by a friend, we would not consider him truly sorry if he said to us: "I am sorry for having set fire to your house and I will pay the damages and never set fire to your house again. But I may slander you to your neighbors."

Lastly, our contrition must be *sovereign*. "Sovereign" is used here in a technical and unusual meaning, but it seems to be the best English word for the purpose. It conveys two ideas with regard to contrition. First, it signifies that the sinner, appraising mortal sin as the greatest of all evils, detests it, grieves over it, and resolves not to commit it again. It is not required that the sinner make any comparisons. He should not, for example, ask himself whether he considers his mortal sins as a greater evil than the loss of his life or his wealth. In practice his sorrow is sovereign if he is firmly resolved not to sin in the future. He will prefer God to any personal satisfaction which might come to him from sinning.

It is important to observe, secondly, that this quality of contrition does not demand any special intensity of feeling. It must reside in the *will*. Feelings of sorrow are praiseworthy and are an accidental perfection of contrition if they result from our internal acts of mind and will. But sorrow can be genuine even though we do not feel it. It could be genuine even despite the fact that we *feel* a physical attraction to sin at the very time when we are making our act of contrition. This should be remembered. If a man is told by his doctor that one glass of whiskey will kill him, he will be firmly resolved not to take whiskey even though he still feels strongly attracted to it.

Contrition also includes a willingness to make amends, to do penance. If the sinner is baptized, it also includes, at least implicitly, a desire to go to the sacrament of penance.

There are two kinds of contrition, perfect and imperfect.

Imperfect contrition or attrition. This proceeds from some supernatural motive which is of lesser dignity than God's own personal goodness. We shall deal explicitly with attrition in the following Conclusion.

Perfect contrition. Its motive is founded on God's own personal goodness, not merely on His goodness to me or to humanity. Since the use of the act of perfect contrition is of great consequence, we shall make a few observations concerning it.

Catholics should make an act of perfect contrition after they commit a mortal sin, even before they go to confession. When they receive the sacrament, they should try to have perfect contrition, though it is not necessary. If a sinner is dying and cannot go to confession, he can save his soul by an act of perfect contrition which includes the desire to confess.

The act of perfect contrition is distinguished from attrition by its motive, not by intensity of feelings or anything else.

Again, an act of perfect contrition requires no great length of time. It could be made in one second.

Noteworthy, too, is the fact that the perfect love for God which motivates perfect contrition does not necessarily exclude attachment to venial sin. Venial sin conflicts with a high degree of perfect love for God, but not with the substance of that love.

In the act of perfect contrition other motives can coexist with the perfect love required. It would be a mistake to think that gratitude to God, humble subjection to Him, fear of hell, would have to be eliminated at the time when an act of perfect contrition is made.

Two considerations can particularly help us to attain to the perfect love required for this act. First, we should reflect on Christ dead on the cross. We know that He died for each one of us, for me. So it is easy to repent of sins by the imperfect motive of gratitude to Him. But I know also that Christ died for all men. How good, then, must He be in Himself. If I repent of my sins because our Lord is so good in Himself that He died for everybody, I have made an act of perfect contrition.

We should also ponder God's goodness as manifested by His

gifts. He has been very good to me. If for this reason I am sorry for my sins, I have imperfect contrition. However, if I reflect further that God has been good to everyone, that He never does anything that is not for the true good of men, it should be easy for me to realize how good He is in Himself. If, then, I repent of my sins because God is so good and generous in Himself, I make an act of perfect contrition.

Perhaps the following illustration will clarify the act of perfect contrition. A son takes his father's car some evening against his father's express command. Moreover, the son, driving recklessly, wrecks the car. He returns home genuinely repentant. He tells his father: "Dad, I am sorry for having disobeyed you and wrecked your car because I owe you so much and because I disobeyed your orders. I'm sorry, too, because I know that you have a right to punish me. But I'm particularly sorry because I offended your own good self." If I repent of my sins because I have offended God's "own good Self," I have perfect contrition.

Is it very difficult to make the act of perfect contrition? Evidently the Church does not think that it is difficult for *Catholics* to do so. She permits a Catholic who is in mortal sin to receive the sacraments of confirmation, extreme unction, orders, and matrimony without first going to confession provided that the person makes an act of perfect contrition. She recommends, of course, that serious sinners go to confession beforehand if possible, but she does not order it.

It is only for the reception of Holy Communion that she obliges the sinner to go to confession. Since the Church must be vigilant so that sacraments will be received not only validly, but also fruitfully, she apparently believes that the act of perfect contrition is easy to make. Otherwise we would be commanded, if we are in the state of mortal sin, to go to confession before receiving the four sacraments of the living mentioned above.

The following act of contrition should be memorized. It contains all the necessary elements which we have explained.

"Oh, my God, I am heartily sorry for having offended Thee, and I detest all my sins because I dread the loss of heaven and the pains of hell. But most of all, because they have offended Thee, my good God, who are all good and deserving of all my love. I firmly resolve with the help of Thy grace to confess my sins, to do penance, and to amend my life. Amen."

The Conclusion has three parts.

First, in order to be saved a sinner must make an act of contrition by necessity of precept.

Second, he must do so by necessity of means.

Third, he must do so by absolute necessity of means. No substitute is available under any circumstances.

Adversaries. Many Protestants do not have a proper concept of contrition. They believe that confidence in Christ and recollection of baptism are sufficient to cover over one's sins.

Dogmatic Note

The first part is implicitly of faith. The Council of Trent (DB. 894; CT. 788) declares that "to obtain grace and justification repentance was necessary at all periods of history for all men who stained themselves with some mortal sin." Accordingly, God must have at least commanded contrition.

That contrition is necessary by necessity of means is definable teaching, though not actually defined. In the preceding quotation from Trent, it is stated that repentance was required "at all periods of history" (*quovis tempore*). Therefore, it was required before God revealed any divine positive laws. It is objectively necessary for man's salvation.

It is Catholic doctrine that this necessity is absolute, not relative or hypothetical.

We shall prove all three parts simultaneously.

Proof 2. From Holy Scripture (Ps. 50:4, 5, 19; Ecclus. 2:22; Jer. 18:8; Ezech. 18:30; 33:8, 9, 12–16; Matt. 3:2, 8; Luke 5:32; 13:3, 15:18; 24:47; Acts 2:38; 3:19; II Pet. 3:9). There are many other texts also. They teach the same lesson. Sin will be forgiven to those who do penance; it will not be forgiven to those who omit penance. ". . . but unless you shall do penance, you shall all likewise perish" (Luke 13:3). This is the gist of all the Scripture texts.

It is evident, then, that God has commanded sinners to do penance in order to save their souls. But from the frequency of the texts and the unanimity of their teaching we can also reasonably conclude that contrition is necessary by necessity of means and by absolute necessity of means. Not a single text even intimates that a sinner's obligation to do penance ceases if he labors under some difficulty. We should, however, expect to find excusing causes mentioned somewhere if the necessity for penance were of precept only. Hence the necessity is of means.

Furthermore, this necessity of means is absolute. If any substitute were available to the sinner, God would certainly have mentioned it in at least one of His frequent references to the necessity of penance. Yet we look in vain for any substitute. One thing, and one thing only, is exacted of the sinner—repentance. Nothing can take its place in any circumstances.

Proof 3. From the Fathers. Some of the Fathers (St. Ambrose, St. Pacian, Tertullian) wrote entire books to inculcate the absolute need of contrition on the part of sinners.

St. Ambrose declares: "Sin is not taken away except by the tears of repentance" (*Epist.* 51, 11; PL. XVI, 1162).

St. Gregory the Great testifies: "The 'wrath to come' is the infliction of final punishment. This the sinner will not evade unless he now has recourse to penitential lamentations" (*In Evan.,* Hom. 20, 7; PL. LXXVI, 1163).

Objections

1. God as supreme Ruler can forgive sins without repentance. So it is false to say that contrition is required from every serious sinner.

Answer. We have proved that every sinner must repent under pain of eternal damnation. This is God's will. God possibly could have decided otherwise, but since He has not, the grave sinner must repent. God who has enacted this rigid decree always gives sufficient grace so that the sinner can be sorry.

2. Both Holy Writ (e.g., Tob. 4:11) and the Fathers often attribute remission of sins to acts of fraternal charity or to some other virtuous act that is not repentance. Hence contrition is not necessary.

Answer. Scripture and the Fathers merely mean that certain acts of virtue are remote dispositions by reason of which God will give grace to the sinner so that he can repent of his sins.

3. An act of perfect love always remits sins. But an act of love is not an act of perfect contrition.

Answer. The act of perfect love is not always an explicit act of sorrow for sin, but it is so implicitly. If the sinner when eliciting an act of perfect love thinks of his sins, he will certainly be sorry for them. No friend can make an act of perfect love for his friend without repenting of past infidelities not yet forgiven.

The acts of perfect love and of perfect contrition are substantially the same. Both forgive all mortal sins. If a sinner does not happen to think about his sinful condition, he will make an act of perfect love. If he is conscious of his sins, he will make an act of perfect contrition.

It should be noted that the act of perfect love, though it always remits serious sins, is not a sufficient disposition for the sacrament of penance. For this sacrament contrition as such is necessary. Hence the penitent must have either attrition or perfect contrition.

*

Conclusion 6. In the sacrament of penance attrition suffices for the forgiveness of mortal sins.

Introduction. We have just learned that God never forgives mortal sins unless the sinner makes an act of contrition, either perfect or imperfect. It follows, then, that, since sins are remitted by the sacrament of penance, the penitent must have at least imperfect contrition or attrition.

We now inquire whether attrition is enough for sacramental forgiveness. We answer that it is, and so perfect contrition is not demanded of the penitent. It is laudable, however, for penitents to make an act of perfect contrition before they approach the sacrament.

Explanation of Terms

1. Attrition. This is the only term that needs clarification. Attrition is sorrow for sin animated by a supernatural motive that is inferior to perfect love for God.

Some of the motives which suffice for attrition are the following: fear of incurring the sense torments of hell; fear of losing the sense joys of heaven; fear of being punished by God in this life because of one's sins; fear of judgment, either the particular or the general judgment; the disobedience to God involved in sin; the ingratitude to God manifested by sin; the loss of merit resulting from sin; the loss of one's divine adoption or of sanctifying grace.

It should be emphasized again that all these motives must be supernatural, i.e., based on faith, on God's revelation. A sinner might repent because he knows by reason alone that his sins were acts of disobedience or of ingratitude to God. Such sorrow would not be supernatural.

We know by God's revelation, as well as by reason, that sin is an act of ingratitude and of disobedience. Attrition elicited from these motives must be based on revelation. Similarly a man may be sorry for his sins because they prevent him from going to Communion with the rest of his family. This would be a natural motive. But if he repents because he cannot receive the spiritual benefits of Communion, his attrition is supernatural.

As we mentioned before, people are often sorry for their sins because of some worthy natural motive, e.g., because they have lost their money, or their health, or their job, or their friends, or their reputation, or because of the natural indecency involved in sin. These motives are helpful, but they are not enough. Only supernatural attrition suffices for the sacrament.

Fear of the sense torments of hell is a common supernatural motive for sorrow for sin, but it must be correctly understood. Its object is the sensible punishments of hell, not the loss of God (pain of loss), which is the severest suffering of the damned. If a sinner repented because of the consideration that he would have lost God forever had he died in his sins, he has perfect sorrow.

Again, the sinner should not be terrorized by the thought of the sense punishments of hell. Rational fear is enough. Terror would be harmful. Furthermore, the sinner must fear hell, but he must not detest it. He should consider it as the just retribution which God threatens to impose for each mortal sin. Fearing this just retribution, the sinner detests his *sins*, and firmly resolves never to sin again. To detest hell itself while remaining attached to one's sins would not be sorrow at all, and would indeed indicate an unbalanced personality.

The fear motive is under attack today from some psychologists. Common sense teaches how ridiculous is this attack. Every time a man carries an umbrella, or takes medicine, or gets out of a draught, he is motivated by reasonable fear for his health. A large number of our everyday actions are inspired by some kind of legitimate fear.

Martin Luther, Baius, the Jansenists, the Synod of Pistoia, and others declared that attrition animated by fear of the sensible torments of hell is wicked. This assertion was condemned as heretical by Trent (DB. 915, 898; CT. 804, 792). Christ Himself approved this kind of attrition when He said (Matt. 10:28): "Fear Him who can cast both soul and body into hell."

It is also noteworthy that for remission of sins in the sacrament of penance attrition must be accompanied by hope of forgiveness. But this act of hope is implicitly contained in the act of attrition. By coming to the sacrament in a spirit of attrition, the sinner evidently hopes to be forgiven. Otherwise he would not receive the sacrament at all.

Adversaries. A few of the early scholastic theologians seem to have believed that perfect contrition was required for the fruitful reception of the sacrament of penance. This opinion is not heretical, but it cannot be, and is not, defended today by anyone.

Dogmatic Note

This teaching is Catholic doctrine. It is derived in different ways from the Council of Trent (DB. 896–98; CT. 790–92), but we shall explain the two simplest arguments only. For the first we need the last reference alone (DB. 898; CT. 792).

Towards the close of this paragraph the council says: "Therefore, certain men falsely slander Catholic writers as though these taught that the sacrament of penance confers grace without a good act on the part of the recipients (*absque bono motu suscipientium*). . . ."

The council, accordingly, states that the sacrament is fruitfully received by those who elicit a "good act." But what is this good act?

In the preceding sentences of the paragraph the council has divided contrition into perfect and imperfect. It has also described imperfect contrition. It says that this kind of sorrow is praiseworthy, that it is "a gift of God and an inspiration of the Holy Ghost."

However, any act of virtue that is a gift of God and an inspiration of the Holy Ghost is a good act. Hence when the council declares that penance gives grace to those who elicit a good act, it must mean that attrition is enough.

We know, too, from the Council of Trent (DB. 896; CT. 790) that the primary purpose of this sacrament is to reconcile the sinner with God (*reconciliatio est cum Deo*). But the sacrament would never obtain this effect if perfect contrition were required for its reception. The sinner would be reconciled with God before he received the sacrament. God, however, would have acted irrationally, had He determined forgiveness as the primary effect of the sacrament and at the same time had postulated a condition (perfect contrition) which would make it impossible for the sacrament ever to attain its primary objective. Therefore, attrition suffices for the sacrament.

Proof 2. From the practice of the Church. When preaching, priests exhort sinners to repent from motives of attrition only. Confessors give absolution daily to sinners who have attrition alone. The Church could not tolerate these practices unless it were certain that attrition is enough for the sacrament. The Church may not tolerate the doubtful administration of sacraments.

OBJECTIONS

1. Attrition which is motivated by fear of sensible punishments is nothing but self-love. Self-love, however, is bad and so attrition is bad.

Answer. Properly regulated self-love is a good thing. In fact, it is commanded by God when He says: "Love thy neighbor as *thyself.*" Attrition prompted by rational fear of hell is properly regulated self-love. Christ ordered us to cultivate it: "Fear Him who can cast both soul and body into hell."

2. If a man is sorry for his sins solely because he fears hell, he really does not repent of his sins. He would commit the sins again if the penalty of hell were removed. Consequently, attrition of this kind is to be rejected.

Answer. We know that the penalty of hell is not going to be removed. Since this is so, a sinner can truly repent of his sins owing to this motive. Perhaps if he existed in some other hypothetical world where hell was not a future retribution for wrongdoing, he might commit sins. But he does not exist there.

3. Nevertheless, the sinner who repents through fear of hell solely, does not detest sin above all other evils. He detests hell more than he detests sin. So this kind of attrition is not to be approved.

Answer. This difficulty proceeds from a misunderstanding of repentance motivated by fear of hell. A man who uses this motive does not detest hell at all. He *fears* hell, realizing at the same time that the fact of its existence is salutary for him while he lives in this world. Moved by this rational fear, he *detests* his past sins and resolves not to sin again. He determines to sacrifice any sinful good which might accrue to him in this world rather than to incur the danger of hell fire.

4. Enlightened people today are never actuated by fear. So fear of hell cannot be a part of Christianity.

Answer. Even enlightened people today are constantly acting through fear. Why do they pay attention to traffic lights if they are not moved by fear of accident or arrest?

5. St. John says (I John 4:18): "Fear is not in charity: but perfect charity casteth out fear. . . ." Therefore, fear of hell is rejected.

Answer. St. John concludes the same verse by saying: "He that feareth is not *perfected* in charity." In other words, once a man is motivated by perfect love, his fear of hell will pass into the background, but it will not be forgotten. Fear is good, but charity is better. This is all that St. John means, and, in fact, is all that he says.

6. St. Paul says (I Cor. 13:2): "If I have not charity, I am nothing." Therefore, fear of hell must be motivated at least partially by charity.

Answer. St. Paul is not speaking of repentance in this sentence. He is extolling charity in general in the entire passage. He means that, if a man does not have the *virtue* of charity and, consequently, sanctifying grace, he is of no supernatural worth in God's sight. No matter what good works a man does, they are not meritorious for heaven unless he possesses the virtue of charity.

Comment 1. The meaning of two expressions in Trent.

The council states that attrition can be motivated "by a consideration of the baseness of sin" (DB. 898; CT. 792), or by consideration of the "foulness" of sin (DB. 915; CT. 804).

The council does not mean that mere natural sorrow proceeding from a realization of the indecency of sin as something opposed to man's natural dignity is sufficient for attrition. It means that sin involves baseness and foulness because it involves disrespect, disobedience, and ingratitude to God. Hence these motives, as proposed by Trent, are supernatural.

Comment 2. Can this sacrament be valid, but unfruitful?

A few theologians of distinction hold that penance can be valid and yet unfruitful. If they are right, the sacrament can in certain circumstances revive and bestow its grace later on when the recipient becomes disposed.

To defend their opinion, these men offer two examples. The first is that of a penitent whose motive for attrition is not sufficiently universal to include all his mortal sins. If a penitent has committed sins both of theft and of perjury, he might in good faith think that he is sorry for both sins even though his motive for attrition is prompted solely by the consideration of God's attribute of infinite truthfulness. This motive does not cover the sin of theft. In this event, since the sinner is in good faith, the sacrament would be valid, but it would not give grace until he afterwards made an act of attrition of sufficient universality.

In the other case, these theologians think that the quality of sovereignness might not be sufficiently accomplished in the act of attrition. The sinner would honestly think that he detests sin more than any other evil, but in reality he does not. Since he is in good faith and is resolved not to sin again, he has attrition, but its quality is sufficient for validity only, not for obtaining grace here and now from the sacrament. If the penitent afterwards raises the quality of his attrition so that he does in fact detest sin above every other evil, he will have his sins removed and receive grace *ex opere operato*.

We cannot share this minority opinion for various reasons.

First, since such penitents would usually go to Holy Communion after being absolved, they would receive this sacrament while they are, though unknowingly, in the state of mortal sin. There is a material or involuntary irreverence in this that we do not believe God would allow to happen so frequently.

Moreover, these communicants would more probably be forever deprived of the graces flowing *ex opere operato* from their Communion, because, as we have seen earlier, the Eucharist does not revive. It is more probable that Communion, when received by a sinner who is attrite and in good faith, produces first grace and removes even mortal sins. But in the two instances cited by these theologians, the sinner does not verify both conditions when he receives Communion. He is in good faith and so does not commit a sacrilege. But he is not sufficiently attrite. If his attrition was incapable of disposing him to obtain grace from the sacrament of penance, neither does it dispose him to receive grace from Communion.

Second, this opinion would be a source of scruples to many people. Who can be certain that he truly detests sin more than any other possible evil that might befall him? Indeed, this opinion seems to make it imperative for the sinner to make comparisons between his hatred for sin and his attractions for personal, sinful satisfactions. This would result in constant worry and would even discourage some sinners from going to confession.

Third, in practice confessors grant absolution to sinners who simply promise to try honestly to avoid mortal sin in the future. Confessors, however, could not do this unless such a resolution were sufficient to obtain grace from the sacrament. The ministers of sacraments are obliged to take care that sacraments are received not only validly, but also fruitfully.

It is true, of course, that the penitent's attrition must be universal. Attrition induced by a consideration of but one of God's attributes does not cover sins which offend against some other attribute. All the motives for attrition which we have cited in the Conclusion are universal. In fact, attrition prompted by only one of God's attributes is so rare that it hardly merits practical consideration. If the penitent does not elicit an act of attrition which embraces all his mortal sins, his good faith preserves him from making a sacrilegious confession, but he more probably does not receive the sacrament at all.

Comment 3. The fear of the sensible pains of hell, even when not accompanied by any incipient act of love for God, is a sufficient motive for attrition.

A few theologians since Trent have contended that attrition, motivated solely by fear, is not sufficient for the sacrament of penance. They do not believe that the sinner is properly disposed unless his fear of hell is also motivated by an imperfect love (*amor initialis*) for God. They support their opinion by recourse to Trent (DB. 798; CT. 562) where the council, when describing the preliminaries of justification, says that sinners "begin to love God as the fount of all justice, and on that account are stirred by a kind of hatred and detestation for their sins. . . ."

In answer to this objection we say:

First, it is arbitrary to transfer to the sacrament of penance this statement from a decree on justification in general. The council may intend to include extra-sacramental, i.e., neither by baptism nor by penance, justification in its decree.

Moreover, the council does not say that all the mentioned preparatory acts are *necessary* before justification. This incipient love could very well be something which is often realized, but which is not necessary.

Furthermore, the statement of the council is verified even in the case of a penitent who has attrition based only on fear of hell, because objectively he wants to be set right with God, to be united with Him. Included in his one act of attrition is an incipient love for God, because he detests sin and is resolved to keep God's laws in the future.

Again, the reasonable way to find out what kind of attrition the council requires for the sacrament of penance is to examine the passage in which it directly discusses attrition. In this passage (DB. 898; CT. 792) the council does not mention a necessity for any kind of love. It declares that attrition which proceeds from fear of hell and punishments and contains a resolve not to sin again and a hope of pardon, is sufficient. Hence no subjective act of incipient love for God is required.

Besides, if this inchoate love were necessary, confessors would be obliged to find out if penitents have it. Since this is not done in practice, no incipient love is necessary.

Finally, the few authors who defend the need of this love do not agree in explaining it. All the explanations are vague.

*

Conclusion 7. To receive the sacrament of penance some kind of external confession must be made by the sinner. Normally this external confession must be objectively complete, but sometimes a subjectively complete confession suffices.

Introduction. When a sinner comes to the sacrament of penance, he must have contrition for his sins. We now say that he must also confess them. Confession forms part of the matter of this sacrament and so we logically treat of it here.

Explanation of Terms

1. Confession. It is the voluntary accusation of one's sins to a qualified priest in order to obtain absolution from him.

2. Some kind of external confession. We do not specify in the first part of the Conclusion the kind of external confession required. This is done in the second part. For the present we merely exclude the idea that a purely internal desire to make a confession would be enough to receive the sacrament.

3. Must be made by the sinner. Some kind of external confession of sins is necessary by absolute necessity of means. Nothing else under any circumstances can substitute for it.

4. To receive the sacrament of penance. We are not speaking about the necessity of an external confession in order to save one's soul, but in order to receive the sacrament. We have already discussed in Conclusion 4 the necessity of the sacrament as a whole in order that a baptized sinner may be saved. For the sake of clarity we shall throughout this Conclusion use the word, "confession," to designate only that part of the sacrament which involves the accusation of one's sins. When we refer to the whole sacrament, we shall say "the sacrament of penance."

5. An objectively complete confession. We deal with mortal sins only. A confession is objectively complete if the sinner confesses every single mortal sin according to number and kinds which he has committed since his last worthy reception of the sacrament of penance.

6. Normally a confession must be objectively complete. "Normally" means that an objectively complete confession is the sole ordinary way of obtaining forgiveness in the sacrament. It is necessary by hypothetical necessity of means.

7. A subjectively complete confession. This is had when a sinner accuses himself of all his mortal sins in so far as he is able to do so. Sometimes a man will forget one of his mortal sins when he confesses. If this happens, the forgotten sin is forgiven indirectly by the absolution, but the sin must be told in the next reception of the sacrament.

Other causes, too, can prevent a sinner from telling all his mortal sins in his confession. He might be semi-conscious so that he can only strike his breast or nod his head to manifest externally that he is a sinner. Even so, his unmentioned sins are remitted, but they must be confessed, if possible, in a later reception of the sacrament.

Only the deliberate concealment of a mortal sin in one's confession makes the sacrament invalid and sacrilegious. If this is done, all mortal sins committed, beginning with and including those of the sacrilegious confession, must be repeated in order that a subsequent reception of the sacrament can be valid.

8. Sometimes a subjectively complete confession suffices. This kind of confession is an extraordinary way of obtaining absolution. It can be used only when the ordinary way, the objectively complete confession, cannot be adopted. Even then, the sinner must desire to make an objectively complete confession. Therefore, "sometimes" means in extraordinary circumstances.

In these circumstances the subjectively complete confession can substitute for the objectively complete one, but there is no other substitute. Some kind of external confession must be made.

The two parts of the Conclusion are clear from its wording. First, unless a sinner manifests his grave sins externally by either an objectively or subjectively complete confession, he cannot receive the sacrament of penance.

Second, the objectively complete confession is the sole ordinary way of obtaining forgiveness in the sacrament, but in extraordinary circumstances the subjectively complete confession can substitute for it.

Adversaries. Besides the Protestants generally, Fr. Ballerini denied the first part. He held that an external confession is required by necessity of precept only. Hence, if an unconscious, dying man has only the intention of making a confession, he can receive the sacrament validly.

Dogmatic Note

It is Catholic doctrine that some kind of external confession is required with absolute necessity of means in order to receive the sacrament. The Council of Trent (DB. 896; CT. 790) says that confession is "a kind of matter" of this sacrament. An intention to make a confession (opinion of Fr. Ballerini) is not a confession.

Furthermore, in its entire discussion of confession the council (DB. 899–901, 914, 916–18; CT. 793, 794, 803, 805–07) makes it clear that it demands an external manifestation of sins.

Finally and most important, it is of faith from Trent (DB. 919; CT. 808) that this sacrament involves a judicial process. Reason teaches that such a process is impossible without some kind of external accusation of guilt.

It seems to be of faith, and is at least Catholic doctrine, that an objectively complete confession is required by hypothetical necessity of means in order to receive the sacrament. Trent (DB. 899; CT. 793) says that sins are to be confessed "specifically and one by one."

At the same time the council (DB. 899, 900, 917; CT. 793, 794, 806) in three distinct places makes room for a subjectively complete confession to supply for an objectively complete one when the latter is impossible owing to a defect of memory. Hence in this extraordinary circumstance the subjectively complete confession suffices. It is the common and certain teaching of theologians that this kind of confession also suffices in other extraordinary circumstances.

Part 1. To receive the sacrament of penance some kind of external confession must be made by the sinner.

Proof 2. From Holy Scripture (John 20:23). We are familiar with this text. From it we have previously proved that this sacrament is essentially a judicial process. It follows, then, with certainty that the offenses of the sinner must be externally manifested. A judicial process by its very nature deals with crimes and other violations of law. It cannot even be begun unless some accusation is externally made. Hence some kind of external confession must be made in the sacrament. The sinner alone can make this external accusation, because he alone knows his sins of thought and desire. Besides, only he knows the malicious extent of his outward sinful actions, since their malice depends upon his interior knowledge and consent.

Part 2. Normally this external confession must be objectively complete, but sometimes a subjectively complete confession suffices.

First, normally the confession must be objectively complete.

Proof 2. From theological reasoning. We have several reasons why under ordinary circumstances the sinner must confess all his mortal sins according to their number and their kinds.

Each mortal sin by itself is enough to require that a person go to the sacrament of penance. Hence, if a man sins seven times in the same way, or seven times in different ways, he should manifest all his sins. He is accomplishing in one reception of the sacrament what another person who committed the same number and kinds of sins, but who went to the sacrament after each one, would accomplish by several receptions of the sacrament.

Besides, each mortal sin destroys sanctifying grace. Consequently, if a man has committed several mortal sins, he should accuse himself of them all.

Again, it would be unreasonable to say that one theft is equal to ten thefts; or to try a man for theft, but not try him for murder if he has been guilty of both; or to say that assassinating the president is the same as killing an ordinary citizen. Even our secular, criminal courts investigate the number of crimes and their different kinds.

Moreover, generally speaking, the confessor should impose a penance proportionate to the number and kinds of sins committed. He cannot do this unless every mortal sin is revealed.

The confessor, too, as a physician and instructor cannot adequately help to cure the sinful maladies of the penitent unless sins are confessed according to number and kinds.

Finally and of great consequence, unless an objectively complete confession is made whenever possible, the penitent can easily lose his reverence for the sacrament. He might approach it without genuine sorrow for his sins. He would also sin more readily in the future. The obligation to tell one's mortal sins specifically and numerically is an effective deterrent to future sins.

Proof 3. From the Fathers. The following quotations show that an objectively complete confession was expected if possible.

St. Jerome, after declaring that the priests of the Old Law were enjoined to distinguish one leper from another, says: "So now [under the New Law] the bishop or priest binds or looses, not merely those who are innocent or guilty, but after having heard the *kinds of sins,* he knows in accordance with his office *who* should be bound or *who* loosed" (*In Matt.,* L. 3, chap. 16, n. 19; PL XXVI, 118).

St. Leo the Great indicates that sins were confessed individually when he writes: "With regard to penance, which is necessary for the faithful, do not allow a written confession of each individual sin to be read publicly, since it suffices to confess secretly to priests alone the guilt of one's conscience" (DB. 145).

All the Oriental schismatics agree that an objectively complete confession must be made if possible.

Nevertheless, it is clear from the constant practice and teaching of the Church that in unusual circumstances the subjectively complete confession can substitute for the objectively complete one. Hence if a dying sinner can do no more than say, "I have sinned," it is the regular practice to absolve him unconditionally. Our doctrine is proposed in catechisms, in books on theology, in sermons, and, as we have seen under the dogmatic note, in the Council of Trent itself.

This teaching is consonant with right reason. Let us assume that the objectively complete confession is so necessary that the subjectively complete one can never substitute for it. We might, then, have the following case actually verified. A Catholic man leads a dissolute life and commits countless mortal sins of many kinds, but at the age of thirty he is converted and lives the life of a saint until his death at the age of seventy. Since his sins have been committed after his baptism, he can have them remitted by the sacrament of penance only. But it is impossible for him to make an objectively complete confession. His mortal sins of thought, desire, and deed are so many that he cannot remember their exact number, nor can he even remember all their kinds.

This man, then, on the supposition that only an objectively complete confession suffices for the sacrament, has no hope of saving his soul despite his forty years of holy living. He cannot recall the exact number and kinds of his sins and so, according to the assumption, cannot receive the sacrament. Neither can he have his sins forgiven by an act of perfect contrition because this act entails, according to the supposition, a sincere intention to make an objectively complete confession in the sacrament. This he cannot intend because it is impossible for him. Hence he cannot be saved.

This conclusion, however, changes God into a tyrant and makes Him disregard the feebleness of the human faculties which He Himself has bestowed upon us.

Moreover, even in secular, criminal courts the judge or jury must often be content with an incomplete knowledge of the case. They do their best to penetrate the crime, but their best is frequently an inadequate knowledge. Yet, so long as they do obtain some substantial knowledge, their verdict is valid. But even so, their ideal always remains to obtain when possible a thorough knowledge of the case.

OBJECTIONS

1. Absolution is granted today to all dying Catholics, even if they make no confession at all. Therefore, no external confession is necessary.

Answer. Absolution is granted only conditionally when no external confession of any kind has been made.

However, we are justified in giving absolution conditionally to any dying Catholic. In such extraordinary circumstances it is possible that a groan, or a movement of the lips, or of the hands, might be an attempt on the person's part to confess. Even these slight external signs under those circumstances *might* be accepted by God as a subjectively complete confession.

2. A confessor can know that a penitent is worthy of absolution without hearing all his sins in detail. Hence an objectively complete confession is not required.

Answer. We have answered this objection in our proofs for the second part of the Conclusion. We merely add here that a confessor frequently would not know from a generic confession if a penitent is worthy of absolution. Quite a few sins, e.g., theft and slander, demand restitution. The confessor must decide whether restitution is necessary, how much is required, how it is to be carried out in practice. He cannot fulfill these duties unless he knows the sins in detail.

3. If a penitent forgets to confess a mortal sin in the sacrament, the sin is forgiven anyway. So it is not necessary to confess all mortal sins.

Answer. Such a penitent makes a subjectively complete confession and his blameless failure to remember a mortal sin is sufficient reason to excuse him from an objectively complete enumeration of his sins.

The forgotten sin is remitted, not directly by the absolution, but indirectly by the infusion of grace. The sin is implicitly included in the penitent's act of contrition. If the unmentioned sin is remembered afterwards by the penitent, he is obliged to tell it in a later confession.

4. The act of perfect contrition remits all mortal sins. Hence sins forgiven by this act should not be confessed.

Answer. The act of perfect contrition involves the intention to do everything commanded by God under grave obligation. So it includes objectively an intention to tell one's mortal sins in the sacrament. Without at least an implicit intention to do this, there can be no act of perfect contrition.

If a sinner has this intention when he makes an act of perfect contrition, all his mortal sins are forgiven instantly, but he must later tell the sins to a confessor. If he deliberately refuses to do this, he does not fall back into the forgiven sins, but he does commit a new mortal sin.

5. To make a detailed confession of mortal sins demands excessive introspection and gives rise to anxieties. So God did not command it.

Answer. All that God demands is a calm, sincere self-examination. The sinner should exercise the same diligence in examining his conscience that he uses in other important matters. Anxiety, scruples, self-torture are unnecessary and deplorable.

*

Conclusion 8. To receive the sacrament of penance the sinner must be willing to accept the penance to be assigned by the confessor. Both the willingness to accept the penance and its actual fulfillment remove temporal punishment *ex opere operato*.

Introduction. Readiness to accept the penance enjoined by the confessor is the third part of the matter of this sacrament. It should be noted, consequently, that the sacrament can be fruitfully received even though the penance is not actually done. Its actual fulfillment is required only for the integrity of the sacrament and in some circumstances may be omitted entirely.

Explanation of Terms

1. Willingness to accept the penance. The act of contrition, which a person makes before going to the sacrament of penance, involves the intention of confessing, the resolution not to sin again, and the intention to accept the penance to be enjoined by the confessor. The latter is sometimes called the intention to make satisfaction. The penitent is not free to choose the outward act of expiation.

It is clear, therefore, that of the three acts of the penitent, contrition, confession, and willingness to make satisfaction, the most fundamental is the act of contrition. It should always be made before entering the confessional and should be repeated while the priest is giving absolution.

Since the matter of a sacrament must always be in some way

perceptible, it might seem that readiness to accept the penance, since it is an internal act of virtue, cannot be a part of the matter of this sacrament. However, this internal act is externalized either explicitly by saying, "Thank you, father," or, "Yes, father," when the confessor assigns the penance; or implicitly by repeating the act of contrition or by the mere fact of making a sorrowful confession of one's sins.

2. The sinner *must* be willing to accept the penance. Readiness to accept the penance is not only commanded by God, but is an essential part of the sacrament. It is necessary by absolute necessity of means. There is no substitute for it, just as there is no substitute for some kind of external confession.

The actual performance of the penance is commanded by God, but when for some good reason it cannot be done, it may be omitted. Hence if a man forgets to do his penance, he has received the sacrament anyhow.

If a man deliberately and without sufficient reason fails to perform his penance, he sins either venially or mortally depending on various circumstances, but his confessed sins have been forgiven by the sacrament, provided that he truly intended, at the time it was assigned, to do it.

If mortal sins are confessed, the priest has a grave obligation to impose *some kind* of penance. If only venial sins are confessed, the priest has a light obligation to assign a penance.

Ordinarily the confessor will enjoin some prayers as a penance. However, it should be noted that he has the right to prescribe other kinds of good works. He may enjoin a visit to a church, fasting, an alms to the poor, a visit to the sick, or some other act of virtue.

In deciding the amount of penance to be done, the priest is guided, first of all, by the kind and number of sins confessed. A person who has missed Mass ten times without excuse, should ordinarily receive a more severe penance than one who has missed Mass but once. Again, a person who has committed murder, should receive a more burdensome penance than one who has missed Mass.

However, the confessor follows also a second norm when assigning a penance. He takes into account the strength, the dispositions, and the other circumstances of the penitent. If a man who has confessed even very serious sins is exceedingly ill, the priest might tell him merely to kiss the crucifix. He may tell a very contrite penitent to perform a comparatively small penance. If a soldier is in haste to join his regiment for battle, the priest may tell him to say one 'Hail Mary,' even though serious sins have been confessed.

Consequently, the man who confesses mortal sins would err if he concluded from the light penance assigned that the priest did not consider his sins as serious. The confessor has some good reason, though he may not mention it, for changing the deserved penance to a smaller one.

3. Remove temporal punishment. The satisfaction or penance enjoined by the confessor removes temporal punishment. This means that the penance takes away some of the sufferings of purgatory to which we are subject after death by reason of our sins. It is a kind of substitute for purgatory. Although the penance has other purposes, this is the one with which we are particularly concerned.

4. Remove temporal punishment *ex opere operato*. It should be carefully noted that we are speaking now, not of the conferring of grace, but solely of the remission of temporal punishment *ex opere operato*. It is clear that the willingness to make satisfaction, since it is an essential part of the sacrament, cooperates in the sacrament's production of grace *ex opere operato*.

We say here that readiness to do the penance, when it is elevated to sacramental efficacy by the priestly absolution, removes temporal punishment *ex opere operato*. Then, too, if the penitent actually does his penance as usually happens, the fulfillment of it remits even more of his temporal punishment *ex opere operato*, even though it is done some time after absolution has been conferred.

Adversaries. Although we could omit any reference to the Protestants because they deny the very existence of the sacrament, it may be well to recall what some of them say about the doing of penance in general. Some of them believe that outward penitential works are useless, even detrimental. They think that such works cast reflection on the infinite satisfaction offered by Christ on the cross.

This view has been condemned as heretical by the Council of

Trent (DB. 923, 924; CT. 812, 813). It is also opposed to Scripture. Not only the gospels, but also the Acts of the Apostles and the epistles of St. Paul frequently urge Christians to do penance. It is true that Christ's satisfaction is of infinite value, but His satisfaction must be applied to men. Our own penitential works derive their value from our Lord's universal and infinite satisfaction.

The Conclusion, then, has two parts. First, the sinner must be willing to accept the penance to be assigned by the confessor.

Second, both willingness to accept the penance and its actual fulfillment remove temporal punishment *ex opere operato*.

Dogmatic Note

That willingness to accept the penance is an essential part of the sacrament may be qualified as Catholic doctrine. The Council of Trent (DB. 896; CT. 790) says that satisfaction is "a kind of matter" for this sacrament. It says "kind of" because this act of the penitent is not a material substance like water in baptism. Since a sacrament cannot exist without its matter, the satisfaction of the penitent is necessary by absolute necessity of means in order to receive the sacrament. Observe, too, that "satisfaction" does not mean the actual doing of the penance, but its acceptance.

It is common and certain teaching that both willingness to accept the penance and its actual fulfillment remove temporal punishment *ex opere operato*.

Part 1. To receive the sacrament the sinner must be willing to accept the penance to be assigned by the confessor.

Proof 2. From theological reasoning.

Since contrition is required, as we have seen previously, by absolute necessity of means in order to have sins remitted, it follows that willingness to expiate by doing some kind of penance has the same necessity. No man is sincerely sorry for an offense unless he is willing to make amends.

Moreover, since the sacrament of penance is a judicial process, the penitent must be willing to accept, not a penance of his own choosing, but one imposed by the priest, who is a judge and acts in God's name. Even in secular, criminal courts the punishment of the delinquent is assigned.

It may happen occasionally that a confessor will forget to impose a penance. In this event, the penitent has no cause for worry. Provided that he was willing to accept the penance, he has received the sacrament.

The Council of Trent (DB. 904, 905; CT. 797, 798) mentions other reasons why the penitent must be sincerely willing to accept, and perform if possible, the penance enjoined.

First, by it he punishes himself for his sins and so repairs the injury done to God by them.

Second, the penance makes him more prompt and more energetic to avoid future sins.

Third, it curbs the evil tendencies which are left in him by reason of his sins.

Fourth, the penance makes him like to Christ who suffered on the cross for our sins.

Part 2. Both the willingness to accept the penance and its actual fulfillment remove temporal punishment *ex opere operato.*

Proof 2. From theological reasoning. The argument follows in form.

The characteristic effect of a sacrament is produced ex opere operato;

But the remission of temporal punishment by the willing acceptance and performance of the penance is a part of the characteristic effect of this sacrament:

Therefore, the remission of temporal punishment by the willing acceptance and the performance of the penance is produced ex opere operato.

Proof for the major. It is admitted by all theologians.

Proof for the minor. The total characteristic effect of the sacrament of penance is to remove mortal sin. Sin, however, includes not only personal guilt, but also the liability to eternal punishment and to temporal punishment. To remove temporal punishment is, then, a part of the characteristic effect of this sacrament.

We need not be surprised that the performance of the penance removes temporal punishment *ex opere operato,* even though the sacrament was administered some time before. The actual fulfillment of the penance is merely the doing in fact of that which was promised at the time of confession, and so is intimately linked with the sacrament.

OBJECTIONS

1. All essential parts of the sacrament should be present at the moment when absolution is given. But the penitent performs his penance after absolution. So the satisfaction or penance cannot be an essential part of the sacrament.

Answer. Willingness to do the penance is the substantial part of the sacrament. Actual performance of the penance is required for completeness or integrity only. At the moment of absolution the sinner is willing to accept the penance to be assigned.

2. If the penance should be proportioned to the sins confessed, the Church has violated this norm. In ancient times she required very severe satisfactions. Today she demands comparatively trivial ones.

Answer. Penances are proportioned not only to the gravity and number of sins, but also to the ability of the penitent, which depends both on his personal circumstances and, to some extent, on general customs, which vary at different stages of history.

In our times people would be repelled from the sacrament if the ancient rigorous penances were imposed.

Besides, today Catholics go to the sacrament much more often than in ancient times, and some temporal punishment is removed by each absolution.

Moreover, nowadays our people gain many more indulgences, which remove temporal punishment in whole or in part.

Finally, the objection forgets that the indispensable part of the sacrament is the readiness to do the penance, not its actual performance.

Comment 1. When one's penance should be performed.

It is advisable to do it immediately after leaving the confessional. However, this is not required, nor is it required to perform the penance before receiving Holy Communion. Ordinarily it should have been done before one's next confession.

Only rarely and for exceptional reasons, does a confessor assign a penance that is to be done during a period of two or more days. If this is done, it is clear that the penitent could go to confession again before his penance is completed.

Comment 2. The doing of one's penance remits temporal punishment *ex opere operantis* also.

This is of divine faith from the Council of Trent (DB. 923; CT. 812): "If anyone says that satisfaction for temporal punishment is not made to God . . . by punishments prescribed by the priest . . . let him be anathema." The least that this can mean is that the actual fulfillment of a sacramental penance remits temporal punishment *ex opere operantis.*

Moreover, every nonsinful action performed by one who is in the state of grace has a threefold value. It is meritorious (wins more sanctifying grace), impetratory (implores God for help), and satisfactory (removes some temporal punishment). Hence if the penitent is in the state of grace when he does his penance, he obtains the removal of some temporal punishment *ex opere operantis* (through his own efforts). This is lost if he performs his penance while in the state of mortal sin. But even in this event, his obligation to do the penance is fulfilled.

Comment 3. Does one's penance remove all temporal punishment?

Even after the penance has been accepted and performed, some temporal punishment may still remain for the sins that have been confessed. The amount of temporal punishment removed depends upon the sorrow of the penitent and the kind of penance imposed. If these two conditions are adequate, the entire temporal punishment due to the sins confessed is remitted by the sacrament *ex opere operato.*

Comment 4. Sinning mortally before doing one's penance.

If the penitent does his penance while in the state of mortal sin, the penance more probably will revive, i.e., it will remove temporal punishment *ex opere operato* when he recovers the state of grace. However, since the good work done as a penance was performed while he was a sinner, it will never remove temporal punishment *ex opere operantis.*

Comment 5. Does the doing of one's penance give grace *ex opere operato?*

Although the fulfillment of one's penance remits temporal punishment *ex opere operato,* it is more probable that it does not confer grace in the same way, but only *ex opere operantis* like any good work done in the state of grace.

*

Conclusion 9. The form of the sacrament of penance is contained in the words "I absolve you."

Introduction. Having explained the matter of this sacrament, we now consider its most important constituent, its form. We deal with only that form which is necessary for validity.

The priest ordinarily says five prayers when he absolves. Four of these may be omitted for a good reason. But the third prayer, which may never be omitted, is: "I absolve you from your sins in the name of the Father and of the Son and of the Holy Ghost."

Only the first three of these words are absolutely necessary. In the Latin form used by the priest the two words, "Absolvo te," suffice because the word "I" is contained in the letter "o" at the end of "absolvo."

Explanation of Terms

The meaning of the Conclusion is sufficiently clear. We merely emphasize that, for the existence of the sacrament, the words, "I absolve you," are necessary by absolute necessity of means.

Dogmatic Note

It is common and certain teaching that the declaration, "I absolve you," suffices for validity.

That "I absolve you from your sins in the name of the Father and of the Son and of the Holy Ghost" suffices is of faith from the Council of Trent (DB. 896; CT. 790).

It is Catholic doctrine that it suffices to say: "I absolve you from your sins."

Proof 2. From theological reasoning. We show by exclusion that the words added to "I absolve you" are not necessary for validity.

The words, "in the name of the Father and of the Son and of

the Holy Ghost," are not required because they are not found in some of the older valid forms; because they were not indicated by Christ, as they were for baptism, when He instituted this sacrament (John 20:23); because they were not mentioned by Him when He promised the sacrament (Matt. 18:18).

Besides, although a judge must pronounce his verdict in the name of his superior, he does not have to *express* the superior in his verdict. The reason why the three divine Persons must be invoked individually in the form of baptism is not because the minister acts in their name, but because the one baptized is consecrated to the Blessed Trinity.

It is not necessary to add "from your sins," because the word "absolve" is evidently directed at sins, since it is pronounced after the confession of sins has been heard. No other object under the circumstances can be referred to.

Moreover, in a secular, criminal court the crime for which the accused is condemned or from which he is acquitted does not have to be expressed in the verdict.

It is disputed whether the word "you" must be expressed in the form. It is a probable opinion that it can be omitted. If this opinion is correct, only the words "I absolve" are necessary for validity.

Comment 1. Further remarks about the words of absolution.

They must be pronounced with the lips or they are invalid. A gesture does not suffice. This is certain.

The penitent must be present to the priest when he gives absolution. If, however, the penitent leaves the confessional before receiving absolution, he is considered as being present to the priest if he is still in the church. He is morally present to the confessor.

Absolution may not be sent by letter or transmitted by telephone.

It is of faith from Trent (DB. 896; CT. 790) that the words of absolution are the form of the sacrament. But it is not certain that the acts of the penitent are its matter. These acts are absolutely necessary to obtain sacramental forgiveness, but they may be merely an indispensable condition.

Scotus held that the words of absolution are both matter and form of the sacrament. They are the matter if considered as mere words or sound without a meaning. They are the form in so far as they mean something. Serious objections can be raised against this explanation, but it is not censurable.

Comment 2. Whether a synonym could replace "I absolve."

Absolutely speaking, synonymous expressions like "I loose," or "I liberate," could substitute for "I absolve." As a matter of fact, synonymous expressions have been used in the past. Besides, these expressions do not alter the substantial meaning of the form.

Nevertheless, some theologians believe that any synonymous expression would be invalid today in the Latin Church. Just as the state may demand that certain specified words be used by a judge when he renders his verdict, so the Church, which has jurisdiction over the administration of this sacrament, may possibly require the one definite word "absolve."

Comment 3. The deprecatory form of absolution.

For many centuries the Church used quite commonly the deprecatory form of absolution. This was expressed in the subjunctive mood and so seemed to signify a wish or request for forgiveness. Such a form would be: "May God absolve you from your sins."

Since a judge must pronounce an efficacious verdict, which postulates the use of the indicative mood, it might seem that all the deprecatory forms were invalid.

This would be an unwarranted conclusion. It is not the mere outward or grammatical expression that must be considered, but the meaning that was attached to it.

A declaratory or indicative meaning can be signified by the subjunctive mood. A superior may say to a subject: "I would like to have you do this," and yet his meaning may be: "I want you to do this." The state, too, may prescribe as a judicial formula of acquittal: "May this powerful commonwealth free you." Yet the meaning would be indicative.

The deprecatory forms of absolution were indicative in meaning. This is clear from the fact that in the whole of tradition the priest who absolved was looked upon as a judge. He truly forgave sins. Hence, regardless of his subjunctive expression, he intended to absolve efficaciously. This is also evident from the context of some of the absolutory forms and from other circumstances.

It is debated by theologians whether a deprecatory form of absolution would be valid today in the Latin Church. If it would be invalid, the reason is that every society has power to set the norms which its official judges must follow. The Church at the Council of Trent (DB. 896; CT. 790) decreed that the form of this sacrament is "I absolve you from your sins." Hence the deprecatory form might be invalid today.

This would not mean that the Church has changed substantially the form of the sacrament. She might merely mean that a priest who would sinfully use the deprecatory form is by that very fact deprived of jurisdiction. He would not have a necessary prerequisite for the conferring of absolution. The substance of the sacramental form would not be altered.

Comment 4. Meaning of the absolution when a sinner has made an act of perfect contrition before coming to confession.

In this case it is difficult to explain the meaning of the absolution. The act of perfect contrition has already remitted the sins, and this act may have been of so high a quality that it removed all temporal punishment also. How, then, is it true for the priest to say: "I absolve you from your sins?"

First of all, the absolution frees the man from his obligation to confess. If he had failed to come to the sacrament, he would have committed a new grievous sin.

But although this is true, the absolution means: "I absolve you from the sins you have committed," not merely: "I absolve you from a future sin." Consequently, the lifting of a grave obligation from the penitent is not enough to explain the significance of the words of absolution.

The best explanation seems to be that the absolution always means: "I give you a *right* to the forgiveness of your sins." Such a right may be given many times even though sins were actually remitted long ago. A father can assure his son repeatedly of pardon by saying "I forgive you," although he truly forgave his son on the very first occasion when he said the words. This is particularly true of the sacrament of penance because each time that the right to forgiveness of sins is conferred, more grace is infused into the penitent's soul.

This also explains why people may go to confession and tell the priest nothing but sins of their past life which have already been forgiven by absolution. They obtain a new right to forgiveness of those sins, a remission of temporal punishment, and infusion of grace, and a title to actual graces by which they are fortified against future sins.

*

Conclusion 10. The sacrament of penance forgives sins so efficaciously that they can never revive even though the penitent commits other mortal sins afterwards. Moreover, when a sinner is absolved, at least some of the sanctifying grace which he possessed before he sinned is restored to him. In fact, all of it is restored.

Introduction. We have already seen that the sacrament of penance truly wipes away sins by infusing grace and restoring God's friendship. We have also learned that this forgiveness remits the eternal punishment incurred by sin, and at least a part of the temporal punishment. Moreover, the reception of this sacrament gives a man a right to actual graces which will strengthen him against future temptations.

At present we shall explain more in detail how completely God remits the transgressions of the repentant sinner. We learn how inexhaustible is the mercy of God.

Explanation of the Meaning of the Conclusion

It is of faith that sins are not merely covered over by the sacrament of penance. But granting this, it may still be possible that God forgives our sins only temporarily. He may remit them on condition that we do not sin mortally in the future. If he did forgive them on this condition, every time that an absolved penitent committed a fresh mortal sin, all his previously forgiven mortal sins would revive, both as regards their personal guilt and eternal punishment as well as their temporal punishment.

The first part of the Conclusion denies that God forgives sins in this way. He so abolishes them that they are absolutely and totally and lastingly wiped away. They cannot revive no matter how much the person sins in the future. Even the man condemned to hell is not punished for sins which he once had remitted in the sacrament of penance.

It should be noted also that this irrevocable forgiveness of sins by God holds true whether sins are remitted by baptism, or by penance, or by an act of perfect contrition, or by extreme unction, though the latter two ways must be accompanied by at least an implicit desire to receive the sacrament of penance.

In the second part of the Conclusion we illustrate still further the efficacy of this sacrament. As long as a Catholic remains in the state of grace, he is constantly winning more grace because of his personal good works (his merits) or because of his reception of sacraments. However, when he commits a mortal sin, he loses all of his sanctifying grace and can gain no more until he repents.

When he comes to confession and has his sins forgiven, it is important to know what happens to all the grace which he had before he fell into mortal sin. Is it lost forever? Does it come back in part only? Or, perhaps, does it all come back?

We say, first, that at least some of it is restored to him. We go even further and answer that all of it is restored. In fact, immediately after receiving the sacrament of penance, he possesses more grace than he had before his sins, since in addition to the recuperation of all his lost grace, he receives some new grace *ex opere operato* from the sacrament.

Here, too, notice that this is also true when a man has his sins forgiven by the act of perfect contrition or by extreme unction.

This is sufficient to explain the meaning of the Conclusion, but concerning the second part of it the student should learn that a man's acts with regard to God are of four kinds. First, some acts are mortally sinful. These can never be altered and so can never be acceptable to God. Second, other acts are fruitless. They are made while a man is in the state of mortal sin. They will never enable a man to gain a higher place in heaven because their value is lost by the state of sin. Third, some acts are fruitful. They are good in themselves and done while one is in the state of grace. Consequently, they are meritorious for heaven. Finally, some acts are fruitful but suspended. These are fruitful acts which have temporarily lost their meritorious value for heaven because their agent has fallen into mortal sin. They regain their meritorious value when the sinner is converted.

The second part of the Conclusion deals only with this last classification of acts. The grace won by them originally, returns to the sinner when he recovers the state of grace. Moreover, any sanctifying grace which he had obtained *ex opere operato* from sacraments is also restored to him.

The Conclusion has, then, three parts. First, the sacrament of penance forgives sins so efficaciously that they can never revive even though the penitent commits other mortal sins afterwards.

Second, when a sinner is absolved, at least some of the grace which he possessed before he sinned is restored to him.

Third, all of it is restored.

Dogmatic Note

The first part is Catholic doctrine.

The second part is also Catholic doctrine.

The third part is more common and more probable teaching.

Part 1. The sacrament forgives sins so efficaciously that they can never revive.

Proof 2. From Holy Scripture. If forgiven sins were to revive when a new sin is committed, God would forgive sins conditionally, not absolutely. The condition would be: "if you do not sin again." However, in the numerous Scripture texts pertaining to the remission of sins, no such condition is ever mentioned.

Moreover, the possibility of such a condition being implicitly present is excluded by the absolute manner in which God is said to forgive sins. Thus we read (John 20:23): "Whose sins you shall forgive, they are forgiven them." The prophet Micheas declares (7:19): ". . . He will put away our iniquities: and He will cast all our sins to the bottom of the sea." If an object is cast to the bottom of the sea, there was, at least in Micheas' day, no method of retrieving it. Furthermore, the prophet Isaias states (1:18): "If your sins be as scarlet, they shall be made as white as snow: and if they be as crimson, they shall be as white as wool." Other texts have the same purport.

Again, when sins are forgiven, the satisfaction of Christ is applied to them (John 1:29; I Pet. 2:24). This satisfaction, when applied, cries out in justice for the remission of our sins. If sins once forgiven were to revive, it would seem to imply that Christ's satisfaction is not sufficient to wipe them away completely. This would reflect on the condign satisfaction of our Redeemer.

Proof 3. From the practice of the Church. If forgiven sins were to revive through the commission of a new mortal sin, the sinner would be obliged to confess not only all the mortal sins since his last confession, but all the mortal sins of his entire past life. This goes contrary to the constant practice of the Church.

Again, when a confessor grants absolution to a sinner, he never does so under this condition: "If you do not sin again in the future."

It should be noted that, if a penitent has some temporal punishment remaining for sins already forgiven, it is not increased by reason of a fresh mortal sin. It remains the same as it was. But he now has more temporal punishment to expiate because of his new sins.

Part 2. When a sinner is absolved, at least some of the grace which he possessed before he sinned is restored to him.

Proof 2. From theological reasoning. If no grace at all were restored to the penitent from his past life, we might be confronted with the following incredible case. A man who has continuously led a good life and often received the sacraments might commit a mortal sin shortly before he died and then confess with mediocre dispositions. If none of the grace obtained during his past life revived, he would receive only a lowly place in heaven. On the other hand, a man who lived his entire life in sin and in neglect of the sacraments, might on his death bed repent with great devotion. He would receive a higher place in heaven than the first man. This seems to be against the mercy of God.

This part is also evident from a statement of Pius XI (DB. 2193) which we shall explain in a moment.

Part 3. All suspended grace is restored.

Proof 2. From the Bull of Pius XI decreeing the Holy Year of 1925. He says (DB. 2193): "During this great jubilee year whoever by repentance fulfill the wholesome directives of the Apostolic See retrieve and receive anew that abundance of merits and gifts which they had lost by sin. . . ."

It is evident from this sentence that *some* of the sanctifying grace possessed before sin was committed is restored by repentance. Hence the preceding part of the Conclusion is Catholic doctrine.

That the penitent regains all of his suspended grace is the more obvious meaning of the quotation for the following reasons.

First, the Pontiff explicitly says that sinners regain the abundance of their merits and gifts "ex integro." This Latin phrase may be translated either by "anew" or by "entirely." The second translation is an explicit enunciation of this part of the Conclusion. This first translation more obviously means the same thing. If "the *abundance* of merits and gifts" is received "anew," all grace must return. If only a portion of it were restored, the Pontiff could hardly say that the *abundance* of it is recovered.

Moreover, according to the Holy Father the sinner regains the abundance of his *merits* and *gifts* (*meritorum donorumque*). Merits can refer only to the sanctifying grace won by good deeds. Hence, the added word "gifts" should include the grace obtained *ex opere operato* by the reception of sacraments. This grace is truly a "gift." Consequently, all sanctifying grace, however procured, is restored to the repentant sinner.

Finally, it should be noted that the fact that this decree refers only to the Holy Year cannot affect the principles involved. The restoration of grace to the sinner depends on God's dispensation, not on the jurisdiction of the Holy Father.

Proof 3. From the Council of Trent. The council (DB. 842; CT. 606) lays down three conditions according to which a person by good works merits eternal life. These conditions are: that the works must be morally good; that they must be done while a person is in the state of grace; that the person must die in this state.

Now if we examine those meritorious works whose sanctifying grace has been suspended because a man has sinned mortally, we find that they fulfill these conditions. They are: good works; done in the state of grace. Besides, the person who did them and afterwards sinned can repent and so die in the state of grace.

Therefore, since the conditions of Trent are verified, all the grace obtained by meritorious acts is restored to the repentant sinner. The council nowhere declares that a man must remain permanently in the state of grace in order that the grace acquired by his good works should be efficacious for heaven.

It should be observed, however, that this argument proves only that grace won by *meritorious* acts revives in its entirety. It does not prove that grace received *ex opere operato* through sacraments is regained.

Objections

1. From the parable (Matt. 18:23 ff.) it is clear that the forgiven sins of the heartless servant return when he refuses to forgive his fellow servant. Therefore, sins revive by the commission of a new mortal sin.

Answer. The student should read the parable in order to understand the following replies to the objection.

First, the purpose of this parable is to inculcate the absolute necessity of forgiving others, not to explain the way in which God forgives sins.

Second, the cruel servant may not have committed any sins at all by falling into debt. It may have been owing to incompetence. In this interpretation there is no possibility of revival of sins because he was not guilty of any. Only the debt would revive.

Third, on the supposition that the servant had actually committed sins and so incurred debt, the parable merely means that, just as he had become subject to eternal punishment by the sins committed before his pardon, so he became subject to eternal punishment again by reason of his cruelty to his fellow servant. He is not liable to this punishment because of his forgiven sins, but because of his new mortal sin of cruelty.

Comment 1. Explanation of a difficulty from Trent.

Those theologians who deny that all suspended grace is restored to the repentant sinner argue particularly from Trent (DB. 799; CT. 563). The council declares that grace is given us "according to the measure which the Holy Spirit freely grants to each person, and according to the individual's disposition and cooperation."

According to this declaration, say these authors, suspended sanctifying grace is regained in proportion to the disposition which the sinner has when he repents. He may excite so excellent a disposition that all suspended grace would be recovered. On the other hand, he may have inferior dispositions of many degrees so that he may regain only a portion of his grace.

However, the statement of the council remains perfectly true even though all suspended grace is restored no matter how inferior (provided that it is adequate) the penitent's disposition may be when he is absolved. The grace won by meritorious works was given to him according to the perfection of his dispositions *at the time he performed them.* Grace was bestowed by sacraments in proportion to the disposition *with which he received them.* All this grace was procured once for all.

When it was removed from his soul by mortal sin, it was, so to speak, merely transferred to a safety deposit vault. As long as he remained in the state of sin, he had no key to this vault and so could not recover the grace. But repentance is the key which opens the vault and enables him to regain his grace. The only grace which he receives according to his disposition at the time he goes to confession or makes an act of perfect contrition is that which comes from the sacrament or from the act.

In short, when there is question of obtaining more sanctifying grace, it is always granted according to one's dispositions. But once grace has been acquired according to one's dispositions, it remains acquired. Mortal sin is an obstacle which alienates it for the time being only.

In connection with this difficulty it should be noted that Pius XI in his Bull decreeing the Holy Year does not demand any special degree of repentance in order to recover suspended grace. He says that it is regained "by repentance" (*poenitendo*). Hence any genuine repentance, even of inferior quality, suffices for the restoration of all suspended grace.

Comment 2. Why the absolved sinner has more grace than ever before.

This should be clear from the fact that any degree of repentance is sufficient to regain all suspended grace. If the sinner repents by reception of the sacrament of penance, he obtains grace *ex opere operato* from it. This grace is added to the entire amount which he possessed before he sinned. If he repents by an act of perfect contrition involving a resolution to go to confession, he acquires grace by this act *ex opere operantis.* This grace, too, is in addition to his restored grace. The same is true if he repents by way of extreme unction (when he cannot confess) or by martyrdom. He always has more grace than he ever had before.

Comment 3. How a forgiven mortal sin can make a new mortal sin objectively more malicious.

Although forgiven sins never return, yet a forgiven sin can add to the guilt of a future sin. Let us suppose that a man commits murder and then has the sin remitted. But afterwards he commits murder again.

The second homicide, supposing all other conditions to be the same as at the first one, is *objectively* a graver sin than the first because it involves not only murder but also ingratitude for the remission of the first sin. Unless the sinner *adverts* to this ingratitude, however, the second murder is no more serious *subjectively* than the first.

This is evidently not the revival of a forgiven sin. Neither the personal guilt nor the liability to punishments return from his first sin. But the second sin is *objectively* more serious than the first because it involves an element of ingratitude which would have been missing had the first sin not been forgiven.

*

Conclusion 11. No one except a priest can administer the sacrament of penance. To do so, even a priest needs special faculties.

Introduction. Having previously considered the material, formal, and final causes of this sacrament, we now deal with its efficient cause, the human agent who acts as Christ's vicar in its administration. Although the sinner must provide the matter for the sacrament, he is not its minister because his acts lack sacramental efficacy until they are energized by the words of absolution.

We treat only of the minister who can validly confer the sacrament. Other conditions are prescribed for licit administration.

Explanation of Terms

1. No one except a priest. A priest is one who has the priestly character bestowed by the sacrament of orders. Hence both bishops and priests are valid ministers. Deacons, subdeacons, all others are excluded.

2. A priest needs special faculties. This means that even an ordained priest must also receive jurisdiction or ruling power in order to absolve validly. Priestly ordination is not enough. The character of the priesthood confers the *sanctifying* power necessary for the remission of sins, but not the *ruling* power which every judge must have.

A bishop or priest can receive this power in either of two ways. He may be appointed to a certain office like the bishopric of a diocese or the pastorate of a parish. Such appointments automatically confer faculties to hear confessions. The same faculties can also be obtained by delegation from a superior, as when a bishop grants them to religious priests. But unless a priest has ruling power, he cannot validly absolve. Mere ordination to the priesthood never confers this power.

The Conclusion, then, has two parts. First, no one except a priest can administer the sacrament of penance.

Second, to do so, even a priest needs faculties.

Dogmatic Note

The first part is of divine faith from the Council of Trent (DB. 920; CT. 809): "If anyone says . . . that priests alone are not the ministers of absolution . . . let him be anathema."

The second part is also of divine faith from the same council (DB. 903; CT. 796) when it states that it ratifies as most true what the Church has always held, namely, "that the absolution which a priest confers on one over whom he has neither ordinary or delegated jurisdiction ought to be reckoned of no worth."

From this statement it follows as Catholic doctrine that a priest does not receive faculties by ordination alone. The council supposes that the minister is a "priest," i.e., validly ordained. Yet it says that his absolution is of no worth unless he has either ordinary or delegated jurisdiction. Consequently, he did not receive this jurisdiction by the mere fact of his ordination.

Part 1. No one except a priest can administer this sacrament.

Proof 2. From the Fathers. It can be proved from Scripture that bishops are empowered to remit sin. Christ gave this power to the apostles (John 20:21–23) and bishops are successors of the apostles. Scripture, however, offers no proof that priests can forgive sins. Hence, we appeal to tradition.

St. Jerome declares: "We read in the book of Leviticus about lepers. . . . Just as in that passage the priest makes the leper clean or unclean, so now the *bishop* or *priest* binds or looses, not the guiltless or guilty, but, as his office requires, those guiltless and guilty whose sins he has heard and who he knows deserve to be bound or loosed" (*In Matt.*, 1. 3, c. 16, v. 19; RJ. 1386).

St. Dionysius of Alexandria (before the close of the third century) reports the following request of the dying old man, Serapion: "Hasten, please, to absolve me as soon as possible. Summon one of the priests for me" (Eusebius, *Eccl. History,* VI, 44).

St. Cyprian testifies that priests were absolving in the African churches (*Epist.* 18, 1; RJ. 570).

That deacons and all others were excluded from absolving is clear from the fact that only bishops and priests are mentioned as ministers. Moreover, St. Ambrose states explicitly: "For this right [to bind and loose sins] is granted to priests alone" (*De Paenit.*, 1. 1, c. 2, n. 7; RJ. 1293).

Part 2. Even a priest needs special faculties.

Proof 2. From theological reasoning. The argument follows in form.

Judicial power involves the exercise of jurisdiction;
But the power to absolve or retain sins is judicial power:
Therefore, the power to absolve or retain sins involves the exercise of jurisdiction.

Proof for the major. A judge binds or looses the wills of men by imposing or liberating from obligations. This involves the exercise of jurisdiction, which he cannot assume on his own authority. He must have public power.

Proof for the minor. It is clear from the second Conclusion.

Proof 3. From the practice of the Church as revealed by the prescriptions of canon law.

The *Code of Canon Law* (Par. 872) states: "Besides the power of orders, the minister, to absolve sins validly, must have either ordinary or delegated power of jurisdiction over the penitent."

From this declaration it is evident that *delegated* jurisdiction to absolve is not conferred by priestly ordination or episcopal consecration. That *ordinary* jurisdiction is not granted follows from the fact that no man receives a parish or diocese by his ordination.

OBJECTIONS

1. St. Cyprian says of dying sinners: "If a priest is not available and death is imminent, they can make their confession to a deacon also, so that, by the imposition of his hands unto repentance, they may go to God peacefully." Hence deacons can absolve.

Answer. This is the only patristic quotation which seems to militate against the first part of the Conclusion.

The case as proposed by St. Cyprian is rigidly circumscribed. A man is dying. The bishop cannot come to him in time. No priest is available. Such qualifications make it plain that St. Cyprian did not consider deacons as *regular* ministers of the sacrament.

However, according to the Conclusion a deacon could never under any circumstances give absolution validly. Therefore, the words of St. Cyprian must be explained.

First, he may have been mistaken. He was not infallible.

Second, he may be referring, not to sacramental absolution, but to reconciliation with the Church in the external forum. In other words, he might have meant that deacons may officially restore such dying persons to good standing in the Church.

Again, he may wish to say that a deacon could act as an intermediary for a bishop or priest. The deacon himself would not bestow absolution from sins, but would simply relay it from the bishop or priest.

Finally, St. Cyprian may mean that deacons could exhort such sinners to perfect contrition. The penitent would confess his sins to the deacon, but would not receive sacramental absolution from him. The confession of sins would be an outward testimony of perfect contrition. The deacon could then impose hands on the sinner to signify that he was reconciled with the Church.

2. Even in the Middle Ages deacons in cases of necessity heard confessions and absolved sinners.

Answer. At that period of history deacons often remained deacons for a long time. *Dying* persons sometimes made their confessions to them when a bishop or priest was not at hand.

Such a confession was not considered as sacramental, but it testified to the sorrow of the dying man and to his *desire* to receive the sacrament. For the same reason the dying were sometimes urged to make a confession even to a lay person if no priest was available.

It is a fact, however, that some deacons forgot their position and attempted occasionally to absolve the dying. They were severely rebuked in the *Synodal Constitution* of St. Odo of Paris (1201 A.D.) and in the Synod of Poitiers (1280 A.D.).

3. We read (Jas. 5:16): "Confess, therefore, yours sins to one another." Therefore, even a lay person can absolve.

Answer. Nothing is said in this sentence about absolution. Confession is not absolution.

However, even if St. James here refers to sacramental confession with absolution, he does not mean that the laity can be ministers. The original text does not say "to one another," but "one to another." If the preceding verses about extreme unction are read, it becomes clear that "another" is a priest, not a layman. It is a priest who is called in to help the sick man. The priest's anointing will remove his sins. But if possible, the infirm man should go to confession and not receive extreme unction only. He should first confess his sins to "another," i.e., the priest.

4. Perhaps jurisdiction is given at ordination, but the Church is empowered to regulate its use.

Answer. If jurisdiction were conferred by ordination, the Church could not take it away. She cannot remove those powers that come directly from God when a sacrament is administered.

5. If jurisdiction must be obtained from the Church, the Holy Father could not go to confession because he cannot be subject to anyone.

Answer. The Pope acting as supreme ruler of the Church grants jurisdiction to his confessor. But when the Holy Father goes to confession, he acts in a private capacity.

Comment 1. Reserved cases.

The Council of Trent (DB. 903, 921; CT. 796, 810) has defined that bishops have the power to reserve cases. This means, first of all, that bishops can specify certain kinds of sins from which priests may not validly absolve. When this is done, e.g., with regard to murder, the priest must have recourse to the bishop in order to obtain faculties to absolve. The sacramental seal is, of course, always safeguarded when such recourse is had.

The bishop can, if he wishes, limit the jurisdiction of a confessor in other ways. He may allow a priest to hear confessions for a limited time, or in only one place. He may even restrict a priest to hearing the confessions of one class of persons.

Comment 2. Absolution for those in danger of death.

The following provision of the *Code of Canon Law* (Par. 882) should be remembered: "In danger of death any priest, although not approved for hearing confessions, validly and licitly absolves any penitent whomsoever from any sin or censure whatsoever, no matter how reserved or how infamous, even if an approved confessor is available. . . ."

SECTION SIX

The Sacrament of
Extreme Unction

*

Section Six

THE SACRAMENT OF EXTREME UNCTION

EXTREME UNCTION or the last anointing is the beautiful sacrament that fortifies us against the trials and temptations to which all of us are subject during critical illness.

It is treated immediately after the sacrament of penance because it deletes the remains of sins and so is often called the complement of penance.

Conclusion 1. Extreme unction is a sacrament.

Introduction. As usual, we begin by establishing the sacramental nature of extreme unction. This is important because it was revealed by God and because it is rejected by all Protestants except the Ritualists.

Explanation of Terms

1. Extreme unction is a sacrament which by an anointing with olive oil, blessed by a bishop, and by the prayer of a priest confers upon a dangerously-ill Christian health of soul, and also of body when this is conducive to the soul's welfare.

This definition is a synopsis of the entire section. It will be amplified and clarified in the rest of the Conclusions.

This sacrament is called *extreme* unction or *last* anointing, not to give the false impression that it is to be received only when a person is on the brink of death, but simply to indicate that it is ordinarily the last in the order of sacramental anointings. An anointing is prescribed for baptism and orders, is essential in confirmation. Usually a person will receive extreme unction after these sacraments and so it is the *last* anointing.

Dogmatic Note

This is an article of divine faith from the Council of Trent (DB. 926; CT. 835): "If anyone says that extreme unction is not truly and properly a sacrament, instituted by Christ our Lord and promulgated by the apostle James, but that it is only a rite received from the Fathers, or a human figment, let him be anathema."

Proof 2. From Holy Scripture (Jas. 5:14, 15). Although Scripture contains no formal promise of extreme unction, it does foreshadow or prefigure the sacrament (Mark 6:13): "And they [the apostles] . . . anointed with oil many that were sick and healed them." The Council of Trent (DB. 908; CT. 832) says that the sacrament "is suggested" by these words of St. Mark.

The letter of St. James was written before the year 62 and was directed not to any one church, but to the whole Church, especially to those Catholics who had been converted from Judaism.

Formerly Protestants omitted this epistle from the New Testament. Today, however, many of them accept it.

Our proof is dogmatically certain from Trent (DB. 908; CT. 832). Apologetically, it is very probable. St. James says:

"Is any man sick among you? Let him bring in the priests of the Church, and let them pray over him, anointing him with oil in the name of the Lord.

"And the prayer of faith will save the sick man: and the Lord shall raise him up: and if he be in sins, they shall be forgiven him."

In these verses we find verified our definition of a sacrament.

First, we find a *perceptible sign* because there is an anointing with oil (v. 14). A prayer by the priest is also mentioned (v. 14).

Second, grace is conferred by the anointing because the rite takes away sins, sometimes even mortal sins (v. 15). When sins are remitted, God always infuses grace. If mortal sins are removed, He gives first grace; if venial sins only, He gives second grace, i.e., an increase of grace. If a person having no sins of any kind is anointed, he, too, receives more grace. This happens because the nature of the rite remains unchanged. If extreme unction can give grace even to sinners, it can *a fortiori* give it to a sinless person.

Moreover, the word "save" (v. 15), used four times in this epistle, means in the other passages "spiritual salvation." Hence it probably means the same thing here.

Spiritual salvation, however, necessarily involves the bestowal of sanctifying grace.

It is true that in other parts of Scripture the word "save" frequently denotes a bodily cure. In St. James, too, this is probably its secondary meaning, because extreme unction does sometimes have a beneficial effect upon physical health. But this cannot be the primary meaning in our text, as the preceding proofs reveal.

Third, the grace is conferred *ex opere operato* because the forgiveness of sins is attributed, not to the merits of the sick person, but to the anointing and the prayer of the priest.

The "prayer of faith" (v. 15) is not the prayer of the sick man because St. James includes people who are so ill that they cannot pray at all. They might be unconscious.

Moreover, the "prayer of faith" refers naturally to the prayer which is mentioned before (v. 14), but this is clearly the prayer of the priest alone ("let them pray over him").

Besides, if the effect was caused by the prayerful efforts of the ailing man, why should he be anointed by the priest?

For these reasons the "prayer of faith" is the prayer of objective faith, the liturgical prayer or rite of the sacrament.

This becomes even more evident if we consider that St. James does not attribute the forgiveness of sins to the subjective prayer of the priest either. He simply bids Christians to "summon the priests." He does not tell them to call *holy* priests. Any priest can perform this rite efficaciously, whereas only a priest in the state of grace could utter a *personal* prayer that would benefit others.

Fourth, *Christ* instituted this rite because it is to be administered "in the name of the Lord" (v. 14). Besides, St. James was an apostle and St. Paul declares that even the apostles were mere "dispensers of the mysteries of God" (I Cor. 4:1).

Fifth, the rite must continue for all time because there will always be Catholics who are dangerously ill and so need this sacrament. Its purpose will be perpetually attainable.

Proof 3. From the Fathers. Until the close of the fourth century it is difficult to find in writings of the Fathers clear references to extreme unction. The reasons for this are as follows.

First, the Fathers did not treat systematically of the sacraments.

Again, the commentaries on St. James' epistle, which were written by some of them, have perished.

Besides, extreme unction is only rarely necessary for salvation.

Furthermore, the Fathers spoke about sacraments only when occasions arose. However, occasions for writing about extreme unction were rare then, as indeed they are now.

Then, too, when the Fathers mention that a person received reconciliation or the sacrament of penance, they may have implicitly included extreme unction if the person was seriously ill, since this sacrament was looked upon as the complement of penance.

It is also noteworthy that it would have often been impossible to give extreme unction in the early centuries. Pagans were in almost every household so that a Catholic member could not have summoned a priest to administer this sacrament. In some instances a priest would not have been admitted into the house, and during times of persecution his life would have been endangered.

Providentially preserved, however, are the comments of Pope Innocent I about the text of St. James (416 A.D.). He interprets it about extreme unction (DB. 99; CT. 829): "There is no doubt that these words [of St. James] should be interpreted or understood about the faithful who are sick. These can be anointed by the holy oil of chrism, which has been blessed by a bishop. Not only priests, but all Christians may be anointed with it when the need arises."

The Conclusion is confirmed from the fact that the Oriental schismatics admit that extreme unction is a sacrament.

We do not know exactly when our Lord instituted the sacrament. He probably did so sometime between His resurrection and ascension.

OBJECTIONS

1. It might be reasonably inferred that St. James is speaking of the same anointing which is mentioned by St. Mark (6:13). But the latter was not a sacrament. Therefore, neither is the former.

Answer. St. James may be implicitly referring to the anointing recorded by St. Mark. But St. James makes it clear that the anointing which he promulgates has an effect not found in St. Mark's. The anointing of St. James remits sins: "If he be in sins, they shall be forgiven him." St. Mark's anointing cured the body only. An outward sign that remits even mortal sins gives grace and so is a sacrament.

2. The entire effect mentioned by St. James is referred to the "prayer of faith." The confidence of the sick man was aroused so that he obtained forgiveness of his sins by his own prayers.

Answer. The effect is attributed by St. James, not only to the "prayer of faith," but also to the anointing. Moreover, the "prayer of faith" is not the subjective prayer of the infirm, but the prayer of the priests who alone are referred to as praying: "Let them pray over him. . . . And the prayer of faith will save the sick man."

Finally, the effect is not caused solely by the subjective prayer of the priests, but by the fact that their prayer is combined with the anointing. In other words, it is owing to the sacramental rite.

3. St. James merely means that some Christian or other who had the gift of charismatic healing should be called in to take care of sick people.

Answer. The gift of healing was a charismatic gift bestowed on a limited number of Christians in the early Church. But this gift was not restricted to priests, whereas St. James explicitly states that priests are to be summoned.

Second, the remission of sins could not have been effected by a gift intended for a bodily cure only.

Moreover, St. James implies that bodily health was not always granted. Otherwise Christians would never have died.

In addition, charismatic gifts were not a part of the regular ministry of the Church. But St. James speaks of the visitation of the sick by priests as though it formed a part of the regular ministry.

Finally, charismatic gifts did not produce their effects by the application of a set and unchangeable rite. St. James, however, portrays the rite of extreme unction as something definitely settled and to be adhered to in all cases.

4. St. James promises the remission of sins, but only conditionally. If extreme unction were a sacrament, it would remit sins unconditionally.

Answer. St. James places no condition to the efficacy of the rite to forgive sins. It can always do so. But some sick people may be free of sins. In their case the sacrament cannot remit sins because they have no sins. Hence, "*if* he be in sins, they shall be forgiven him."

5. In biographies of the early Fathers we find no record that they received extreme unction when they were dangerously ill. So the sacrament did not exist until after their time.

Answer. The so-called *argument from silence* is valid only when it can be proved that the matter in question ought to have been mentioned. This cannot be shown of extreme unction in the lives of these Fathers.

First, most of these biographies are very brief. Consequently, they often fail to mention even that a Father was confirmed or received Viaticum.

Again, many of these Fathers did not receive extreme unction because they were martyred.

Furthermore, this sacrament, since it is not ordinarily necessary for salvation, may not have been administered as commonly as it is today.

Last, Pope Innocent I in the year 416 speaks of extreme unction as a regular ministration of the Church. Yet, not even he would have mentioned it, had he not been questioned by Decentius (DB. 99; CT. 829).

*

Conclusion 2. The remote matter of extreme unction is olive oil that has been blessed by a bishop. The proximate matter is an anointing of the body. The form must be addressed to God as a prayer.

Introduction. We now deal with the matter and form, the intrinsic causes, of extreme unction. We are concerned with their validity only. For liceity the *Code of Canon Law* (Pars. 937–947) lays down other prescriptions.

It is exceedingly important to know the requirements for validity. If they are fulfilled, the sacrament is truly administered even though the accidentals have been omitted or wrongly performed.

Explanation of Terms

1. Remote matter. Here, as in baptism, it is a material substance.

2. Olive oil. This is oil pressed from olives. The Latin Church does not allow small quantities of other fluids to be mixed with the olive oil. If so much of a foreign substance were mixed with the oil that it would no longer be commonly reckoned as olive oil, the matter would be invalid.

3. Blessed by a bishop. A bishop has the power to bless the oil by his episcopal consecration without any authorization from the Holy See. Hence, he is called the *ordinary* minister of the blessing. To give this blessing priests must obtain special delegation from the supreme pontiff and so they are called *extraordinary* ministers.

In some of the Oriental churches priests regularly bless the oil, but they always remain extraordinary ministers.

It is more probable that the oil must be blessed specifically for use in extreme unction. Hence, the chrism of confirmation or the oil of catechumens would be invalid matter. These oils could be used in cases of necessity, but the sacrament would be given conditionally and should be repeated afterwards if possible.

4. Anointing of the body. The proximate matter consists of the application of the remote matter to the sick person. We call

the application of oil to the body an anointing. Although for liceity six anointings are prescribed, one anointing, accompanied by the short form, suffices for validity. Furthermore, this anointing may be applied to *any part* of the sick person's body. Although in practice the one anointing is made on the forehead, this is not necessary for validity.

5. The form must be a prayer. Since the form specifies or determines the matter, it must always express, at least in a general way, the purpose of the sacrament. However, this purpose can be expressed either as a declaration in the indicative mood or as a request or imploration in the subjunctive mood. A prayer as such should be in the subjunctive mood because it is a petition addressed to God. Thus in the Latin form of extreme unction we have the subjunctive "indulgeat" (may the Lord pardon).

Yet, the forms of extreme unction as we find them in older liturgical books differ widely. Some of them are assertions in the indicative. Such forms would seem to have been invalid, since they were not a prayer.

However, although *expressed* in the indicative, their *meaning* was in the subjunctive mood. They are often preceded or followed by expressions which make it clear that they were intended as requests. When such expressions did not surround the form, the meaning of the latter became a prayer by the intention of the minister.

That this explanation suffices is evident from our own ways of speaking. A friend, for instance, may say to another: "I want you to do this for me," when he really means: "Please do this for me." His words are indicative in expression, but subjunctive in meaning. The Conclusion, then, says that the valid form of extreme unction must always be a prayer, if not in its wording, at least in its meaning.

We had a similar difficulty with the sacrament of penance. There we saw that the form had to be indicative in meaning, though it could be subjunctive in wording. We explained the deprecatory forms of absolution by the same principles which we use here.

The three parts of the Conclusion follow. First, the remote matter of extreme unction is olive oil that has been blessed by a bishop.

Second, the proximate matter is an anointing of the body.
Third, the form must be addressed to God as a prayer.

Dogmatic Note

It is of divine faith from the Council of Trent (DB. 908; CT. 832) that olive oil is valid matter.

It is certain and common teaching that only olive oil is valid matter.

It is also certain and common teaching that the oil must be blessed by either a bishop or a delegated priest.

As regards the second part, Trent (DB. 908; CT. 832) has defined that the body must be anointed (*unctio*).

That one anointing accompanied by the short form suffices for validity is certain and common teaching.

It is very probable that the one anointing may be made on any part of the body.

Concerning the third part, Trent (DB. 908; CT. 832) defined that the form used in the Latin Church today is valid. Its initial words are cited by the council.

It is certain and common teaching that every form must be a prayer, but it is very probable that forms expressed in the indicative or imperative moods may be subjunctive in meaning and so valid.

Part 1. The remote matter is olive oil that has been blessed by a bishop.

Proof 2. From Holy Scripture. St. James says (5:14): ". . . anointing him with *oil* in the name of the Lord." In Scripture the word "oil," when used without qualification, always means olive oil. Today in our country "oil" would not have this meaning. It would ordinarily signify a lubricant for some mechanical device.

We cannot prove from Scripture that the olive oil must be blessed by a bishop, but this is clear from the tradition of the Church. It is contained in the statement of Innocent I (DB. 99; CT. 829) which we quoted in the first Conclusion. It is also explicitly mentioned in the Councils of Florence (DB. 700; CT. 830) and of Trent (DB. 908; CT. 832).

It is proved from the practice of the Church and from the *Code of Canon Law* (Par. 945) that the Holy See may empower a priest to bless the oil.

Part 2. The proximate matter is an anointing of the body.

Proof 2. From Holy Scripture. St. James states (5:14): ". . . anointing him with oil."

However, St. James does not tell us how many anointings are necessary. But the practice of the Church, sanctioned by the *Code of Canon Law* (Par. 947), proves that one anointing suffices. For instance, in Cook County Hospital, Chicago, the short form, owing to lack of time, is used regularly with one anointing.

Neither does St. James tell us where the body is to be anointed. By examining, however, the parts of the body which were anointed in diverse liturgies, we conclude that the anointing can be made anywhere on the body. So varied are the parts of the body that have been anointed that the only common element seems to be an anointing of the body in some part or other.

This, too, seems to be the meaning of the *Code of Canon Law* (Par. 947) which says that the one anointing is made "more properly on the forehead," or on "one of the senses." Since the sense of touch is everywhere, we infer that the body can be anointed in any spot.

It should be noted that, for validity, the anointing may be made with an instrument instead of with the thumb. It is, however, forbidden to use an instrument except in cases of necessity, e.g., danger of contagion.

Part 3. The form must be addressed to God as a prayer.

Proof 2. From Holy Scripture. St. James indicates this when he says (5:14): "Let them *pray* over him." He does not tell us how this prayer is to be expressed.

That indicative or even imperative forms may be valid because of the subjunctive mood intended, is quite clear from the practice of the Church which has tolerated such forms in various places and for a long time. Reason, too, as we mentioned previously, teaches the same lesson. Sometimes when we pray to God we say: "Lord, make me holy," or "Lord, I want to be holy." Thus we use the imperative and the indicative moods, but we certainly intend a request.

OBJECTIONS

1. St. James does not say that the oil must be blessed by anyone.

Answer. This is true, but Scripture is not the only rule of faith. Tradition teaches that the oil must be blessed, and by a bishop as the ordinary minister, by a priest as extraordinary minister.

2. All scholastic theologians teach that at least the five senses must be anointed. Therefore, one anointing never suffices.

Answer. These theologians merely mean that, for liceity, at least the five senses must be anointed. They admit that one anointing is enough for validity.

3. If a man receives but one anointing, the Church orders him to receive unconditionally the rest of the anointings afterwards, if this is possible. Hence one anointing is doubtfully valid.

Answer. The rest of the anointings are conferred upon him afterwards, not because they are required for the validity of the sacrament, but because the Church wishes her sacramental rites to be administered in their entirety. When the missing anointings are supplied later, they have no efficacy *ex opere operato,* but are regarded as sacramentals.

4. St. James does not say that the prayer of the priest is the form of the sacrament.

Answer. He does not say so explicitly, but he implies it because the effect obtained is referred to the prayer of faith as well as to the anointing.

Comment 1. When does extreme unction produce sanctifying grace *ex opere operato?*

If, in case of necessity, only one anointing is made, it is evident that sanctifying grace is conferred *ex opere operato* as soon as the matter and form are united and the last word of the form is pronounced.

Ordinarily, however, the sacrament is administered by a series of six anointings, each of them having its own form. The anointings follow this sequence: eyes, ears, nose, mouth, hands, and feet. The anointing of the feet may be omitted for any good reason.

A partial form accompanies each anointing. Thus when the eyes are anointed, the priest says: "Through this holy unction and His own most tender mercy, may the Lord pardon thee whatever debt thou hast incurred *through thy vision.*" The same form is uttered at the following anointings except that its ending is adapted to the part of the body being anointed: by hearing, smell, taste, touch, walking.

Since it is certain that the six anointings compose but one sacrament, we are led to inquire precisely when the sacrament produces its sanctifying grace *ex opere operato.*

Although other opinions may be held, it is much better to say that no grace is conferred until the last anointing has been completed. This is the view of St. Thomas, Suarez, and many others.

No sacrament produces grace until the full significance of its form is expressed. In extreme unction each of the forms uttered at the individual anointings has but a partial significance. It is only after the last partial form has been expressed that the preceding forms unite with it to signify that the debts incurred by misuse of *all* the bodily faculties are removed.

*

Conclusion 3. Extreme unction confers on the sick person a sense of security. It can remove all his sins and all the temporal punishment due to sins. Sometimes it restores his bodily health. Its principal special effect is to confer a sense of security.

Introduction. Extreme unction produces *ex opere operato* sanctifying grace, the effect common to all the sacraments, and, since it is a sacrament of the living, it ordinarily bestows an increase of grace. This sacrament also revives when it is received validly but unfruitfully.

We now inquire into its special effects, those, namely, which are proper to it either in themselves or in the manner in which they are achieved.

Explanation of Terms

1. A sense of security. When in danger of death, a sick person is bound to be afflicted by disturbing thoughts. Some of these

arise from the remembrance of past sins; others from one's present state of infirmity with its resultant feelings of depression and impatience; others, again, from the imminent trials to be encountered both before and after death.

Against the misgivings emerging from one's past infidelities, extreme unction bestows confidence. Against the uneasiness evoked by one's present pain and lassitude, it imparts peace and tranquillity. Against the fears generated by the dangers lying ahead, it confers courage. In short, extreme unction gives the sick person a sense of security which counteracts all tribulations.

This effect is accomplished by the bestowal of actual graces which flow *ex opere operato* from the sacrament after its reception. But the effect will not be obtained unless the sick person cooperates with these graces.

The actual graces continue to come as long as the infirm person is in danger of death. Once out of danger, they cease. Consequently, a sick man who relapses into danger of death, should be anointed again.

Since all the mental and physical trials connected with death are the result of Adam's sin, which introduced death into the world, the sense of security stimulated by the sacrament is a removal of one of the consequences of sin.

2. All his sins.

First, extreme unction in certain circumstances can remove all *mortal* sins.

When we considered the necessity of the sacrament of penance for a person who had sinned grievously after baptism, we saw that extreme unction was one of the substitutes that could be used for it in extraordinary circumstances. If a man is dangerously ill and is not likely to have another opportunity to go to the sacrament of penance, he is obliged to confess his mortal sins before receiving extreme unction, because the sacrament of penance is the only ordinary means of having such sins remitted.

But let us suppose that a man guilty of mortal sins has fallen unconscious. Although we give him conditional absolution, it is doubtful if he receives the sacrament of penance. If, however, before falling unconscious, he made an act of attrition only, extreme unction certainly takes away all his mortal sins. When, therefore, a sick man cannot go to the sacrament of penance, is in good faith, and has at least habitual attrition, extreme unction removes his mortal sins. It is only more probable that the other sacraments of the living can do this, but it is certain regarding extreme unction. This sacrament was instituted by Christ to remit serious sins, but only under the aforementioned conditions.

The student, however, should remember that extreme unction is a sacrament of the living. Hence, if a sick sinner is conscious and foresees his anointing, he is obliged to acquire the state of grace before receiving this sacrament.

It is customary and laudable for every person always to go to the sacrament of penance before being anointed, but this is not strictly required even if one is conscious of mortal sins. An act of perfect contrition including the intention of confessing suffices. If a man fails to make such an act but honestly thinks that he has, extreme unction will delete his mortal sins. He is in good faith and has at least attrition.

When mortal sins are remitted by extreme unction, it is evident that this effect results *ex opere operato* and immediately. The sick person does not have to cooperate with any actual graces emanating from the sacrament after its reception.

Second, extreme unction can remit all *venial* sins, both deliberate and semi-deliberate.

All theologians admit this truth, but they do not agree about the *manner* in which the sacrament removes the personal guilt of all venial sins.

Some believe that they are remitted *ex opere operato* and immediately at the instant of fruitful reception, provided that the recipient has at least a general resolve not to commit any venial sins again, or, according to others, if he has genuine attrition, either explicit or implicit, for all his venial sins. This latter opinion means that the sick man must not only be determined not to sin venially again (first opinion), but must in addition grieve over all his past unforgiven venial sins in a general way.

Other theologians think that, even if a sick man elicits a general retractation of all his venial sins, the personal guilt of only *some* of them is remitted *ex opere operato* when the sacrament is received. Full remission of these sins depends on the recipient's cooperation with the actual graces which follow after the sacrament's reception.

Either of these opinions may be held, but it should be noted that all agree that the sacrament *can* delete all venial sins by its own efficacy.

3. All temporal punishment due to past sins. Since temporal punishment is a liability to punishment in purgatory, it follows that extreme unction *can* enable a sick person to escape purgatory entirely.

Here again, it is certain that some temporal punishment is removed *ex opere operato* and immediately when grace is infused by the sacrament.

It is disputed *how* the sacrament takes away *all* temporal punishment. It is more probable that the complete effect is obtained by cooperating with the actual graces produced by the sacrament. But note again that all admit that the sacrament by its own power *can* delete *all* temporal punishment.

It should be observed that all the effects so far considered depend upon a fruitful reception of the sacrament. The sick man must either be in the state of grace when he receives it, or he must obtain sanctifying grace from or after its reception.

4. Restoration of bodily health. This restoration is sometimes complete, more often partial only. To obtain it the sacrament must be received fruitfully. Another condition, too, must be fulfilled. The Council of Trent (DB. 909; CT. 833) says that health is restored only "when it is conducive to the soul's welfare."

Theologians generally add a third condition. They say that the sacrament must be received before the natural bodily forces of recuperation are completely exhausted. This condition, however, is not universal because, in rare cases, the restoration of health can be miraculous. This is an infrequent occurrence which no one can expect.

The recuperation of health is produced by the sacrament supernaturally. God, by reason of its fruitful reception, either augments or cooperates with one's natural powers of recuperation, or, at times, He may by a special providence provide some external circumstance which will better one's health.

Theologians disagree about the translation of Trent's phrase, "when it is conducive to the soul's welfare." Some translate: "when it is conducive to the soul's eternal *salvation.*" This second translation may be defended, but it leads to conclusions which we would not want to admit.

It would follow, for instance, that a sick man who regained his health from the sacrament (a fact about which we can be sometimes morally certain), would be predestined. He might sin even repeatedly after his health is restored, and yet he would be certain to die in the state of grace. Otherwise, it would not have been conducive to his eternal salvation to have his health restored by the sacrament.

Again, it would seem to follow that those people, no matter how holy they are, who do not regain their health from the sacrament's reception, would have lost their souls, or would, at any rate, have deteriorated spiritually, if they had lived longer.

It would also follow from this translation that the efficacy of a sacrament would be dependent upon a future condition (eternal salvation). This is difficult to accept because sacraments operate as do natural causes. These, however, depend upon present conditions only.

Hence we prefer to translate the clause, "when it is conducive to the soul's *welfare,*" i.e., when it is conducive to the complete cleansing here and now of the sick man's soul. In short, extreme unction *can* restore baptismal innocence.

Sometimes, however, an improvement of health will assist the sick person to perform the acts of virtue, prompted by the graces of the sacrament, which will effect this innocence. In this case, extreme unction will benefit the body, regularly if it is received in plenty of time, rarely if it is delayed until the physical forces are almost exhausted. According to this explanation the restoration of health is no gauge of the spiritual condition in which the sick person who has recovered his health will finally die.

It is not only a revealed truth, but a fact of experience to which many doctors, nurses, and priests will attest, that extreme unction sometimes betters the recipient's health. However, here again we do not know for sure *how* the sacrament does this. Being a secondary special effect, it is only granted dependently on the principal effect, the sense of security.

Thus some cases of restoration of health can be explained by the fact that the sick man has cooperated with the actual graces which follow the sacrament's reception. Knowing that his sins are forgiven and inspired with confidence and peace, he will improve in health because the soul's condition necessarily reacts upon the body. This explanation has a solid foundation in the Council of Trent (DB. 909; CT. 833), in the Roman Catechism, and in St. Thomas.

However, it is quite clear that it does not explain all cases. Some organic ailments like cancer or angina pectoris cannot be ameliorated by one's psychological condition. Furthermore, some patients are so nervously exhausted that they cannot cooperate with the actual graces bestowed by the sacrament.

To explain such cases, some theologians believe that the improvement in health may be produced before the other special effects. It is granted in order that the person can *obtain* the total cleansing of his soul and a sense of security, not as an *effect* of this cleansing. The betterment of health results from the sacrament *ex opere operato* and immediately. According to the first explanation, it is produced *ex opere operato* but indirectly by cooperation with the actual graces.

Finally, some theologians suggest that the prayers said by the sick man when he cooperates with the graces springing from the sacrament may be endowed with a special impetratory value with reference to obtaining bodily health. As a result, God may enlighten the doctor to use a more efficient remedy, or He may see to it that some circumstance arises which will effect a restoration of bodily health.

It is quite probable that all three of these explanations are valid. One explanation will apply to some cases; the others to different cases. In some instances the restoration of health may result in all three ways.

5. A sense of security is the principal special effect. All the effects mentioned in the Conclusion are special, but among them the sense of security has the primacy. This means that God wants this effect to be attained above all the others and that they are subordinate to it. They are conferred either with a view to obtaining it or as a consequence of it.

Finally, it should be observed that all admit that God's purpose in instituting this sacrament was to enable the sick man, if he dies, to enter heaven without delay.

There are, then, five parts to the Conclusion. First, extreme unction confers a sense of security.

Second, it can remit all sins, mortal and venial.

Third, it can delete all temporal punishment due to sins.

Fourth, it sometimes restores bodily health.

Fifth, the conferring of a sense of security is the principal special effect.

Adversaries. The only disagreement among Catholics is about the fifth part. Many Scotists, following the opinion of St. Bonaventure and Scotus, believe that the primary effect is the full remission of venial sins.

Dogmatic Note

The first part is of divine faith from the Council of Trent (DB. 927; CT. 836): "If anyone says that the sacred unction of the sick does not confer grace, nor remit sins, nor *comfort the* sick . . . let him be anathema." The meaning of "comfort the sick" is evolved by the council (DB. 909, 907; CT. 833, 831).

From the same canon of Trent it is of faith that extreme unction remits at least venial sins ("nor remit sins").

It is certain and common teaching that the sacrament has the power to remove *all* venial sins.

It is also common and certain teaching that the sacrament deletes mortal sins under the specified conditions.

Concerning the third part, it is Catholic doctrine that the sacrament takes away *some* temporal punishment. Whenever the personal guilt of sins is removed, some of the temporal punishment due to them is also forgiven. Moreover, Trent (DB. 909; CT. 833) declares that this sacrament "wipes away the remains of sin." It is likely that this expression does not refer merely to the evil inclinations which remain as a result of sins committed, but also to their temporal punishment.

It is certain and common teaching that the sacrament *can* delete *all the* temporal punishment.

It is of divine faith from Trent (DB. 909; CT. 833) that extreme unction restores or benefits bodily health. The council says that the sick person "sometimes receives health of body when it is conducive to the soul's welfare."

It is more probable that the sense of security is the principal special effect. This seems to be indicated by Trent (DB. 907; CT. 831) when the council declares: ". . . similarly, (our most merciful Redeemer) has fortified the close of life by a kind of sturdy rampart, the sacrament of extreme unction." These words refer more obviously to the sense of security and, by mentioning only this effect in its introduction to the sacrament, the council seems to mean that this is its principal effect.

Part 1. Extreme unction confers a sense of security.

Proof 2. From Holy Scripture (James 5:14): ". . . the Lord will raise him up." We argue from the words "raise up" (*alleviabit*, i.e., arouse, excite, lighten). The proof is dogmatically certain because Trent (DB. 927, 909, 907; CT. 836, 833, 831) adopts the word "alleviabit" from St. James and explains it as meaning a sense of security. Apologetically, the proof is probable.

The word "alleviare" (to arouse) denotes in Scripture either a spiritual or a bodily excitation. Hence we cannot argue from its use in Scripture generally.

However, in our text the word, although it contains secondarily the meaning of bodily excitation because the sacrament does sometimes restore bodily health, denotes primarily a spiritual arousing.

This is true because, if a bodily cure were the only effect referred to by St. James, Christians would never die because they could keep a priest on hand to give them extreme unction. Moreover, the bodily cure would always be obtained since St. James does not attach any condition to it: ". . . the Lord will raise him up." Consequently, he must be referring primarily to some spiritual effect produced by the sacrament.

Furthermore, this effect is not merely the conferring of sanctifying grace because "alleviare" always signifies *activity* and *proximate* activity. Although sanctifying grace, as our supernatural nature, implies *remote* activity, this activity does not become fruitful except by the use of actual grace and the infused virtues. Just as the direct use of the voice or hand is necessary to awaken a sleeping person, so extreme unction directly arouses or awakens spiritually a sick one. This suggests that extreme unction confers actual graces on its recipient. If he corresponds with them, as the senses of a sleeping person do to a call, he will be comforted.

The meaning of a sense of security is beautifully explained in the *Catechism of the Council of Trent* (*Roman Catechism*, Part II, Chap. 6, Q. 14). This is a separate proof that a sense of security is an effect of extreme unction. This catechism has a special dogmatic value because it was written at the request of the council and by theologians who were present at the council.

Part 2. Extreme unction can remove all sins.

Proof 2. From Holy Scripture (James 5:15): ". . . if he is in sins, they shall be forgiven him." This proof is dogmatically certain, apologetically very probable.

No solid reason is advanced to restrict the meaning of "sins" to venial sins only. In fact, in Scripture the word "sins" commonly refers to mortal sins.

It does not follow that extreme unction forgives sins independently of the sacrament of penance. The words of St. James must be interpreted in the light of John 20:23. From this text we previously proved that all mortal sins must be submitted to the tribunal of penance. It is the one ordinary means of forgiveness.

Proof 3. From the form of extreme unction. It is a theological axiom that the form of a sacrament truly effects what it signifies. In pronouncing the form of extreme unction the priest says: ". . . may the Lord pardon you whatsoever debt you have incurred" (*quidquid deliquisti*). The most burdensome debt incurred by men is their sins, mortal and also venial. Since, then, the form of the sacrament signifies the cancellation of this debt, extreme unction can remit all sins.

Part 3. Extreme unction can remit all temporal punishment.

Proof 2. From the consent of theologians. All of them admit that this sacrament can win for its recipient immediate entrance into heaven. This teaching implies that all temporal punishment can be remitted.

Proof 3. From the form of the sacrament. Temporal punishment is a spiritual debt incurred by reason of sin. Hence, extreme unction, since its form expresses pardon for spiritual debts (*quidquid deliquisti*), should remove temporal punishment. Moreover, it can remove all this punishment because its form does not express any limitation.

The plenary indulgence of the apostolic benediction is given to the sick person immediately after extreme unction. This indulgence takes effect at the moment of death.

It does not imply that extreme unction is unable to delete all temporal punishment, but is intended to remove any temporal punishment incurred *after* the reception of the sacrament and also any that may remain owing to faulty cooperation with the actual graces flowing from the sacrament. The granting of this indulgence reveals the Church's desire to have us escape purgatory.

Part 4. Sometimes extreme unction restores bodily health.

Proof 2. From Holy Scripture (James 5:15): ". . . the Lord will raise him up." Although "raise up" (*alleviabit*), as we have seen, denotes primarily a spiritual comforting, it is interpreted by the Fathers and theologians as referring secondarily to an improvement of health.

Proof 3. From tradition. In all the liturgical books we find that the prayers used to consecrate the oil of extreme unction contain an appeal that it may benefit the bodily health of the future recipient. This fact manifests the constant and universal belief of the Church that this sacrament restores health when the conditions are verified.

Part 5. A sense of security is the principal special effect. The argument follows in form from theological reasoning.

That special effect which can be obtained by every *sick person and* only *by a sick person is the principal special effect;*

But a sense of security is the only special effect which can be obtained by every *sick person and* only *by a sick person:*

Therefore, a sense of security is the principal special effect.

Proof for the major. *Every* sick person should be able to obtain the principal special effect of a sacrament that is intended for the sick. All admit, and we shall prove it later, that *only* a seriously ill person can receive extreme unction.

Proof for the minor. *Every* sick person cannot obtain the other special effects. Some of the sick may not have any mortal sins, or venial sins, or temporal punishment. They may have eliminated all these by confessions, by good works, by indulgences.

Moreover, restoration of bodily health cannot be the principal special effect because many anointed persons do not obtain it.

The only effect which *every* sick person can obtain is a sense of security. Depression, faintness, fear are the common lot of the sick.

It would not be a valid objection to say that some infirm people are unconscious and so cannot obtain a sense of security because they do not need it. To use the actual graces given by any sacrament, the recipient must be conscious. According to such an objection we should have to say that strength to profess the faith bravely is not the principal special effect of confirmation, because unconscious people are also confirmed.

Consciousness is merely an indispensable natural condition which makes it possible for the recipient of extreme unction to obtain its principal effect. The conscious or unconscious condition of the recipient is extrinsic to the sacrament and has no part in determining which of the several special effects is the primary one.

The other special effects do not pertain *only* to the sick. It is obvious that sins and temporal punishment can be forgiven to those who are not sick.

Restoration of bodily health cannot be the principal special effect because, although it can be granted to the sick only, it cannot, as we have seen, be granted to all of them.

It is true, of course, that many others besides the sick need a sense of security. The soldier about to go to battle, the criminal mounting the scaffold are much perturbed and need comforting. It seems, then, that a sense of security is not the principal special effect because it does not apply to sick persons only.

But the healthy, regardless of their unfortunate circumstances, do not need a sense of security *in the same way* as the sick. The man who receives extreme unction must be in danger of death from sickness or accident or old age. His natural bodily forces, his nervous system, have been dealt a severe blow. His disturbed state of soul is caused by a very special condition which is not verified in the soldier or criminal. These, when in danger of death, retain their natural strength and can gain a spirit of confidence by prayer and by cooperating with the graces coming from confession and Communion. But the sick man has lost his natural strength and so is in an extraordinary condition. Accordingly, he requires a singular remedy, extreme unction, which provides him with special graces to overcome the unique state of weakness which afflicts him. In this sense, only the sick need a sense of security.

OBJECTIONS

1. Often the sick who have been anointed do not manifest a sense of security, but rather more anxiety than they had before. So extreme unction does not comfort the seriously ill.

Answer. The fact is that almost all the recipients of this sacrament manifest a peace that was previously wanting.

If someone would, after being anointed, manifest great perturbation of soul, we would explain this as follows. First, the man may not have received the sacrament validly and fruitfully. We cannot, however, reach this uncharitable conclusion simply from external signs of worry which he manifests.

Again, spiritual comfort is not obtained unless the sick man cooperates with the actual graces conferred.

Third, a person may, owing to human frailty, manifest outward signs of worry and at the same time be interiorly comforted.

2. Baptism and penance were instituted by Christ to remit sins. Therefore, this is not a special effect of extreme unction.

Answer. Extreme unction is a sacrament of the living. Hence its recipient should, when possible, be in the state of grace when he receives it. Baptism and penance are sacraments of the dead.

The remission of sins by extreme unction differs from the remission procured by baptism or penance. Baptism remits antebaptismal sins only. Extreme unction remits postbaptismal sins.

Both penance and extreme unction have postbaptismal sins as their object, but penance is the only independent way of having mortal sins forgiven. Extreme unction can in some circumstances remit them, but only dependently on penance.

Remission of sins is a special effect of extreme unction, but it is limited to the comparatively few people who cannot, except in desire, receive penance.

3. If extreme unction removed all temporal punishment, the Church would not urge us to have Masses said or prayers offered for those who die immediately after being anointed.

Answer. It is certain that extreme unction *can* remit all temporal punishment, but it is always doubtful whether it actually does so. It is more probable that the obtaining of this effect in its entirety depends upon the cooperation of the sick man with the actual graces issuing spontaneously from the sacrament. Hence, full remission of temporal punishment is not achieved until some time elapses after the sacrament's reception. So it is evident that Masses and prayers should be offered for one who dies immediately after receiving extreme unction.

It may be held, however, that all temporal punishment is removed at the very time when the sacrament is received provided that the dispositions of the recipient are sufficiently perfect. Even so, Masses and prayers should be offered for the deceased because we have no way of knowing what dispositions he had when he was anointed.

If, in fact, the anointed person now dead has no need of our Masses and prayers, they will not be fruitless because they will benefit others as well as ourselves.

4. According to this Conclusion extreme unction, since it opens heaven immediately, is the equivalent of martyrdom. But the Church has always regarded martyrdom as unique.

Answer. In order to obtain all the spiritual effects of extreme unction, the sick person must cooperate with the graces of the sacrament after it is received. The martyr needs a disposition only at the instant of his death. Besides, martyrdom ordinarily wins a higher degree of glory than extreme unction. We pray *to* martyrs; we pray *for* those who die after being anointed.

5. The primary effect of a sacrament is expressed by its form. But the form of extreme unction expresses the remission of sins, not a sense of security. So the primary effect of this sacrament is the remission of venial sins.

Answer. The general primary effect of every sacrament is the infusion of sanctifying grace. Yet, even this effect is only implicitly expressed in the forms of the various sacraments.

So, too, the principal special effect of a sacrament may be only implicitly expressed by its form. The form of extreme unction does implicitly express a sense of security because the worries besetting the ailing man arise either from his own sins or from the sin of Adam. If Adam had not sinned, there would be no death with its concomitant anxieties. Hence, since the form of extreme unction implores pardon for "whatever debts you have incurred," it implicitly petitions the bestowal of a sense of security. In our proof we offered reasons why the remission of venial sins cannot be the principal special effect of this sacrament.

6. Every person is guilty of venial sins. So the remission of these sins can always be obtained by extreme unction and should be the primary effect of the sacrament.

Answer. Venial sins are forgiven in many ways. Hence it is not only theoretically, but practically possible for the recipient of extreme unction to be free of all venial sins at the time when he receives the sacrament. So the remission of venial sins, since it is not applicable to *every* sick person, cannot be the principal special effect.

Comment 1. Extreme unction confers sanctifying grace on the unconscious.

It should be recalled that the supreme effect of every sacrament is the conferring of sanctifying grace *ex opere operato*. This effect is procured even if the disposed sick person is unconscious and so does not need the actual graces which foster the sense of security.

Comment 2. The revival of extreme unction.

This sacrament bestows its sanctifying grace and also its actual graces after it is received, if it was valid but unfruitful at the moment of reception.

Thus a grave sinner who is unconscious but at least implicitly wished to receive the sacrament, receives it validly even though he has no sorrow for his sins. If he becomes conscious afterwards and makes an act of attrition, grace comes to him from the sacrament *ex opere operato*.

Comment 3. When extreme unction should be received.

Although theologians dispute *how* the total remission of venial sins and of temporal punishment and also *how* the restoration of bodily health are achieved, all agree that this sacrament should be received in plenty of time. They deprecate the fairly common practice of delaying the sacrament until the patient is at the brink of death. The priest should be called as soon as real danger of death exists. Early reception of the sacrament enables the sick person to prepare for it and to cooperate with the graces emanating from it. Delay until death is imminent makes this preparation and cooperation difficult and sometimes impossible. As a result, the efficacy of the sacrament is impeded.

Comment 4. The symbolism of extreme unction.

This sacrament, like the others, is a *mixed* sign. Its effects are symbolized by its matter, olive oil. This will be clear if we examine the nature of this oil.

First, it aids digestion and is itself of nutritional value and so gives a feeling of lightness and of strength to the body. So it symbolizes a sense of security or buoyancy.

Besides, oil is a source of light and of heat and, consequently, symbolizes the light of faith and the warmth of confidence which are involved in the sense of security.

Moreover, olive oil when rubbed on aching muscles or joints relieves the pain. In this way it symbolizes the removal of sins, the pains of the soul.

Again, when oil is applied to cuts or abrasions, it helps them to scarify and to disappear. Thus it symbolizes the removal of temporal punishment, the scar remaining from our sins.

Finally, this oil, both as an internal medicine which facilitates bodily functions and as an external remedy which alleviates aches and cures wounds, symbolizes the betterment of health which may result from extreme unction.

Accordingly, all the special effects of the sacrament are symbolized by the anointing with olive oil.

*

Conclusion 4. The minister of extreme unction is any priest, but only a priest. The recipient must be an adult who has been baptized and is in danger of death.

Introduction. So far we have considered the intrinsic causes (matter and form) and the final cause (effects) of extreme unction. We now treat of its efficient cause (the minister) who places the sacrament as Christ's vicar.

Moreover, since every sacrament must be administered to some one, it is important to know who can receive extreme unction.

In both parts we deal with validity only. For liceity on the part of both minister and recipient, other conditions are prescribed. If the requirements explained in this Conclusion are not fulfilled, no sacrament is conferred even though the outward rite may be perfectly performed.

We assume that the general conditions for any valid sacrament are verified. Matter and form must be correct, and properly united. The priest must have a virtual and internal intention. The recipient must elicit at least an implicit habitual and an internal intention.

Explanation of Terms

1. Any priest. We make no exception. The priest can be from a foreign land, of an Oriental rite, a stranger, an apostate. He needs no authorization or jurisdiction from the Church.

2. Only a priest. The minister must possess the character which is imprinted on the soul by ordination to the priesthood. Bishops, of course, have this character as well as ordinary priests. Deacons have the character of orders, but not the character of the priesthood, and so cannot administer extreme unction. All others are excluded, even a cardinal if he should happen to lack the priestly character.

3. The recipient must be an *adult*. Hence infants, and the insane who never at any time in their lives had the use of reason, cannot receive this sacrament validly. A child who has sufficient use of reason before the age of seven may receive the sacrament.

4. The recipient must be *baptized*. Baptism is required for the valid reception of any other sacrament.

5. The recipient must be in danger of death. Healthy people cannot receive this sacrament. Neither can all those who are in danger of death. The danger must arise from some cause *already present within the body*. Hence soldiers going into battle and criminals about to be executed cannot be anointed. The danger

must be caused by sickness, disease, old age (which is a combination of diseases or a general malfunctioning of the life processes), or by accident or injury.

Danger of death does not mean that death must be imminent, though, of course, extreme unction should be given then if it has not been administered before. It could be a mortal sin against charity for relatives to wait until the sick person is beyond hope of recovery before they summon a priest to confer the sacrament.

The anointing may be conferred even if the danger of death is merely remote. In practice, the proximity of the danger is to be judged from the nature of the illness and from the opinions of doctors, nurses, priests, the sick man himself, and his close relatives.

The danger of death attendant upon diverse diseases varies with time and other circumstances. It depends on the advancement of medical knowledge, the general health of the sick person, the medical equipment on hand, and so on.

Before the advent of surgical operations, an attack of acute appendicitis placed a person in great danger of death. This is usually not true today if the person can undergo an operation. However, it is still probable that the victim of such an attack may be anointed before the operation.

Formerly tuberculosis of the lungs was nearly always fatal, but not so in most cases today.

On the other hand, some diseases such as certain kinds of cancer are still incurable. If a man contracts one of these types of cancer, he may be anointed even though he will most likely live for a considerable time.

Two parts, then, make up the Conclusion. First, the minister must be a priest, and only a priest.

Second, the recipient must be an adult, baptized, and in danger of death.

Dogmatic Note

It is certain and common teaching that *any* ordained priest can be the minister.

The Council of Trent (DB. 929; CT. 838) has defined as an article of faith that only a priest can be the minister: "If anyone says that . . . a priest *alone* is not the proper minister of extreme unction, let him be anathema."

It is Catholic doctrine, inferred from Trent (DB. 909; CT. 833), that the recipient must be an adult. The council mentions three effects—the remission of sins, the remission of temporal punishment, the obtaining of a sense of security—which evidently can be received by adults only.

It is also Catholic doctrine that the sick person must be baptized.

It can be inferred from Trent (DB. 910; CT. 834), and so is Catholic doctrine, that the recipient must be in danger of death. The council declares that the text of St. James means "that this anointing is to be applied to the *sick*, particularly to those who are so dangerously ill that they seem about to expire." It is, therefore, plain that the sacrament is to be given to those also who are not in any immediate danger of death, but who are seriously ill.

Part 1. The minister is any priest, but only a priest.

Proof 2. From Holy Scripture (James 5:14): "Let him call in the *priests* of the Church." The text is dogmatically certain, apologetically probable, with regard to both points.

St. James mentions no other qualification of the minister except that he be a priest. The priest does not need holiness or charismatic gifts or jurisdiction or anything else. He is to use the sanctifying power rooted in his sacramental character. The exercise of this power does not depend for validity upon the subjective dispositions of the priest because extreme unction is a sacrament and gives grace *ex opere operato.* So any priest can be the minister.

St. James mentions priests alone, but does he intend to exclude all other ministers? Perhaps he means that priests are the ordinary ministers, but that deacons or laymen could in case of necessity administer the sacrament validly.

This interpretation is possible, but not likely. St. James uses the same Greek word, "presbuteroi," (literally, "old men") which occurs in the *Acts* and in the epistles of St. Paul and which means either bishops or priests (Acts 11:30; 14:22; I Tim. 4:12, 14; 5:17–22; Tit. 1:5).

Proof 3. From the *Code of Canon Law* (Par. 938): "Every priest and only a priest administers this sacrament validly."

Part 2. The recipient must be an adult, baptized, in danger of death.

Proof 2. From Holy Scripture (James 5:14, 15). St. James says: ". . . if he be in *sins.*" He supposes that the recipient is capable of sinning and so that he is an *adult.*

Moreover, he says: "Is any one sick among *you?*" Since the letter is addressed to Catholics only, he takes for granted that those to be anointed are *baptized.*

Furthermore, we can infer from the text that the recipient must be *seriously ill.* It would be ridiculous for St. James to inculcate so much solemnity for a person having a slight illness like a cold or a headache.

Besides, he says: "Let him *call in* the priests of the Church." He intimates, therefore, that the ailing man is so sick that he is not able to go to see the priest, as we would expect him to do.

Proof 3. From the *Code of Canon Law* (Par. 940): "Extreme unction cannot be conferred except on one of the *faithful* who, after *attaining the use of reason,* is in *danger of death* by reason of sickness or old age."

OBJECTIONS

1. St. James says (5:14): "Let him call in the *priests* of the Church." Therefore, one priest cannot administer the sacrament.

Answer. St. James uses the plural to designate a class of persons. Sometimes we speak the same way. We might say, referring to a sick person: "Let him call in the doctors." We would merely mean that he should summon one doctor, a man belonging to the medical profession. It should be remembered, however, that several priests can administer extreme unction, as we shall explain in a Comment.

2. St. James by "priests" simply means an aged man. This is the true meaning of the Greek word which he employs.

Answer. We admit that etymologically and in profane usage the Greek word has this meaning. In the New Testament, however, it does not ordinarily retain this meaning. It usually designates a class of persons having an official function in the Church. That this is the signification intended by St. James becomes more clear from the fact that he does not merely say "priests," but "priests *of the Church.*" No Christian would have dreamed of calling in an aged pagan or non-Catholic to administer the rite. Hence it was not necessary to add "of the Church," if St. James meant that a Catholic *aged* person should be summoned. Consequently, "priests of the Church" means those who are ordained priests and so have official duties in the Church.

The Council of Trent (DB. 929; CT. 838), after examining tradition, defined that "priests" in this text means priests in the strict sense.

Comment 1. Can several priests administer extreme unction?

Yes, they could do so validly, but not licitly in the Latin Church. To be valid, the sacrament would be administered in one of the three following ways.

First, all might perform the entire series of anointings in this manner. The first priest would anoint the eyes and say the corresponding form; the second priest would then do the same; the third priest would repeat the same anointing; and so on if there were more priests. Thereupon the first priest would anoint the ears and say the prescribed form; the second priest would repeat the same anointing; and so for the other priests.

Second, all might perform the entire rite successively. The first priest would perform all the anointings while saying their corresponding forms. The second priest would then repeat all the anointings. So would the third and the others.

Third, the first priest might anoint the eyes and say the form. The second priest would then anoint the ears and say the form. The third priest would anoint the lips and recite the corresponding form.

The sacrament would be invalid if one priest were to anoint while another uttered the form.

Comment 2. The necessity of receiving extreme unction.

Generally speaking, this sacrament is not necessary by necessity of means to attain salvation. It is, however, necessary by necessity of precept, but it is safe to say that ordinarily this precept does not oblige under pain of mortal sin. This is the more obvious meaning of the *Code of Canon Law* (Par. 944).

To omit the sacrament out of contempt, or in circumstances which might occasion serious scandal, would be a mortal sin.

The student should recall that in some instances extreme unction is absolutely necessary for the salvation of a sick man. This occurs when a grave sinner is unconscious, but has made an act of attrition before falling unconscious. In this case, extreme unction can supply for the sacrament of penance so that without the anointing the man cannot be saved, since it is unlikely that he can receive the sacrament of penance.

Comment 3. Repeating extreme unction.

It is certain that a man can and should receive this sacrament each time that he falls into serious illness during his life.

However, during the same illness the sick often undergo improvements and regressions in health, though the illness abides. Angina pectoris and tuberculosis are examples.

It is safe to say that, if a sick man, once anointed when in danger of death, relapses into this danger after an interval of some time during which danger of death from the same illness became remote, he may be anointed again. No obligation seems to exist to confer the sacrament, but it *may* be repeated.

SECTION SEVEN

The Sacrament of Order

*

Section Seven

THE SACRAMENT OF ORDER

WE now come to consider the first of the two sacraments which are primarily destined for the welfare of the Christian society, as distinguished from the welfare of the individual. From the viewpoint of the status or functions which it confers, order is the noblest of all sacraments. It is also absolutely necessary for the continuance of the Church.

Conclusion 1. The rite by which some orders are conferred is a true sacrament.

Introduction. It is clear from the previous sections that the apostles and their successors received from Christ the power to sanctify others by administering the sacraments. Baptism and matrimony are the only sacraments that can be administered by the laity.

Nevertheless, it is not yet proved that Christ wished His ministers to receive their sanctifying power by the conferral of an external rite or ordination ceremony. Moreover, even if Christ did wish and command such a ceremony, it would not necessarily follow that this ceremony would be a sacrament. Despite the fact that Christ did not institute any inefficacious or non-sacramental rites, we ought to prove for the benefit of non-Catholics that the ordination ceremony is a genuine sacrament.

343

In this Conclusion we do not prove that any definite ordination is a sacrament. We shall deal with the individual ordinations later. Our only object here is to prove theologically and apologetically that Christ did institute *some* ordination ceremony that is a sacrament.

Explanation of Terms

1. Orders. It is a sacrament which, by the imposition of a bishop's hand and his accompanying prayer, confers upon a man spiritual power to sanctify others.

2. A true sacrament. We shall prove that there is an ordination ceremony which fulfills our general definition of a sacrament.

Adversaries. Some Protestants have an ordination ceremony, but all of them except the Ritualists deny that it is a sacrament.

Dogmatic Note

It is of divine faith from the Council of Trent (DB. 963; CT. 846): "If anyone says that orders or holy ordination is not truly and properly a sacrament instituted by Christ the Lord; or that it is a kind of human figment devised by men unskilled in eccesiastical matters; or that it is merely a ceremony for choosing ministers of the word of God and of the sacraments; let him be anathema."

Proof 2. From Holy Scripture (II Tim. 1:6, 7): "For this reason I admonish thee to stir up the grace of God which is in thee by the imposition of my hands. For God has not given us the spirit of fear, but of power and of love and of prudence."

From this text it is dogmatically certain (DB. 959; CT. 842), apologetically probable, that orders is a sacrament.

In these words of St. Paul addressed to Timothy, bishop of Ephesus, we find the essential elements of a sacrament.

First, there is a *perceptible sign,* the "laying on of my hands."

This imposition of hands does not refer to confirmation for various reasons. First, it is clear from other passages of Scripture that an imposition of hands was used in ordaining ministers (Acts 6:6; I Tim. 4:14; 5:22).

Again, confirmation does not bestow the spirit of "prudence" which St. Paul ascribes to this particular laying on of hands.

Besides, all Christians received confirmation, whereas this text refers to a special gift received by Timothy alone: "which is in *thee*."

Moreover, confirmation was usually conferred immediately after baptism in the early Church (Acts 8:12–18; 19:2–6). Since Timothy was already a Catholic when St. Paul first met him (Acts 16:1), he had probably been already confirmed.

Finally, it is evident from both letters to Timothy that the grace which he is admonished to stir up is more than that of confirmation. He is to teach, preach, counsel, reprimand, govern, and ordain others.

Second, this laying on of hands *conferred grace* on Timothy. The word "grace" (*charisma*) used in the text had only two possible meanings for St. Paul. Either it signified a charismatic gift like the gift of healing, or sanctifying grace. We know that charismatic gifts depended upon the inspiration of the Holy Spirit for their exercise. But the "grace" referred to in this text depends upon the *free will* of Timothy. He is to "stir it up." Hence it must be sanctifying grace, a perpetual possession.

Third, this grace is bestowed *ex opere operato*. St. Paul does not attribute it either to his own virtues or to those of Timothy, but to the laying on of hands. The rite itself, then, must have functioned in the production of the grace.

Fourth, the rite was *instituted by Christ* because all grace-giving rites owe their origin to Him. The apostles were merely "dispensers of the mysteries of God" (I Cor. 4:1).

Finally, this rite was to continue *perpetually* because the very existence of the indefectible Church depends upon it. There could be no Mass, no Holy Communion, no sacrament of penance, without the sacrament of orders.

Proof 3. From the Fathers. Speaking of one who has just been ordained, St. Gregory of Nyssa writes: "Granted that he looks the same externally; but internally his soul has been purified by the invisible power of grace" (*Orat. in bapt. Christi;* PG. XLVI, 582).

St. Gregory the Great declares: "Externally we receive the sacraments of sacred orders from teachers of the Church, but internally we are strengthened by the omnipotent God through the power of these sacraments" (*In I Reg.,* 1. 4, chap. 5; PL. LXXIX, 299).

For additional patristic quotations, consult Pohle-Preuss, *The Sacraments*, IV, 59–61.

Proof 4. From the consent of the Oriental churches. These schismatical churches existed long before Protestantism. They were, too, unwilling to accept anything from the Catholic Church. Yet all of them hold that orders is a sacrament.

Objections

1. In II Tim 1:6 the Greek word which is translated in the Vulgate by "imposition of hands," simply means the uplifting of one's hands to cast a vote. Therefore, it might be inferred that Timothy was chosen by popular vote, not by a sacramental rite.

Answer. There was no popular vote. St. Paul says that Timothy was ordained "by the imposition of *my* hands."

Moreover, a popular vote could not bestow sanctifying grace.

Finally, although in profane usage the Greek word employed in this text frequently meant the raising of hands to cast a vote, this is not its ordinary Scriptural usage. In fact, the Greek word used in I Tim. 4:14, where St. Paul also refers to the ordination of Timothy, necessarily means a physical laying on of hands. Clerics were never consecrated by popular vote. Sometimes bishops were chosen by popular demand, but they were always ordained by another bishop.

2. St. Peter calls all Christians "a holy priesthood" (I Pet. 2:5) and "a royal priesthood" (I Pet. 2:9). So all Christians are priests and no sacrament of orders confers special powers on relatively few.

Answer. All Christians by baptism and confirmation may be called priests in a general way. They can offer "spiritual sacrifices" to God, as St. Peter himself explains (I Pet. 2:5). These spiritual sacrifices are internal acts of worship and of praise. We have already clarified the meaning of this general priesthood of the laity in the Conclusion on the sacramental character and in our treatment of the Mass.

3. We do not find any record of the institution of the sacrament of order in the gospels. Christ said nothing about it.

Answer. Christ in the gospels explicitly conferred the two outstanding powers, to say Mass and to absolve from sin, upon the apostles and their successors.

Our Lord does not say *how* He wanted these powers transmitted to future generations and so says nothing in the gospels about the *rite* of orders. When, however, we find the apostles, shortly after the ascension, ordaining others by imposing hands, we reasonably infer that they had been instructed by Christ to do this.

Christ personally instituted this sacrament and, more probably, on some occasion between His resurrection and ascension; certainly before His ascension.

*

Conclusion 2. The subdiaconate and the minor orders do not belong to the sacrament of order.

Introduction. Having proved that there exists a sacrament of order, we now face the problem of deciding which of the various orders belong to the sacrament. For we find eight different orders in the Latin Church. The first four are: the bishopric, priesthood, diaconate, and subdiaconate. These are called *major* orders because the vow of celibacy is attached to them. In addition, we have the four *minor* orders which by distinct rites create acolytes, exorcists, readers, and doorkeepers.

All eight orders are very ancient and are enumerated by Pope Cornelius (DB. 45) in the year 251. Trent (DB. 958; CT. 841), too, declares that all of them were known "from the very beginning of the Church."

In the very early writings of St. Ignatius of Antioch (died about 107) we find only bishops, priests, and deacons mentioned. Even today in the Oriental churches, three of the four minor orders are wanting. They have readers only, but they do have all four major orders.

Explanation of Terms

1. Subdiaconate. As the name implies, the subdeacon is empowered to assist the deacon at solemn Mass. He pours water into the chalice, chants the epistle, presents the paten to the

deacon, and gives the latter general assistance. He also washes the corporals and sacred linen used at Mass. It should be noted that the subdiaconate is a *major* order and of a more sacred character than the minor orders, but it does not belong to the sacrament. The subdeacon takes a vow of celibacy before his ordination.

2. Four minor orders.

Acolytes assist the higher clergy at Mass, especially by carrying lighted candles and presenting the water and wine.

Exorcists are deputed to pronounce the formula of exorcism either at baptism or at other times. At present the Church does not allow them to exercise this function. Only priests are permitted to do this.

Readers are authorized to read publicly at sacred services.

Doorkeepers receive power to perform the duties of sextons, sacristans, and ushers.

Most of these functions of the four minor orders are performed commonly today by those who have never been ordained.

3. Do not belong to the sacrament. We simply mean that these five rites do not fulfill our general definition of a sacrament, especially that they do not give grace *ex opere operato.*

Adversaries. Some great scholastic theologians like St. Albert the Great, St. Bonaventure, and Scotus seem to have taught as more probable that these five orders belong to the sacrament. A few reputable theologians of today follow this opinion.

Dogmatic Note

It is much more probable that these orders do not belong to the sacrament. Personally we believe that this is now certain. The Constitution, *Sacramentum ordinis,* (Nov. 30, 1947, DB. 3001; CT. 852) of Pius XII states that the sacrament of order must have the same matter, and decides that this matter is the imposition of hands for the bishopric, priesthood, and diaconate. Since no imposition of hands occurs in the subdiaconate and minor orders, they cannot belong to the sacrament.

Proof 2. From theological reasoning. We have two such arguments. The first follows in form.

Rites not instituted by Christ, but by the Church, are not sacraments;

But the subdiaconate and minor orders are rites not instituted by Christ, but by the Church:

Therefore, the subdiaconate and minor orders are not sacraments.

Proof for the major. It is admitted by all and was proved in an early Conclusion.

Proof for the minor. It is substantiated from history. These orders vary in number at different times and in diverse places. Even today in the Oriental churches we have only the subdiaconate and the lectorate.

They would have to remain permanently everywhere if Christ had instituted them. The Church cannot suppress anything that He established.

The second argument follows in form.

Rites not having the matter of the sacrament of order do not belong to the sacrament;

But the subdiaconate and minor orders are rites not having the matter of the sacrament of order:

Therefore, the subdiaconate and minor orders do not belong to the sacrament.

Proof for the major. Each sacrament must have its own determinate matter. If the same sacrament were to have two specifically different matters, it would not be one sacrament, but two.

Proof for the minor. It is a fact that no imposition of hands is conferred in the subdiaconate and minor orders. Yet imposition of hands, and it alone, is the matter of the sacrament, and this is Catholic doctrine.

OBJECTIONS

1. The subdiaconate and minor orders may not be repeated. Hence they impress a character; but only sacraments do this.

Answer. The fact that the Church does not repeat ordinations to the subdiaconate and minor orders simply shows that she does not want to repeat them, not that they imprint a character. Indeed, there is no reason for repeating them. When men are deputed to any public function, even secular, this deputation is not ordinarily repeated even though no physical mark accompanied the original deputation.

2. The *Decretum pro Armenis* (DB. 701; CT. 839) evidently means that the subdiaconate and minor orders are part of the sacrament.

Answer. We shall discuss this decree later. It has very little, if any, dogmatic value. It does, however, seem to teach what the objection asserts.

Comment 1. Are there eight or seven orders?

Some theologians and the Council of Trent (DB. 958; CT. 841) say that there are seven orders, whereas we have said that there are eight and have named them.

The discrepancy arises from the fact that some authors include ordinations both to the episcopate and to the priesthood under one term "priesthood." The Council of Trent also does this, but it should be noted that the heading or title, "Concerning the *Seven* Orders," is not the work of the council itself.

It was formerly disputed, but is now certain that the bishopric is a distinct sacramental rite from that of the priesthood. Hence we should speak of eight orders, not of seven.

The tonsure or cutting of the hair which precedes the conferring of the minor orders is not an order. It is an ecclesiastical ceremony which places a man in the clerical state. It confers no power whatever.

Comment 2. Implicit institution of the subdiaconate and minor orders.

1. A few authors explain the historical variations of the subdiaconate and minor orders by saying that Christ Himself instituted them when He instituted the diaconate, so that these five orders are implicitly contained in the diaconate. Consequently, the Church is empowered to suppress them and reintroduce them according to her needs. But they were established by Christ, and so one of our arguments from theological reasoning has no force.

However, Pope Pius XII in his *Constitution* "Sacramentum ordinis" has declared that the only matter for the diaconate is the imposition of hands. Yet no imposition of hands occurs in the five ordinations in question, but only a transmission of the instruments.

Hence the proffered explanation must admit that one and the same sacrament can have two specifically different matters. This is untenable. We would then have several sacramental signs and, consequently, several sacraments of orders. This is heretical.

Moreover, if the Church could divide up the diaconate, as these authors affirm, why could she not also divide up the higher orders? Why, for instance, could she not suppress the diaconate itself (which she has never done), since all powers of a deacon are possessed by a priest? Why does she not suppress the diaconate today in many places, since deacons are not necessary? At solemn Mass priests regularly perform the functions of the deacon.

Would it be allowable to say that the Church could divide up the powers of the priesthood or the bishopric? Could she ordain a priest merely to say Mass or to hear confessions? Could she consecrate a bishop who could confirm only? Why not, according to the principle proposed to explain the historical appearances and disappearances of the subdiaconate and minor orders?

*

Conclusion 3. Ordination to the diaconate belongs to the sacrament of order.

Introduction. We shall now prove briefly that each of the three higher orders forms part of the sacrament. We begin with the diaconate.

Explanation of Terms

1. Ordination to the diaconate. The essentials of this ordination will be given explicitly in a later Conclusion. According to the *Roman Pontifical* this ordination bestows on the recipient the power "to minister at the altar, to baptize, and to preach." Deacons having the pastor's permission are allowed also to distribute Holy Communion. Then, too, they need the pastor's permission to administer solemn baptism and to preach.

In general, deacons are those men who by their ordination are empowered to assist bishops and priests in the performance of sacred functions.

The so-called "deacons" of some Protestant churches are either auxiliary preachers or caretakers of the poor or administrators of external affairs.

2. Belongs to the sacrament. The ordination of a deacon fulfills our general definition of a sacrament and, especially, it confers grace *ex opere operato*.

Dogmatic Note

It is Catholic doctrine. The Constitution, *Sacramentum Ordinis,* (DB. 3001; CT. 852) takes for granted that this ordination belongs to the sacrament.

The same truth can be inferred from the Council of Trent (DB. 964; CT. 847) which declares: "If anyone says that the Holy Spirit is not conferred by holy ordination and so that the bishops say in vain: 'Receive the Holy Ghost' . . . let him be anathema."

When ordaining deacons, the bishop says: "Receive the Holy Ghost." Consequently, according to the council, these words are not said in vain, but the Holy Ghost, i.e., sanctifying grace, is conferred by the ordination.

It should be observed, however, that the words, "Receive the Holy Ghost," are not the *form* of the ordination. But the bishop does utter them and the council states that they are effective—not that they themselves produce the effect, but that the truth which they express is accomplished by the rite.

Proof 2. From Holy Scripture. Deacons are mentioned explicitly by St. Paul (Phil. 1:1; I Tim. 3:8, 9, 12), but these texts do not prove that their ordination is a sacrament. The classic passage (Acts 6:1–6) is declared by Trent (DB. 958; CT. 841) to refer to the ordination of deacons. The passage itself does not say so. We argue especially from verse 6: "These [seven men] they set before the apostles: and they praying imposed hands upon them."

The proof is dogmatically certain from the interpretation of tradition. Apologetically, it has some probability. As usual we seek in the passage the essential elements of our definition of a sacrament.

Since there is an imposition of hands and a prayer, we find a *perceptible sign* without difficulty. But it is not clear that this rite conferred grace, much less that it did so *ex opere operato.*

A power to supervise the distribution of temporal goods was given by the ordination. Furthermore, spiritual power seems to have been conferred because we find Philip (Acts 8), one of the seven deacons, preaching to and baptizing the Samaritans, and also instructing and baptizing the courtier of Queen Candace.

However, the only Scriptural argument which even indicates that the deacons received grace as well as power is drawn from the fact that the rite of imposition of hands, when it is mentioned elsewhere in the Acts and epistles of St. Paul, usually bestowed grace *ex opere operato*. So the same effect should have been produced by ordination to the diaconate.

The rite, if it confers grace, was *instituted by Christ* (I Cor. 4:1) and *must last to the end of time* because any grace-giving rite is an essential part of the indefectible Church.

Proof 3. From the Fathers. St. Ambrose says: "The functions of levites [deacons] are not unimportant since our Lord said of them: 'Behold, I have selected levites.' . . . We know that levites are not ranked among the laity, but above them, since they have been selected from among them all and have been *sanctified*" (*De Officiis*, 1, 249; PL. XVI, 99).

Proof 4. From the rite itself. It consists, according to all the liturgical books, of an imposition of hands and a prayer invoking divine grace. Consequently, it has the matter and form of the sacrament of order.

We find confirmation of our proofs from the Oriental churches, all of which hold that this ordination belongs to the sacrament.

*

Conclusion 4. Ordination to the priesthood belongs to the sacrament of order.

Introduction. The priesthood confers powers far exceeding those of the diaconate. Hence, since ordination to the diaconate is a sacrament, we should expect priestly ordination to be one also.

Explanation of Terms

1. Ordination to the priesthood. Here again we refer only to the essential rite, which will be specified in a later Conclusion.

A priest is one who by the character imprinted on his soul by his ordination is empowered to consecrate and offer the Eucharistic sacrifice. This definition, drawn from Trent (DB. 961, 949, 957; CT. 844, 757, 840), mentions only the principal power of the priest.

His second greatest power is to forgive or retain sins (DB. 961; CT. 844). The other powers which stem from his sacramental character are explained in the Conclusions which treat of the minister of the various sacraments.

During the ordination ceremony the bishop proclaims that the priest has power "to offer, to bless, to rule, to preach, to baptize." Not all of these powers are attached to the priestly character. Ruling power and blessings and preaching may be granted to others who have the Church's delegation, though ordinarily these functions are reserved to priests. The Church would be obliged to restrict them to priests, if they depended for their exercise upon the sacramental character.

2. Belongs to the sacrament of order. We simply prove that priestly ordination fulfills the essential notes of our general definition of a sacrament, particularly, that it confers grace *ex opere operato*. We do not prove that it bestows the powers which we have explained.

Dogmatic Note

It is of divine faith from the constant teaching of the Church. It may also be qualified as implicitly defined because the Council of Trent (DB. 960; CT. 843) declares: "Since in the *sacrament of order,* as in baptism and confirmation, a character is imprinted which cannot be deleted or removed, the sacred council rightly condemns the opinion of those who assert that *priests* of the New Testament have a merely transient power and that, although they have been duly ordained, they can again become laymen if they do not exercise the sacred ministry."

In this sentence the council attaches the priesthood to the sacrament of order. That "priests" is to be understood of priests in the ordinary sense and not of bishops is clear from the following canon (DB. 961; CT. 844) to which this sentence refers, and from the remainder of the same chapter (DB. 960; CT. 843) in which priests (*sacerdotes*) are distinguished from bishops (*episcopi*).

Proof 2. From the ordination rite itself. All the rituals, even the most ancient, contain a ceremony for ordaining priests and it consists of an imposition of hands and a prayer invoking the grace of the Holy Ghost. Accordingly, ordination to the priesthood has always had the matter and form of this sacrament and so belongs to it.

Our proofs are confirmed from the consent of all the Oriental churches.

Comment 1. Did the Church always have priests as distinguished from bishops?

We mentioned under the section on extreme unction that the Greek word for priests means literally "old men." In Scripture this meaning is occasionally retained (John 8:9), but more often it means men, regardless of their age, who rule and sanctify others. It includes both bishops and priests (Acts 11:30; 15:4–6; 16:4; Jas. 5:14; I Tim. 4:14; I Pet. 5:1 ff.).

The sole text which quite evidently refers to priests to the exclusion of bishops is I Tim. 5:17–22. This text mentions an imposition of hands and, more probably, refers to the imposition of hands at the ordination of a priest. However, no sanctifying effect is mentioned and so the text does not prove that priestly ordination is a sacrament.

St. Ignatius of Antioch (died about 107) clearly distinguishes in several passages between bishops and priests. We know, then, that priests exercised their duties in the Church from the very beginning. It should be noted, however, that the Fathers often include both bishops and priests in the Latin word, "sacerdotes," which, taken literally, means priests.

*

Conclusion 5. The ordination of a bishop also belongs to the sacrament of order.

Introduction. This ordination is usually called a consecration. Formerly scholastic theologians disputed whether it belonged to the sacrament. The disagreement arose from failure to understand in the same way what it means to say that the bishopric belongs to the sacrament.

The only question to be answered is: "Does the consecration of a bishop fulfill our general definition of a sacrament and, especially, does it confer sanctifying grace *ex opere operato?*" If the question had been so presented, all theologians would probably have answered affirmatively.

Explanation of Terms

1. Ordination of a bishop. A bishop is one who, besides the powers of a priest, has by reason of his episcopal consecration the power to ordain others and to administer confirmation. Although priests may confer confirmation, they can never do so because of their priestly ordination alone. Besides the priestly character they need delegation from the Holy See. But a bishop needs no delegation. Even excommunicated bishops could validly ordain and confirm, though they would sin grievously by doing so.

Bishops are empowered to perform other sacred functions. They rule dioceses, and within his diocese the bishop can legislate, judge in the external forum, and punish. Bishops alone can bless certain objects like churches and altars. They grant faculties to hear confessions, to assist at marriages, to preach.

However, the most sublime function which a bishop can exercise is none of these. It is his power to offer the Eucharistic sacrifice. This power is possessed by priests also.

We wish, then, to prove that episcopal ordination contains the essential elements of a sacrament and, particularly, that it bestows sanctifying grace *ex opere operato.*

Dogmatic Note

It is at least Catholic doctrine from the *Apostolic Constitution* of Pius XII (DB. 3001; CT. 852) in which the bishopric is treated as part of the sacrament of order and its matter and form given. *Proof 2.* From Holy Scripture (II Tim. 1:6). This text was cited in our first Conclusion. As we mentioned there, it is dogmatically certain (DB. 959; CT. 842) that the text proves order *in general* to be a sacrament.

However, it is neither dogmatically nor apologetically certain that the text establishes the sacramental nature of *episcopal* consecration. It is possible that St. Paul ordained Timothy to the priesthood and bishopric by one and the same imposition of hands.

More probably, though, this was not the case. St. Paul seems to be thinking only of episcopal consecration when he says, "by the imposition of my hands," because the rest of the letter deals with Timothy's duties as a bishop. Hence, the text, placed at the very beginning of the letter, seems to mean that Timothy should "stir up the grace of God" which he had received by the imposition of hands which constituted him a bishop.

Proof 3. From the rite itself. All the rituals, past and present, contain a rite for episcopal consecration and prescribe for it an imposition of hands and a prayer invoking the grace of the Holy Ghost. So the true matter and form of the sacrament of order are found in this ordination.

Proof 4. From theological reasoning. The argument follows in form.

A rite which produces a character is a sacrament;
But episcopal consecration is a rite which produces a character:
Therefore, episcopal consecration is a sacrament.

Proof for the major. No theologian denies this.

Proof for the minor. It is certain that even the Holy Father cannot take away from a bishop his powers to validly ordain and confirm. Hence, these powers must come from Christ and must be vested in a permanent reality, a character, bestowed by episcopal consecration.

OBJECTIONS

1. As regards the Eucharist, a bishop has no more power than a priest. Accordingly, the bishopric as distinguished from the priesthood is not a sacrament.

Answer. We do not prove the sacramental nature of the bishopric by considering the powers conferred, but by showing that it gives grace *ex opere operato.*

However, the objection has no force even from the viewpoint of the powers conferred. Only a bishop can ordain priests. Therefore, a bishop has more power with regard to the Eucharist than a priest, because only a bishop can ordain others to offer the sacrifice of the Mass.

∗

Conclusion 6. The matter of the sacrament of order consists of the imposition of hands alone. The forms for the three sacramental orders are to be found in definitive sentences which express the sacramental effect of each order.

Introduction. Having established the existence of the sacrament of order and determined which orders belong to it, we now deal with its intrinsic causes, its matter and form. We take for granted that only the three higher orders belong to the sacrament.

Moreover, we are concerned with validity only. For liceity the complete rites as prescribed in the *Pontificale* must be observed.

Since order is but one sacrament, its matter must be the same in all three orders. The forms will differ because each order imparts a diverse spiritual power, but they will possess a common element—the calling down of the grace of the Holy Spirit. The form of each ordination follows shortly after the imposition of hands so that the two are morally united.

It is exceedingly important to note that we treat only of the matter and forms which are necessary for validity *now* and *in the future.* We say nothing about the past. The defenders of specific institution maintain that imposition of hands was always the sole matter of order, but this is denied by those who hold generic institution.

Explanation of Terms

1. Matter. In this sacrament it is an action, not a material substance as in some other sacraments.

2. Imposition of hands.

In the ordination of a deacon only one imposition of hands occurs. It takes place immediately after the epistle of the Mass. The bishop imposes his right hand upon the head of the candidate.

All other antecedent and subsequent rites are unnecessary for validity. They are, however, sacramentals and so deserve our esteem because they make the ordination more impressive and obtain favors for the candidate through the Church's intercession.

At the ordination of a priest two impositions of hands take place. The second follows the postcommunion of the Mass and is not necessary for validity. The first and necessary one follows the epistle of the Mass and immediately before the last sentence of the gradual. The bishop imposes both his white-gloved hands upon the head of each candidate and says nothing. All other preceding and following rites are unnecessary for validity.

Only one imposition of hands occurs at the consecration of a bishop. It, too, takes place after the epistle of the Mass and, more precisely, after the gradual. The consecrating bishop places both hands upon the head of the candidate. Although three bishops are required for the liceity of episcopal consecration and all three impose hands on the candidate, it is certain that only the consecrating bishop confers the sacrament. The many other rites performed before and after this consecration are accidental to the sacrament.

3. Forms. The words of each form determine the matter. An imposition of hands, though it is an apt way to symbolize the conferring of grace and spiritual power, is undetermined in meaning. By itself it might be merely an expression of good will. But when the words are pronounced, its meaning becomes plain. The three forms must express the grace of the Holy Spirit and the bestowal of spiritual power.

Although other sentences from the three rites could objectively be the forms so far as their meaning goes, the Holy Father has designated the exact sentence for each ordination. If this were omitted, the ordination would be invalid.

Adversaries. Since the appearance of the *Apostolic Constitution* of Pius XII, no Catholic can be opposed to this Conclusion. Some interesting reading about former controversies is found in Pohle-Preuss, *The Sacraments,* IV, 62–70.

Dogmatic Note

The entire Conclusion is Catholic doctrine from the *Apostolic Constitution* of Pius XII (DB. 3001; CT. 852) which was published in the *Acta Apostolicae Sedis* for January 28, 1948, and which took effect on April 28, 1948.

Concerning the matter of order the Holy Father (Par. 4) declares: ". . . the only matter for the sacred orders of the diaconate, the priesthood, and the bishopric is the imposition of hands." To make it clear that in the priesthood only the first imposition of hands is required, the Holy Father adds: "In the ordination of a priest the matter is the bishop's first imposition of hands which takes place in silence."

The forms, translated from the *Constitution*, are as follows.

For the diaconate. "Send forth upon them, we beseech Thee, O Lord, the Holy Spirit that they may be strengthened by Him, through the gift of Thy sevenfold grace, unto the faithful discharge of Thy service."

For the priesthood. "We beseech Thee, almighty Father, invest these Thy servants with the dignity of the priesthood. Do Thou renew in their hearts the spirit of holiness, that they may hold the office, next to ours in importance, which they have received from Thee, O Lord, and by the example of their lives point out a norm of conduct."

For the bishopric. "Accomplish in Thy priest the fullness of Thy ministry and endow him with the adornments of complete glorification, and sanctify him with the dew of heavenly anointing."

Part 1. The matter is the imposition of hands alone.

Proof 2. From Holy Scripture. No other rite can be found in Scripture except the imposition of hands (Acts 6:6; 14:22; I Tim. 4:14; 5:22; II Tim. 1:6).

All other ceremonies were added gradually by the Church. It is possible, however, that the imposition of hands which is made by all priests attending a priestly ordination and which follows immediately after the essential imposition of hands by the bishop, goes back to apostolic times. It seems to be contained in St. Paul (I Tim. 4:14), "with imposition of hands of the presbytery." It is certain that this imposition is accidental to the ordination.

Proof 3. From the consent of the Oriental churches. All of these never had any other matter for order except the imposition of hands. Yet we know for sure that their ordinations were valid. In the consecration of a bishop the Orientals did place the book of gospels on the head and shoulders of the candidate, but this rite cannot be traced back further than the fourth century and was never considered essential.

Part 2. The forms.

All the forms cited from the *Constitution* express the giving of grace and the conferring of spiritual power. Hence they determine the meaning of the imposition of hands, as is required of the form of every sacrament.

Comment 1. A few general remarks.

Even if the bishop when ordaining fails to actually touch the head of the candidate, the ordination is valid. This is mentioned explicitly in the *Constitution*.

The fact that the bishop wears gloves is no obstacle. Neither would it matter if the candidate were wearing a wig.

Although the bishop imposes both his hands when ordaining a priest or bishop, it is very probable that the imposition of only one hand would suffice for validity.

Even before the *Constitution* appeared, the more common opinion placed the matter of the sacrament in the imposition of hands alone.

Comment 2. Difficulties from the *Decree for the Armenians*.

This decree was approved by the Council of Florence in 1439 A.D. It contains eight sections of which the fifth deals with the sacraments. The decree is accurate in its exposition of six sacraments, but the paragraph dealing with order presents several difficulties. It reads as follows (DB. 701; CT. 839): "The sixth sacrament is order whose matter consists of the object by the transmission of which the order is conferred: so the priesthood is conferred by the giving of the chalice containing wine and the paten on which is bread; the diaconate by the giving of the book of gospels; the subdiaconate by the transmission of the empty chalice with the empty paten on top of it; and so for the other orders, by the giving of those objects which pertain to the ministry of each. The form of the priesthood is as follows: 'Receive the power to offer sacrifice in the Church for the living and the dead in the name of the Father and of the Son and of the Holy Ghost.' And the same is true for the forms of the other orders, as they are contained here and there in the Roman Pontifical. The ordinary minister of this sacrament is a bishop. The effect is the increase of grace so that a man may be a worthy minister."

The decree occasions three difficulties particularly. The first concerns the matter of order. According to the decree the matter is the transmission of the various sacred objects to be used by each of the orders. The imposition of hands is not even mentioned.

A second difficulty arises from the fact that the decree seems to mean that the subdiaconate and the minor orders belong to the sacrament. Cf. Conclusion 2, Objection 2.

Third, the form offered for the ordination of a priest is wrong. It is not the one prescribed in the *Constitution* of Pius XII.

It would be possible to offer various interpretations of this paragraph and so possibly show that the errors are only apparent. Such interpretations, however, would not eliminate the fact that the obvious meaning is that which the difficulties present. Rather than answer the difficulties singly, we shall obviate all of them by showing that this decree has little if any doctrinal value.

It is certainly not an infallible pronouncement for several reasons.

First, it is directed to the Armenians alone, not to the entire Church.

Second, in introducing this fifth section about the sacraments, the council does not speak with the solemnity which we would expect in an infallible pronouncement. It says: "For the easier comprehension of the Armenians, both present and future, we summarize the truth concerning the Church's sacraments according to the following compendious formula."

Third, at the close of the entire decree its contents are divided into "chapters, declarations, definitions, traditions, statutes, and doctrine." Evidently, then, some sections of the decree are not infallible pronouncements. Since four of the eight sections are plainly of faith because they are taken from previous ecumenical councils, it is likely that this fifth section was not intended as a definition. It probably comes under the word "statutes."

Fourth, if the decree were infallible, the Church could not have permitted so many theologians to contradict it.

Fifth, this section repeats almost verbatim a writing of St. Thomas called "Concerning the Articles of Faith and the Sacraments of the Church." Rarely, if ever, does the Church define the private works of any individual theologian, even of one as great as St. Thomas.

The decree more probably has no dogmatic value. It is simply a directive issued to the Armenians. The council merely meant: "Since you Armenians wish to be united with Rome and would like to administer the sacraments in the same way that Rome does, we offer you the following norms for your guidance."

Comment 3. Unity of the sacrament of order.

Since it is of faith that there are only seven sacraments, order must be a single sacrament. Yet, as we have proved, the diaconate, the priesthood, and the bishopric individually confer sanctifying grace *ex opere operato* and also imprint a character. It would seem, then, that each of them is a separate sacrament. Consequently, we must explain how they are parts of one and the same sacrament, both from the viewpoint of the powers conferred and from that of the bestowal of grace.

First, from the viewpoint of the characters or powers conferred.

Order is but one sacrament from this angle because the totality of the spiritual powers which it gives always remains the same. This totality is received only by the bishopric. A bishop, in addition to his specific powers, is able to do everything that a priest or deacon can do. A priest can perform the functions of a priest and also those of a deacon, but not those of a bishop. He has the principal powers of order, but not the totality of its powers. A deacon can perform his own functions, but not those of a priest or bishop. Hence he has the least part of the sum-total of the powers that can be transmitted by the sacrament.

Deacons and priests, therefore, have received the sacrament of order, but not its totality. Order bestows its powers by way of gradation, but their totality is always constant, and so the sacrament is one from this point of view.

Second, from the viewpoint of conferring grace *ex opere operato.*

A similar explanation seems to be the best one for this difficulty also. There is but one sum-total of grace that order can confer. This totality of grace can be received only if a man is consecrated a bishop. Then only, so far as the objective power of the sacrament to confer grace is concerned, does he receive the fullness of its grace, and he receives it according to his dispositions at the time of his episcopal consecration.

However, when a man is ordained deacon, he receives some grace *ex opere operato,* but this ordination is not capable of producing all the grace which the sacrament can effect. Consequently, no matter how perfect his dispositions, the deacon does not receive *ex opere operato* all the grace which the sacrament as a whole can impart.

The same is true of ordination to the priesthood. This ordination, too, gives grace *ex opere operato.* It has the objective efficacy to confer more grace than the diaconate, but it cannot give the total amount of grace possible from the sacrament even if its candidate's dispositions are most excellent. It is only when the bishopric is received that order exhausts its power to bestow grace. Since, therefore, order can impart but one sum-total of grace, it is one sacrament from this aspect also.

Comment 4. Anglican orders.

These orders are invalid. Pope Leo XIII in his letter, "Apostolicae curae," of September 13, 1896 authoritatively declared that Anglican orders are invalid. Consequently, neither deacons, priests, or bishops exist in any of the Anglican churches.

Their orders are invalid according to the Holy Father because, first, they used an inadequate form for too long a time, and, second, their intention was defective.

These essential requisites for the sacrament were wanting in the Anglican church for 112 years, from 1550 to 1662. Before the year 1550 their orders were valid because they had been received from validly consecrated bishops. But the period of time during which the invalid form, "Receive the Holy Ghost," and the defective intention (priests were not ordained to say Mass) prevailed was so long that all validly consecrated bishops had died and so there were no validly consecrated bishops to confer the sacrament. The papal pronouncement is clear (DB. 1963-66). The entire matter is discussed in Pohle-Preuss, *The Sacraments,* IV, 70, 71.

Comment 5. Sacramental grace and characters of orders.

It is Catholic doctrine that each of the three sacramental orders gives a title to actual graces. These graces will come to the recipient during his entire subsequent life, but he must cooperate with them. They will enable him to perform his sacred duties properly and to foster his personal sanctity (DB. 701; CT. 839).

Pope Pius XI in his encyclical *Ad Catholici Sacerdotii* of December 20, 1935 (DB. 2275) speaks about this sacramental grace with regard to priests, and, implicitly, with regard to bishops. If these actual graces are attached to sanctifying grace, as many theologians say, one who is in the state of mortal sin does not receive them. If, however, they are linked to the character, as some say, the ordained minister will receive them even if he is a sinner.

It is of faith that the *priesthood* confers a character. It is certain that the diaconate and the bishopric do the same. However, it is disputed whether these three characters are objectively distinguished from one another or whether the priesthood and the bishopric merely intensify the one character imprinted by the diaconate. In short, are there three distinct realities or qualities etched on the soul by the three ordinations, or is there but one quality which is intensified or enriched by subsequent ordinations?

It is unnecessary to discuss the opinions of theologians about this matter. It is more probable that each of the characters is really distinct from the others. However, as we have explained previously, order is one sacrament capable of producing but one totality of spiritual powers. This is a good reason for saying that the characters of the priesthood and bishopric simply intensify the original character of the diaconate.

The student should recall that these characters are objectively in the soul, that they truly modify it, though only accidentally.

Comment 6. Reasons for celibacy of those in major orders.

Non-Catholics sometimes ask: "Why don't priests get married?"

We should know how to answer this question, especially since a few of the apostles were married.

The Church could, if she wished, allow her ministers to be married. Celibacy is her law, not Christ's, though the pattern of celibacy was formed by Christ Himself. Indeed, He (Matt. 19:12) recommends virginity even to the laity who are called to it. So does St. Paul (I Cor. 7:8).

Briefly, then, some of the reasons why priests do not marry are these. First, the priest is "another Christ" and so should strive to follow our Lord's example.

Again, if priests were married, they would be exposed to greater danger of violating the seal of confession and of using information obtained in confession. For instance, a married priest would be tempted to warn his wife or children against associating with a neighbor who had confessed certain kinds of sins.

Besides, it would be difficult for a married priest to exhort his people to the highest sanctity, even to virginity.

Then, too, a married priest would be encumbered in the performance of some of his pastoral duties. For example, it might be necessary for him to stay at home to care for his sick wife when he should be doing apostolic work for others.

Furthermore, he would be reluctant to risk his health by caring for the sick afflicted with contagious diseases.

Finally, it would be more difficult for him to go to the foreign missions or to become a chaplain in the armed forces.

No injustice is done by the law of celibacy. It is accepted freely and only by those who have reached the age of twenty-two. It involves no disrespect for the noble state of matrimony. Nor is celibacy something purely negative. By it the priest, induced by the loftiest motives and relying on God's grace, positively consecrates his body to God.

The highest medical authorities testify that the observance of celibacy does not injure one's bodily health. If scandals sometimes occur because of the law of celibacy, this is accidental to the law. Scandals happen in every walk of life.

*

Conclusion 7. The minister of the sacrament of order is a bishop alone.

Introduction. The validity of most of the sacraments depends upon a spiritual power possessed by the minister. Hence it is always important to know who can validly confer a sacrament. We now inquire who is the valid minister of order.

We treat of the three highest orders only, not of the subdiaconate and minor orders. It should be noted that a bishop is the ordinary minister of these also, but a priest may be empowered by the Church to confer them.

Explanation of Terms

1. Sacrament of order. We include only the diaconate, the priesthood, and the bishopric.

2. A bishop alone. The minister must have received episcopal consecration. The power to ordain is inherent in the bishop's sacramental character and cannot be taken away by the Church. No priest or deacon or other inferior can ordain validly.

Adversaries. A few theologians believe that a priest could be delegated by the Holy See to ordain another priest. Quite a few theologians think that a priest could be authorized by the Holy See to ordain a deacon.

Dogmatic Note

It is of divine faith that bishops alone are the ordinary ministers of this sacrament. The Council of Trent (DB. 967; CT. 850) declares: "If anyone says that bishops . . . do not have the power to confirm and ordain, or that the power which they have is common to priests also . . . let him be anathema."

This canon does not state whether priests could be given the faculty to ordain by the Holy See and so become extraordinary ministers of the sacrament.

However, it is Catholic doctrine that a deacon or one inferior to him could not be given the power to ordain.

It is certain that a priest could not be delegated to consecrate a bishop.

It is far more probable that a priest could not be authorized by the Holy See to ordain another priest.

It is probable that a priest could not be empowered to ordain a deacon.

Proof 2. From Holy Scripture. The proof is more probable, both dogmatically and apologetically. Not enough instances are recorded in Scripture to make it certain. The argument follows in form.

In Scripture only the apostles, and the bishops, Timothy and Titus, are ministers of the sacrament of order;

But bishops alone are successors of the apostles:

Therefore, bishops alone are ministers of the sacrament of order.

Proof for the major. We find the apostles ordaining (Acts 6:6; 14:22; II Tim. 1:6). The bishops, Timothy and Titus, are also empowered to ordain (Tit. 1:5; I Tim. 5:22).

Proof for the minor. This is proved in the treatise about the Church and is defined doctrine (DB. 960; CT. 843).

Proof 3. From tradition. Diverse councils, all the rituals even the most ancient, various Fathers testify that only bishops are ministers of order.

St. Epiphanius (died 403 A.D.), writing against the heretic Aerius, who was no more than a priest, declares: "When he [Aerius] tries to equate bishops and priests, every sensible person readily perceives that he is uttering absolute foolishness. How can such an allegation be sustained? The chief duty of the episcopal rank is to generate fathers. It is the bishop's function to propagate fathers within the Church. A priest, since he cannot generate fathers, produces sons for the Church by the laver of regeneration, but not fathers or teachers. How, then, could he [Aerius] possibly produce a priest since he has no right to impose hands for his production?" (*Adv. Haer. P.,* 75, 4; RJ. 1108).

This tradition is echoed in the *Code of Canon Law* (Par. 951).

Proof 4. From theological reasoning. If the Church has the power to delegate priests to ordain other priests, she knows it and she should have occasionally exercised it. But she never has. In times of dire persecution when the salvation of many souls depended upon having more priests available, she has allowed priests to confirm, but she has never authorized them to ordain other priests.

1. St. Paul says (I Tim. 4:14) that Timothy was ordained "with the impositions of hands of the presbytery." Therefore, priests can consecrate even bishops.

Answer. We have refuted this difficulty under the objections to Conclusion 1. St. Paul expressly states (II Tim. 1:6) that Timothy had been ordained "by the imposition of *my* hands." Other priests imposed hands on him merely to add solemnity to the rite.

2. In ancient times the choreopiscopi, who were mere priests, received delegation from their metropolitan bishop to ordain priests and deacons. So priests can administer order.

Answer. The choreopiscopi were genuine bishops. Permission to ordain priests and deacons was necessary for liceity only.

3. Pope Innocent VIII in 1489 granted Cistercian abbots the faculty to ordain their own subjects as deacons. These abbots were not bishops.

Answer. Cardinal Gasparri examined in the Vatican archives this Bull of Innocent III and said: "It contains no mention of the diaconate."

4. Why can a priest be delegated to confer the subdiaconate and minor orders, but not the higher orders?

Answer. Because the subdiaconate and minor orders are of ecclesiastical origin. As a result, the Pope can decide who administers these orders. The sacrament was instituted by Christ who determined that its minister must be a bishop. The Church cannot alter this.

5. Did not the Bulls of Boniface IX (Feb. 1, 1400) and of Martin V (Nov. 16, 1427) authorize certain religious priests to ordain their subjects both to the diaconate and the priesthood?

Answer. The meaning of these Bulls is not clear. They probably mean that the abbots of two monasteries were given permission to have their subjects ordained deacons and priests by other bishops than those in whose dioceses the monasteries were located.

For a fuller discussion of the objections, consult Pohle-Preuss, *The Sacraments*, IV, 122–124.

Comment 1. The recipient of the sacrament of order.

We deal with validity only. The *Code of Canon Law* (Par. 968, 1) states: "Only one of the *male* sex can be validly ordained." This holds for all eight orders.

It is Catholic doctrine that women cannot be validly ordained. Scripture offers a probable proof (I Cor. 14:34, 35; I Tim. 2:11, 12). Scripture testifies that our Lord granted spiritual powers to men only, His apostles. Christ was assisted by women, as was St. Paul, but He never gave them the sacrament of order.

In the whole history of the Church there is no instance of a woman being ordained. It is certain that the exclusion of women from the reception of this sacrament is by divine law.

It is Catholic doctrine that baptism is by divine law an essential prerequisite for the reception of the three sacramental orders. By ecclesiastical law baptism is required for the subdiaconate and minor orders.

Every baptized male, even a baby, can be validly ordained. This statement is surprising but it is supported by the *Instruction*, "Inter sollicitas," (May 4, 1745) of Pope Benedict XIV.

A baby, however, if it were, contrary to the law, ordained, would be informed of this later and at the age of twenty-one could choose whether or not to follow the sacred ministry. If he does not wish to do so, he has no obligation whatever. He may marry, he is not obligated to the recitation of the breviary or to any other functions of the ministry. Yet he always has the sacramental character imprinted by his ordination.

It is certain that every baptized male can be ordained validly to the diaconate without previously receiving the minor orders and the subdiaconate.

It is likewise certain that every baptized male can be validly ordained a priest without previously being ordained a deacon or receiving the lesser orders.

However, the more probable teaching is that a baptized male cannot be validly consecrated a bishop unless he has previously been ordained a priest. This seems to be evident from the form of episcopal consecration: "Accomplish in Thy *priest* the fullness of Thy ministry." The priesthood is supposed.

Comment 2. The necessity of the sacrament of order.

It is obvious that the priesthood and the bishopric are absolutely necessary for the continuance of the Church. If this sacrament were not conferred, the Mass and most of the sacraments would perish.

However, it is more difficult to determine precisely what obligation rests on the individual boy to respond to a vocation to the priesthood. It will vary according to the clarity of the call, the needs of the Church or diocese, and other circumstances. Speaking only in general, we may say that the obligation does not bind under pain of mortal sin.

SECTION EIGHT

The Sacrament
of Matrimony

*

Section Eight

THE SACRAMENT OF MATRIMONY

EVERY kind of marriage is a means by which husband and wife can generate and educate their offspring, develop their own personalities, and improve and increase the human family.

This is true of Christian marriage also, but in a superior way. The baptized man and woman who contract matrimony generate children to become the adopted sons of God; they train them not only in natural learning and goodness, but also in supernatural faith and wisdom. Then, too, the Christian husband and wife can develop their personalities not only naturally, but also supernaturally inasmuch as the graces of the sacrament help them to attain the beatific vision. Christian marriage betters and expands the nation and the human race, and, in addition, the Church of God.

These supernatural fruits derive from Christian matrimony because it is a sacrament which confers sanctifying grace when it is received, and because it bestows actual graces upon the partners as long as the marriage endures.

Conclusion 1. For the baptized matrimony is a sacrament.

Introduction. The Catholic who ponders this Conclusion will never forget that marriage has a sacred character, a truth which is widely disregarded today. Jokes about marriage will be repugnant to him.

Since even Protestants generally deny the sacramental nature of marriage, it is important to establish this point at the beginning.

Explanation of Terms

1. Matrimony. It is a sacrament which bestows on a baptized man and woman who have lawfully made the prescribed contract, the graces which will enable them to fulfill their matrimonial obligations. We shall now explain this definition.

First, it is a *contract*. We understand contract in its strict meaning. It signifies an agreement, freely made, but, once made, imposing a serious obligation to share the rights and duties of the married state. The agreement or consent must be internal (sincere), simultaneous with the making of the contract, externally manifested, voluntary.

Second, the contract must be made *lawfully*. Both the man and the woman must be baptized and they must be free from diriment or invalidating impediments (these render a marriage null and void), and also from impedient or illicit impediments (these do not make marriage invalid, but they make it sinful). Only diriment impediments make marriage impossible. We shall name these impediments in a later Conclusion.

Third, the partners will receive actual graces *to fulfill their matrimonial obligations*. These obligations arise from the very nature of matrimony and cannot be altered by any subjective ideas of the contracting parties.

The primary purpose of the marriage contract is the procreation and education of offspring. Since sexual intercourse (also called the marriage act or the marriage debt) is necessary for procreation, the contract confers the *right* to this intercourse. However, two persons may be validly married even though they promise each other beforehand that they will never exercise this right. If, after marriage, they mutually decide to void the promise, they may perform the marriage act without any sin whatever.

It should also be observed that the right to the marriage act means the right to perform this act in the proper way so that a child can be conceived. Hence any deliberate performance of the act which would impede procreation is mortally sinful.

However, so long as the marriage act is properly performed, it may be enacted by married people even though they know that procreation is impossible. Thus elderly spouses, and a wife who has had her ovaries removed, may perform the act.

The secondary and dependent purposes of marriage are two. It serves, first, as a remedy for carnal concupiscence and, second, it provides each of the partners with a helpmate in material, psychological, and moral needs.

Hence, although the common good, the increase and education of the human family and of the subjects of the Church, is the primary purpose of marriage, it also aims at assisting the spouses to overcome the difficulties, both domestic and personal, which hamper the attainment of their eternal salvation.

Marriages are classified into four kinds.

First, we have the *legitimate marriage*. The word "legitimate" is used here technically. It means a true, natural marriage between two parties, neither of whom is baptized. We also include marriages validly contracted by a baptized party with an unbaptized party although they are not technically called "legitimate." When such a marriage occurs, it is very likely that the baptized person does not receive the sacrament. The resultant bond is a natural one.

Second, a legitimate marriage can become a *legitimate, consummated marriage*. This merely means that the marriage act has been performed by those who have contracted a *legitimate marriage*.

The third kind is called a *ratified marriage*. This technical expression designates a marriage entered into by two baptized parties who have not yet performed the marriage act.

Finally, a *ratified, consummated marriage* signifies that the two baptized parties who have contracted a *ratified marriage* have also performed the marriage act.

The student should be sure to learn these four kinds of marriage. They will be referred to subsequently.

It should be observed that the same initial marriage contract might progressively become all four kinds of marriage. For instance, two pagans, having no diriment impediments, get married before a justice of the peace (a legitimate marriage). After the contract they perform the marriage act (a legitimate, consummated marriage). Later on, they both become baptized (a ratified marriage—no renewal of the contract required). Finally, after their baptism they perform the marriage act (a ratified, consummated marriage).

Noteworthy, too, is the fact that the sacrament of matrimony is the contract itself. Hence the sacrament as such is transient, but it produces a permanent effect, the state of matrimony.

Any two baptized persons, whether Catholics or not, receive this sacrament, if no diriment impediment blocks their marriage.

Dogmatic Note

It is of divine faith that matrimony is a sacrament from the solemn definition of the Council of Trent (DB. 971; CT. 857): "If anyone say that matrimony is not truly and properly one of the seven sacraments of the evangelical law, instituted by Christ our Lord, but that it has been invented by men in the Church, and that it does not confer grace: let him be anathema."

Proof 2. From Holy Scripture (Eph. 5:22–33; 6:1–9). It is dogmatically certain that the passage from chapter five furnishes *some* evidence that marriage is a sacrament because Trent (DB. 969; CT. 855) states that St. Paul here "intimates" (*innuit*) that such is the case. Apologetically, the proof is probable.

Synopsis of the entire passage.

It is not St. Paul's purpose to prove that marriage is a sacrament. He wishes to inculcate the rights and duties which the various members of a Christian household have towards one another.

He deals first with husband and wife. Just as Christ, the head of the mystical body, rules that body, so the husband, as head of the wife, should rule her (5:22–24). The wife, therefore, should obey her husband. The husband, since Christ loves the Church as His own body, should love his wife as his own body (5:25–31).

St. Paul deals next with children and parents. Children should obey their parents (6:1–3). Fathers should educate their children religiously, but should not provoke them to anger (6:4).

Finally, St. Paul considers the slaves or servants in the household. Slaves should obey their masters from a supernatural motive (6:5–8). Masters, on the other hand, should be good to their slaves and, particularly, should refrain from threatening them (6:9).

St. Paul supposes that both husband and wife are Christians. The wife is to obey her husband as the Church obeys Christ. She could not act from this supernatural motive unless she were a Catholic. Nor could she obey her husband, if he were a pagan, as the Church obeys Christ, since a pagan could not typify Christ the head of the Church. The same conclusion could be reached by considering the supernatural love which St. Paul inculcates. He is, therefore, speaking about Christian marriage only.

Remembering, then, this preface, we argue especially from chapter 5:31, 32: "For this reason a man shall leave his father and mother and shall cleave to his wife; and the two shall become one flesh [a quotation from Gen. 2:24]. This is a great sacrament: I mean in reference to Christ and the Church."

We shall progressively show how the elements of a sacrament are found in these verses.

Christian marriage according to St. Paul symbolizes the union of Christ with His Church (v. 32). He says that Christian marriage ("this") is a great mystery with reference to this union. He means that it is a mystery how marriage, which is in itself a natural thing, can signify one of the most profound supernatural mysteries of faith, the union of Christ with His mystical body. It is beyond our comprehension *how* marriage can symbolize this union ("a great mystery"), but there is no doubt that it does.

The pronoun "this" in verse 32 must refer to matrimony for two reasons: first, because its immediate antecedent is matrimony (v. 31); second, because if it stood for the union of Christ with the Church, as some Protestant commentators allege, the meaning of verse 32 would be absurd. We should have to say: "The union of Christ with His Church is a great mystery: I mean with reference to the union of Christ with the Church." This does not make sense.

Christian marriage is, therefore, a perceptible sign of the mystical body.

Moreover, matrimony, since it symbolizes the union of Christ with the Church, must also symbolize sanctifying grace, at least as a theoretical sign. The principal bond of union between Christ and His members is sanctifying grace. Since, then, matrimony signifies this union, it, too, should signify grace.

However, this argument is only probable because St. Paul may be merely emphasizing the *intimacy* of the union between Christ and the Church in order to inculcate the *intimacy* which should flourish between husband and wife. He may not intend to indicate the *manner* in which this intimacy between Christ and the Church is effected.

A second and more probable way of showing that marriage, at least as a theoretical sign, signifies grace is as follows. St. Paul demands the exercise of permanent, supernatural virtues by both husband and wife. These virtues are, particularly, obedience and love. They are to be exercised constantly, as is plain from the text and context (5:22–30). They are to be supernatural because they are to be like the obedience of the Church to Christ and like the love of Christ for the Church. This obedience and love are evidently supernatural because the union itself of Christ with the Church is supernatural.

We know, however, that the constant exercise of supernatural love supposes the presence of the supernatural virtue of love, and the presence of this virtue always entails the presence of sanctifying grace. Indeed, some theologians identify grace and the virtue of love.

Accordingly, Christian marriage probably signifies sanctifying grace, at least as a theoretical sign.

But, perhaps only the *state* of marriage has this signification, whereas we must prove that the rite itself, the contract, the sacrament has it.

St. Paul indicates that the rite itself symbolizes grace because the contract or rite is the efficient cause of the state of matrimony and, consequently, the state could not signify grace unless it derived this signification from its cause, the contract. Unless the contract itself signified the union of Christ with the Church, the state could never do so.

Besides, St. Paul (v. 31) hints at the contract when he quotes Genesis: "For this cause shall a man *leave* father and mother. . . ." What St. Paul really means in verse 32 is: "This *getting married* (the contract) and the state resulting from it are a great mystery: I mean with reference to Christ and the Church."

If the contract or rite of Christian marriage theoretically signifies sanctifying grace, as we have shown, the contract must also *produce* it *ex opere operato*. We know this from St. Paul himself who calls the rites of the Old Law "weak and needy elements" (Gal. 4:9), thus implying that the rites of the New Law are efficacious.

Furthermore, if the contract produces grace, it must have been instituted by Christ. No perceptible rite can give grace unless Christ designated it for this purpose. He alone has the power of excellence, one of the functions of which is to attach the production of grace to visible signs. Moreover, Christ alone merited all grace and so He alone could dispose of it by instituting outward signs which confer it. Then, too, St. Paul states that he is but a dispenser of the mysteries of God (I Cor. 4:1).

Finally, Christ must have intended Christian matrimony to be perpetual because its purpose remains until the end of time. The Church would vanish if marriage were to cease. Married Christians will always need the actual graces coming from the sacrament.

Consequently, we find all the elements of a sacrament in the marriage contract—a perceptible sign, instituted in perpetuity by Christ, to bestow sanctifying grace *ex opere operato*.

Proof 3. From prescription. The argument follows in form.

Any teaching held as of faith by the whole Church for three centuries before Protestantism, was revealed in the deposit of faith;

But the teaching that marriage is a sacrament is such:

Therefore, the sacramental nature of marriage was revealed in the deposit of faith.

Proof for the major. It was proved both dogmatically and apologetically in Conclusion 2 of the *Sacraments in General*.

Proof for the minor. The second Council of Lyons, held in 1274, was ecumenical and so reflected the belief of the entire Church. The council (DB. 465; CT. 660) explicitly names matrimony as one of the seven sacraments.

In the twelfth century Peter Lombard wrote: "Let us now treat of the sacraments of the New Law which are: baptism, confirmation, the bread of benediction . . . *marriage*" (*Sent.* IV, D. 2, chap. 1).

Objections

1. Matrimony is the same now as it was before the coming of Christ. It has always consisted of the contract. Therefore, Christ did not institute the sacrament of matrimony.

Answer. We grant that Christ did not institute the matrimonial contract. However, He endued the contract with power to produce grace *ex opere operato*. Without changing the essence of the contract, He transformed it into a sacramental rite.

2. This answer is not satisfactory because the Fathers and theologians admit that matrimony, even before the time of Christ, represented the union of Christ with His Church. So matrimony gave grace before Christ's advent.

Answer. Before Christ marriage symbolized the union of Christ with the Church, but only imperfectly. Since the Church did not yet exist and Christ had not yet become man, marriage antecedent to Christ could have represented this union only in an imperfect way. Once the Church was actually established, Christian marriage symbolized this union much more adequately.

Moreover, no rites of the Old Law conferred grace *ex opere operato* and causally. Much less did *pagan* marriage do this.

3. Virginity is superior to matrimony. Yet virginity is not a sacrament which confers grace.

Answer. Virginity as a state is superior to matrimony, but not as a rite.

4. This answer is insufficient. Since virginity as a state is more difficult than the state of matrimony, the very rite which initiates the state of virginity should give grace. The virgin needs more grace than the married.

Answer. Comparatively few people are called to the state of virginity. This state, too, is intended primarily for the sanctification of the individual, not for the benefit of others. Married people, however, need grace to bear with each other and also to educate their children.

Finally, virgins have more means of obtaining grace by receiving the sacraments and by prayer. Consequently, they can obtain all the graces which they need without having them conferred by the rite itself.

5. Some of the earlier canonists denied that marriage is a sacrament.

Answer. A few of the earlier canonists did deny this. They opposed the common teaching of theologians and also the more common opinion of canonists.

They favored this false opinion because the priest was given a stipend when he assisted at a marriage. They did not understand how money could be given for a sacrament.

It is evident that this reasoning is false. The man and woman are the ministers of matrimony. They confer the sacrament on each other. Consequently, they cannot give money for the sacrament. They usually tender a stipend to the priest because of the time and services he gives them, not because of the sacrament.

Comment 1. When did Christ institute the sacrament of matrimony?

He did so on some occasion before His ascension, but we do not know exactly when. Some theologians think that He instituted the sacrament when He attended the marriage at Cana (John 2:1–10). Others believe that He did so when He banned all divorce (Matt. 19:2–12). It is more probable that He established the sacrament after His resurrection "for forty days appearing to them and speaking of the kingdom of God" (Acts 1:3).

*

Conclusion 2. The essence of the sacrament of matrimony is to be found in the marriage contract. Consequently, no marriage of baptized parties is valid unless it is also a sacrament.

Introduction. Once we have established the existence of this sacrament, we logically treat of its matter and form, its constitutive causes. Although various external rites ordinarily accompany the marriage contract, such as the blessing of the ring, the blessing of the spouses, and various prayers, we say now that the essential matter and form are located in the contract itself.

This contract is made by the man and woman who, therefore,

administer the sacrament to each other. The essence of the contract consists of the following questions asked by the officiating priest and of the answers of the bridegroom and bride respectively: N., wilt thou take N. here present, for thy lawful wife, according to the rite of our holy Mother the Church? I will. N., wilt thou take N. here present, for thy lawful husband, according to the rite of our holy Mother the Church? I will.

It should be noted that the answers, "I will," are in the present tense. They mean "I want," or "I do." The Latin word is "volo" which is the present indicative.

This Conclusion is of great practical import. Since the sacrament and the contract are ontologically, objectively identified, it follows that only the Church, not the state, has jurisdiction over marriages among the baptized. Sacraments were entrusted by Christ to the Church, not to the state. Hence the state has no authority over the substance of the contract.

The state can legislate only with regard to the purely civil effects of sacramental marriages. It may, for instance, establish laws regarding inheritance; or laws permitting husband and wife to keep property separately rather than jointly; or laws requiring the registration of such marriages with civil authorities.

Explanation of the Meaning of the Conclusion

Until comparatively recent years there were Catholic adversaries of this Conclusion. They had a common objective—to enable baptized persons to be validly married without receiving the sacrament and, as a result, to give the state jurisdiction over even the marriages of the baptized.

One group taught that the matter and form of matrimony were to be found in the priest's blessing, not in the contract. Accordingly, two Catholics could be validly married by making the natural and civil contract, but they would not receive the sacrament until they obtained the priest's blessing.

Others believed that the matter of the sacrament was located in the contract, but the form in the priest's blessing. Nevertheless, two Catholics would be validly married even though they never obtained this blessing.

Others said that both matter and form were in the contract, but that two Catholics could be validly married even if they did not intend to receive the sacrament. If they *intended* to receive it, they did; if they did not intend to receive it, they were married anyhow so long as they gave true matrimonial consent.

All these adversaries denied the Conclusion, since, according to them, the sacrament and the contract are not ontologically identified, but separable.

On the contrary, we say now that the entire sacrament, both its matter and form, is to be found in the contract alone, not in the priest's blessing (nuptial blessing). The sacrament and the contract are so objectively identified that, if two parties were to make the contract while positively rejecting the reception of the sacrament, they would not receive the sacrament nor would they be married at all. One cannot be had without the other.

The contracting parties, however, do not have to *know* that matrimony is a sacrament; neither do they have to *believe* this. Even those who know and believe this are not obliged to *expressly* intend to receive the sacrament. They *implicitly* intend to receive it by intending to get married, because the contract and the sacrament are one and the same. To make their marriage invalid, they would have to make a positive act of the will whereby they would refuse to accept the sacrament.

Dogmatic Note

This is Catholic doctrine from the authoritative declarations of several pontiffs. Leo XIII in his encyclical *Arcanum divinae sapientiae* of Feb. 10, 1880 says (DB. 1854; CT. 870): ". . . in Christian marriage the contract is inseparable from the sacrament and, therefore, the contract cannot be true and legitimate without being a sacrament as well."

Further on, he adds: "For Christ our Lord amplified marriage with the dignity of a sacrament; but *marriage is the contract itself* whenever that contract is lawfully enacted. . . . Hence it is clear that among Christians every true marriage is, in itself and by itself, a sacrament, and that nothing can be further from the truth than to say that the sacrament is a kind of added adornment or outward endowment which can be separated and torn away from the contract by the caprice of men."

Pius XI (DB. 1640) in his allocution *Acerbissimum vobiscum* of 1852 is equally clear.

Proof 2. From the *Code of Canon Law* (Par. 1012, 1, 2): "Christ the Lord raised to the dignity of a sacrament the matrimonial contract itself when made by the baptized.

"Accordingly, among the baptized the matrimonial contract cannot be valid without being at the same time a sacrament."

No other certain proof is given for the Conclusion. However, the Fathers did not think that the priest's blessing was a constituent of the sacrament. Although deprecating the so-called clandestine (without the public approval of the Church) marriages, they admitted their validity even though no priestly blessing had been conferred. Furthermore, they considered second marriages after the death of a previous partner as valid, but they did not bless them.

OBJECTIONS

1. Every sacrament must signify grace. But the mutual consent expressed in the marriage contract does not signify grace. Hence the contract alone cannot constitute the sacrament.

Answer. The sacraments are signs of grace not naturally, but by Christ's free choice. When He raised matrimony to sacramental dignity, He decided that whenever two baptized people would make the contract the expression of their consent, though not differing from a purely natural matrimonial consent, would confer grace.

The giving of sanctifying grace is not explicitly mentioned in the form of any sacrament. It is true, however, that in the rest of the sacraments the conferring of grace is more directly indicated by their forms than it is in the sacrament of matrimony.

2. A sacramental marriage which is not consummated can be dissolved. One that is consummated cannot be dissolved. This shows that the consummation is an essential part of the sacrament and so the contract is not enough.

Answer. Consummation adds an accidental perfection to marriage, but the contract alone represents the union of Christ with the Church. The consummation represents the union of Christ with His human nature by His incarnation. This union is absolutely indissoluble.

Even the state admits that marriage is essentially completed by the contract. Every couple who perform the civil ceremony are considered as truly married independently of the consummation.

According to this objection a dying person could not get married.

The fact that under certain circumstances non-consummated marriages can be dissolved merely shows that Christ wanted the contract in such cases to be less durable than in others.

Hence the marriage contract is not merely an engagement or solemn promise of marriage. It is the marriage itself which, as we have proved, is identified with the contract.

Comment 1. The matter and form of the sacrament.

Even after all theologians agreed that the matrimonial contract and the sacrament are identified, they disputed *how* the matter and form are found in the contract.

It is the common opinion today that the matter is the contract in so far as this involves the mutual *offering* of the right over each other's body. The form is the contract in so far as it denotes the mutual *acceptance* of the right over each other's body. Just as the offering of any gift does not get its meaning of a gift until it is accepted, so in the marriage contract the reciprocal offering of the parties to each other does not get its full meaning until the offering is reciprocally accepted. The form lends a definite meaning to the matter.

Briefly then, in the sacrament of matrimony the *remote matter* about which the contract is to be made is the mutual right over each other's body; the *proximate matter* is the actual offering of this right to each other; the *form* is the actual acceptance of this offering by each party.

Comment 2. The sacramental nature of certain kinds of marriage.

Although two baptized parties cannot get married without receiving the sacrament, they may not obtain sanctifying grace *ex opere operato* from it, because matrimony is a sacrament of the living. If both parties are in the state of grace, they both receive *ex opere operato* an increase of sanctifying grace when they make the contract. If one party is in the state of grace, the other not in this state, only the one in the state of grace obtains more grace at the time of the contract. However, this sacrament very probably revives and so will bestow its sanctifying grace later when one or both parties regain the state of grace.

If a Catholic, having obtained a dispensation from disparity of cult, marries an unbaptized person, the marriage is valid, but it seems certain that the Catholic party does not receive the sacrament of matrimony and so does not obtain its grace. The bond of such a marriage is a natural one.

If a baptized Protestant marries an unbaptized person, no impediment of disparity of cult exists and so no dispensation from it is necessary. Furthermore, such a marriage may in certain circumstances be dissolved by the Holy See. It seems certain in this case too that the baptized Protestant does not receive the sacrament. Only a natural bond results from the marriage.

If two unbaptized persons get married and only one of them is baptized afterwards, the baptized party does not receive the sacrament. The bond remains a natural one.

If two unbaptized parties enter marriage and *both* are later baptized, theologians agree that they receive the sacrament of matrimony without renewing the contract. Some say that the baptisms together with a tacit or explicit renewal of consent to the marriage, make the original contract sacramental.

Today, however, the far more common opinion holds that the marriage becomes a sacrament by the mere fact that the two parties are baptized and at the moment when both parties are baptized, so that no renewal of consent is necessary since the former consent still persists.

Accordingly, if they are properly disposed for baptism, they receive sanctifying grace *ex opere operato* not only from baptism, but also from matrimony. They are also vested with the rights to the actual graces of both baptism and matrimony.

*

Conclusion 3. The Church has received from God the power to establish diriment impediments to Christian marriage.

Introduction. This is a corollary of the preceding Conclusion. Since the sacrament and the contract are identified, the Church, to which Christ has entrusted the sacraments, must have the power to determine the conditions according to which marriage is to be contracted.

We presuppose that certain conditions, affecting the persons particularly, must be verified in the making of any contract, especially one which is indissoluble and has a weighty bearing upon the common good. We now prove specifically that the Church is empowered to legislate impediments which make marriage invalid, and that she has this power from God, not from the state.

Explanation of Terms

1. The Church. We mean the supreme ruling power of the Church, the Holy Father himself or an ecumenical council approved by him. Bishops do not have this power.

2. From God. The Church does not derive this power from the state, but rightfully possesses it by her own constitution as instituted by Christ.

3. Christian marriage. We deal only with marriages among the baptized, or with those in which at least one party is baptized. Since, in the latter case, at least one person is her subject, the Church has the right to apply her impediments to that person directly, and so indirectly to the other person.

It should be noted, too, that baptized non-Catholics are bound by all diriment impediments flowing from the natural law and the divine positive law; also by all ecclesiastical impediments except disparity of cult.

However, baptized non-Catholics are not bound by the *form* of Catholic marriages. This means that non-Catholics are not obliged to be married in the presence of a priest and two witnesses.

This is not, strictly speaking, an impediment. An impediment affects the *persons* intending to make the contract. The *form* pertains to the circumstances in which the marriage is contracted. Hence other things besides the diriment impediments can render a marriage invalid.

4. Diriment impediments. These are obstacles which affect either one or both parties wishing to get married and which make an attempted marriage null and void.

They differ from *impedient impediments*. The Church has the right to legislate these also, but if a marriage is contracted without a previous dispensation from them, the marriage is valid. However, sin is committed if the parties know about the impediment beforehand.

Diriment impediments, then, make marriage impossible; impedient impediments make it unlawful.

Note, too, that diriment impediments flow from the natural law, the divine positive law, and ecclesiastical law. The Church can dispense from only those diriment impediments which are established by her own laws. She cannot dispense from impediments of the natural or divine positive law.

There are twelve diriment impediments: lack of the required age, impotence, bond of prior marriage, disparity of cult, sacred orders, solemn religious vows, abduction, crime, consanguinity, affinity, public propriety, spiritual relationship.

A thirteenth diriment impediment is called legal relationship, but in its regard the Church allows her subjects to follow their local civil law. If that law makes legal relationship a diriment impediment to marriage, so does the Church; if not, neither does the Church.

The *Code of Canon Law* (Pars. 1067–1080) explains the various impediments. A more detailed explanation is given in *Canon Law,* Bouscaren and Ellis, p. 465 ff.

Observe, too, that diriment impediments are not arbitrarily set up by the Church. They are necessary (though some of them may cease to be necessary and new ones may become necessary, depending on circumstances) either for the good of the family, or of society, or of the Church, or to preserve due reverence for the sacrament of matrimony.

The Conclusion, therefore, has two parts. First, the Church has the power to establish diriment impediments to Christian marriage. Second, she has this power from Christ, not from the state.

Dogmatic Note

Both parts are of divine faith and were defined by Pius VI in his Constitution, *Auctorem fidei*, of August 28, 1794. The Holy Father (DB. 1559) condemns the following assertion of the Synod of Pistoia as heretical: "The teaching of the synod which asserts 'that in the beginning only the state was empowered to establish diriment impediments to the matrimonial contract'

. . . as though the Church was not able at all times and today *by her own authority* to set up impediments which not only prohibit, but nullify matrimony, and which bind Christians everywhere even in pagan lands . . . is contrary to matrimonial canons 3, 4, 9, 12 of the Council of Trent and is *heretical.*"

The note is established without the canons of Trent, but, if the student wishes to read these, he will find them in DB. 973, 974, 979, 982; CT. 859, 860, 865, 868.

Part 1. The Church has the power to establish diriment impediments to Christian marriage.

Proof 2. From Holy Scripture (Matt. 16:18): "And I [our Lord is speaking] say to thee: 'Thou art Peter; and upon this rock I will build My Church, and the gates of hell shall not prevail against it. And I will give to thee the keys of the kingdom of heaven. And whatsoever thou shalt bind upon earth, it shall be bound also in heaven: and whatsoever thou shalt loose on earth, it shall be loosed also in heaven.'"

The text is dogmatically certain; apologetically, very probable. The argument follows in form.

A power pertaining to the Church's primary purpose (men's salvation) belongs to the Church;

But the power to enact diriment impediments to matrimony is a power pertaining to the Church's primary purpose:

Therefore, the power to enact diriment impediments to matrimony belongs to the Church.

Proof for the major. Our Lord is speaking to St. Peter as the head of the Church, as the "rock" upon which it is to be founded. As such, St. Peter receives the keys to the kingdom of heaven with power to bind and loose whatever conduces to or hinders from the attainment of that kingdom.

Proof for the minor. Diriment impediments are enacted by the Church to prevent men from doing something which will impede their salvation. All these impediments protect the good morals of the family and of society, and also the dignity of the sacrament. The impediment of crime, for example, is a deterrent to adultery, and, in some cases, even to murder. Thus a man who commits adultery with a married woman incurs this impediment and cannot marry her after her husband's death. If he murders her husband in order to marry her, he incurs another species of this same impediment and cannot marry her.

Proof 3. From the ancient practice of the Church. The general principle of setting up impediments was indicated by the martyr, St. Ignatius, (about 100 A.D.): "It is fitting that engaged couples enter marriage with the bishop's approval so that their marriage may be according to the Lord and not according to lust" (*Ad Polycarpum*, 5, 1; RJ. 67).

The Council of Neocaesarea (314 A.D.) legislated the diriment impediment of affinity: "If a woman marries two brothers, let her be excommunicated until death; but if at that time she promises that, in the event of her getting well, she will disrupt the marriage, let her out of mercy be given penance."

The Council of Elvira (about 300 A.D.) decreed the diriment impediment of disparity of cult. The Council of Carthage (398 A.D.) set up the diriment impediment of vow or religion. The Council of Trullo (692 A.D.) established the diriment impediment of spiritual relationship arising from baptism.

Pohle-Preuss, *The Sacraments,* IV, 222–224 gives additional historical evidence of this practice of the Church.

Part 2. The Church has this power from Christ, not from the state.

Proof 2. By reasoning from the preceding proofs.

First, as we have seen, it was Christ Himself (Matt. 16:18, 19), not the state, who communicated to the Church the power to legislate diriment impediments.

Second, the councils that established such impediments did so on their own authority without recurring to the state for approval.

Proof 3. From theological reasoning.

First, the Church has jurisdiction over the sacraments and, consequently, over the diriment impediments to matrimony. Again, the Church has set up these impediments even when they were contrary to the civil laws. Pope St. Gregory the Great (about 600 A.D.), for instance, enacted the diriment impediment invalidating marriages between first cousins, although such marriages were allowed by Roman law. Besides, the Church obliges even sovereign civil rulers by her matrimonial impediments.

Since the Church has the power to establish diriment impediments, she also has the power to dispense from them when there are justifiable reasons. But she cannot dispense from the diriment impediments which God Himself, either by natural law or divine positive law, has enacted.

OBJECTIONS

1. God in the Old Testament revealed the impediments to marriage. Therefore, the Church cannot alter them or establish new ones.

Answer. The Mosaic Law does not bind Christians. Although the Church esteems the impediments revealed in the Old Testament and even uses them as a general norm in formulating her own laws, they have no binding force unless the Church confirms them.

As we have mentioned before, changes of circumstances may make it necessary to abolish some diriment impediments or to establish new ones. Accordingly, the power to remove or inaugurate such impediments must belong to the Church.

Comment 1. The state has no power to legislate impediments to Christian marriage.

Although it is clear that the Church has the power to legislate diriment impediments and to do so on her own authority, it may be possible that the state, too, has, independently of the Church, the same power. Both authorities may have the same right. This may even seem reasonable because marriage is not only a religious, but also a civil contract upon which the continuance and prosperity of the state depends.

It is Catholic doctrine that the state has no power at all to set up impediments to Christian matrimony. Additional reasons are these. Christian marriage is now a supernatural contract and so the Church, as the sole supernatural society, can establish diriment impediments to it. The state does not suffer as a consequence. Its continuance and prosperity are guaranteed by the observance of the Church's diriment impediments. Moreover, to avoid conflicts, only one authority can possess the power to determine diriment impediments. Suppose that the state would enact a diriment impediment which the Church would not recognize, or vice versa? This would entail discord and various legal and ecclesiastical difficulties.

It should be noted, however, that theologians dispute whether the state can establish diriment impediments for marriages in which both parties are unbaptized. All agree that, if even one of the parties is baptized, the Church alone has jurisdiction over the marriage and only her diriment impediments are binding.

*

Conclusion 4. The bond resulting from Christian marriage is so restricted that polygamy is invalid by divine positive law.

Introduction. The matrimonial contract has two basic properties or qualities, unity and indissolubility. Unity means that the bond of matrimony can exist between but one man and one woman. Indissolubility means that this bond between one man and one woman cannot be severed.

At present we treat of unity only. Afterwards we shall consider indissolubility. Since in the United States the unity of marriage is upheld by the civil laws, this Conclusion is not of great practical importance. However, it is part of God's revelation and any news from God Himself deserves our esteem and study.

Explanation of Terms

1. The bond. This refers to the marriage tie, the state of marriage which results from the contract.

2. From Christian marriage. The Conclusion is true of all marriages, but we speak only of Christian marriages, i.e., of two baptized persons.

3. Polygamy. This means that one woman has more than one husband living with her (polyandry) or that one man has more than one wife living with him (polygyny). Since polyandry is opposed to the primary function of matrimony and so has been repudiated by all peoples, we shall say no more about it.

When we use the word "polygamy" during this Conclusion, we mean that one man has more than one wife living with him. Hence we rule out the possibility that a man could validly marry two or more women at the same time, or that he could marry one wife, afterwards add a second or a third and so on, always re-taining the previous women also as his wives.

4. Invalid. A man can have one wife only. Any others he may attempt to marry, can never be his wives.

5. By divine positive law. This is God's own legislation, known by His revelation. Hence, the Church cannot dispense from it. Under the Old Law God Himself dispensed and at times allowed polygamy. This dispensation was revoked by Christ.

The Conclusion has two parts. First, once a man has validly married, he cannot marry another woman even though he retains his first wife. Second, this legislation originated with God's posi-tive law.

Dogmatic Note

The first part is Catholic doctrine from the encyclical *Casti Connubii* of Pius XI (DB. 2231; CT. 874): "Hence this mutual fidelity demands especially the *absolute* unity of marriage, as the Creator Himself exemplified in the marriage of our first parents for which He refused to have more than one man and one woman. Although, afterwards, God, the supreme legislator, relaxed to some extent and temporarily this original law, there is no doubt that the law of the gospel restored entirely that pristine, perfect unity and abrogated all dispensations from it, as the words of Christ and the constant teaching and practice of the Church make abundantly plain."

If polygamy were merely prohibited by law, exceptions would take place. However, the Holy Father excludes the possibility of an exception and so polygamy is invalid.

The second part is also Catholic doctrine because the Holy Father in the preceding citation expressly says: "as the words of *Christ* . . . make abundantly plain." Since Christ revealed the law, it is of divine institution.

Since polygamy is invalid, it follows that it is also illicit or gravely sinful. This has been defined by Trent (DB. 972, 969; CT. 858, 855).

Part 1. Once a man has validly married, he cannot marry another woman even though he retains his first wife.

Proof 2. From Holy Scripture. We have two direct proofs. The first is derived from St. Paul (Rom. 7:2, 3): "For the woman that hath a husband, whilst her husband liveth, is bound to the law. But if her husband be dead, she is loosed from the law of her husband. Therefore, whilst her husband liveth, she shall be called an adulteress if she be with another man." The text is dogmatically certain; apologetically certain against polyandry; apologetically very probable against polygamy.

St. Paul says that a woman cannot have more than one husband, whether she is living with him or is separated from him. She is "bound to the law," i.e., to the matrimonial bond, the law of having but one husband. Only the death of her husband permits her to marry another man.

Furthermore, to attempt to marry a second husband when she is already married is not only illicit, but invalid, because, if she does so, she will be guilty of adultery. If the second man were a true husband, she would not be guilty of adultery by having sexual intercourse with him.

Although the text aims specifically at polyandry, it is also against polygamy, since according to St. Paul (I Cor. 7: 2, 3) both wife and husband are *in the same condition* with regard to their marital obligations.

The second proof is also from St. Paul (I Cor. 7:39): "A woman is bound by the law as long as her husband liveth; but if her husband die, she is at liberty: let her marry to whom she will; only in the Lord." This text, too, is dogmatically certain; apologetically, very probable.

According to this text a woman cannot take a second husband while her first husband is alive. It makes no difference whether she separates from her first husband or continues to live with him. In either case it is against the "law," the bond of matrimony, to marry a second husband.

Although the text specifically excludes polyandry, it virtually excludes polygamy for the reason mentioned above (I Cor. 7:2, 3). We can conclude from the text that polyandry and polygamy are illicit, but not with certainty that they are invalid.

The New Testament offers an indirect proof against polygamy in as much as it never even hints at the possibility of a man having more than one wife. All the texts refer to the marriage of one man with one woman (Matt. 19:4–6, 9; Mark 10:11, 12; Luke 16:18; I Cor. 7:2–4, 10, 11).

Proof 3. From the Fathers. Many of them condemned polygamy. St. Ambrose, for example, declares: "You may not take another wife, while your wife is alive; to take a second while you have your first is the crime of adultery" (*De Abraham*, 1, 7, 59; RJ. 1322).

Proof 4. From theological reasoning. There is but one Christ and one Catholic Church, the bride of Christ. Christian marriage represents this union between Christ and His Church and, consequently, should be between one man and one woman.

Proof 5. From philosophy.

First, when a man marries a woman, the law of his rational nature prompts him not only to remain with her all his life, but also to remain with her *alone*.

Again, the birth-rate of each sex is approximately the same. This is an indication that God wills each man to have only one wife and each wife to have only one husband.

Part 2. Polygamy is invalid *by divine positive law*.

This part needs no development. The Scripture texts opposing polygamy are God's revelation and so His positive law.

OBJECTIONS

1. Polygamy is not against the natural law. Therefore, Christ did not abolish it.

Answer. Polygamy is not contrary to the primary purpose of marriage, the procreation and education of children, because it is possible for one husband to beget children by several wives and to provide for their education.

However, polygamy militates against the secondary aims of marriage and so is against a secondary precept of the natural law. It would be very difficult, if not impossible, for one husband to treat two or more wives equally, to satisfy the desires of all, to prevent discords and jealousies, to treat all his children impartially.

Consequently, polygamy destroys that reciprocal equality which should subsist between married partners. Hence, as nations become more civilized, they see the wrong of polygamy and abolish it, as our own country has done.

Comment 1. The history of polygamy.

Polygamy was not practised at the outset of human history

(Gen. 2:22–25; Matt. 19:4–6). Marriage was probably monogamous up to the time of the deluge. At some time after the deluge polygamy was permitted by God either for the more rapid expansion of the race, or to avert greater evils like idolatry.

Comment 2. Polygamy among the unbaptized.

It is certain that polygamy is invalid for the unbaptized also. The fact that our Lord cites Genesis (Matt. 19:4, 5) shows that He was legislating for all marriages.

Besides, polygamy is contrary to secondary precepts of the natural law. Hence, only God could allow it and He has not done so in the Christian dispensation. In fact, He revoked the tolerance of polygamy which He had accorded under the Old Law.

*

Conclusion 5. The marriage bond cannot be dissolved by one or even both of the married partners, no matter what their reasons may be. It cannot be dissolved by them even if adultery has been committed by one or both partners.

Introduction. We now consider the second property of the marriage bond, its indissolubility. This matter is of great practical moment in the United States where all the states except one allow divorce.

Although two persons are at liberty to enter marriage and by this voluntary contract establish the marriage tie, they cannot, as they can in some other contracts, break the tie on their own authority.

Before studying this Conclusion the student should make sure that he grasps the difference between unity and indissolubility. Unity is violated when the bond is multiplied by adding one or more wives. Indissolubility is violated when a man severs the bond and afterwards marries another woman. He does not intend ever to live with his first wife again and so he never has more than one wife at a time. Sometimes the violation of indissolubility is called "successive polygamy," but this phrase is misleading.

Explanation of Terms

1. The marriage bond. We deal with only the sacrament of matrimony, with marriages in which both parties are baptized. We include both ratified and ratified, consummated marriages. However, the Conclusion is true of *all* marriages.

2. Cannot be dissolved. We mean that the bond of marriage cannot be sundered so that the separated partners are free to contract a new matrimony. Mere separation of spouses is sometimes allowed. Only when adultery has been committed, however, may the innocent partner on his own authority withdraw permanently from the other party. There are other causes for separation, but if it is to be permanent, the bishop's approval is to be secured.

3. By one or even both of the married partners, no matter what their reasons may be. Hence they cannot break the bond on their own authority, even if they both agree to its rupture and even if one or both may have most cogent reasons.

We do not now consider the possibility of having the marriage bond severed by an authority which is outside and independent of the partners. The Church, as we shall see, can in some cases sunder the marriage bond when both or at least one of the spouses are baptized.

But no other authority is empowered to dissolve a marriage. The state is helpless to rupture, not only a sacramental, but any duly contracted marriage.

In the United States and most other countries divorce is granted by the state, not solely by the personal decision of one or both of the married parties. From the viewpoint of morality, this is a better condition of affairs than if the married partners by themselves could dissolve the bond, because compulsory submission to a legal process prevents the dissolution of many marriages that would otherwise be terminated. The cost and publicity curtail the number of divorces.

Nevertheless, divorce granted by the state is in fact divorce effected on the authority of the spouses, because the state has no power to sever any legitimate marriage bond. It usurps authority when it does so.

4. Adultery. This is the weightiest single cause for divorce. It is an act directly opposed to the matrimonial contract and is also a most serious sin against the virtue of purity. Adultery is implicitly included in the first sentence of the Conclusion, but we mention it specifically because some people have the idea that, though the bond cannot be dissolved for any other reason, it can be sundered if a spouse commits adultery.

On the contrary, not even adultery permits an innocent spouse to break the marriage bond. Neither can it be broken if both partners commit adultery.

The Conclusion has two parts. First, once two Christians are validly married, the bond cannot be dissolved by one or even both of the married partners, no matter what their reasons may be.

Second, it cannot be dissolved by them even if adultery has been committed by one or both partners.

Adversaries. Nearly all modern Protestants deny this Conclusion.

Dogmatic Note

That Christian matrimony cannot be dissolved by reason of *heresy* or *incompatibility* or *desertion* is of divine faith from the Council of Trent (DB. 975; CT. 867): "If anyone says that the bond of matrimony can be dissolved because of heresy or incompatibility or the desertion of a spouse, let him be anathema."

This canon deals with marriages among the baptized because Trent is concerned with the sacrament.

The council includes both a ratified marriage and a ratified, consummated marriage, because the contract alone constitutes the sacrament. The consummation of the marriage is not necessary.

Dissolution of a marriage by mere withdrawal of consent on the part of one or both partners is the simplest and easiest way of disrupting a marriage. Since the council states that marriage cannot be dissolved for the reasons cited, it must *at least* mean that the bond cannot be severed simply because the married parties wish to do so.

It should be noted, too, that desertion is, after adultery, probably the most compelling reason for rupturing a marriage. Desertion frequently involves adultery and always denotes a refusal to fulfill the obligations contracted by marriage. Hence any other reasons for breaking the marriage bond would be less cogent than desertion. Yet Trent defines that not even desertion suffices.

Nevertheless, since the Conclusion affirms that Christian marriage cannot be dissolved *for any reason whatever,* the dogmatic note is Catholic doctrine. The first part of the Conclusion is not only readily deduced from Trent, but is also taught expressly by Pope Pius XI (DB. 2236; CT. 876).

Trent (DB. 977; CT. 863) makes a solemn pronouncement about the second part: "If anyone says that the Church errs when she has inculcated and continues to inculcate, in accord with evangelical and apostolic teaching, that the bond of marriage cannot be dissolved by reason of adultery on the part of one spouse; and that both parties, even the innocent one who gave no reason for adultery, cannot contract a new marriage while the other spouse is alive; and that both the man who marries another wife after dismissing an adulterous one commits adultery, and the wife who marries another husband after dismissing an adulterous one commits adultery, let him be anathema."

It follows for the same reasons given after the preceding canon that this definition is concerned with Christian marriage, both ratified and ratified, consummated, and that it excludes the possibility of dissolution on the authority of one or both partners.

Furthermore, although the canon mentions adultery explicitly and deals with it alone, it is worded in a special way in order not to make more difficult the reunion of the Oriental schismatics with the Holy See. In practice these Orientals were allowing divorce for adultery, but they never assimilated this practice into their formal teaching. Consequently, the canon does not condemn these Orientals as heretics, since they do not officially *teach* "that the Church errs when she . . . teaches that the bond of matrimony cannot be dissolved by reason of adultery."

Since, however, the Church does not err when she *teaches* that adultery cannot sever the bond, it is definable that *in practice* adultery does not sever it.

Both parts will be proved simultaneously.

Proof 2. From Holy Scripture. There are four outstanding texts of which we shall analyze the first only.

It is part of the gospel teaching to which Trent (DB. 977; CT. 863) refers and is found (Mark 10:2–12):

2 "And the Pharisees coming to Him asked Him: Is it lawful for a man to put away his wife? tempting Him.

3 But He answering, saith to them: What did Moses command you?

4 Who said: Moses permitted to write a bill of divorce, and to put her away.

5 To whom Jesus answering, said: Because of the hardness of your heart he wrote you that precept.

6 But from the beginning of the creation, God made them male and female.

7 For this cause a man shall leave his father and mother, and shall cleave to his wife.

8 And they shall be two in one flesh. Therefore now they are not two, but one flesh.

9 What therefore God hath joined together, let not man put asunder.

10 And in the house again his disciples asked Him concerning the same thing.

11 And He saith to them: Whosoever shall put away his wife and marry another, committeth adultery against her.

12 And if the wife shall put away her husband, and be married to another, she committeth adultery."

The proof from this passage is dogmatically certain (DB. 977; CT. 863); apologetically, very probable.

First, the passage deals explicitly with divorce (v. 2). It was about this that our Lord was questioned.

It is plainly stated that neither the husband (v. 11) nor the wife (v. 12) can break the bond. They are both in the same condition with regard to it.

The passage does not expressly treat of the case in which both husband and wife would agree to sever the bond, but it does so implicitly by quoting Genesis and by simply declaring: "What therefore God hath put together, let not man put asunder" (v. 9).

Our Lord's words are mainly concerned with divorce attempted on the authority of the partners: "Whosoever shall put away his wife" (v. 11), "If the wife shall put away her husband" (v. 12).

Since divorce is absolutely forbidden, the least possible meaning is that husband and wife cannot disrupt the bond merely because they wish to do so.

Neither can the state dissolve a marriage. "Let not *man*" (v. 9) more obviously includes the state. The state, although it derives its power from God, does not receive any revelation from Him.

Whether the Church is empowered in some instances to dissolve a marriage will depend on a further revelation of God. The passage prescinds from this subsequent revelation. It simply restores matrimony of every kind to its pristine indissolubility.

Our Lord certainly included Christian marriages because there are additional reasons why such marriages should be indissoluble. They are efficacious signs of grace and represent the permanent union of Christ and the Church. Such marriages, then, *a fortiori* can never be severed on the authority of the spouses.

Furthermore, Christ on this occasion was giving a revelation which was to be entrusted to His Church for preservation. He must, then, be including the sacrament of matrimony which is an essential part of His revelation.

Moreover, the passage pertains to ratified marriages as well as ratified, consummated ones, because it embraces all genuine marriages in which a man may call a woman his wife and a wife call a man her husband. This is true of a ratified marriage.

Our Lord not only prohibits divorce, but He makes it invalid. Otherwise, the parties who attempt divorce would not be guilty of adultery (vv. 11, 12).

Nor is there any justifying cause for any divorce. Moses allowed divorce if the wife committed some kind of "uncleanness" (Deut. 24:1). This would include adultery. Christ, however, on this occasion expressly revokes this permission of Moses. Accordingly, not even adultery is sufficient reason for divorce and, consequently, no other reason would justify it.

Besides, Christ declares without any qualification: "What therefore God hath put together, let not man put asunder" (v. 9).

Another dogmatically certain, apologetically very probable, gospel proof can be found in Luke 16:18.

The *apostolic* teaching referred to by Trent (DB. 977; CT. 863) is enunciated in I Cor. 7:10, 11, 39; 2–5. The text is apologetically very probable.

St. Paul provides another text (Rom. 7:2, 3) which is also quite clear and excludes both polygamy and divorce.

Proof 3. From the Fathers. Commenting on Rom. 7:2, 3, St. John Chrysostom writes: "What is that law which St. Paul has given to us? 'A woman,' he says, 'is bound by the law.' Hence she must not be divorced from her husband as long as he is alive. She must not add a second husband to her first. She must not attempt a second marriage. Notice, too, the careful exactness with which he spoke. He does not say: 'She must live with her husband as long as he is alive,' but 'A woman is bound by the law as long as her husband is alive.' Consequently, even if he gives her a bill of divorce, even if she leaves his home, even if she deserts him for another husband, she is bound by the law and is an adulteress. . . . Forbear from quoting to me extraneous civil laws which permit the giving of a bill of divorce with a right to a new marriage. For on judgment day God will not sentence you according to these laws, but according to those which He Himself has established" (Hom., *De libello repudii,* 1: RJ. 1212).

St. Jerome, too, speaks very plainly: "The apostle [St. Paul] sheared off all reasons for divorce when he explicitly legislated that the woman who married a second husband commits adultery if her first husband is still alive. He may have committed adultery or sodomy or all other crimes and have been forsaken by his wife for those reasons. But as long as he is alive, he is her husband and she is not allowed to marry another" (*Epist.* 55, 3; RJ. 1351).

St. Jerome also testifies that what is not permitted to the wife is not permitted to the husband either: "Among us Christians what is forbidden to women is also forbidden to men. Both are in the same state with regard to their obligations" (*Epist.* 77, 3; RJ. 1352).

Other quotations may be found in Pohle-Preuss, *The Sacraments,* IV, 196–198.

Proof 4. From theological reasoning. Christian matrimony symbolizes the union of Christ with His Church. Since this union is abiding, Christian marriage should also be indissoluble.

Proof 5. From philosophy. We give this proof because the matter is so important and because, in discussing divorce with non-religious persons, only philosophical reasons can be advanced.

First, indissolubility flows from the natural promptings to conjugal love. When a man and woman so love each other that they desire matrimony, they instinctively want the bond to be lasting. This natural instinct finds expression even in our popular songs in which lovers are made to chant that they will remain with each other "forever," "until the moon changes its color," and so on.

Second, indissolubility is necessary for the attainment of the purposes of marriage. If a child is born, it needs the guidance and help of both parents for many years. Succeeding children are also born ordinarily, and these, too, need parental guidance and support for many years. Accordingly, it is evident that for the *education* (in the broadest sense) of the children, a marriage should endure for so long a time that the partners would hardly think of remarriage. Furthermore, the mutual assistance promised by the parties when they marry is completely voided if the marriage ends in divorce.

Finally, the common good of society demands the permanence of marriage. Public morality is weakened if divorce is allowed. For instance, the possibility of securing a divorce sometimes leads to the practice of artificial birth control, because children will be a future encumbrance if the marriage is terminated. Moreover, divorced men and women more readily commit adultery. Often enough the newspapers tell us of divorces which result in murder or suicide or both.

Then, too, a certain amount of enmity necessarily arises between divorced partners and their relatives and friends. Thus disunion is engendered in society.

Divorce also produces severe psychological strain upon children. Very often they become maladjusted and quite frequently true, juvenile delinquents. To verify this statement, it is only necessary to trace the records of our youngsters who are consigned to industrial or reform schools. Most of them come from broken homes. Furthermore, all our citizens must pay for the support of these schools which are necessary, mainly because some parents have failed to abide by their marriage vows.

OBJECTIONS

1. When two persons make a contract, they can revoke it if they both agree to do so. Therefore, married people should be able to sever the marriage contract if they both consent to its dissolution.

Answer. Many contracts can be dissolved by mutual agreement if only personal interests are involved. If, however, the common good is endangered by dissolution of the contract, the contracting parties may not revoke it. For instance, in time of war a steel company contracts to sell so much steel at regular intervals to another company which makes fighter planes for the government. These two companies may not cancel their mutual contract simply because it would be advantageous for them to do so. The common good of the country demands that they fulfill the contract.

So it is with marriage, which is not a contract involving only two persons. The contract itself is concerned with the common good of the country—with the begetting of citizens and with the upkeep of morality.

2. When Christ made marriage a sacrament, He would not have imposed any obligation contrary to natural law. But natural law sometimes permits the extrinsic dissolution of a marriage as when, for instance, a wife is sterile, or so sick that she can never render the marriage debt.

Answer. This objection is not directly against the Conclusion, which deals with *intrinsic* dissolubility, i.e., on the authority of the married partners themselves. This is never allowed by natural law because of the breakdown of morality that would follow.

All theologians hold that Christ determined that no marriage can be dissolved merely because a wife is sterile or sick.

Some, however, have admitted that, prescinding from Christ's decree and viewing such cases from a purely rational standpoint, they could be dissolved *extrinsically*, i.e., by an authority independent of the spouses.

But most theologians deny this. The common good requires that every marriage, whether sacramental or not, be indissoluble. If a single cause for divorce is admitted, partners who desire to sever their marriage will find ways of "proving" that they have this cause. The common good must always be preferred to the individual's good.

3. The New Law should not be more burdensome than the Old. Since, then, God allowed divorce for some reasons in the Old Law, it should be allowed in the New Law for similar reasons.

Answer. It is false to make the general statement that the New Law should be less burdensome than the Old. It is more burdensome in many ways. For instance, our Lord commanded Christians to love even their enemies, a more burdensome precept than any enactments concerning fraternal charity under the Old Law. It is true that, all things considered, the New Law is less burdensome than the Old, because of the spiritual compensations obtained by observing the harder requirements of the New Law.

Moreover, divorce is not contrary to a primary precept of the natural law, but to a secondary one. Owing to special circumstances, God allowed divorce under the Old Law and so He providentially provided for the ensuing evils. But He has expressly revoked this permission in the New Law, as we have seen in our proofs.

4. Our Lord said (Matt. 19:9): "And I say to you, that whosoever shall put away his wife, except it be for fornication, and shall marry another, committeth adultery; and he that shall marry her that is put away, committeth adultery." Therefore, our Lord allowed divorce when one partner commits adultery.

Answer. The student should read the entire passage (Matt. 19:3-10). It is the parallel passage of Mark 10:2-12 which we developed in our Scripture proof.

Catholic exegetes are not agreed upon the interpretation of verse 9, which constitutes the essence of the objection. All exegetes do agree, however, that Christ does not permit divorce by reason of adultery or fornication.

It is an elementary rule of hermeneutics that an obscure passage of Scripture is to be understood in the light of other passages. According to this rule it is clear from our proofs (Mark 10:2-12; Luke 16:18; I Cor. 7:10, 11, 39; Rom. 7:2, 3) that Christ banned divorce for any reason whatever. Nor does Matthew mean anything different.

First, as regards verse 9 itself, it is not important what the word "fornication" means. Some translate it as "immorality": others as "adultery." Some say that it signifies any extraordinary sin against chastity. It probably means adultery.

We believe that the interpretation of verse 9 which was offered at the beginning of the fifth century by St. Augustine is the best. According to this explanation the verse should be punctuated as follows: "And I say to you, that whosoever shall put away his wife except it be for adultery—and shall marry another, committeth adultery. . . ."

This is a logical explanation. The clause "except it be for adultery" limits only "whosoever shall put away his wife." It has no connection with "shall marry another."

If Christ had wanted this clause to apply to both the "whosoever" clauses, He should have said: "And I say to you, that whosoever shall put away his wife and shall marry another, except it be for adultery, committeth adultery. . . ." This He does not say, though He should have if the objection is to have any force.

This explanation is even more plausible if we recall that "putting away one's wife," i.e., separation from cohabitation, was well known to the Jews, as it is by natural law to all peoples. It is sanctioned by our own civil laws which make room for suits for separate maintenance. If a wife commits adultery, the innocent husband can by Christ's permission and by natural law itself, "put her away."

Moreover, verse 9 closes with these words: ". . . and he that shall marry her that is put away, committeth adultery." If the restrictive clause in the first part of the sentence were limiting both the "whosoever" clauses, it should have been repeated here. Our Lord should have said: "and he that shall marry her that is put away, *except it be for adultery*, committeth adultery."

Furthermore, the context lends support to this explanation. The disciples told Christ afterwards: "If the case of a man with his wife be so, it is not expedient to marry" (v. 10). Being Jews and habituated to the Jewish law which allowed divorce at least for adultery, they are astonished at our Lord's words. What they really mean is this: "If there is no possibility at all of disrupting a marriage, it is not expedient to marry."

Hence we read (Mark 10:10): "And in the house again the disciples asked Him again concerning this same thing." The disciples were acquainted with the two Jewish currents of thought about divorce. The followers of Hillel permitted a husband to divorce his wife for anything that displeased him. The school of Shammai permitted divorce only when the wife committed adultery or some other crime against purity. If Christ had sided with either of these schools, the disciples would not have inquired privately about His meaning. Either meaning would have been compatible with their mentalities. But they thought that Christ had rejected both schools. He had outlawed divorce entirely. This was to them a novel and incredible teaching and they wanted to be sure that they had not misunderstood Him. Our Lord simply answered (Mark 10:11): "Whosoever shall put away his wife and marry another, committeth adultery against her." He had not favored either school. He had abolished divorce for any reason whatever.

From this explanation, it follows that the passage of St. Matthew, especially verse 9, is not a solid objection, but rather an additional Scripture proof for the Conclusion.

5. Christ said (Matt. 5:32): "But I say to you, that whosoever shall put away his wife, excepting the cause of fornication, maketh her to commit adultery: and he that shall marry her that is put away, committeth adultery."

Answer. This objection has no force. Nothing is said in the first part of the verse about a second marriage. It simply states that, if a wife commits adultery her husband is not obliged to live with her any longer.

This verse confirms our previous exegesis of Matt. 19:9. There we said that "except it be for adultery" limited only "if a man shall put away his wife." Here "excepting the cause of adultery" evidently restricts only "whosoever shall put away his wife." Hence separation from cohabitation was well known to the Jews.

If a man puts away his wife for other reasons, he makes her, i.e., he exposes her to the commission of adultery. However, if he dismisses her by reason of adultery, he does not expose her to this crime because she has already committed it. But no matter why he puts her away, the marriage bond is not broken because "he that shall marry her that is put away, committeth adultery."

Comment 1. Remarriage after the death of a spouse.

If one of the partners dies, the other is permitted to remarry. The survivor may marry several times if his previous spouses have successively died.

Remarriages of widows and widowers were not encouraged by some of the Fathers, but they never considered such remarriages as invalid.

In itself, of course, it is more perfect if widows and widowers remain single, but sometimes it is preferable for them to enter another marriage. It could even happen that some of them might be obliged to remarry. Accordingly, Catholics should never look askance at such remarriages.

It is Catholic Doctrine that remarriages of this kind are permissible. The Council of Lyons II (DB. 465; CT. 660), held in the year 1274, declares: "If a lawful marriage has been terminated by the death of a spouse, he [Michael Paleologus, who had denied it] admits that a second and a third and subsequent successive marriages are permitted so long as no other canonical impediment is in the way."

St. Paul gives the same testimony (I Cor. 7:30): "A woman is bound by the law as long as her husband liveth; but if her husband die, she is at liberty: let her marry to whom she will; only in the Lord."

*

Conclusion 6. Neither the Church nor the state can dissolve a legitimate matrimony.

Introduction. In the preceding Conclusion we have learned that no marriage can be dissolved on the authority of one or both of the married parties. We now investigate whether any authority independent of the married persons can ever disrupt the marriage bond. The only two possible authorities are the Church and the state, since all other societies are subordinate to these two.

In the following Conclusions we shall deal with various kinds of marriages and decide whether they can be dissolved either by the Church or by the state. We begin with the legitimate marriage. Since many unbaptized Americans get married, this matter is of practical importance.

Explanation of Terms

1. The Church. We mean the Catholic Church. Protestant sects do not themselves grant divorce, but nearly all of them allow their members to obtain a divorce from the state.

2. The state. We include particularly the supreme civil power of a country. Civil power has many subdivisions. In the United States it is exercised over the country as a whole, over the individual states, over each county, over townships and municipalities. The rulers of each of these sections has some civil power. We now say that even the supreme civil power of a nation may not dissolve marriage and, consequently, that the lesser civil powers cannot do so.

3. A legitimate marriage. This, as we mentioned previously, is a marriage contracted by two unbaptized persons both of whom remain unbaptized after their marriage. As long as both of them remain unbaptized, neither Church nor state can dissolve their matrimony. This is true whether the marriage has been consummated or not.

Adversaries. Very many Americans including most Protestants believe that the state can terminate a legitimate matrimony.

Since the Church explicitly professes that she has no jurisdiction over the unbaptized, we shall prove only that the state cannot disrupt a legitimate matrimony.

Dogmatic Note

This is Catholic doctrine from the encyclical *Casti connubii* of Dec. 31, 1930. In it Pius XI (DB. 2235) declares: "Hence our predecessor of happy memory, Pius VI, very wisely replies in writing to the bishop of Erlau in Hungary: 'It is, therefore, perfectly plain that marriage even in the state of nature, and certainly long before it was elevated to the dignity of a genuine sacrament, was so instituted by God as to entail a perpetual and indissoluble bond *which accordingly cannot be broken by civil law.* Consequently, although, as happens among unbelievers, the sacramental quality can be absent from marriage, nevertheless in such a marriage, since it is a true marriage, the perpetuity of the bond must be preserved and preserved absolutely. For from the very beginning divine law has so intimately linked this perpetuity with marriage that *it is not subject to any civil power.'*"

In this quotation Pius XI ratifies for the entire Church the words of Pius VI which comprise nearly the whole paragraph.

The statement clearly rules out the power of the state to dissolve a legitimate marriage, whether merely legitimate or also legitimate and consummated.

Our Holy Father, Pius XII, in an Allocution to the cardinals of the Roman Rota on October 6, 1946, stated: "But marriages once duly contracted even among the unbaptized are sacred things of the natural order. Hence *civil courts have no power to dissolve them* and the Church has never recognized the validity of decrees of divorce in such cases.

"However, this does not interfere with mere decrees of nullity regarding such marriages since such decrees are quite rare compared with decrees of divorce. In certain circumstances decrees of nullity can be issued by a civil tribunal and afterwards be recognized by the Church."

Proof 2. From theological reasoning. In the preceding Conclusion we proved that divorce is contrary both to the natural and the divine positive law. The state is bound to uphold these laws. If it is to dispense from their precepts, it must provide evidence that God has given it that right. Such evidence is wanting. As a result, the state cannot allow divorce even for legitimate marriages. Under the Old Law God Himself dispensed from the indissolubility of marriage in certain circumstances. He revoked that dispensation with the establishment of the New Law, as we proved previously.

Comment 1. Control over legitimate marriages.

Any kind of marriage has a public aspect and so must be regulated by either the Church or the state. Since unbaptized persons are not subject to the jurisdiction of the Church, she does not regulate legitimate marriages except in so far as she rightfully upholds the natural and divine positive law for all men. Hence the state has some jurisdiction over legitimate marriages.

It may issue a decree to nullity for such marriages provided that the reasons for it are valid. Such a decree is not a divorce even though the separated parties are free to marry. The decree simply decides after careful examination that the supposed marriage was really no marriage at all from its very inception. Consequently, there is no question of dissolving a marriage because no marriage ever took place.

The state may also affix diriment impediments to such marriages, but these impediments must not go contrary to natural or divine positive law. Otherwise they would be invalid.

*

Conclusion 7. The Roman Pontiff can dissolve even a consummated marriage contracted by a validly baptized non-Catholic and an unbaptized person.

Introduction. In the preceding Conclusion we treated of a marriage between two persons neither of whom was baptized before the marriage. If neither becomes baptized after the marriage, their marital bond can never be severed.

However, cases arise quite often in which a validly baptized non-Catholic marries an unbaptized person, or when two parties who were never baptized contract marriage and one of them is baptized afterwards. In this Conclusion we deal with the first group only. Can the bond of their matrimony ever be severed?

The matter is of some consequence because in the United States many marriages are contracted between a validly baptized Protestant and an unbaptized person. In such cases the baptized party is not bound by the diriment impediment of disparity of cult, nor by the Catholic form of marriage, i.e., the marriage does not have to be celebrated in the presence of a priest and two witnesses. Consequently, these marriages, unless some other diriment impediment is in the way, or an essential condition of the contract is lacking, are valid. We now say that the bond of such marriages can sometimes be dissolved by the Holy See.

Explanation of Terms

1. The Roman Pontiff. The power to dissolve these marriages belongs to the Holy Father.

2. Even a consummated marriage. Since the Holy Father can disrupt the bond of these marriages even after the marriage act has been performed, it is clear that he can dissolve them if they have not been consummated.

3. By a validly baptized non-Catholic and an unbaptized person. As soon as a person is baptized, he becomes subject to the laws of the Catholic Church whether he realizes it or not. Non-Catholic baptisms, as we have learned, are valid if they are properly administered, and so their recipients come within the scope of the Church's jurisdiction.

When a *Catholic* marries an unbaptized person before a priest and two witnesses and after having obtained a dispensation from disparity of cult, he, too, is validly married. We do not include these cases in the Conclusion.

Dogmatic Note

The Conclusion is certain from the recent practice of the Holy See.

A well-known example of the dissolution here considered is the Helena case about which the Holy Office gave its reply on November 5, 1924. In this case an unbaptized man had married a baptized Anglican woman. Divorce followed and the woman remarried. Sometime after the divorce, the man desired to become a Catholic and to marry a Catholic girl. The bishop of Helena, Montana, presented the case to the Holy See and the Holy Father dissolved the bond of the first marriage.

Other cases have occurred in the meantime. The Holy Office handles these cases.

Such marriages are dissolved for the good of the faith in general, or for the salvation of souls.

Our sole proof, therefore, is from the practice of the Holy Father, who, as Christ's vicar, decides if and when this kind of marriage is to be dissolved.

Comment 1. Control over this kind of marriage.

In the Comment which followed the preceding Conclusion

we learned that the state may at times issue a decree of nullity for marriages contracted by two unbaptized parties both of whom remain unbaptized after the marriage ceremony. We also learned that the state may, within the limits of the divine law, whether natural or positive, legislate even diriment impediments for the marriages of two unbaptized people.

However, the diriment impediments of the state are not applicable to a marriage between an unbaptized and a baptized person. Since one of the parties is her subject by baptism, only the Church has jurisdiction over such a marriage. Neither can the state issue a decree of nullity for these marriages.

When persons, one of whom is unbaptized and the other was validly baptized as a non-Catholic and has not been converted to the Catholic Church, wish to enter marriage, they are bound by all the diriment impediments of the Church except disparity of cult. They are also, as we mentioned earlier, excused from being married in the presence of an authorized priest and two witnesses.

Consequently, the Church alone has control over this kind of marriage.

Comment 2. Another way of dissolving such marriages.

A natural marriage bond of this kind would be changed into a ratified bond upon the conversion of the unbaptized partner. Hence, it could be dissolved, at least sometimes, as a ratified, but unconsummated marriage. In the Helena case, for instance, let us suppose that the unbaptized man had been baptized a Catholic after the baptized woman had definitively separated from him. By the very fact of the man's baptism, the marriage became ratified. However, it would never have become ratified and consummated because the two parties never performed the marriage act *after* the man's baptism. Hence, for a justifying cause the marriage could have been dissolved as a ratified, unconsummated marriage if the Holy See had decided that there was adequate proof for its non-consummation after the man's baptism. We shall prove in a subsequent Conclusion that the Holy Father is empowered to dissolve a ratified, unconsummated marriage.

Comment 3. Use of the power to dissolve these marriages.

The Holy Father does not, and cannot, use his authority indiscriminately in dissolving this kind of marriage. Every valid marriage bond is highly regarded by the Church. It is not severed unless its dissolution redounds to the benefit of the faith or the salvation of souls.

The student should remember that the state cannot rupture the bond of any valid marriage.

*

Conclusion 8. A legitimate, consummated marriage can be dissolved by the Pauline Privilege.

Introduction. We have seen that neither the Church nor the state can rupture the bond when two unbaptized persons validly marry and remain unbaptized. The Church, however, can sometimes sever the bond if one of the parties was validly baptized at the time of marriage.

Now we shall consider another kind of marriage. Two unbaptized persons marry validly. *Afterwards* only one of them is baptized a Catholic. Are there any circumstances in which the bond of this marriage can be dissolved in favor of the faith?

Yes, it can be dissolved, without the intervention of papal power, by the Pauline Privilege. The use of this privilege is supervised by the Church in order to prevent abuses and to be sure that the conditions required by God are verified. But the dissolution of the marriage does not result from any jurisdictional act of the Church. It is accomplished by the fulfillment of the conditions laid down by God.

This privilege, too, is granted for the advancement of the faith. If one of two unbaptized parties gets married and afterwards desires to become a Catholic, he or she might fail to embrace the faith through fear of losing the married partner or of making their conjugal life very burdensome.

This Conclusion is of great importance in the United States where so many unbaptized persons marry, some of whom afterwards wish to be converted. A marriage can be dissolved by the Pauline Privilege within a comparatively short time, without recourse to Rome, at little, or if necessary, no expense. It is taken care of within the dioceses.

Explanation of the Pauline Privilege

First, both parties must be unbaptized at the time of their marriage, and, after the marriage, one of the parties, but only one, must receive baptism.

If both parties were to be baptized after the marriage, the original marriage would at once become a ratified or sacramental marriage. Furthermore, if the marriage act were to be performed after they are both baptized, the original marriage would become ratified and consummated. Such a marriage can never be dissolved, as we shall prove later.

Second, the marriage act can be performed both before and after the baptism of one partner. Hence the marriage is not dissolved by baptism.

Third, the convert is baptized in the Catholic Church. However, the baptism could be conferred in an heretical or schismatical church if the person became a Catholic after baptism.

Fourth, there must be some kind of disassociation or alienation of the unbaptized partner from the converted spouse after the latter's baptism. This alienation might be simple desertion from the convert, a physical separation. It might also be an alienation of affection or good will which would make life burdensome for the convert or entice the convert to commit some kind of mortal sin.

The *motive* for the unbeliever's disassociation is relatively unimportant. It is the *fact* of disassociation which must be proved. Moreover, the convert cannot use the privilege if, after baptism, he or she has given a just cause to the unbeliever to disassociate himself.

Fifth, in order to make sure of the fact of alienation, the unbeliever is to be interrogated by the "appellations." He or she is asked these two questions: Do you wish to be converted and to be baptized? Do you, at any rate, agree to live together with your baptized partner in peace and without offending your Creator?

If the unbeliever answers "No" to both questions, the alienation is evident. If the answer to the first question is "Yes," but to the second, "No," the convert can use the privilege. If, however, an unbeliever answers "No" to the first question, but "Yes" to the second, the privilege cannot be used.

These specific interpellations are always required for the *liceity* of the Pauline Privilege. For its *validity* the alienation of the unbeliever must in every case be juridically established. If this is accomplished by other means than the technical interpellations, the Privilege, according to a probable opinion, may be used validly. In practice, however, recourse should be had to the Holy Office *before* the convert remarries.

If the unbeliever cannot be located to obtain his answers to the interpellations, or his disassociation cannot be proved by other means, a dispensation from the interpellations must be secured from the Holy See.

Sixth, when the Pauline Privilege takes effect, the bond of the first marriage is dissolved. Moreover, it is dissolved by the subsequent marriage rite performed according to the laws of the Church. Then, too, it is dissolved by the marriage of the convert alone. The unbeliever is not free to remarry unless and until the convert remarries. Consequently, neither the baptism of the convert nor the alienation of the unbeliever dissolves the legitimate marriage.

Dogmatic Note

This Conclusion is Catholic doctrine from the constant practice of the Church. Pope Innocent III (DB. 405) states the essence of the teaching in a letter of May 1, 1199: "If one of two unbaptized spouses is converted to the Catholic faith with the result that the other spouse absolutely refuses to live any longer with the convert, or will not do so without inducing irreverence to God or inciting the convert to mortal sin, then the forsaken convert may enter a second marriage if so desired. In such a case we find the teaching of the apostle: 'If the unbeliever depart, let him depart: a brother or sister is not under servitude in such cases (I Cor. 7:15).'"

Proof 2. From Holy Scripture (I Cor. 7:12–15). In the preceding context of this passage St. Paul speaks first (vv. 7–9) to *Catholic* men and women who either have not married or whose spouses have died. To them he recommends continued virginity if they are called to it by God. Otherwise they should marry.

Next (vv. 10, 11), he tells married partners who are both Catholics that only death can disrupt their marriage bond.

Lastly, in our verses (12–15) he considers the case of a convert who is married to an unbeliever. His words follow:

12 "For to the rest I speak, not the Lord. If any brother hath a wife that believeth not, and she consent to dwell with him, let him not put her away.

13 And if any woman hath a husband that believeth not, and he consent to dwell with her, let her not put away her husband.

14 For the unbelieving husband is sanctified by the believing wife; and the unbelieving wife is sanctified by the believing husband: otherwise your children should be unclean; but now they are holy.

15 But if the unbeliever depart, let him depart. For a brother or sister is not under servitude in such cases. But God hath called us in peace."

Our proof is dogmatically certain, apologetically probable.

As regards the words: "For to the rest I speak, not the Lord," all agree that the privilege is granted by God, not merely by St. Paul. The apostle probably means this: "Christ when on earth did not speak explicitly about the case that follows, but I do so now in His name and with His authority."

We now search the passage to find the conditions necessary for the use of the Pauline Privilege.

First, both parties were unbaptized at the time of their marriage. St. Paul says (vv. 12, 13): "if she [he] consent to dwell with him [her]." Consent was mutually present at the time of their marriage or there would have been no marriage. Something intervened afterwards to make one party wish to withdraw the marital consent. The cause of this is indicated in the entire passage by St. Paul's insistence on "believing" and "unbelieving." The presence of the Catholic faith on the part of one and lack of it in the other might impel the unbeliever to withdraw consent to the marriage.

Hence, both were unbaptized at the time of their marriage

and consented unqualifiedly to it, but the later unexpected conversion of one spouse might have occasioned a rejection of consent in the unbelieving partner.

Second, only one spouse is baptized after the marriage. This is clear from all four verses, in which there is a contrast between the believer and the unbeliever. The believer is baptized, the unbeliever is not.

Third, the marriage may be consummated after the baptism of the one partner. This is evident from verse 14 especially: "Otherwise your children should be unclean, but now they are holy." St. Paul supposes that children may be generated after the baptism of one party and he says that the children, as a result, are sanctified. It follows that baptism did not dissolve the legitimate marriage.

Fourth, the convert is baptized a Catholic. This is true because the letter is addressed to the Catholics of Corinth. We would not expect St. Paul to tell us whether those baptized by heretics could use the privilege. We know, however, from the interpretation of reliable theologians and canonists that one who is baptized in heresy and afterwards becomes a Catholic may invoke the privilege.

Fifth, the unbaptized partner must initiate some kind of disassociation from the convert. St. Paul refers to both moral and physical withdrawal. He says (v. 15): "If the unbeliever depart, let him depart." This pertains to actual desertion or physical separation.

He also adds (v. 15): "But God hath called us in peace." Thus he indicates that if married life would be in turmoil as a result of the conversion, the unbaptized party would be morally or affectively withdrawing from the convert.

However, it is only from the interpretation of the Church that we know precisely what constitutes moral withdrawal. Mere solicitation to commit any kind of mortal sin is enough.

It is likewise from the interpretation of the Church that we know that the motive prompting the unbeliever's separation is of little consequence. From the words of St. Paul we would be inclined to conclude that the alienation would have to be motivated solely by dissatisfaction over the conversion.

Note, too, that disassociation or withdrawal initiated by the *convert* would never allow the use of the privilege.

Sixth, the interpellations must be made for validity. St. Paul does not tell us this expressly. He does say that the unbeliever must disassociate himself, but he says nothing about *how* this withdrawal is to be ascertained.

Yet he implicitly requires some kind of proof. Otherwise great abuses would occur. A convert might falsely attest that an unbelieving partner had withdrawn. Then, too, even if the unbeliever had actually deserted the convert, it would not follow that he did not intend to return. He must be given a hearing if possible. This is done by the interpellations. Of course, an answer to these from the infidel is not always necessary. If they are sent by registered mail and no answer is received after a reasonable time, it may be taken for granted that he has withdrawn.

Seventh, the legitimate marriage is truly dissolved. St. Paul says (v. 15): "If the unbeliever depart, let him depart. A brother or sister is not under servitude in such cases." The word "servitude" refers to the bond of matrimony because the preceding sentence already supposes that the unbeliever has departed from cohabitation. Hence the convert is no longer merely separated from the unbeliever, but free from the servitude of the bond itself.

Moreover, "servitude" means the bond, as is clear from verse 39: "If her husband die, she is at liberty; let her marry whom she will, only in the Lord." One who is "under servitude" is not "at liberty." Accordingly, when St. Paul says that "a brother or sister is not under servitude," he means that they are "at liberty," i.e., free to contract another marriage as is the Catholic woman whose husband has died.

Besides, in verses 10 and 11 St. Paul, referring to two married Catholics, says that the wife should not depart from her husband and "if she depart, let her remain unmarried or be reconciled to her husband." We find the opposite here in verse 15. When the unbeliever departs, the apostle does not tell the convert to remain unmarried or be reconciled with the unbeliever. He says: "Let him depart." In other words: "You are not under servitude."

The convert, however, would be under servitude if remarriage were precluded.

However, the bond of the legitimate marriage is not dissolved by the convert's baptism or by the unbeliever's disassociation, but by the second marriage only. St. Paul seems to mean that it is ruptured by the departure of the unbeliever, but we know from the Church's interpretation that this is not true.

Furthermore, the dissolution is effected by the second marriage of the *convert*. This is clear from the tenor of the whole passage. It is the "brother" or "sister" that is "not under servitude." Hence the unbeliever cannot validly remarry until the convert has done so.

Eighth, the convert must enter the second marriage with a Catholic. In practice, then, both parties to the marriage will be Catholics. If the Catholic convert wishes to marry a validly baptized Protestant, a dispensation has to be obtained from the Holy See, not from the bishop unless he has received special faculties. If the convert desires to marry an unbaptized person, a dispensation from disparity of cult has to be secured from the Holy See. It is rarely granted because most cases of this kind would not seem to be for the benefit of the true faith.

Objections

1. The Pauline Privilege seems to favor unbelief, because the unbaptized partly is also allowed to remarry after the baptized party does so.

Answer. The privilege of remarrying is granted to the baptized party only. Furthermore, unbelief is not promoted by the remarriage of the unbaptized person who remains an unbeliever anyhow. On the other hand, the Catholic faith is furthered since the baptized party joins the Church and marries another Catholic.

2. It would also be in favor of the faith to dissolve a ratified, consummated marriage if one partner becomes an apostate or heretic. Yet this kind of marriage can never be ruptured.

Answer. In such cases it is true that ordinarily it would be *easier* for the Catholic partner to live as a Catholic if the marriage were dissolved. However, since the Catholic already has the faith, he receives special grace to bear the evils resulting from the defection of the other partner.

Moreover, this type of objection rests on a false assumption. It tries to tell God what He should do and why. As we shall prove later, God absolutely forbids in all circumstances the dissolution of a ratified, consummated matrimony.

Comment 1. Additional remarks about the Pauline Privilege.

It is called a *privilege* because it is an exemption from the general law forbidding the dissolution of any marriage.

It is called the *Pauline* privilege because God revealed it to St. Paul and inspired him to put it in writing.

Since it is a privilege, the convert is not obliged to use it.

The privilege may be invoked even after the unbeliever has lived in peace for many years with the convert, provided that the conditions are verified.

The dissolution of a marriage by this privilege is not an intrinsic (on the authority of the convert alone), but an extrinsic dissolution. It is not accomplished by mere revocation of marital consent on the part of the convert, but by the fulfillment of the conditions demanded by God who revealed the privilege.

Comment 2. Another way of dissolving a legitimate, consummated marriage.

The Holy Father is empowered to rupture a consummated marriage contracted by two unbaptized persons if one of them afterwards wishes to become a Catholic and to marry another Catholic. This can be done by the Holy Father even though no interpellations are made and so it is not the Pauline Privilege strictly speaking. Moreover, the unbeliever may be unwilling to have the marriage dissolved and yet the Supreme Pontiff can dissolve it in favor of the faith.

This papal power is mentioned in the *Code of Canon Law* (Par. 1125). It is explained in *Canon Law* (Bouscaren-Ellis), 554–560.

Comment 3. Practical utility of the last three Conclusions.

The student can hardly expect to retain the contents of these Conclusions. However, as he goes on in life, he is apt to meet persons who would like to become Catholics, but who think that a previous marriage blocks the way. When this happens, the student should remember that, if neither, or only one, of the partners is baptized, there is a possibility that an antecedent or existing marriage can be dissolved. He should not give any assurances, but should merely direct the prospective convert to a priest.

*

Conclusion 9. The Roman Pontiff as God's vicar can dissolve a ratified, non-consummated marriage.

Introduction. So far we have been considering the possibility of dissolving non-sacramental marriages. We now inquire whether a marriage that is a sacrament can ever be ruptured.

Explanation of Terms

1. The Roman Pontiff as God's vicar. The Holy Father uses vicarious power when he dissolves such a marriage. Consequently, he must have a sufficient reason for severing it.

However, he alone can judge the sufficiency of the reasons. Some reasons would be: probable nullity of the marriage from the beginning; moral impossibility for the married partners to live together; fear of future scandal; fear of adultery on the part of at least one of the spouses.

2. Can dissolve. We speak of perfect divorce with right to remarry, not merely of separation from cohabitation.

3. A ratified, non-consummated marriage. Both parties are baptized at the time of marriage, but they never perform the marriage act. It should be recalled, however, that if only one party is baptized at the time of the marriage and the other party becomes baptized afterwards, their marriage becomes a sacrament. Yet, if they do not perform the marriage act after the baptism of *both* partners, the marriage is ratified, but not consummated and so might possibly be dissolved.

Dogmatic Note

This is Catholic doctrine from the encyclical *Casti connubii* of Pius XI (DB. 2236; CT. 876): "But if this indissolubility of marriage seems to admit exceptions, though very rarely, as happens . . . in the case of Christian *ratified, but not yet consummated* marriages, the exception does not depend on the will of men or of any merely human power, but on the divine law whose sole custodian and interpreter is the Church of Christ."

The *Code of Canon Law* (Par. 1119) states: "A non-consummated matrimony between baptized parties . . . is dissolved . . . by a dispensation granted for a sufficient reason by the Apostolic See. Both parties may make the petition, or only one, despite the unwillingness of the other."

Proof 2. From the practice of the Church. Such marriages have been dissolved for several centuries and by many pontiffs from Martin V (1417 A.D.) to our present Holy Father. If the Church did not have the power to dissolve these ratified, unconsummated marriages, she would have inculcated a false morality because she has severed them so often and for so long a time. Confer Pohle-Preuss, *The Sacraments*, IV, 201–203.

Proof 3. From theological reasoning. We have two such reasons.

First, although the marriage contract is the cause of a lasting bond, the bond is strengthened when the marriage is consummated. By the marriage act husband and wife become more closely united in every way. Children are likely to be conceived and this makes more urgent the permanency of the bond. Thus we can understand to some extent why God permits the Church to dissolve a ratified, unconsummated matrimony, but not a ratified, consummated one.

Second, an unconsummated marriage does not perfectly verify the words of Christ quoted from Genesis: "And they shall be two in one flesh" (Matt. 19:5). It would seem, then, that the Church should be empowered to disrupt such a marriage for good reasons.

OBJECTIONS

1. Christ Himself said (Matt. 19:6): "What God has joined together, let not man put asunder." Therefore, the Roman Pontiff cannot dissolve a ratified, unconsummated marriage.

Answer. Our Lord meant that men on their *private* authority or on the authority of the *state* cannot dissolve a true matrimony. He prescinds in this text from the powers which He will later confer upon the Church.

2. If the Roman Pontiff can dissolve these marriages, we contradict all the philosophical reasons which we formerly presented to prove that divorce is against the natural law. The evil effects of divorce will follow if the pontiff dissolves ratified, unconsummated marriages.

Answer. This objection is unfounded for several reasons. First, ratified, unconsummated marriages are rare. Their dissolution is even rarer. Besides, there must be justifying reasons in every instance. Moreover, there are no children to be neglected. Furthermore, no immorality results. Finally, if perhaps some evil effects accompany the dissolution of these marriages, God in His providence will provide for them since He has given the Church the power to dissolve ratified, unconsummated marriages.

Comment 1. Dissolution of ratified, unconsummated marriages by solemn religious profession.

The Council of Trent (DB. 976; CT. 862) has infallibly defined that such marriages can be dissolved by solemn religious profession also. In practice, this happens so rarely that it hardly merits thorough treatment. The following conditions must be verified in every case.

1. A baptized man and a baptized woman are validly married.

2. They never perform the marriage act. The marriage is ratified, but not consummated.

3. Either one or both of them wants to enter religious life.

4. Permission to do so is obtained from the *Holy See.*

5. One or both enters a religious order (one in which solemn vows are taken), not merely a congregation with simple vows. This is a noteworthy condition because most religious societies have simple vows only.

6. It is the taking of *solemn* vows, not of *first* vows nor the reception of orders, which dissolves such a marriage. A married man might become a priest, and even a bishop, outside a religious order and yet his unconsummated marriage would not be dissolved.

If one of the married partners remains in the world, he or she cannot get married again until the other party actually takes solemn vows. These vows might be given earlier than usual to a married religious. However, it would be more advisable for one or both of the married partners to apply to the Holy See for a dissolution of their ratified, unconsummated marriage before one of them enters a religious order.

It is clear, then, that the dissolution of such a marriage by solemn religious profession is very rare indeed.

*

Conclusion 10. Even the Church cannot dissolve a ratified, consummated matrimony.

Introduction. This is the last kind of marriage whose possible dissolution we have to consider. All theologians agree that God *could* have empowered the Church to rupture the bond of a ratified, consummated marriage. They also agree that God has not conferred this power upon the Church.

Explanation of Terms

1. The Church. We mean the Catholic Church. No other church has legitimate power from God. Not even the Holy Father can dissolve these marriages.

2. Cannot dissolve. Separation from cohabitation is, as we have seen, sometimes permitted, but not perfect divorce with a right to remarry.

3. A ratified, consummated matrimony. Such a marriage is contracted by *two* baptized persons who afterwards consummate it by performing the marriage act. This is the ordinary case. However, if one baptized party marries validly an unbaptized party who afterwards is baptized, the marriage becomes ratified and consummated if they perform the marriage act after the baptism of both. So, too, if two unbaptized persons validly marry and both are afterwards baptized, their marriage becomes ratified and consummated by performance of the marriage act after they are both baptized.

Hence, we do not speak of a marriage that is only ratified. It must be both ratified and consummated. We suppose, of course, that the marriage is valid. Otherwise, a decree of nullity is possible.

Dogmatic Note

This is Catholic Doctrine from the encyclical *Casti connubii* of Pius XI (DB. 2236; CT. 876): "No power of this kind [to dissolve marriage] for any *reason whatever* can ever be exercised over a Christian *ratified and consummated* marriage. For, as the marriage contract is completely achieved in this kind of marriage, so also it reflects the highest solidity and indissolubility and is not to be dissolved by any human authority."

Proof 2. From the practice of the Church. The Church has never dissolved such marriages, even though petitioned many times and even by kings.

This fact by itself would not prove for certain that the Church does not have the power to dissolve them, since the nonuse of a power even for many centuries does not necessarily mean that the power is nonexistent.

However, if the Church possessed this power, she *should* have used it because in some instances thousands of souls would have been helped by it to attain their salvation. Recall the single case of King Henry VIII. England would have most likely retained the faith, had the Pope dissolved the king's ratified and consummated marriage with Catherine of Aragon. But he refused to do so. Diverse popes have refused to dissolve such marriages for other rulers like Lotharius, Philip I and Philip II, and Napoleon I.

The present practice of the Church is clearly expressed in the *Code of Canon Law* (Par. 1118): "A valid ratified and consummated matrimony cannot be dissolved by any human power and for any cause except death."

Proof 3. From theological reasoning. A ratified and consummated marriage typifies not only the union of Christ with His Church, but also the union of the Eternal Word with His human nature. This latter union is absolutely indissoluble.

OBJECTIONS

1. It is evident from Matt. 16:19 that Peter and his successors can dissolve any moral bond whatever. Therefore, the Holy Father can dissolve a ratified, consummated marriage.

Answer. The Holy Father has the power to dissolve any moral bond that furthers the supernatural purpose of the Church and is not otherwise forbidden. He alone can judge how far his power to loosen moral bonds extends and he explicitly declares that he cannot dissolve this kind of marriage.

Although it might conduce to some individual's good, even to his spiritual good, to have a ratified, consummated marriage disrupted, this would never benefit the common good. Rather, by reason of the wicked inclinations of men, many evils would result.

Catholic fathers and mothers derive great consolation from knowing that neither of them can sever their marriage.

2. The Roman Pontiff can dissolve a ratified, unconsummated marriage. Therefore, he should be able to dissolve a ratified, consummated one, because the two marriages do not differ essentially.

Answer. Although the two marriages are essentially the same in as much as both are constituted by the marriage contract, nevertheless, the ratified, consummated matrimony adds solidity to the contract and completes its meaning. Consequently, the ratified, consummated marriage has an added spiritual signification. It represents not only the union of Christ with His Church, but also the absolutely inseparable union of the Second Person of the Blessed Trinity with His human nature.

May the student join with the author in giving all praise and glory to the Most Blessed Trinity, to the Father, to the Son, and to the Holy Ghost. Amen.

INDEX

Ambrose (St.):
on diaconate, 353
on institution of sacraments, 42
on minister of penance, 302
on necessity of contrition, 266
on polygamy, 397
on transubstantiation, 143
Amen: expression of emphasis, 118
Angels: not ministers of sacraments, 48; not recipients of sacraments, 62
Angina pectoris: action of extreme unction upon, 325
Anglican orders: invalidity of, 364 f.
Annihilation: beyond man's power, 188; not verified in a conversion, 136
Anointing: essential for confirmation, 98; essential for extreme unction, 315 ff.; prescribed for baptism and orders, 310; purpose of, in Mk. 6:13, 313
Apostates: baptism by, 52; definition of, 48; reception of sacraments by, 63
Apostles
baptized before Pentecost, 102
married state of some, 366
obliged to consecrate Eucharist, 123
reaction of, to promise of Eucharist, 119 f.
subjective condition of, at Last Supper, 126
Apostolic Benediction: plenary indulgence, 329
Appellations: dispensation from, 418; necessity of, for Pauline privilege, 418, 421; omission of, 423
Appendicitis, acute: reception of extreme unction in case of, 336
Aramaic (language): used by Christ, 133; words for "signify" found in, 133
Arcanum divinae sapientiae of Leo XIII: on contract and sacrament of matrimony, 385
Ascension (of Christ): confirmation promised before, 94, 101; sacraments instituted before, 39, 41 f.

Ash Wednesday: postcommunion prayer of Mass for, 180
Aspersion: *see* Sprinkling
Attention (of sacramental minister): external and internal, 56; meaning of, 55; necessity of, 56
Attrition: *see also* Contrition; Contrition (perfect)
defective sovereignness in, 272 f.
definition of, 267
explanation of two phrases in Trent concerning, 272
fear of hell as motive for, 268, 274
for sacraments of the living, 23 f.
insufficiency of particular motive for, 272-4
motives for, 267 f.
necessary disposition for martyrdom, 81
necessity of, for sacrament of penance, 267 ff.
not necessarily accompanied by love, 274 f.
objections against sufficiency of, in penance, 270 f.
proofs for sufficiency of, in penance, 269 f.
Auctorem fidei of Pius VI: on Church's power to establish diriment impediments, 390
Augustine (St.)
on baptism of heretics, 51
on the character, 29
on effects of baptism, 79
on exegesis of Matt. 19:9, 408
on institution of sacraments, 42
on martyrdom, 85 f.
on necessity of baptism, 85
on necessity of penance, 257
on production of grace by sacraments, 18

Baius (heretic): on fear of hell, 269
Ballerini (theologian): error of, on necessity of external confession, 277
Balm: ingredient of chrism, 97 f.; symbolism of, 104
Baptism of blood: *see* Martyrdom
Baptism of love (desire)
conditions necessary for use of, 83
dependent on baptism, 83